TED WILLIAMS
A BASEBALL LIFE

MICHAEL SEIDEL

With a new foreword by the author

UNIVERSITY OF NEBRASKA PRESS
LINCOLN AND LONDON

⊗

First Nebraska paperback printing: 2000

Library of Congress Cataloging-in-Publication Data
Seidel, Michael, 1943–
Ted Williams: a baseball life / Michael Seidel; with a
new foreword by the author.
p.   cm.
ISBN 0-8032-9308-9 (pbk.: alk. paper)
1. Williams, Ted, 1918–   2. Baseball players—
United States—Biography.   3. Boston
Red Sox (Baseball team)   I. Title.
GV865.W5S44   2003
796.357′092—dc21
[B]   2003047301

For Eileen, Dan, Matt, Tim, and Mick

Contents

"The only real game in the world is baseball."
—Babe Ruth

MICHAEL SEIDEL

Foreword

Ted Williams was simply the best pure hitter the game has known. He managed, by two years, to do what Joe DiMaggio barely missed doing: outlive the century that nurtured his extraordinary talent. On 5 July 2002 Ted Williams died. The days following his death seemed to repeat the shape of his career in microcosm: first came the honorifics, then a raging controversy, and, finally, a few moments of genuine emotional warmth during a celebration in his honor at Fenway Park in Boston.

What was it about this volatile individual and superb ballplayer that made the arc of his public exposure so predictable? I have been thinking about that question for many years. His reality was immediate and it was always insistent: *it's my turn.* Williams was not a considered and deliberate man. Everything about him—except the technical precision of his swing or the uncanny accuracy of his fly-fishing casts—was impulsive, almost as if the body spoke before the words formed. He was always on the move, fidgeting, gesturing, chattering. He spoke often and loudly, and did not listen very well or at all. He drew others into his world not by invitation but by decree.

When I began research for a biography of Ted Williams I wanted to find the earliest remembrances of what he was like as a youngster in San Diego. One of his junior high school teachers recalls a child screaming as loudly as he could for his ups on the schoolyard field: "My turn!" It is no accident that Williams titled his autobiography *My Turn at Bat.* He would hold onto that bat during his voluble on-field interviews with sports-writers, many of whom had the distinct impression that he would just as soon take his turn by swinging at them.

But, oh, could he hit a baseball! However objectionable he was to some, that which Williams did best is what memorializes him most. To have been in Williams's presence is to imagine him always young and always ready to launch a ball into the crowd of white shirts in Fenway's bleacher seats. He could scowl and scream and bully, but his swing was pure—hips slightly gyrating, hands wringing the bat, left elbow cocked back, right hand pulling the bat on its upward arc, and left hand turning over in a split second at the apogee of the swing. It was a swing that most pitchers would prefer to forget, and one that only the true fans among those pitchers deign to remember.

The same few film clips of Williams at the plate played over and over again on the television news broadcasts on the Friday of his death. A day later the story broke of Ted's son, John Henry Williams, arranging to have his father's body frozen and put in cold storage. Physically Williams was such a presence in life that it is strangely fitting that his body should be at the center of the first controversial moments after his death. Ted's daughter from his first marriage, Barbara Jo, publicly added a touch of scandal to the already bizarre circumstances by charging (in a lawsuit, subsequently withdrawn) that her half brother intended to sell her father's DNA for profit and, presumably, should the state of cryonics cooperate, for long-term clonic futures into the Baseball Hall of Fame.

America is a country in which 90 percent of the population claims to believe in some conventional form of religious doctrine. Though to a degree tolerant of cremation—said to be Williams's first wish—conventionalists do not readily cotton to the idea of freezing dead bodies. Perhaps freezing impedes the egress of the soul. Even in death Ted Williams was once again at the center of a public brouhaha. Many insisted that the son contravened the father's wishes in the matter. But I am not so sure. It is hard to know what an ill man says to his son or a son says to a father living his last days. Most likely neither cryonics nor cremation would have made that much doctrinal difference to Ted Williams. From his early days in San Diego when he listened to his mother preach the principles of the Salvation Army, it was not the spiritual import of her doctrinal work that impressed Williams but her insistence on self-reliance. As far as doctrine went, Williams despised any that he did not conjure up himself. What allegiance he had to the way things in this world worked had more to do with demonstrable and possibly foreseeable principles of physics than with metaphysics. Cold storage could easily have been for Williams what it was for Walt Disney, a hedge against present-day ignorance of the future.

Granted, Williams was neither well nor particularly sharp in the last stroke-depleted months of his life. John Henry may have dreamed the deep freeze dream all on his own. The key point is that even in better health Ted would not have figured the predictable public shock waves of such a notion, whether his son's notion or his own. He rarely thought much about the implications of things he did or said. Many comments he made or actions he took that were morally and socially neutral in his mind seemed to bother sportswriters and the general public in ways he could not or would not imagine. Before World War II he used what influence he had among highly placed friends to lessen his chance of being drafted. Such an action was for Williams more a civic right and a matter of proper paperwork than a crisis of failed patriotism, even though the only thing the public saw in Ted's reclassification was cowardice. Reluctantly, after Pearl Harbor and after a chastisement from former Detroit Tigers catcher Mickey Cochrane, Ted gave in and enlisted in the Naval Air Corps. He did so not out of contrition but out of a new conviction that Cochrane had a better long-range sense of things than he had. Ted's learning curve tended to be after-the-fact.

To understand the many controversial moments in Ted Williams's career and the way he mismanaged them is to understand something of the way he found himself ushered out of this world in July of 2002. Whatever his role in the cryonics controversy, his goal was surely not to be deemed outrageous. He had no such goals; he merely reacted with the first thing that entered his head. When alive he had recourse to clarification. He might spend the next few days trying to explain his words or, better yet, the next few days tearing the cover off the ball on the field, which was his preferred way of deflecting controversy into career statistics. After his death his teammates had to intercede for him. They did. In a moving and warm ceremony at Fenway Park the old Red Sox players who so admired him—Dom DiMaggio, Johnny Pesky, Walt Dropo, and his only true roommate on the road, Broadway Charlie Wagner—provided the dignified and touching tribute that convention required. Williams was back in the fold and what was best about him was taken to where it belonged: the baseball diamond.

Preface

BEFORE I BEGAN THIS BOOK, one of my graduate students at Columbia University, a young woman from Holland, asked me whether I was working on something new. I said I was planning a book on Ted Williams, one that interweaves his complex career with the special quality of his sport in America in the pre- and postwar years.

"I know who he is," she said. "He plays basketball for a team in Boston, the Celtics, yes?" She pronounced Celtics with a hard *k* as in Keltic Revival.

"Well, plays basketball isn't exactly right," I said, "and neither is Celtics, with a soft *c* as in celery, but he did play baseball in Boston for the Red Sox from 1939 to 1960."

"Why is he so famous?" my student asked.

"Because," I replied, "he was the best hitter of the last half century, surely the best left-handed hitter—okay, maybe even the best all-around left-handed hitter in the history of baseball."

"Anything else?" my student probed, blissfully unaware that sentiments such as these lead to barroom brawls.

"Yes," I continued. "He was crucial to the game in its most glorious decades, and he was a very controversial ballplayer, *very* controversial."

"Was that because he was left-handed?" she asked.

We had reached an impasse. But my student may have stumbled at least upon a point at which to begin. Ted Williams does not even remember why or when he took his first cuts left-handed on the playgrounds of San Diego, but he never made a decision with quite the same degree of importance for him, and he never subordinated his love of hitting a baseball to anything else for the rest of his career. "Hitting was my life," as he said on any number of occasions.

Much of the controversy surrounding Williams over the years has to do with the priority he placed on getting and taking his cuts at the plate. Even the title of his autobiography, *My Turn at Bat*, bears this out. Its first sentence may have an almost epic ennui about it—"I'm glad it's over," exactly what he said after the difficult loss to the Cards in the 1946 World Series—but he takes his cuts all over again as a memoir writer. A crusty friend of mine in San Francisco gave me his worn and leafed copy of *My Turn* many years ago. "Read it; it's damn good," he advised. I did. And I have done so repeatedly over the years. Williams does not merely write in his book; he makes noises, he grunts, he hisses, he taunts. His locutions are at once as nervous and as noisy as his at-bats.

Motion and emotion are as contrapuntal in Williams's career as hitting and talking. His nature was hyper. A *Sporting News* profile from 1941 caught him supposedly at rest: "At the hotel, he strides around the room, taking his swings, then flopping into a chair and vigorously shaking one foot, talking volubly all the while." A profile a few years later viewed him "relaxed" at home: "He's like a lightning bug on a hot griddle, a St. Vitus–acting kind of guy. He gulps his juice in the morning, jumps up and down to turn on and turn off the radio, says he's hungry or he's not hungry on a whim, and can't sit still to save his soul."

Williams's title, *My Turn at Bat*, not only describes his eagerness to hit a baseball and his inclination to talk about it but it harbors all the exuberant egoism that inspires this great big perpetual kid. "My turn," after all, is the emphatic playground demand of the young, the impulsive staking of turf and logging of time that is at best innocent and at worst greedy. Lelia Brown, a fifth-grade teacher at Garfield Elementary in San Diego, remembers a blatant Ted Williams shouting "first ups" every time the kids hit the playground: "If he didn't get them, hats flew and feet stomped."

There is much to be gleaned from titles. They are temperamental epitomes. How different is *My Turn at Bat* from Joe DiMaggio's almost-wistful, public relations–inspired *Lucky to Be a Yankee*. Di-Maggio's title reflects a humility that folds itself inside an institutional dynasty. As Williams himself pointed out, the Corporate Yankee always supersedes the Embattled Man because players like DiMaggio enjoyed the impregnable support of the ball club for which they played and of the city in which they played. Williams often wondered about the difference between exposed and protected players, complaining that when he walked out on the public limb there was never a scarcity of front-office volunteers, local baseball pressmen, and the Fenway wolf pack ready to help him saw it off. In this sense, his turns at bat were a kind of self-defense, or, better yet, a kind of revenge.

◊

While researching this book at the Hall of Fame Library in Cooperstown I ran into Mike Epstein, who played for the Senators in 1969 when Williams managed the ball club. Epstein had his little boy, Jake, with him, and the kid was marveling at his father's recollection of Williams. What inspired Epstein, who never saw Williams play, was the magnitude and sheer sound of the man. Epstein began "doing" him: standing tall, hands thrust on hips like some Rodin bronze, head cocked to the side, and voice booming constantly. "Gotta get the flow of the swing. Then vhoom! Be quick. Right there, there! 'Attaboy. Flow. Vhoom!'"

Epstein wrung the handle of an imaginary bat: "Come on, what's the count—two balls? two strikes? Gotta be ready." Epstein cocked his right leg as he jerked his shoulders back as if he had a kind of tic douloureux; he squeezed the bat, still talking in Williams patois: "With two strikes, never, I mean never, get beat on a fast ball. Ready, trigger it, wait on it, hips and ass, yeah, EEPHUS-EIPHUS, yeah, Whoosh! Get that bat around."

The real bounty of Williams's career is the awesome beauty of the way he got that bat around, and the 7,706 official at-bats that accompanied his swings. Though the era in which he played ended recently enough that many fans still carry powerful memories of him, those memories are beginning to dim or they are beginning to take on the glow of legend. Oscar Wilde warned that "memory is the diary we all carry about with us, but it often chronicles things that have never happened." My goal is to chronicle the things that did happen, and to provide, in the bargain, as full and as fair a record as

I can of Williams's life as a professional ballplayer during one of the greatest eras baseball has ever known.

Williams's career touched upon four great decades of American baseball—from just before World War II through the golden decades of the '40s and '50s—before the sport was blown out of proportion by extensive television coverage, by screwy new rules, by divisional play, by artificial turf, by homogenized parks, and by multimillionaire .220 hitters. The Boston Red Sox were competitive for most of Williams's great years, with teams of immense talent and just enough weaknesses and deficiencies to make them wildly unpredictable. For every losing skein on the road, for which the Red Sox of the '40s and '50s were notorious, fans could expect devastation at home within the confines of Fenway. Once the St. Louis Browns came into Boston for a two-game set, and they left Boston forty-eight hours later after scoring eight runs—not a bad showing for the Browns. But the Red Sox chalked up 49 runs in those two games, winning 20-4 and 29-4. Playing the Red Sox at their best in Fenway was like falling into a huge turbine engine.

The pages that follow tell the story of Williams's time as a ballplayer, of the Boston Red Sox during the years he played, and of the temper of major league baseball in America in the 1940s and 1950s. My intent is to provide what is notably lacking in the mass of material produced over the years on Williams: continuity and inclusiveness. Though Williams's own autobiography holds pride of place in any review of his life in baseball, its very forcefulness, its stridency, and its special pleading ensure a selective bias that is there by design. And the only other creditable full-length biography on his life, Ed Linn's *Ted Williams: The Eternal Kid*, has been characterized even by novelist John Updike, a truly unreconstructed Williams fan, as a "hagiography." Williams deserves something other, though many would say something less, than sainthood. At least he deserves a look from a vantage point different from that accorded on bended knee.

I have tried to review the accomplishments and controversies, to reconstruct the events and sequences of Williams's baseball life by contacting those directly involved with him and by researching the contemporary records with a persistence that also turned out to be a great pleasure. I have had a great deal of help from a great many people, first and foremost the dozens upon dozens of former ballplayers who spoke to me or wrote to me, primary among them Bobby Doerr, Bob Feller, Dominic DiMaggio, and Johnny Pesky. The staff of the Hall of Fame Library was invaluable, especially Tom Heitz, Bill Deane, and Pat Kelly. For additional help in researching newspaper archives, I am indebted to Nancy Gagnier, Ted Cleary, and Carol Howard. Jack Artenstein of RGA Publishing has been instrumental in the launching and completion of this book, as have my editor, Nancy Crossman, and my project editor, Craig Bolt.

Many friends have helped me, some of them voluntarily. The lately deceased commissioner of baseball, Bart Giamatti, loved the Red Sox, and he never tired of chatting about them on occasions when I sought his help. Pete Williams, son of the longtime New York sportswriter Joe Williams, made available to me invaluable personal tapes of Williams. David Quint was vigilant on behalf of Red Sox history and protected the team, as best he could, from enemies all around. Sean Wilentz, a Yankee fan and a passionate student of the game, leavened idolatry with healthy skepticism.

Most of all, I thank Eileen Mullady for listening to me talk about baseball by the hour, though insisting that her favorite, Billy Williams of the Cubs, had every bit as lovely a swing as Ted Williams. My young sons, Danny and Matt Seidel, were the best fact checkers a writer ever had. They love baseball and its lore, and they pursued questions for me until they found the answers or ran up against the barrier of bedtime.

Introduction

WE LOCATE IN GREAT ATHLETES, sometimes with a sense of apt discovery and sometimes with a sense of embellishing embarrassment, types who make up the myths and legends of the race. Babe Ruth was properly Gargantuan, like the eponymous figure from Rabelais. He simply filled out the imaginative space before him. Ted Williams was a different heroic presence—a loner, a brooder, a technician whose skill in the batter's box reigned supreme but whose actions elsewhere proved unsettling and perplexing—more pointedly like the great Greek warrior Achilles, who spent a fair share of time sulking in his tent, who had difficult relations with the local press, but who hit with extreme authority at home and on the road. No one ever questioned Achilles' will to engage when the power was upon him.

The traditional line on Williams in baseball lore, surely a legitimate one to some extent, is that his career was marked by an overriding paradox: How could a ballplayer so controlled, precise, and patient at the plate turn into a monster of temperament, precipitateness, and verbal disarray away from it? Williams's theory of hitting depended on split-second assessments of ordained hitting zones and an almost eerie self-discipline regarding the nature and frequency of his swings. But away from the plate he seemed to swing savagely and wildly at whatever sucker pitches were tossed up to him.

Why would Williams exhibit qualities outside the batter's box that he would never have tolerated within? Could he have staked out a small piece of turf 60 feet 6 inches from the mound where he behaved differently than he did anywhere else? Perhaps a more intriguing view is to see Williams as a man for whom temperament was not divorced from performance. His theory of hitting, which was also his practice of hitting, was really too surgical for such things as bad press clippings to debilitate it; he thus stirred controversy to serve, or better yet, to pique the very concentration that made him a better, keener hitter.

As an intermittently excitable, exuberant, and oddly diffident man, Ted Williams in a sense cultivated his nature as a ballplayer in a way comparable to Ty Cobb, who used his orneriness as a piece of field artillery. Cobb's antics were fungible—he could convert them into winning strategies. Though Williams was of a more generous and likable nature, he, too, aggravated reactions against him as much as he suffered reactions to him. His career was a case study in exacerbation. He sensed, whether knowingly or intuitively, that the irritant voice can stimulate the quiescent bat.

Williams, of course, would have his excessive reactions understood and perhaps even forgotten in light of the times when he acted generously and sanely. The reflex is not unheard of. His tantrums came with justification in his own mind; and the measure of that justification was not to recognize the effect his ranting produced on others but to harbor deep in his soul the resentments that caused them.

As is the case for many sensitive extroverts, Williams never forgot a slight. If a particular writer irritated him, it was a sure bet the writer would suffer not only for the localized point of irritation but for everything else that he might have written, for everything that might have appeared in his paper or magazine, and for much of what the entire community of writers in his time zone may have written. Even writers Williams didn't know bore the brunt of his swagger: "I never met you before, but you're no good."

Though most ballplayers who played with Williams expressed a fondness for him—as Tommy Henrich put it, "It's hard to understand how anyone would not like the big guy"—many writers simply detested him, and for defensible reasons. He treated them like dirt; they were the flotsam and jetsam of the ballpark, parasites, muckrakers, agitators. Roger Kahn, in a 1959 profile on Williams and Stan Musial, noted how confrontational Williams could be: "It's all very staccato, very shallow, with pat answers ready from a man who has been interviewed more times than he remembers or cares to. Touch a nerve, break the pattern of questions he prefers and Williams explodes or walks away. 'Take my answers and be glad I'm talking,' he still seems to say. 'I never needed anybody. I always had my bat.'"

Woe to the writer who protested Williams's unfairness; Williams got even madder when challenged. His temper was a horror. If approached near the dugout, he would move out to the field proper, inscribing more territory, evoking more sound. Abuse is never attractive and usually crosses the Rubicon of decency in short-enough order: a writer who may have begun as the object of Williams's wrath was now a mere mote in his maddened eye. He was Hercules Furens, Lear on the heath, an outraged Job seeking the ear of God.

To a considerable degree Williams may have courted what he supposedly dreaded. He was aware that the problems he faced with the press—indeed, the problems he sometimes created for himself— were partly strategic. Roger Birtwell of the *Boston Globe* remembers walking by Williams and Dom DiMaggio on a train from Chicago to St. Louis and hearing Dom rib Williams: "You buy every newspaper you can get your hands on and spend half your time reading them— just to find someone to get mad at." When I asked Williams once why so few pitchers drove him off the plate, he answered in a way that suggested pitchers were more savvy than the press and the public in figuring out his psychology. "They knew I hit better mad."

"Mad" is a word that, for better or worse, inhabits a prominent niche in Williams's psyche. He returns to it over and again in describing the state of mind important to hitting. He once told Clif Keane of the *Boston Globe* what he looked for in a young player: "I prefer a kid who gets mad at himself, displays anger, over one who doesn't. It helps a player to explode a little bit and show his concern about what's going on." To a young Jimmy Piersall during spring training Williams said, "Kid, there's only one way for you to become a hitter. Go up to the plate and get mad. Get mad at yourself and mad at the pitcher." In a Ted Ashby *Globe* feature article, he echoed his refrain: "I hit better when I'm mad. I'm sharper. My reactions are quicker. My sensibilities keener." He went so far as to point out that the only good days he had when he wasn't angry were days when "the pitcher was a little bit off his game."

To listen to Williams is to begin to understand the method to his madness. In a profile for *Harper's* magazine John Cory asked him how he managed to navigate his fiery and shell-racked jet fighter back to base after a mission during the Korean War. "I fly better mad." Williams had a shrewd sense of what focused him and excited his energies. He also said that the more frightened he was the madder he got. But even in the instance of his crippled plane, his fear was less at the danger he experienced than at the consternation he felt in its presence. He hated to lose control: his expertise was at issue; he was momentarily inferior to his circumstances. And if anger could refocus him, so be it. He would feel it or find a way to generate it.

Over the years, as Roger Kahn put it, "Williams nurtured his rage." The abuse heaped at his feet by those he found a way to irritate incited the very anger that kicked him into a higher hitting gear. Whenever the usually obliging baseball press were slow to attack he would find a way of quickening the process. Clif Keane asked Williams what made him blow up on the field. Williams admitted it was not the booing of the fans alone but something written in the papers that, to his mind, precipitated the fan hostility or put him in a frame of mind to react: "In every instance that's ever occurred, it's because I've been so peeved about what some ham-and-eggs writer has written about me that I want to just blow up." The box scores, of course, tell the other half of the story. Williams invariably went on a batting tear after one of his on-field or off-field tirades. He felt that rhythm and, indeed, forced it.

Williams has written of the town in which he played that "there were forty-nine million newspapers in Boston, from the *Globe* to the Brookline *Something-or-Other*, all ready to jump us." It is the hyperbole of the forty-nine million and the insouciance of the Brookline *Something-or-Other* that marks Williams's rhetoric as it defines his tactics. The unnamed masses out there prime him, challenge him, stiffen him. He says it again and again, whether about the hordes of newspaper writers or the wolf pack of Fenway fans: "I know there are regulars at Fenway who love to hate me. They get more kicks out of giving me the old razoo than out of watching the game. For them I have nothing but contempt. But I'll tell you something. I actually think I'd be a better ballplayer if I was booed every day. The boos stir me up."

The image of Williams as a lonely victim of Boston's newspaper circulation wars was therefore not an entirely passive one. Rather, the reaction to Williams in Boston cut to the essence of American image making in sports: the complicity of the player in creating the various voices that represent him. Harold Kaese of the *Boston Globe*, who knew Williams better than any writer in town, put the matter succinctly: "He may throw his bait upon the water, but we're the poor fish who grab it."

Dominic DiMaggio told Kaese off the record a simple truth: "Ted wants to look good. When the edge is off, so is he." The edge for Williams was not just something the fates delivered to him. If the blade was dull, he sharpened it. While hanging around the Red Sox batting cage, as was his custom, Kaese listened hard to the chatter among the players. He picked up an exchange between Williams and Dom DiMaggio during spring training of 1947 that reveals something of the way Williams conjured up irritants.

DiMaggio was clicking along at about .400 that spring and Williams told him, "Hell, you could take the title if you keep it up."

Dominic looked at Williams and said, "Yeah, well if I did I wouldn't get any more money."

"Why not?" asked a slightly perplexed Williams.

"Because I haven't got any color," DiMaggio shot back.

"Well," said Williams, "pop off a little. Get your name in the papers."

Then DiMaggio, in a kind of ellipsis from a conversation that had obviously transpired in different forms a dozen times before, said with savvy forcefulness, "You had the newspapermen all over you. Then you made them eat their words. Every one of them."

Williams smiled his smile.

◇ 1 ◇

Country of the Sun

THEODORE SAMUEL WILLIAMS was born on August 30, 1918. San Diego, his birthplace, was founded in 1769 by Father Junipero Serra, the Franciscan padre who was empowered to build a series of missions that would give Spain grounds for defending the land of Alta California from Russia—of all countries—which had already staked claim to territory in the extreme northern reaches of the continent by the middle of the 18th century. Ted Williams's heritage reflects, in a way, the missionary fervor and imperialistic zeal that helped shape the land of his birth. His mother, May Williams, nee Venzer, of Mexican and French parentage, was a zealous Salvation Army foot soldier who would be well known in the San Diego area for nearly half a century. His father, Sam Williams, claimed the honor of riding with Teddy Roosevelt's cavalry regiment and, later, serving in the Philippines during America's first imperialistic war, the Spanish-American War of 1898.

The San Diego of Ted Williams's early years was a vibrant place spawned from a lazy Southern Pacific Railroad branch line town of the 19th century. During the early decades of the 20th century funds poured into the city from the entrepreneurial coffers of wealthy northern California baronial families, from water-seeking magnates of southern California, and from the United States Navy, whose Pacific Fleet and its support services moved into the harbor area. By the 1930s San Diego was the largest hub of activity in America for the navy and the marines, with bustling supply depots, hospitals, training stations, and bases. The young Ted Williams, and the best high

1

school players mustered for the occasion, earned their spurs playing pickup games against the navy ball teams. They also spirited a lot of baseball equipment from the navy when backs were conveniently turned or winks conveniently flashed.

Edmund Wilson once said that every loose marble in the country seemed to end up in San Diego, as if the United States were somehow tilted toward the southwest. This was surely true during the Depression years of the 1930s, when the dust-bowl migration put pressure on local resources, manufacturers, agriculture, and service industries. Moreover, the dust-bowl migration sustained the main occupational activity of the Williams family, the relentless saving of souls that focused the energy of May Williams. Ted recalls that his "mother was gone all day and half the night, working the streets for the Salvation Army. I didn't see much of my dad. He had a little photographic shop on Fifth Avenue downtown, taking passport pictures and pictures of sailors with their girls, and he wouldn't get home until nine, ten o'clock."

Sam's response to May's charitable activities was to work late and make himself remote, even taking a little nip here and there since there was no drinking at home in front of May or the two boys (Danny, Ted's brother, was born in 1920). Ted tried his best to play ball all day and avoid any Salvation Army outings with his mother, though she would drag him and Danny to the naval installations on charity runs because she knew the sailors tended to dig a little deeper into their bell bottoms when the kids were along.

May Williams was a familiar figure, with nicknames such as "Salvation May," "the Sweetheart of San Diego," and "the Angel of Tijuana." From the streets of San Diego to the border flop houses of Tijuana, she belonged heart and soul to the Salvation Army, more regular as a noncom than George Bernard Shaw's Major Barbara was as an officer. From the time she settled in San Diego with Sam Williams in 1915, she was indefatigable in the battle for lost and found souls, especially during those trying years of the 1930s in America, when souls were all too easily lost and none too easily found. Had she not made the mistake of marrying outside Army ranks, she might have gone much higher within the organization: rules against exogamous marriage kept her but a colorful foot soldier in the cause for which she devoted her life.

California was always "Salvation gold," according to the Army's newsletter. The "Soldiers of Jesus" saw the chance for reformation up and down the rough coast, and the movement grew by leaps and bounds. Salvation May patrolled San Diego and environs when the population of the city hovered around 150,000. She was known by everyone, contributors to as well as renegades from her cause. "No" was at best a provisional answer to her solicitations. Gentleman Joe Morgan, the San Diego Union's police reporter, remembers May coming up to a group of his friends outside a club called the College Inn, at Fourth and C, during the Depression days. The lot of them were dead broke. May asked for a donation, and Morgan responded, "Gee, May, we don't even have the price of a cup of beer." She reached in her purse, gave him 15 cents, and said, "Here, let the Army buy you one." This was a surprising response in view of her own as well as the Army's attitude toward alcohol; May Williams obviously understood one of the more designing strategies of fundraising: offer a little something but expect a whole lot more in the long run. Gentleman Joe, after all, remembered the story, and it's a good bet that Salvation May touched him for contributions over the years because of it.

Salvation Army troops had to be tough and inexhaustible; May Williams was. The Army's mixture of rigor and admonition dominated Ted Williams's early life through the mere presence of his mother. Salvation Army doctrines were as clear and present in the Williams home as they were in the slums of Victorian London, where they originated. Here is a passage from the Soldier's Teaching Manual under the heading "When We Sin, We Suffer" that, read in a general way, has a bearing on what the young Williams experienced and what the older Williams became:

> Feed too much power to an electrical appliance and there will be a fuse; tighten a guitar string too much and it will break; put too much weight on springs and they will snap. Try to put a screw into wood by turning it the wrong direction and it will never go in; plane the wood against the grain and there will be trouble; use the plane on the wrong kind of surface and the blade will suffer. Be selfish, but suffer for it.

In very real ways for a child, such doctrines and the relentless tone in which they were expressed are always remembered, or, to put it more subtly, never quite forgotten. Ted Williams grew up reading

Salvation Army literature; to this day he knows the slogans and the jargon by heart. He was both stimulated and mortified by them. His character is a mix of selfless discipline and rebelliousness; he is, in a way, both the product of Salvation Army life and its greatest challenge. As a kid, he knew full well what his mother expected of him and of life, but he also wanted to stick his head in the sand at the public sight of his mother's Salvation Army activities. After all, there is something a bit American Gothic about the Salvation Army brat in San Diego who longed to be rid of a stigma that his pride would barely let him admit: the tireless, yet embarrassing, efforts of a Salvation Army mother to hustle contributions on the streets of San Diego while a largely absentee father took passport photos and love-and-lust exposures of sailors and their floozies in a small shop on Fifth Avenue.

Even a very young Ted Williams preferred his charity a little more subdued just as he preferred his religion a little more private, more a matter of conscience than compulsion. He would rather gravitate toward the neighborhood park for his public expression, and only under strict orders did he march to Salvation May's drumbeat. More so than most religions, whose practices are confined to the meeting house or church, the Salvation Army displayed its full wares on the streets. Roustabouts and spoilers mocked the Army's uniforms, its militancy, its language. Williams still smarts at the memory of the looks and sometimes even the slurs directed at his mother.

The Salvation Army was one among many groups that struck some of the harder livers and drinkers in this border town as meddlesome and batty. Williams felt the reaction on the streets, exclaiming against "the prejudice people had in southern California!" Throughout his career Williams always spoke with a tone that suggested he had given the matter real thought and much preferred that judgments be made on the basis of what a person does and how he or she does it. This is a position from which he rarely wavered in theory, though in practice he built up healthy reserves of prejudice against those ungainly human species whose native habitat was the left-field seats or the press box at Fenway Park.

However much the ridicule of his mother's activities made the young Ted Williams cringe, May simply bore right through it. Ted felt the sting where May felt the challenge: "I was embarrassed that my mother was out in the middle of the damn street all the time. Until the day she died she did that, and it always embarrassed me and God knows I respected her and loved her." His later extreme sensitivity to the taunts of the crowd—he said he had ears so fine he could pick out one insult from ten thousand cheers—looks back to these awkward days in San Diego. For Williams the predictable taunts from the fans in left, especially near the beginning of the 1942 season, when his draft reclassification was based on his claiming his mother as a dependent, must have taken him back to the street corner solicitations of his youth in trying ways—"Hey Williams, ya' mother sucks eggs!" Though in his more sober moments Williams could recognize the distinction among insults between the randomly general and the excruciatingly particular, the boy in him always registered the localized embarrassments of the past in the taunts of the present.

In 1924 the Williamses moved into what might charitably be called the Spreckles house, a six-room structure on 4121 Utah Street, conveniently close to North Park playground in University Heights, where Ted spent most of his waking hours when not in school. The home was in effect donated to May Williams with a $4,000 loan from John D. Spreckles, head of a California family with massive real estate holdings in San Diego, a loan silently forgiven because of May's Salvation Army fame.

Sam Williams was a peripheral figure in all of this. May kept him at a distance to avoid a doctrinal crisis in the house, and he kept himself at a distance to avoid May. He remained intermittently at home during Ted's early years earning a modest living; only after Ted's departure from home did he begin to do better through a connection in the administration of Governor Merriam of California. The veneer of the marriage completely crumbled, and Sam went his independent way in 1939 as an inspector for state prisons and road gangs. His itinerancy came as a blessing.

Ted had very little good to say about his father. He was a negative force, almost an allegorical figure of lack. Sam Williams always claimed to have had a semiheroic past: he rode, so he said, in Teddy Roosevelt's brigade during the Spanish-American War, though it seemed clearer to him than to Ted that he was telling the truth. At least Sam wished to sustain the impression of his exploits by naming his son after the blustering Teddy. It is a forgetfulness bordering on absurdity that Williams cannot grasp the significance of the name "Teddy" on his birth certificate: "I'm not even sure where I got my name. The birth certificate reads 'Teddy Samuel Williams.' I never did like that 'Teddy,' so I always signed my name 'Theodore.'" His middle name, Samuel, he could understand; that name belonged to his mother's brother, claimed Ted, forgetting, perhaps, that Sam was his father's name too.

With his father not there, in a sense, even when he was there, a young Ted Williams was left with the double curse of aloneness. He resented his mother's long hours and, whether or not he could really put his finger on it, resented the estrangement in temperament and in will that kept his father's presence muted and ineffective. His tactic as a child, as a youth, and even as a man, was to make do with surrogates. He sought them out, cultivated their friendship, valued their concern. The list of surrogate fathers is a long one. He drew himself toward them and felt drawn by them.

Johnny Lutz, a Utah Street neighbor and poultry retailer, taught Ted how to fire a rifle and actually hit something. He was a marksman who competed in target shoots. Chick Rotert, a game warden, taught him how to fish. Les Cassie, the father of a boyhood friend and the handyman at the high school, took Ted fishing off Coronado pier and got him his only graduation present, a fountain pen. Floyd Johnson, the principal of Hoover High, remembers a relaxed kid visiting him in his office and trying to angle a way for the two of them to play a little hooky and go fishing.

Perhaps most important, Williams latched on to Rod Luscomb, the director of North Park playground, where Ted learned to play ball: "I tagged after Rod Luscomb almost every day of my life for six or seven years, hanging around like a puppy waiting for him to finish marking the fields or rolling the diamond." The guy who takes care of the local field is a great choice for a friend. It makes life easier when bigger kids, as is their impulse, tell the smaller ones to take a hike.

Even later in his life Williams spoke with an almost filial fondness for those who took the time to respond to him, from Joe Cronin, his first manager at Boston, to Joe McCarthy, his manager in 1948, 1949, and part of 1950. He was a bit more circumspect with Tom Yawkey, owner of the Sox, with whom he was known to shoot pigeons after day games at Fenway, but, then again, he had to negotiate his yearly allowance from that paternal surrogate. Listening to Williams speak now, even beyond the age of 70, one still hears a reverence for relationships he struggled to create as a child and continued to create as a grown man.

Pete Williams, the son of Joe Williams, head of the sports desk for the *New York World Telegram*, taped a conversation with Ted during the 1987 Red Sox spring training in Winterhaven. The writer's son and the old veteran joked a bit about Joe Williams because clearly Ted considered him pretty much a son of a bitch. But as the conversation meandered, Ted struck a special tone with Pete Williams.

Pete described how his dad was a little long in the tooth when he was born and on the road for much of the time, anyway. He wondered if he might have missed something from his childhood. This touched Williams—you could hear it in his voice. His bantering ceased; his chatter calmed: "You want to know your father." So Pete Williams paused after Ted's wistful remark and tried to change the subject. Ted wouldn't quite leave it. He warmed a bit on the subject of Joe Williams, then he meandered onto the subject of older ballplayers, legends, heroes. He spoke about admiring Bill Terry when he was a kid and how he later got to know Terry and talked hitting with him. But the memory of one person he had not met nagged at him. "I have one great regret about the time I played," Williams admitted. "Year after year when we headed north after spring training I never stopped off in Greenville to visit Joe Williams." "You mean Joe Jackson, Shoeless Joe?" Pete corrected. "Oh, yeah. Yeah! Joe Jackson," said Williams. The slip is obvious enough. Two Joes, two Williamses, fathers, sons, regrets, and a mishmash of names. But the slip is telling, nonetheless.

◇

A Chamber of Commerce flier in the 1920s described the city of Ted Williams's birth as "a place where you may be out-of-doors every day and at every hour of the day during the entire year." For the most part, Williams was. Ted Williams grew up hitting. Many who learned the sport before the time of organized youth leagues remember the rhythm and ritual pacing of days at the local park. The same kids were always out there; the same games, versions of over-the-line or hit-the-bat, were always played. Base runners, more often than not, were imaginary because running time took away from hitting time. The trick was to keep the concocted game down to few enough players so that at-bats came hard upon each other. If the playground was jammed with kids, the more innovative ones spun off and found a niche of the field that could still accommodate, with special revisions of ground rules, a healthy dose of hitting—pure hitting.

There is a mystique about taking the field on a warm, sunny day— a feeling that remains powerful throughout one's life. And there is a kind of exhausted serenity in remaining for hours until the last vagrant soul willing to stay out there with you has left. Then, through the power of fantasy, you stay out there alone and play a projected game, finding a concrete wall and hitting rubber balls against it, catching those hits when they zoom off the wall at next-to-impossible angles or heights. You are an entire infield, an entire outfield.

Hannibal Coons, a writer with a name out of a Faulkner novel, spoke at length to Williams's mother in San Diego during the 1948 season and came away with the story that as a kid Ted idolized Babe Ruth. But May didn't know any other ballplayers. Like many distracted mothers of baseball-obsessed kids, she groped for the only name that fell readily off the tip of her tongue. The truth was that Pepper Martin of the Gas House Gang St. Louis Cardinals occupied a more treasured place in Ted's pantheon, such as it was, than Ruth because of the way Martin ran the bases. Even for a young Williams, running was the most difficult part of the game; his recurring nightmare was crawling on his hands and knees to home after rounding third base. Pepper Martin was to base running what Ted Williams would become to hitting: the best.

As for pure left-handed hitters, a young Williams looked to Bill Terry of the Giants, though a kid from San Diego in the 1930s mostly *hears* about major league ballplayers; the only actual glimpse he might catch of them is on a newsreel at the movies. So of his early efforts Ted Williams merely recalls that he hit left-handed in North Park for no particular reason: "I don't know why but from the time I was old enough to carry a bat to the sandlots of San Diego, I hit lefty." His dream as a youth was to hit off Wilbur Wiley, a kid who could fire it past him until Ted was 14.

An old playground acquaintance tells a story about Williams that may or may not be true. Ted Laven, a navy brat, used to hang out with the kids at North Park playground when Williams was 9 or 10. He remembers a game on the softball field that had a shallow left field with a high wire fence and a more spacious right field with a reasonably disposed fence. Local rules gave incremental points for drives to the far reaches of the outfield. Right field simply had farther reaches, and Laven recalls Williams switching to the left side of the plate in pursuit of more hitting territory. He did just fine and stayed put. Laven embellishes the story a bit by supposing the kids subtracted points for the nuisance factor of balls hit from the right side over the left-field fence. But this seems implausible. No kid in his right mind would willingly accede to such a rule.

Whatever the origins of his famous swing, Williams had no trouble putting distance on the ball from portside as he grew older and taller (if not heavier). In January 1934, at the end of Ted's last semester in junior high school, some older friends escorted him over to take a few cuts with the local high school team as the coach, Wos Caldwell, looked on. The Hoover High varsity was beginning spring-term workouts on the field, so the potential recruits were swinging from an auxiliary playground. Not yet 16 years old, Williams put one completely over the school lunch arbor and then another up against a building over 300 feet distant. "I'm Ted Williams," he told Caldwell. "I go to Horace Mann Junior High, but we get out next week—and I'll be back." It was a variation of this remark that he would repeat to the Red Sox outfield when Boston sent him down to Minneapolis halfway through spring training in 1938.

Ted Williams played outfield regularly and pitched a bit for Hoover High in his freshman year. As a tenth grader he hit over .300. But he went on a special tear in 1935, his junior year, jacking up to a remarkable .583. As a senior, he tailed off to .403, but he was concentrating on his pitching that season. His fastball was never dynamite, but he had fine control for a kid and an excellent curve.

Williams played ball constantly in those days; the high school schedule was just a slice of the action. Much of his baseball world inscribed a northern arc that extended from the California-Mexico border to the communities of the greater Los Angeles area, from the local school districts of Hoover High and San Diego High to Fullerton and Exposition Park in Los Angeles. In the spring and summer before he took his first paying job with the Padres, Williams played regular-season high school ball, postseason traveling tournament ball, summer American Legion ball, pickup games with the local military team, and even a bit of semipro with a team sponsored by a local bakery. But May Williams drew the line at Ted's $5-a-game chance to play for the Texas House Liquor team: imagine playing for a liquor-supply house while Mother May was trying to scrape the winos off Broadway!

During these months Ray Boone, a future major leaguer himself, was a 13-year-old lad in San Diego. He was batboy for the "Fighting Bob" Post American Legion team on which Williams contributed mostly his pitching services. Every once in a while the older kids would sneak Boone into right field if the score was lopsided. But Boone's most vivid recollections of Williams in San Diego are not what he remembers from Legion ball but from those wondrous high school games for two years when he was part of a group of grammar school and junior high youngsters who rode to Hoover High games on their bicycles. The bicycle-brigade kids just loved to see Williams hit them and hit them high. "My, he could hit 'em high. Far, okay, okay, but high was the thing. That's why we biked wherever he played. We wanted Williams to hit one, and we just squealed when he put it up, so far up in the air, and then so far out of the park." Boone's voice became more animated: "Ya' know, I remember those shots. And he still hit them that way in the majors. Whenever I saw him hit one I remembered those days in San Diego, all of us kids perched on our bikes, screamin' and screamin'."

Ted Williams began to attract attention from local baseball people in his junior year, when his hitting and pitching were stupendous. Floyd Johnson, principal of Hoover High, remembers his favorite game—a Bay City League game with Santa Monica. Williams struck out 23 and hit a homer, long and high as usual. The boy began receiving some attention. Herb Bennyhoven of the Cardinals made the most serious exploratory foray, talking Ted into a tryout camp at Fullerton even though he was hobbling on a sore foot. Williams knew the Cards were interested in jackrabbits and didn't think he measured up. But Bennyhoven told him they also were looking at a kid from Fullerton, a big, lumbering slugger named Lou Novikoff, the future

"Mad Russian." So why not give it a try? Ted showed up, took a few cuts, couldn't dig in well with his sore foot, and impressed no one but Bennyhoven. Branch Rickey was there and batted not an eye. Still, Bennyhoven got the Cards to take a chance on Williams soon after.

Others looked but had their doubts. One scout, Marty Krug of the Tigers, told May Williams, "If you let this boy play baseball now, it will kill him." Ted was carrying about 150 pounds dripping wet on a gangling 6'3" frame. When he ran the bases he looked like a flamingo on a mating run. That same year Elmer Hill, a friend who knew the family, contacted Yankees scout Bill Essick in Los Angeles. Hill, a San Diego fireman, pitched for a semipro team sponsored by Cramer's Bakery. He knew Essick and thought he should take a look at the kid. By that time, Herb Bennyhoven already had Williams working out with a Cardinals' recruit team, the Juniors. Hill invited Essick down to watch a game in which he himself pitched against the Juniors. This was no setup. Hill's competitive juices began to flow and he threw a one-hitter at the raw recruits. He also got his protégé, Ted Williams, on strikes three times.

Even so, Bill Essick liked the looks of the kid's swing, and after the game he, Hill, and Williams went to speak to May and Sam Williams at their home on Utah Street. Sam Williams only perked up when money was on the agenda. Father Sam had even been in touch with the Los Angeles Angels of the Coast League on Ted's behalf. Essick made an offer: $250 per month and a chance to make Oakland's ball club in the Pacific Coast League. If Ted made it, the offer would go to $400 per month. May and Sam said they would make no decision until next year, Ted's senior year, but the deal looked pretty good and they would probably sign if Essick left the contract.

Williams began playing with Hill's Cramer Bakery semipro team on Sundays and even got a job driving the van for the bakery on Saturdays. In his senior year, Hill took Ted's mother up to a postseason tournament in Pomona. Essick was there again and watched with renewed interest as Williams pitched well and hit much better than he had the previous year. The San Diego papers splashed the victory all over the local sports pages, the *Union* proclaiming, "HOOVER WINS DIAMOND TOURNEY: Rising to the heights behind a brilliant three-hit mound performance by lanky Ted Williams, Herbert Hoover High yesterday defeated arch rival San Diego High 6-1 in the Stadium to capture the championship in the first annual American Legion Invitational Interscholastic Baseball championship. Williams, the limber-armed right-hander who usually shows more power at the plate than on the mound, struck out 13 and walked 7."

At this point Sam Williams got into the act with Essick in an annoying but still, in Elmer Hill's estimation, workable way. He began to finagle for a signing bonus of $1,000 and for slightly jacked-up contracts of $275 or $425 per month, whichever one materialized. Hill told Sam that he couldn't imagine that would be much of a problem and would get back to him after he spoke to Essick. This was on June 25, 1936. On June 26 Bill Lane, of the newly installed San Diego Padres, cut a different deal with May Williams. Elmer Hill knew the jig was up. He sensed that Ted wanted to sign with the Yanks, but that "being a minor, he didn't have much choice." Hill went on, "I was burning plenty, called Ted's dad, told him the least he could do was wire Essick and explain. This he did. Bill sent me his wire, which I still have." Sam Williams may have smoothed Essick's feathers, but not Hill's.

Later, Hill reconstructed the evening. "Bill Lane and Frank Shellenback, manager of the Padres, must have gotten to May Williams the very night I spoke to Sam. I don't know for sure what the deal was, but it was rumored that Mr. Williams was offered a couple of hundred bucks for signing on the spot and grabbed it. Ted played for a little bit of nothing." For May, the linchpin of the deal was a promise extracted from Bill Lane that Ted would not be optioned out of San Diego immediately, and that if his contract were later to be sold, she and Sam would get a percentage cut of the sale price. No one else was interested in signing the lad to a stay-at-home deal, and no one else but Lane really could. From May's point of view her boy's options at just under 18 years of age were limited to the Salvation Army (not likely), the United States Navy (not desirable), or the San Diego Padres (passable). She chose, and Ted was chosen for, the last.

Actually, Bill Lane had begun talking to the Williams family and those serving as their intermediaries—Wos Caldwell, Ted's high school coach, and Herb Bennyhoven, who still had a notion of keeping Williams local until the Cards could nab him—around June 20. Ted was then still playing tournament ball for Hoover—a few days before he signed he got shellacked on the mound in an 8–3 loss to Escondido High—but that week, before signing, he also began working out with the Padres.

San Diego Union sports columnist Monroe McConnell provided an account on June 23 of an exhibition game between the Padres and the Navy All-Stars. This is the first inkling that Williams was on the premises. McConnell said little in his story except that the Padres worked themselves into a 12-0 lead, which gave manager Frank Shellenback the chance to fiddle with some camp followers: "Once out in front with a seemingly safe margin, the Padres gave up their places to young high school players who have been working out at the park daily. Ted Williams went to left field." The high schoolers almost frittered away the Padres' lead and the score ended up 12-10, but Williams ripped a single in his only time at the plate.

Bobby Doerr, only 18 himself and playing regular second base for the Padres, remembers the scene. The high schoolers were shagging flies and taking grounders with the club, but some of the vets wanted them out of the batting cage—that is, until their curiosity about Williams got the better of them. "Let this kid hit," one vet implored manager Shellenback. "Yeah, sure, hit a few, kid," Shellenback muttered, realizing all the while what Bill Lane intended. Williams slammed several out of Lane Field, the brand-new combined base-ball-football complex, toward the rail yard tracks near the harbor. Bobby Doerr heard the vet growl, "They'll sign him." Indeed they did.

◇ 2 ◇

Minor Key and Major Talent

A FEW MONTHS SHY OF HIS 18th birthday, on June 26, 1936, Ted Williams signed with the consent of his family to play ball for the San Diego Padres of the Pacific Coast League for $150 a month. He would join the team immediately. In addition to Bobby Doerr starring at second base, the Padres could boast of a slick-fielding shortstop, George Myatt; an experienced catcher, Gene Desautels; and the oldest of the hard-hitting DiMaggios, Vince, in left. This was the Padres' first year in San Diego, though seemingly not a banner one at the time they signed Williams. They were floundering in sixth place with a 37–42 record. No one thought Williams was the answer. In fact, the Padres placed their hopes on a journeyman ballplayer from Indianapolis, Ivey Shiver, who would join the team in a couple of weeks, shine for a couple of months in the outfield, and then bag it all to coach college football, much to the rookie Williams's delight.

Lane's deal with the raw Williams was more a future's stake than anything else. He signed the kid with an agreement to season him at home—that is, not to option his contract to anyone for the balance of 1936 and through 1937, though Williams probably ought to have played a notch down from the Coast League's Double-A ball in 1936. Lane figured Ted probably belonged on a lower level in 1937 as well, but to honor his deal with May Williams he kept the boy as part of his local baseball portfolio.

No matter what perspective Lane put on his signing of Williams, it was a landmark week for Ted and a generally interesting one in Depression-racked America. The signing of the local high school star hit the San Diego newspapers on June 27, and the Saturday edition of the *Union* featured the event on its pages: "Ted Williams, Herbert Hoover High School diamond hero and one of the best natural prospects developed in this area in some time, signed a contract with the San Diego Padres yesterday and will be in uniform with the Coast League club today." The Padres even provided some of the contractual small print: "Under the terms of his contract, Williams will be kept with the Padres for the remainder of the season and all of next without being farmed out." Manager Shellenback's reaction was noncommittal: "He will be given the opportunity to show what he can do under fire."

Along with the story of Williams's contract, local papers on the morning of June 27, 1936, carried the news that Lucky Luciano had just been put away for 30–50 years by the dapper special rackets prosecutor of New York State, Thomas E. Dewey, who had methodically tied Luciano to a network of 300 brothels run by organized crime along the eastern seaboard. Also in the news, Mrs. Gloria Morgan Vanderbilt petitioned the courts to release $4,250 of the estate of her twelve-year-old daughter Gloria so that she might take care of the girl for the one month a year stipulated at the infamous Vanderbilt custody trial. Her request glosses the style to which some of the rich had grown accustomed during the Depression. Mrs. Vanderbilt argued that, among other things, she must dole out $12 a day for the protection afforded by a private detective, $30 a month for goodies at Bloomingdale's, $75 a month for an assistant to the gardener, and $113 a month for automobile expenses.

Internationally during the last week of June, the British government refused to continue political or economic sanctions against Mussolini for the Italian military invasion of Ethiopia. The government's decision met with jeers in the House of Commons, and the well-known foreign correspondent John Elliott, thinking as much about the Germans in the Rhineland and Franco in Spain as about Mussolini's mechanized thrust against Ethiopian spear carriers, wrote in his syndicated dispatches: "All along the line dictatorships are triumphant and everywhere democracies have been beaten." Most Americans in 1936 did not wish to hear this sort of talk any more than the British government did, but voices were nonetheless raised early for those ready to listen.

On the American political scene, Father Charles E. Coughlin of
the National Union for Social Justice party announced his support of
third-party presidential candidate, Representative William Lemke,
who was running against Alf Landon, just selected by the Republicans, and Roosevelt, then ensconced in his first-term presidency.
Coughlin ranted that the American worker was dying on the vine,
working on the average only half the year and earning a mere $1,000.
The United States had just gone $6 billion over the previous year's
national debt—a ringing $34,331,355,867. This was the largest in-
crease since 1919.

Elsewhere around the nation at the end of June 1936, the Marx
brothers were rehearsing a stage production of A Day at the Races,
soon to become a movie; Jeanette MacDonald was starring in San
Francisco, the disaster film of the '30s; and The Great Ziegfeld was
booming at the box office. In Boston, the unthinkable happened at
Harvard University's June commencement. Mrs. Mary Curley Don-
nelly, daughter of Boston mayor James M. Curley, inadvertently
followed her father into Harvard Yard for graduation exercises. This
was a literal faux pas. The mayor's daughter was the very first woman
to set her official foot on this all-male ground in 300 years of the
school's history. Commencement marshals escorted her out with
dispatch and a certain graceless horror.

In major league baseball at the time Ted Williams signed, his
favorite team, the St. Louis Cardinals, held a two-game lead over the
Cubs, and the Yanks were five games up on Boston. Lou Gehrig, in
the middle of his consecutive-games-played streak, led American
League hitters at .388, and one of Williams's favorites, Pepper Martin, led the National League at .374. Jimmie Foxx and Mel Ott were
the big home-run hitters in June, Foxx with 18 for Boston and Ott
with 12 for the Giants. Joe DiMaggio, in his rookie year, was hitting
at a .347 clip for the Yanks, and Bobby Feller, also a rookie, was
burning up the league for Cleveland. The Sporting News had its eye
on several hot prospects in the minors, featuring three "can't-miss"
phenoms: Joe Gordon, Tommy Henrich, and Rudy York. None of
them, in fact, did miss.

The Joe Louis–Max Schmeling fight of a week earlier was still hot
sports news. On June 19 Max Schmeling stunned Louis, an odds-on
favorite, in front of 45,000 fans at Yankee Stadium. Heavyweight

champ James Braddock was there to check out his next likely contender in this major nontitle bout. Schmeling beat Louis to the punch all night long with sneak rights, putting him down in the 4th, exhausting him by the 10th, and finally shelving him in the 12th with unrelenting right hooks and crosses. As referee Art Donovan counted, Louis lifted his shoulder from the mat at 5, raised to his elbow at 7 and shook his head clear, then staggered and swayed to a London Bridge position as Donovan hit 10. The next day Schmeling was properly Third Reichian: "I knew I could beat him, and I would not let any Negro beat me. . . . Any man who holds his left out like so," he stated as he waved his fist, "can be hit with a right, no?" *Yes*, Joe Louis must have thought, as he made a mental note for his return match.

Naturally, Adolf Hitler sent his golden boy Schmeling a congratulatory telegram the next day, June 20. On that same day Jesse Owens, a brilliant black runner from Ohio State University, set what appeared to be a world record of 10.2 seconds in the 100 meters during an NCAA meet at Stagg Field, in Chicago. But the time was disallowed as wind-aided. Later in the summer of 1936 Owens and his black teammates would have a run at Hitler's Aryans and the rest of the world in the Munich Summer Olympic Games. The glory of their performances would send the bilious führer out of his own stadium in a huff.

The day after Williams signed, he enjoyed—or, more accurately—suffered his first at-bat as a professional ballplayer. On June 27 he struck out looking off Henry "Cotton" Pippen of Sacramento, a pitcher he later faced with better results in his first game for the Red Sox at Fenway in 1939 when Pippen pitched for the Philadelphia A's. Williams came into the game as a pinch hitter for Padres pitcher Jack Hill in the second. Hill looked horrible on the mound in the top of that inning, and Shellenback wanted to get him out of there before the game was blown wide open. He ended up using 18 men on his roster, including Williams, and the Padres finally pulled the game out 7-6.

The only action Williams saw in the next few days was before the umpire said "play ball." He threw batting practice. Shellenback, with a king's ransom of outfielders, wasn't sure what he was going to do with the kid, and he wanted to see if Williams could pitch. He had his doubts. A few days later, July 3, against Los Angeles, Williams had himself quite a day. With the Padres getting whacked around and trailing by 10 runs, he came into the game as a pinch hitter in the sixth and singled off Glen Babler for his first hit as a pro. But this time he remained in the game to single again off Joe Berry. Ted then pitched 1⅓ innings, getting blasted for a pair of runs on solo homers by Steve Mesner and Wes Schulmerich. The left-field blast by Schulmerich tore into a tree 450 feet away and ripped off most of its branches. Shellenback had seen enough. Williams was through as a pitcher, though it looked as though he could hit a bit.

Shellenback gave Williams his first start the next day, July 4, in the opening game of a doubleheader in Los Angeles. He went 1 for 4 with a double, his first extra-base hit. The next day the clubs played another doubleheader, and Williams got the nod in both games. But Shellenback did not like what he saw. Ted did about as fast a fade as a rookie could. He took the collar in both games, with a couple of walks. Shellenback put him right back on the bench and went shopping for more veteran outfielders.

Ted Williams had his own personal scoop on Shellenback early. He wrote in his autobiography that Frank was "a wonderful, wonderful man, a man I respected as much as any I've known in baseball, but I don't mean to say he was all out for young ballplayers." Only the newness of the life and the thrill of the travel and the promise of the future masked the boredom of Williams's rookie season, much of which he spent putting a high gloss on the wooden bench with his Padres flannels. This was as planned by owner Bill Lane, who, like many shrewd minor league executives in the first half of the century, was willing to nurture Williams for a richer payoff in a few years. Everyone in the Padres organization also knew that Shellenback liked to go with veterans, wherever he could find them. The Padres' outfield in 1936 was an open invitation to experienced players, the last of which, shortly after Williams signed, was Ivey "Chick" Shiver. On July 7, the Padres purchased Shiver from Indianapolis, and he took over permanently—for the time being—in right, as Vince DiMaggio held down left and Williams's veteran roommate, Sid Durst, roamed center.

The Padres were not doing well, and Bill Lane was on edge for a number of reasons, some of them having less to do with his players on the field than with the dirtiness of league politics. Minor league ball marched pretty much to its own drumbeat in the Pacific Coast League of the 1930s, and those who presently find the contemporary shenanigans of professional baseball to be small-minded should measure the following episode for its ethical fit. In a game against the Angels in San Diego on July 19, the local fans turned on the umps for some dicey calls. The display was ugly and unrelenting. Lane was in attendance with the league president, W. C. Tuttle, and the two men left their seats and repaired to Lane's private office, where they issued instructions to warn the fans that the game would be called if calm were not restored. Calm was not, and the umpires were told to suspend the ball game in the fourth inning.

But things were just warming up. The Los Angeles papers, especially the *Herald Examiner,* went berserk, charging their smaller San Diego neighbor to the south with a crime akin to cattle rustling. The next time the two teams played in San Diego, Lane responded by banning the *Herald Examiner* writers from the press box. He claimed the whole incident was a put-up job by John Connolly, a sports editor on the *Examiner* who was openly campaigning for Tuttle's job as league president. Lane claimed that when he and Tuttle left their seats during the game in question, Connolly concocted a wild tale that the league president was threatened with assault by fans for incompetence. Lane was getting even for what he saw as a journalistic outrage.

Most of this silliness took place while Williams sat on the bench, but he got a dose, at least, of how seedy relations between baseball and the press could be. Shellenback kept his young outfielder sitting for nearly a month until an August 9 doubleheader against Portland, when Williams played both ends because Sid Durst had pulled a muscle. He broke out, slamming three hits and driving in a couple of runs as the Padres swept. The club was playing better ball and creeping up in the standings to within three games of first. *San Diego Union* columnist Monroe McConnell, who had tracked Williams from his high school days, wrote: "Young Ted Williams, Padre recruit who got his chance in the outfield when Sid Durst was out of the lineup temporarily because of a pulled muscle, delivered like a veteran and Padre fans probably will see more of him."

Delivering like a veteran was about the only thing a rookie could do to impress Shellenback, but another shrewd observer of talent was in the stands for that August doubleheader: Eddie Collins, the general manager of the Boston Red Sox. The former great second baseman of the A's and White Sox was in town to take an option on the contract of a potential prize property, Bobby Doerr, for Mr. Tom Yawkey's Red Sox. Doerr was good and Collins knew it. At the time, Bill Lane was also touting the value of shortstop George Myatt, but Collins had other notions. In the midst of seeking another option on catcher Gene Desautels, he asked about the kid in right, that youngster Williams, whose swing looked good and who seemed able to drive in runs. Lane demurred, claiming the kid was just 17 and he had made a deal with his mother. So Collins backed off, but he cajoled Lane into a verbal agreement that the Padres' owner, to his credit, honored. Lane would not peddle Williams to anyone else without first consulting with Collins.

Collins left town after his quick look-see at potential Red Sox properties, and Williams was back in his rut. On August 13 he went 0 for 7 in a doubleheader and, even with Durst out, Shellenback sat Ted again, digging up a reserve named Wirthman to play in his stead. These were not good times, though Bobby Doerr said that Williams never lost his natural exuberance, even taking a header one day on the polished floor of a hotel lobby while swinging an imaginary bat. Moreover, the travel was new and fresh—Williams was seeing country in northern California and up the coast into Oregon and Washington that enchanted him. And chowing down with the team was a special delight. Williams went way over Uncle Bill Lane's daily meal allowance, but the owner let it ride. Bobby Doerr said that this, in itself, was something. Lane was a gruff old coot and his players were a bit intimidated by him. But he softened on Williams. His property, after all, was a growing boy and had to be nurtured.

Through most of August Williams sat. And sat . . . and sat. He was nowhere in a poll that ranked the Padres' most popular players, a list headed by his injured roomie, Sid Durst, with Bobby Doerr, Georgie Myatt, Gene Desautels, and Vince DiMaggio following. However, on September 1 San Diego faced one of its several ludicrous crisis points during the year. The slick-fielding Ivey Shiver, singled out in July as the apple of Frank Shellenback's eye, told the team he had a chance to coach football in Georgia. For Shiver this was, in his mind, a career opportunity. Any chance for the majors seemed already behind him.

Bill Lane was perplexed at this turn of events because San Diego was actually making a run for the pennant. They were in second place and closing at two games behind Portland. The day before Shiver's sudden departure, Shellenback put Williams in the outfield for a charity game against a local semipro team. Ted got four hits, including his first home run as a Padre, even if it didn't count in league play. But the performance earned him another crack at the lineup. Back in the regular action the next day against Sacramento, Williams broke loose. He went 2 for 3 with power—a triple, a double, and two runs batted in. He also made two fine running catches in left. Monroe McConnell, always ready to praise the youngster, commented in his column on the fans' short-lived ire at Ivey Shiver's departure and their delight in Williams's work: "After seeing young Ted Williams cover his left-field sector like a blanket and smack out a double and triple in three times up, most of the fans were willing to join in on the chorus of a sad little ditty for Shiver, 'We're plenty glad you're gone, you rascal you.'"

With the pennant on the line, Williams soon got a taste of the glory. He coasted for a couple of games and then earned his first banner headline for two games against Sacramento on September 6: "PADRES TAKE DOUBLEHEADER: TED WILLIAMS SHINES." He smashed a double, a single, stole a base, and "reached over the fence to spear a drive by Peters to go along with three other spectacular catches on the day." A Sacramento reporter in the press box complained to the *Union's* McConnell that "the kid was a thorn in our side all day." Inadvertently, the writer mumbled a nickname that would stick when the Kid showed up a year and a half later for the Red Sox spring training in 1938.

The Padres and Portland fought it out during the last days of the season, but San Diego ended up 1½ games out of first, close enough to earn a playoff berth. In the Pacific Coast League, teams could win the pennant and then lose in postseason play, a kind of round-robin involving the top four teams in the division. On September 15 the playoffs began with the Oakland Oaks taking the first game from the Padres 6–3. But Ted Williams did something in the game he had not been able to do during the regular season—he hit his first official home run as a minor league ballplayer in the eighth inning off one of the premier pitchers on the coast, Wee Willie Ludolph, a.k.a. the Oakland Ghost.

The rest of the playoffs were uneventful. San Diego managed but one win in the best-of-seven series, and Williams rounded out his rookie year by banging out two singles in the last game. For the regular season he hit a respectable .271 in 42 games. He came to the plate for 107 official at-bats and managed 8 doubles and 2 triples. Bobby Doerr, whose career would roughly parallel Williams's with the Sox through the early '50s, hit a solid .342 for the Padres in 1936.

In 1937 Williams was eager. He came to the Padres' spring training early with pitchers and catchers to work with Sid Durst, a former Yankees outfielder now 40 years old, on hitting and, especially, fielding. Bill Lane was intent this year on refining the talents of his investment, and Durst was the first refiner. He had the good sense not to touch Ted's swing, but he emphasized something Williams never forgot: bat speed relies on the pivot of the hips, and a hitter is nothing without quickness. The swing must explode from the pivot; the movement of the torso frees the arms for the tuck-and-pull action of the swing.

Williams arrived not only raring to go but tuned up. During the off-season he had pestered and nagged Padres catcher Gene Desautels, also living in San Diego, to go with him to the park and pitch to him. Desautels was willing enough but not quite at the pace Williams desired. Nonetheless, he recalls hitting with Williams by the hour that winter. All the while Desautels was serving Eddie Collins, who had called and told him to keep tabs on Williams. Desautels later advised Collins to purchase the kid's option. He had no doubts.

In March the rest of the Padres returned to San Diego for spring training. The big news in California was the planned around-the-world flight of the aviatrix Amelia Earhart, who took off from Oakland on March 18 on the first leg of a long and ultimately sad journey. The *San Diego Union* featured Earhart on the opening day of spring training, and it also began its traditional thumbnail sketches of the Padres. Of Williams, the feature recalled his legendary .430 career average at Hoover High, breezed over his .271 for the 1936 season, and dwelled on his one hobby, at least the one he revealed for the sketch: "Oh, I like to go to the park and hit."

This year Williams was determined to start for the Padres, though already Frank Shellenback had pulled another outfielder out of his hat—the exciting and powerful Tommy Thompson. Nobody was penciling Williams's name in yet, and the Padres' season opened with Williams in that familiar spot he had occupied most of the previous year: the bench. Shellenback, playing sudden and unpredictable whims, started Williams in a doubleheader on April 11 against the San Francisco Missions. He hit his first regular-season home run in the minors off lefty Stew Bolen. Then he sat again. After hitting a homer on April 27, he played a few more games and was subsequently benched for a doubleheader on May 2.

Shellenback simply did not consider his outfield anyone's safe haven, but as his club slipped five games behind the San Francisco Seals (there were two San Francisco clubs in the league then), he thought he would give consistency a try. Shellenback settled with Sid Durst, Tommy Thompson, and Hal Catchet garnering most of the outfield play. Ten days went by during one stretch in late May with Williams playing nary a game. This was not the stuff that dreams were made of. Through June, he played a couple of games and sat; played three straight and rested, and so on. He moped on the bench and pressed on those few occasions when he got the opportunity to hit. If he struck out or popped up, the pain would register all too readily on his face.

Then Williams got a chance. On June 22, the same day that Joe Louis shook the Max Schmeling bogeyman off his back by knocking out James Braddock in the eighth round for the heavyweight championship of the world, Williams scored the winning run in a 3-2 game by blasting one into the far reaches of deep center at Lane Field for an inside-the-park home run. The local press rewarded the effort with a banner headline: "TED WILLIAMS HOMER WINS FOR PADRES." But, more significant, the fabled national baseball newspaper *The Sporting News* picked up the item the next week for its minor league highlights column: "Ted Williams, 18-year-old San Diego leftfielder, broke up a pitcher's duel between Tiny Chaplin of the Padres and Barnacle Bill Posedel of Portland June 22 when he cracked a 400' homer inside Lane Field."

In the next several games Williams began belting them out on an almost daily basis: one on June 24, another the next day, two more on June 27, another on July 2. Shellenback got the message. With San Diego creeping up on league-leading Sacramento, he had himself a regular outfielder. The Padres took over first place on the same day the United States Navy, after a long, fruitless effort in the Pacific, reluctantly gave up the search for Amelia Earhart.

During the dog days of August, the Padres barely clung to their lead, though an increasingly confident and powerful Williams continued to break up ball games with long blasts. He began to tire in late August, and Shellenback decided to rest him on August 20. But he needed a pinch hitter in the eighth inning of a close game against Sacramento. Williams came in and doubled to keep the Padres in the game and then homered in the 11th to win it. The game was notable because umpire Jack Powell yanked a couple of fans out of their seats and began beating the hell out of them on the field. It turned out he was umping while roaring drunk and had to be escorted from the field by the police. He could have used the services of Williams's mother but had to settle for Padres infielder Jimmy Reese, who came down to the jail and bailed him out.

As the 1937 season entered its final weeks, Williams continued to drive the ball and the club. He won a game against the Seals on August 31 with a home run in the eighth that, according to sportswriter Monroe McConnell, landed in the shed of the railroad freight yard. He had never seen anything like it at Lane Field. McConnell wrote that "Ted Williams had an answer for his severest critics, whose chief complaint is that he is weak against southpaw pitchers. All Theodore did yesterday to refute the argument was to sock a double in the first and catapult a homer over the right-field wall in the eighth off lefty Frank Lamanske." The next day he hit two more, and the day after that he helped his club score nine runs in the ninth inning to tie a game 15–15 against the Seals, only to lose in the next inning, 16–15.

This tough loss began a San Diego slide. Though Williams was hitting well, the team began to fade in the stretch. Of course, the Padres finished high enough for the playoffs, a way to still win after losing. San Diego began with a 6–4 win over the Sacramento Solons. Williams led the way with a triple, a double, and two base hits. Three days later the Padres swept the first installment of the playoffs when Williams blasted one out against Tony Freitas. It took them another four games, and another sweep, to win the league championship from Portland, with Williams and Tommy Thompson leading the way at the plate.

These games, eight playoff wins in a row, were wonderful ones for Williams. He ended his first full minor league season with a major display of power and prowess, finishing up at .291 with 23 home runs during a season in which he began playing only intermittently. Veterans in the league were talking about him, including the veteran pitchers, whose litmus test for a youngster is simple: Can he hit breaking stuff? At season's end, Williams was ripping into anything thrown to him. He had a future. His fondest memory of the season was a newspaper article he read in San Francisco in which the manager of the Seals, the former great major leaguer Lefty O'Doul, said Williams was the best left-handed hitter in the Coast League since Paul Waner.

In the 1937 winter meetings of minor league owners, at the Palmer House in Chicago, Bill Lane held to his promise to Eddie Collins the year before and told him that the bidding was opening on Williams. The Boston Braves were interested; so, too, were the Giants, Tigers, and the Dodgers. Collins had to talk Red Sox owner Tom Yawkey into the purchase price for Williams's contract. Yawkey was less keen than he had been in the recent past on shelling out large sums for baseball talent, though in the case of Williams his manager and shortstop, Joe Cronin, chimed in on Collins's side, "Sure, we gotta get that camel-gaited kid with rubber wrists."

Yawkey's Red Sox had gone through a major rebuilding program over the last several years, highlighted by the purchase of Joe Cronin's contract from the Senators at $250,000 in 1934. Cronin was married to the daughter of the Senators' owner, Clark Griffith, but there was no law on the books about selling your son-in-law. In any event, Yawkey was more intent on developing the players already in his farm system than on buying up others. When he purchased the Red Sox in 1933 he began with a surplus of $498,572, and by year's end he had worked himself into a deficit of $310,286. The tab kept going up, and now Yawkey wanted some payoff on the lower-end models. Former major league umpire Bill Evan was director of

Boston's farms. In 1935 there were a mere 25 players under development; by Williams's rookie year in the majors, 1939, Evan would have over 200 young ballplayers under minor league contracts. He had working arrangements with some clubs, such as San Diego, and direct affiliate relations with others: Minneapolis, until a 1939 switch to Louisville (American Association); Little Rock (Southern Association); Scranton (Eastern League); Canton (Mid-Atlantic League); Danville (Bi-State League); Clarksdale (Cotton States League); Rocky Mount (Piedmont League); and Centreville (Eastern Shore League).

Eddie Collins and Joe Cronin kept on Yawkey about Williams's contract. The decision had to be made. Giants scout Heinie Groh, for one thing, was ready to close a deal with Lane. Indeed, he thought he had one, but Giants manager Bill Terry demurred. Terry said he was genuinely worried about rumors he had heard of Williams's temper when he failed to connect at the plate: "The kid is too high-strung for New York." With the Giants out of the picture, the Boston Braves stepped in. In on the action was Casey Stengel, then managing the Braves, who forever after kept telling Ted he almost nabbed him in '37. Casey always had a fond spot for "that Williams fella" in his heart.

Lane needed an answer from Eddie Collins. He put it to him right on the line. Now or never. Collins then put his reputation on the line with Yawkey, who remained reluctant to pursue the deal. But Collins prevailed. Boston would get Williams and Bill Lane would get options on Dominic Dallesandro and Al Miemiec and two other minor leaguers, shortstop Bunny Griffith and outfielder Spencer Harris, whose contracts had to be purchased by the Sox for $35,000 in order to be able to offer them to San Diego. Williams would get $3,000 his first year and $4,500 his second, a boost from the $200 a month he was then pulling in with the Padres. This may not seem like much, but it beat the average Depression wage in America by a handsome margin. To measure with a finer gauge, a young man then in the Cardinals organization was pulling down $65 a month playing D ball for Monessen of the Penn State Association. His name was Stan Musial.

Even after the Red Sox cut their deal with Lane, the bidding was not entirely over. Larry MacPhail, who had been buying up players for the Dodgers right and left, had been interested in Williams from the time of the winter meetings—he had even written a memo to Bill Lane promising three players and cash—but Lane told him Collins and the Red Sox had first refusal. MacPhail then made an appointment to visit Eddie Collins in Boston and talk money. But when MacPhail arrived after the meetings Collins shut him down. Yawkey, who himself had to be talked into Williams as a prospect, now wanted his prize harbored. MacPhail was convinced that Ed Barrow of the Yankees had gotten to Yawkey to keep Williams away from the Dodgers, a rival New York draw, and place him in the American League where everyone might benefit if he hit it big. But Yawkey by then needed no external prodding. MacPhail took the train back to New York empty-handed.

The Red Sox paid off on the percentage cut promised to May and Sam Williams by Bill Lane when and if he should sell Ted's contract. Ted's parents, in a disintegrating marriage, gained $1,000 from the deal. It surely did not go into a trust fund for either of their kids. *The Sporting News*, in a brief back-page story that included the paper's first photograph of Williams, summed up the potential pitfalls of the deal as well as the potential rewards: the lad was described as a great prospect but he has yet to master an "uncertainty in fielding flies, and a tendency to get caught off base."

The *San Diego Union*'s McConnell took a different tack, one at once poignantly innocent and decently hortatory. Would that McConnell had gazed a little deeper into his crystal ball.

> Through all this praise, Williams has marched to the front without getting the big head. He appreciates all the kind words written about him and he always shows his appreciation to the scribes by thanking them. Boston fans are going to like this lad, and if he's treated right he's going to like Boston.

◊

In February 1938 torrential downpours were wreaking havoc in southern California—rail lines were shut, communication lines were down, roads were impassable. Two hundred people lost their lives in flooding, and property damage soared to $50,000,000. The Depression was bad enough without this. Bobby Doerr and Boston Braves outfielder Max West planned to head east to El Paso, Texas, by whatever means of transportation were available and to catch a train from there to spring training in Sarasota, Florida. Eddie Collins called Doerr at his home in Los Angeles and asked if they would mind hooking up with Ted Williams in San Diego. Doerr had been in the majors during 1937 and recalled only the spotty first year of Williams's career, but his father had been writing him from Los Angeles about Ted's 1937 exploits: "That young fellow Williams you played with is a better hitter than DiMaggio." Doerr didn't quite know whether to believe it yet, but he was willing enough to travel with his old pal if they could connect up.

Although Eddie Collins had gotten through from Boston, Doerr couldn't make the local phone connection to San Diego. But at Williams's urging a couple of ham radio operators were able to get a message through. Bobby and Ted arranged to hook up in Indio to travel to El Paso, but the Los Angeles trains couldn't get out of the station because of the floods. Doerr and West headed to El Paso by bus, and Williams traveled alone on the first leg of the trip by train from San Diego.

By now no one in Florida expected the California contingent on time. As eager as he was to get to the Red Sox camp, Ted Williams ended up immensely enjoying what would amount to a five-day delay. After he met Doerr and West for the train trip to Florida the trio was joined by another traveling companion, Babe Herman, who had played the year before in Detroit. Babe was fated to spend the next several years in the minors before one last hurrah during the war, but this was spring training—everyone is a .400 hitter before the season starts.

However much Herman was fading at the plate, he was still formidable as a talker. And the young Williams would talk to the conductor about hitting if he thought he could get something out of him. Mouth-to-mouth, Herman and Williams were a match made in hitting heaven. Williams wanted to know everything Herman had to tell him. Babe had to search back a bit—he only came to the plate 20 times for the Tigers in 1937—but this was a slugger who had a combined five-year batting average of .346 with Brooklyn in the late 1920s. In 1930 he batted .393 with 241 hits and 35 home runs. The man had the numbers, but he didn't have sufficient theory for

Williams, who drove him nuts with questions: "How can you say hitting is in the legs? It's the hips and the snap of the swing!"

Doerr and West were beleaguered witnesses to all of this. They couldn't even sleep with Williams chattering away at Herman's curtain-closed berth. The porter had to wrest his pillow from him in the middle of the night because he was using it as a bat in the aisle of the sleeper. When the trip was over Max West told Doerr, "Thank God I don't have to listen to that kid anymore."

With spring training in March 1938 came another of Hitler's moves in Europe, the Austrian Anschluss, part of an annexing strategy that would test—indeed stretch—the limits of western indulgence to the breaking point. Under the banner headline, "JEWS LOSE JOBS," a reporter pointed out that the Nazis had just suspended the medical license of Sigmund Freud. At the same time, the new American ambassador to the Court of St. James in England, Joseph P. Kennedy, put the British in an altogether depressing funk with his warnings about the lack of commitment in this country to any impending European hostilities.

In a story datelined Ravello, Italy, an even more famous isolationist made her famous comment, or a version thereof. Greta Garbo, traveling with Leopold Stokowski, appeared at a press conference to deny wedding rumors. She said she only wanted to see beautiful things in the world before "cruel events happening today make it impossible to do so" and told reporters following her every move, "I only want to be left alone."

In America, as spring training opened in 1938, so did Walt Disney's cartoon feature *Snow White* and the wonderful Cary Grant–Katharine Hepburn screwball comedy *Bringing Up Baby*. A front-page photo in the *Boston Globe* revealed something of a different tone to life in America during the 1930s. A local sheriff in Baltimore, Maryland, was depicted whipping a man tied to a post. The man was a wife beater. Any number of things can be gleaned from this, among them that sensibilities about wife beating ran high in Baltimore County. More notable is the penchant of the Boston press for sensationalizing and admonishing at the same time, something Ted Williams, in a completely different context, would soon learn about.

Williams's early troubles in spring training of 1938, however, did not come from the press. The Red Sox were joined in Sarasota every spring by a group of Boston patriots called the Royal Rooters. These were an old-time cadre of fans and supporters who arranged vacations and trips to Florida to coincide with the team's arrival. The Royal Rooters were an institution, and, like so many of that ilk, had a thousand memories to match a thousand opinions. Rookies were raw meat for them, and the idea of a rookie who had not yet hit Boston was a palatable delight. Needless to say, the veteran Boston writers hanging around camp for the long weeks of spring training were honorary members of the Royal Rooters; surely, at any rate, they shared many of their prejudices.

With his one pair of pants and his red West Coast sport shirt, Williams was a sight around the camp and at the hotel from the first moments of his arrival, though he wasn't the only Theodore who was attracting local attention. The hot rookie in camp that year, a "can't miss" future Lefty Grove, was Ted Olson, of Squantum, Massachusetts, a stringbean lefty who threw smoke. Every spring training has such a prospect. He got bombed in training camp—apparently the Sox regulars had no trouble hitting straight smoke. Ted from Squantum quickly blew out, leaving the Royal Rooters one focal point: Ted from Cow Country.

Williams was unrefined, desert sundrenched, and loose. He was dubbed "California" immediately by those Boston regulars who sought a neutral nickname and "Meathead" by those like Joe Cronin who understood, whether subliminally or not, that the historical San Diego was indeed cow country. The *Boston Globe* ran a small feature on the new arrival, as radiant as California sun: "WILLIAMS SHINES." The writer, Hy Hurwitz, who would find himself constantly embroiled with Williams in one controversy or another over the years, took notes from Cronin: "The kid is fine. He's as loose as can be with the club. He's got strong wrist action. He's a hitter of the Babe Herman type and everybody knows how Babe could wallop the pill." Doerr and West must have put Herman's name in Cronin's head— he was giving back some of the palaver he no doubt heard. When Williams finally did break in with the Sox in 1939, the comparisons were to Babe, all right, but Ruth rather than Herman.

For the time being, the writers were having a field day with the colorful rookie. His muscles, one said, in the midst of a rank session with the Royal Rooters, looked like eggs rolled in a handkerchief. Williams's volubility, his open-handed greetings—"Hiya, sport"—and his complaints about Florida humidity—dry semidesert heat was in his blood—set the Rooters off: "How the hell can this fellow come here complaining about moisture in the air when they just had 11 inches of goddamn rain in California?" They were merciless. The old Boston coots dubbed him "California Cracker" and the "San Diego Saparoo."

Williams was the Mr. Glad Hand of camp, cocky and anything but recessive. He tried to trap Moe Berg, perhaps the smartest man who ever played the game, on the old riddler, "Can a man marry his widow's daughter?" Berg just stared at him and shook his head, which indeed was very smart. Cronin and Williams were at a Mexican standoff from the start. For every intemperate "Hiya, sport" from the brash rookie, the Red Sox manager came back with a scornful "Meathead." Over the years Williams jettisoned the Gatsbian "Sport" and, almost as a testimonial, adopted the all-purpose nickname "Meathead" or the economy version, "Meat."

Stories began circulating that both tickled and irritated the fans from Boston, the Royal Rooters, the press corps, and the regular Red Sox ballplayers. Doerr was supposed to have asked Williams if he'd seen Jimmie Foxx hit yet, and Ted snapped, "Has he seen *me* hit?" Williams claimed he never said any such thing; in fact, he wrote home about the most impressive thing that happened to him in spring training—*listening* to Foxx hit. The sound of Foxx's bat, driven by those huge arms, crushing the ball is something a rookie remembers, and Williams later said he never heard such a sound again until Mickey Mantle broke in.

But even if he did boast to Doerr—and it's a natural enough bantering remark to a friend with whom you have just traveled across country—it wasn't Williams's brashness that drummed him out of the Sox complex. It was a visible lack of seasoning and consistency against major league pitching. In his first appearance he took the collar, 0 for 4, in a March 13 exhibition game against the Cincinnati Reds. A few days later it became clear that Williams was on the way out, and Hurwitz provided the party line in the *Globe*: "Ted 'Baby-face' Williams will be farmed out. The cocky West Coast youngster is lacking in experience and was easily fooled by Hutchinson [Ira Hutchinson, then in the Braves organization], who fanned him. Ted will probably go to Minneapolis."

It was neither in Boston's nor in Williams's best interests to break him in that year. To pick up the story from the opposite side of the street is to understand what the Red Sox had in mind from the start. An item in the *Minneapolis Tribune* set out a scenario: "Donie Bush announced Thursday that he would go to Sarasota next week to get a line on the players promised the Minneapolis club by Eddie Collins, general manager of the Boston Red Sox, who are training there."

Donie Bush was the manager of the Minneapolis Millers—also called the Kels, after their owner, Mike Kelly—and he was coming to pick up a specially promised prize—Ted Williams. When Williams left camp for Daytona Beach, where the Millers trained, he did not do so in confusion or consternation. He knew he would return to the Sox, and he knew he would return a better ballplayer. Most of all, he knew he needed another year in the minors and said so. Unlike Bobby Doerr, who came to the majors so young and played with the Sox in 1937, Williams was a raw hitter; he could do fewer things for a ball club in a general sense, and his one great talent had to be finely honed before he was ready. Doerr played the whole diamond; Williams's home was the batter's box. And he was not yet registering enough about pitchers, about sequences of pitches, about the adjustments at the plate essential to hitting in the majors, especially hitting with power in the majors.

In leaving the Red Sox camp, Williams was understandably down but far from dispirited. For him, the real pain of the Minneapolis move was the burden of the razzing, good-humored or hostile, by some of the Red Sox. As was always the case with Williams, just beneath the man's bravado was the boy's embarrassment. Joe Cronin, who had doled out his fair share of abuse to the young Williams in camp, was savvy enough to relent at the end. He told Johnny Orlando, the clubhouse man, to usher the kid to the bus depot and not make a big public deal of it. Williams spent the time with Orlando assessing his own prospects. He knew that the combined Boston outfield (Doc Cramer, Ben Chapman, and Joe Vosmik) was not long for the world, and he said good-bye to Orlando riding high, despite the razzing from others on the parent team: "Hey, California, where are ya' going?" Williams responded: "Look out for your job—I'll be back." To be back for Williams, who had not yet set eyes on the city of Boston, meant what it always meant: back to an activity rather than back to a place, back to hitting a baseball.

The Millers couldn't have been happier. The team's public relations machinery cranked into gear. Upon Williams's acquisition on March 21, the line went out to the Minneapolis press: "Baseball critics acclaim him another Joe DiMaggio." Williams was humble enough; he told Dick Hackenberg of the *Minneapolis Star*: "I guess I could stand some more experience." On March 23, he got some. In his first appearance for the Kels he fouled out with the bases loaded against the Chattanooga Lookouts. Williams took the collar for the day in an 8-7 loss. He repeated his hitless performance the next game. The briefly ecstatic Minneapolis baseball writers began reporting on what Williams made available to them—foul balls: "Ted Williams became the first Miller to lam the ball out of the Cypress Street park Thursday morning, the kid caressing two of them foul, over the 350-foot right-field wall." His first hit for the Kels was a more modest, but fair, single to center.

All the talk in the spring training camps, even in the minor league camps, of 1938 centered on the holdout of Joe DiMaggio from the fold of the New York Yankees. As Williams adjusted his sights downward for the 1938 season, DiMaggio was peering toward the stars. He wanted Yankees owner Colonel Ruppert, a very wealthy brewer, to jack his salary up from $15,000 a year to an even $40,000. He wasn't seriously planning to stay at that figure, but he wasn't seriously planning to descend to $25,000, the figure Ruppert offered, either. Ruppert called DiMaggio "the most stubborn young man I have ever met. Why, $25,000 is enough to make him financially independent for the rest of his life."

Colonel Ruppert, who kept his brewery workers on modest salaries during the Depression whether or not there was work for them, apparently didn't feel that DiMaggio had much right to lay in against the future. He himself, of course, was worth $150,000,000 and held only a little less of New York's real estate than the Astors. Ruppert, along with other sportsmen who happened to own teams— Tom Yawkey, Walter Briggs, Powell Crosley, and Phil Wrigley—

could, on any given day during the Depression, ante up a billion dollars among them for a friendly card game if they so chose.

Cooling his heels in San Francisco, DiMaggio wasn't drumming up a great deal of support among the ballplayers in spring training. Williams remembers Rogers Hornsby, who had an informal relationship with the Minneapolis Millers—something between Master Hitting Instructor and Friend of the Owner—as especially bitter on the DiMaggio holdout: "Shit, he ain't Ruth. And he won't be, either." DiMaggio's holdout would last until April 21. Friends advised him to make himself look good in these Depression days and take the $25,000. DiMaggio was laconic about it: "I figured I'd be the sport." Colonel Ruppert stroked back in a roundabout sort of way, the spoils belonging to the victor: "This is the toughest young man I've ever had to negotiate with. He left my office January 21, and I didn't hear from him again until yesterday."

Williams spent as much time as he could at Daytona Beach hanging around Hornsby, and the great old-timer took to him in an ornery sort of way, trying to focus the kid on more aspects of the game than hitting. Williams liked Hornsby's stories, and his eyes must have opened wide when Hornsby got around to the subject of gambling, a bit of an indulgence for him and others during the high life of the 1920s and even through the Depression years of the 1930s. Hornsby recalled winning $78,000 one day at the track, and he also laughed about an incident in which the commissioner of baseball, Kenesaw Mountain Landis, had called him and a young Bobo Newsom in to the office to talk about another big day at the races near Boston. It seems the two had taken up a collection among players and umpires to bet on a 24–1 long shot. So many were in on it that news reached upstairs. When Landis confronted Newsom he tried to frame the issue in a way that would make the pitcher squirm: "Let me put it this way. Who would you be thinking about at post time if the bases were full and DiMaggio were batting in a tie game and you had $500 on a race? Would you be thinking about DiMaggio or the horse?" Newsom gave the commissioner an absolutely baffled look: "Are you kidding? The horse." Landis just sighed.

Though Hornsby spent most of his time with Williams trying to get the kid to think about the whole game, not just hitting, he did impart some advice that, to an extent, Williams already practiced. He said that great hitters know as much how *not* to swing at certain pitches as how to swing at others. By this he meant that the great hitter is a selective hitter; he does not hit the pitcher's best pitch but waits for the pitch he can hit best. This, of course, is much easier said than done, but Hornsby's point was that great hitters find a way to do it and mediocre ones don't.

Meanwhile, Hornsby's hitting advice wasn't doing Williams much good; his slow spring with the Millers continued. "TED WILLIAMS GOAT OF THE GAME," read the *Minneapolis Star* headline for April 3, with a subheading: "Former Bosox Rookie Makes Two Costly Mistakes," including the "bonehead" play of failing to run out a just-fair ground ball on the assumption it was foul. Hornsby kept hacking at Williams: "Kee-rist, there's more to this game than swingin' the bat." And so did the *Star*'s Dick Hackenberg: "It is questionable whether Ted Williams, the $25,000 youngster optioned to the Kels by the Boston Red Sox, can make us forget about Dusty Cooke in right field." The memory of the unforgettable Dusty Cooke seemed more secure in March than it would in June.

The Minneapolis club concluded spring training with Williams penciled in at fourth in the batting order. "Ted Williams Will Bat at Cleanup Spot Against Indians on Saturday," the *Star*'s story proclaimed, even though "the order of hitters occasioned some surprise as it showed the youthful Ted Williams in the cleanup position. While the Pacific Coast sensation failed to hit as expected in spring games, Donie [Bush] has implicit faith in the youngster and is confident he will hit his stride as soon as the pennant race gets under way."

Bush was obviously drooling at the prospect of Ted Williams's swing matched up to the extremely short right-field fence, 280 feet down the line, at Nicollet Park, but the configurations of parks around the league were not all so cozy. Some, like the pastures of Indianapolis's Perry Field, where the Millers were to open the season, were stupendous. The legend of Williams's home-run swing, so memorable to Ray Boone from the playgrounds of San Diego, was rekindled at batting practice for the opening game of the season. George Barton of the *Star* described the scene, with a host of writers and minor league aficionados replacing the bicycle brigade of Williams's youth: "Williams, the 19-year-old prospect, with his age on his back, number 19, had several hundred spectators gasping with excitement at Perry Stadium Thursday afternoon by polling three long drives over the right-field fence near the 375-foot marker and then parking a fourth wallop approximately 470 feet on the fly in center."

At game time, however, a pressing Williams left his swing in the batting-practice cage. The Millers lost their opener 5–4, and Ted went 0 for 5, though one of his outs was an absolutely scorched liner to right speared on a dive by Glenn Chapman for the play of the game. The next day was worse. Indianapolis handed it to the Millers 13–5, and Williams got collared again, 0 for 4, amusing, after a fashion, the hometown writers with his gangling efforts in right field: "Ted Williams looked very amateurish charging in on Glenn Chapman's hit with the bases filled in the fourth inning. He should have held the blow to a single but foolishly tried for a one-handed stop and missed the ball entirely, the pellet rolling to the right-field wall. Three runners raced home and Chapman sprinted to third before Williams rounded up the ball and returned it to the infield."

When the Millers lost again, 4–3, and Ted went 0 for 3, Bush moved him up in the order. In the dugout the struggling Williams, his concentration shattered, heard a train whistle and mumbled to his manager, "That's what I want to be. An engineer. I'm no good for baseball." Two years later, in 1940, contemplating a salary he called chicken feed, he saw his uncle, a fireman from Mount Vernon, New York, lounging in the sun-field bleachers at Yankee Stadium, and changed his wish list: "That's what I want to be, a fireman."

Bush told the young man to calm down, that no one was railroading him out of town just yet. Besides, Bush had other problems. Pat Malone, his big right-handed pitcher, had that very day staggered stinking drunk past the Miller's owner, Mike Kelly, in the hotel lobby. Kelly insisted Bush suspend the ex-Cubs and ex-Yankees hurler with 134 wins in the majors. Bush didn't want to lose the pitcher but had to do the owner's bidding. Malone came back with a classic Depression line: "Hell, I don't need this. I can make $75 a day doing nothing in Hollywood." That did it. Pat got his walking papers two days later. He was gone with the wind—indeed, he could have tried his hand in that very film, then shooting in Hollywood.

In the midst of the Malone eruption, the *Star* sports page on April 19 recorded a move by the Millers that must have struck Williams as ominous: "BUSH BIDS FOR SLUGGING LEFT-HANDED HITTER." He had a line on someone in the lower minors because, as the story's subhead told it, "Lack of Power Slows Kels." Williams was then 0 for 12. Who could Bush mean? Williams always knew what was in the papers, and he always reacted accordingly. He couldn't buy a base hit, and he might have gone all loose at the joints at the charge that the Millers had no power hitters from the left side. But he didn't.

In the next game, a 10–4 win over the Louisville Colonels on April 19, Williams walked five times, refusing to give in to the impatience generated by a slump. He got a base hit in his other at-bat, but that registered less than the walks. He was following Hornsby's advice: he was waiting for pitches he could hit. Pitchers do not, as a rule, waste time with ineffective pitching sequences. Some are stupid enough to do so, but most will adjust to what they think they have to do to get a man, at the very least, to swing. That Williams could display such patience under the pressure of a season-opening slump revealed a good deal about the kid.

The next day the Millers won again, 13–6, and Williams began to let it out, going 2 for 5 with a long double. On April 21, all hell broke loose, even though the Kels lost 6–2 to Louisville. Williams hit two massive home runs: his first, off Jack Zising, bounced high and rolled to a distance of 470 feet; and the other sailed 450 feet on the fly over Nick Tremark's head and rolled to a stop 512 feet from the plate (someone measured the distances after the game). The headline in the paper read: "LOUISVILLE 6, TED WILLIAMS 2." Williams stopped talking to Donie Bush about trains. *Star* sportswriter Bob Beebe began comparing him with the giant swingers of yore: "He has his shortcomings afield but when he connects he has such power as ten hitters can boast. It's no ordinary slugger that can hit two balls in an afternoon that both travel over 450 feet on the fly."

With the Millers still on the road but soon returning home, Donie Bush joked with the baseball writers: "We were thinking that it would be wise in the interests of economy to cut down the kid's batting practice at Nicollet. He might run up a terrific ball bill." A couple of games later, at Toledo on April 26, Williams belted a tremendous shot high and clean over the right-field fence and into the street 450 feet away. Bob Beebe figured out that if he hit nine more that distance, he would have hit a mile's worth of home runs.

On April 29 the Millers arrived in Minneapolis for their home opener against Louisville. They won it 14-4, "paced," as the papers put it, "by the slugging of Ted Williams." The kid put a high arc shot over the right-field fence onto Nicollet Avenue. Right field at the foul pole had an inviting sign—280 feet. But, as Bob Beebe pointed out, the sign had nothing to do with the destination of this rainmaker: "The Kid looks great at the plate," he wrote, making sure to capitalize the nickname. "The Miller ball club put on quite a show for the home folks at Nicollet Friday afternoon, but that towering home run by Ted Williams was easily the high spot—yes, mighty high. It seemed mighty near as high as it was long, and it was plenty long because it carried easily 100 feet beyond the right-field wall, which is 280 feet from the plate at the foul line."

George Barton chimed in that "nothing the likes of this has occurred in town since Joe Hauser used to pole them out during the years he wore a Minneapolis uniform." Joe Hauser, a pretty good ballplayer for the Philadelphia A's in the 1920s, played for the Kels in 1933 and poled 69 home runs, most of them left-handed, over the short porch in right. Williams seemed to be catching up to that pace. On May 1 the Millers killed Louisville 15-5, and Ted hit two more well beyond the fence in right, the first a modest 400 feet; the second, off lefty Johnny Owens, a stinger: "The ball, driven against a strong wind, cleared the advertising signs atop the right-field wall at about 350 feet from the plate, then sailed the proverbial mile in the air and landed on the far side of Nicollet Avenue. It traveled approximately 450 feet on the fly."

A spell of Midwest weather soon set in and interrupted the monumental hitting of a now deeply contented Ted Williams. Freak rainstorms rained out seven games in a row; the weather was the worst since 1892, when the Millers were rained out an almost biblical 27 straight games. By May 10, a sports headline in the *Minneapolis Star* simply read: "Note to Printers: Keep This Headline in Type— MILLERS RAINED OUT AGAIN." They ought to have kept another in type as well: "WILLIAMS HOMERS." When play resumed so did his extraordinary slugging. He drove in the only run in a 7–1 loss to Columbus with a 400-foot blow to left center, and he hit his eighth of the year the next day, one of those high parabola shots to right center against St. Paul.

The Millers got some needed right-handed power now that left-handed power was no longer the issue. In late May Jim Tabor, the hard-drinking third baseman, joined the squad. It began to look as if the team might go somewhere; they were hovering but a few games out of first. These were sprightly days for the young Ted Williams. Dizzy Trout, then pitching for Toledo, remembers that in batting practice, with the record player blaring music over speakers, Williams climbed the fence behind home plate and began announcing the selections and singing along with them, playing the appropriate "Tall, Tall Timber" as big Jim Tabor stepped up for his cuts.

On the serious side, Tabor's acquisition gave Williams some protection in the lineup, and he kept blasting them, his 11th by May 26 and his 12th by May 30, the day before Lou Gehrig played in his 2,000th consecutive game for the Yankees and Barney Ross lost in 15 rounds to Henry Armstrong for the welterweight title of the world.

The only thing that seemed to disturb the steady litany of Williams's home runs in his spring surge was his fielding. On June 4 against the colorfully named Toledo Mudhens, he hit two home runs but gave up the ghost on an easy fly: "Williams had plenty of time to camp under the ball, and after striking a characteristic pose the Kid made an inglorious muff." "Characteristic" is the giveaway. Williams just didn't look comfortable in the field; his bean-pole 6'3" frame seemed as though it was hunching itself into a question mark as the ball ascended, which helped sustain the impression of what was likely to happen when it fell. Even if, as Williams insisted, he was a secure and practiced outfielder, more so as he got older, his muffs were the stuff of farce: he looked like Plastic Man fumbling for loose change.

Manager Donie Bush came to Williams's defense. Though he said there were times he wished he could wring his rightfielder's neck, Williams rarely made tactical errors all season long—throwing to the wrong base and the like—nor did he make excessive mistakes charging grounders, misjudging flies, or misplaying hitters. It just *seemed* that way. Bush primarily complained about Williams's exuberance and his attention span. He recalled the day the opposition "had the bases drunk, 3-2 on the hitter, and I look out and there's Williams in right waving to some kid perched on a building behind the fence." Or he would look out toward the outfield and see Williams with his back to the plate practicing his swing. Bush grew hoarse yelling at his star to "get in the goddamn game, ya' meathead." Stan Spence, who played center for the Kels, had to make sure that "Ted wasn't talking to the boys running the scoreboard with a ball coming his way. But that kid sure murders the potato with a bat in his hands."

In early June the Red Sox checked in to see how their prospect was doing. Yawkey, Collins, and Cronin were thinking of cashing in their present 1938 outfield and sizing up Boston for a new look. The contract of Stan Spence was purchased for 1939; Cronin eventually intended to pair him with Williams in the outfield. Eddie Collins spoke with *Star* columnist George Barton: "Ted Williams has dispelled all doubt. The Kid's got it. When you lump those long fences in Kansas City, Indianapolis, Louisville, Toledo, and Columbus, then you know the youngster is blessed with genuine power. He's a cinch to attain stardom in the big show."

On June 11 Williams was hitting .340 with a bone-crushing 16 home runs in 43 games. He was doing far better than the entire lineups of the Boston Bees and Brooklyn Dodgers in the major leagues, who had the misfortune that week to face Johnny Vander Meer, a 23-year-old lefty for the Cincinnati Reds, who tossed back-to-back no hitters at them. During the days Vander Meer accomplished his feat, Williams hit four more home runs for Minneapolis, skyrocketed his average, and carried a 21-game hitting streak. Irvin Rudick wrote in the *Star* of June 18:

> From the throats of a thousand youngsters, members of the "Knot-hole Gang," came the chorus: "We want a home run! We want a home run!"
>
> They were calling to Ted Williams, the four-base specialist, and who is Ted to deny these lads their desires?
>
> Williams strode to the plate swinging three bats as though they were hardly more than a bandleader's wand. He chose one to his liking and hardly had the bat contacted the sphere than these same youngsters, seated in a special section of the left-field stands, rose as one and cheered Williams all the way around the bases as he smote a mighty home run to send three runs home and give the Millers a 5–3 victory over Toledo at Nicollet Park Saturday afternoon.
>
> It was no ordinary homer that Williams propelled over the right-

center wall. The Kid doesn't do things that way. He lashed the
pellet to the left of the major league scoreboard and on across
Nicollet Avenue, the Ruthian swat traveling fully 440' in the air.

And on Sunday, Rudick still couldn't contain himself.

> The most colorful rookie to appear in this league in many a year
> put on another spectacular show for the spectators, not only with
> his bat but with his brilliant fly grabbing and throwing.
> It's a bad afternoon when the 19-year-old youngster doesn't
> provide the customers with a few thrills. Williams was quite a show,
> not only at the plate but mostly in right field, where he snared
> drives with leaping gloved-hand catches, up against the fence and
> racing in and near the foul line. He also cut loose with a throw
> from right field to third base to cut down a runner.

At a time when Williams was riding so high, another great American sportsman avenged the bitterest night of his career, a night just
prior to the time Williams signed back in 1936. Joe Louis knocked
out Max Schmeling in 2:04 of the first round at Yankee Stadium on
June 22. This was the quickest knockout in heavyweight history and
a gratifying turnaround for Louis. Little love was lost between the two
men, Schmeling having spoken with undisguised racism about the
possible mortification of losing to a black man. So when a reporter
shouted to Louis—"Will you give him another fight, Joe?"—the
answer was typically terse but untypically acerbic: "What for?"

Louis crumpled his German rival early with a stupendous body
punch to the kidney. Art Donovan, the ref, said he heard Schmeling
scream when Louis hit him. Later, the medical report revealed two
damaged vertebrae in Schmeling's lower back. He was nearly para-
lyzed by the body punch and slumped into the crossing right to his
jaw that finished him off. Schmeling's cornerman threw in so many
towels it looked as though they were at a White Sale. In Germany,
Goebbels and Hitler consoled Schmeling's actress wife, Anny Ondra,
who seemed to think punching was against the rules: "It's terrible
they permit such things."

Louis's win occurred four days after the infamous event in Germany known as Kristallnacht, when uniformed Nazis raged against
Jewish shop owners. Sometimes the argument is made that Americans
were shielded from the reality of Nazi terror in Europe, but the

newspapers in Minneapolis had no difficulty fixing blame and iden-
tifying what so many denied—the existence of concentration camps:
"A merciless official campaign against the Jews, reinforced by mob
action, was extended to all Germany today by secret police orders. At
Buchenwald . . . 63 army buses were coming nightly from Berlin
filled with Jews."

During these alarming times in Europe, Williams kept rolling in
Minneapolis. By June 26 he did something that always thrilled him—
he took over the Triple Crown, leading the league in average at .356,
in homers at 22, and in runs batted in at 56. The local writers were
even praising his newfound ability "as a fly hawk," with "sure
hands," a "fast break" toward the ball, and "no faulty maneuvering,"
"few, if any, mistakes," and a "fine arm." He was chosen unani-
mously by the league's sports writers for the All-Star Game.

Ted Williams tuned up with his first grand slam of the year, over
the center-field fence at Columbus, on July 13. For the next day's All-
Star Game he managed a single in four tries, as the league-leading
Milwaukee Brewers, with their star Whit Wyatt pitching, beat the
rest of the league's All-Stars 6-3. A few days after the game, one of
the most bizarre events of the decade took place. On July 18,
Douglas G. Corrigan flew 3,150 miles to Ireland in 28 hours and
13 minutes. The only hitch was that he was supposed to be flying
across America in the other direction: "The pivot of my compass
stuck and didn't come loose until near the end of the flight. I came
east instead of heading for California."

"I'm Douglas Corrigan," the disoriented flier told U.S. Ambassador
John Cudahy, a crony of Charles Lindbergh. Corrigan claimed cloud
cover marred his entire flight and he thought he was sighting the
California coast. The plane may be old and rickety, he noted, but it
"gets good mileage." For the time being, officials suspended his
flying license. "I made a mistake," the newly named "Wrong Way"
Corrigan told reporters in one of the classic understatements of the
century.

Through the heat of July and into August, the Millers made their
one sustained move on the pennant, with Williams carrying them on
his lanky back. By July 23 he was up to 27 home runs and 84 runs
batted in, but he began to wilt a little in the summer sun. In San
Diego Frank Shellenback had given him plenty of chances, many

more than he wanted, to rest. Not so in Minneapolis. He was the ball club. George Barton noticed that he looked "indifferent on the field." This was never a pose Williams masked very well; and he tended to sulk when he wearied or when he lost his intensity at the plate. But Barton's comments snapped him out of it. In early August he busted loose for three more homers, raising his total to a robust 32.

The Millers were hovering within striking distance of first place on August 3 when Williams came to the plate in the fifth inning against Wild Bill Zuber of the Milwaukee Brewers; he had already doubled and singled. Zuber had seen enough of the young slugger. He threw one at his head—and hit it. Williams was knocked cold with a concussion and was carried off the field. During his few days of paid leave he could rest, relax, and gear up for the stretch run.

Williams got back in the lineup on August 6 and hit home run number 33; the next day he chalked up 34. He was going so strong that the sportswriters in town had little to do but chide him on his fielding, though the tone taken was downright jovial. A headline for August 8 read: "TED WILLIAMS NOTE: OUTFIELDER FIELDS BUNT AT KNOXVILLE." The Knoxville pitcher, first baseman, and second baseman all went for Lou Bush's popped-up bunt and collided. The ball rolled to the lip of the outfield and rightfielder Van Robays was the only one left standing to make the play.

George Barton, the columnist who came down on Williams in late July, began to sing a different tune in early August.

> It is pleasing to see Ted Williams shake off the editorial comment and boos directed at him two weeks ago and prove his mettle by bearing down all the harder to convince all and sundry that he has plenty of what it takes to be a great ballplayer.
>
> What was said about Williams by baseball writers of Minneapolis was for the youngster's own good. It was thought from his actions on the field that he was indifferent. Maybe the youngster was misunderstood. Whatever the cause, Ted quickly got back into stride and demonstrated he could take the "heat" without getting him down.
>
> The way he bounced back showed he possesses grand competitive spirit, and that's all he needs to attain stardom in the major leagues. The kid has it in him to vie with Joe DiMaggio for the headlines in the American League.

He was already doing his fair share of vying in the American Association, leading the league by mid-August in hitting, .358; in home runs, 35; and in runs batted in, 111. After an earlier 21-game hitting streak, Williams was in the midst of another that would last 26 games. By the end of the month he was up to 41 homers, having slugged his last one clear over a building and into an alley between Nicollet and First. His average was up to .360, and he had knocked in 130 runs.

In early September the Millers met cross-town rival St. Paul for a big series. St. Paul was three games up in first place, and the Kels had the chance to stick it to them. They didn't. Instead, they lost three of four in front of local crowds. Williams was pressing in the first inning of a game against Lloyd Brown because the Kels had three men on and he had the count his way at 3-1. A pitch came in that had the alley behind right field written all over it, but Williams's swing barely missed; he got under the ball and popped it up. He came back to the dugout fuming, paced a bit, and then turned on a five-gallon water cooler as if it were Max Schmeling, putting his fist right through its gut. Glass exploded and water flowed all over the place. Williams had his hand bandaged and went back in the game, but for Donie Bush this was just another of those instances that made him contact the Red Sox about the powderkeg virtuoso in their repertoire. Bush figured early on that Williams's temper could get him in trouble.

The season ended quietly for the Millers as they descended the league standings. But Ted Williams surely went out with a bang, collecting five hits in a doubleheader and his 43rd home run. He finished with the Triple Crown. In 1941, the year he hit .406, Williams lost the Most Valuable Player award in the American League to Joe DiMaggio; this year in the minors he lost out to pitcher Whit Wyatt and Ollie Bejma, a second baseman for St. Paul. Both had 52 votes to Williams's 47. There was little to do but go home to San Diego, the last time Williams would do so for a long stretch in the fall and winter. He would, as always, hang out at the playgrounds, talking anyone on the scene into pitching and shagging for him. Ray Boone remembers seeing Williams in the winter of 1938. Even after the year he had in Minneapolis, he still felt the inclination to sharpen his swing under the postseason southland sun.

In the fall of 1938 the Red Sox made a move that fairly well indicated their intent for the next year. They gave regular outfielder Ben Chapman his walking papers—Williams was coming up. The front-office brass were sure of it. Though Chapman could hit—he finished at .340 in 1938 and also led the league in stolen bases—he was something of a thorn in player-manager Joe Cronin's side. Cronin hated his chronic second-guessing and constant bellyaching. Chapman, who could run like the wind earlier in his career, had even angered owner Tom Yawkey when he failed to show for a match race with George Case of the Senators, claiming an injury to his leg. He still demanded that Yawkey, who had put up part of the stake, pay him $250 for his efforts. Yawkey was in some doubt as to what, exactly, his effort consisted of. But he was in little doubt about what to do with Chapman—dump him. Ted Williams would join Doc Cramer and Joe Vosmik in the Boston outfield for 1939.

◇ 3 ◇

Baby Ruth
1939

THERE WAS LITTLE DOUBT in anyone's mind that when Ted Williams arrived in Sarasota for spring training in 1939 he was a major leaguer. As early as February 10, a month before camp opened, *Globe* sportswriter James O'Leary simply assumed "that Williams is booked as a regular along with Vosmik and Cramer." Right field was vacant with Ben Chapman's departure to the Indians. Williams's only competition for the position came from Red Nonnenkamp, whose name hinted at the result of his challenge to the Red Sox superrookie: Not-in-camp.

The world in the spring of 1939 was a volatile and violent place. No one in America knew at the time exactly what form the political crisis in Europe would take, but even those appalled by Hitler's activities wanted to know precisely what President Roosevelt meant when he said that the "American frontier is on the Rhine." At the same time the country was trying to determine its posture toward imminent world war, American Bund rallies in major cities across the country were getting uglier and uglier. In one riotous meeting on February 10 in Madison Square Garden, speakers kept referring to "our Jewish President Rosenfeld." Dorothy Thompson, a syndicated political correspondent for the *Boston Globe* and an outspoken opponent of fascism, covered the event; the crude Bund slander brought her to her feet with screams of "Bunk!"

Though Thompson's position was clear, the fervent desire in the United States to keep out of the conflict in Europe produced a curious assumption, held tenaciously by millions in those prewar days, that Germany's intentions were still honorable. Hence, the newspapers in the country were printing vignettes of Nazi life on the social pages. Such tidbits as a photo of a smiling Hitler oozing Bavarian charm while chucking an American dancer under the chin appeared on the feature pages of the *Globe* in February. "What a wonderful man," the dancer purred. The editors of the paper may have known what they were doing; but, like the Neutrality Act itself, which dictated national policy, they seemed to be playing it both ways.

Springtime in America in 1939 brought the opening of the World's Fair in Flushing Meadows, New York. The fair, with its bright orange and blue colors (the uniforms of the New York Mets, who play their games in a stadium built on the former site of the fairgrounds, still bear these colors) took "Dawn of a New Day" as its theme. The Perisphere and Trylon, the wonderful General Motors Futurama, with its highways and cities of tomorrow, and the whimsical Westinghouse robots and gadgets were the focus of attention. The indefatigable Middleton family of the comic strip designed to promote the fair seemed to inhabit the fairgrounds 24 hours a day, standing in lines for the Singing Tower of Light; for Elektro, The Moto-Man, a robot who, among other things, smoked cigarettes; and for the most thrilling contraption of all, real live television. At a time when Europe faced its doom, the fair predicted a bright and hopeful future of peace and progress.

The fantasy world of Hollywood in 1939 billed Lana Turner as its new can't-miss "*It* Girl." Turner had enough of whatever "it" was not to miss by much. On screen, *Gunga Din*, with Cary Grant and Sam Jaffe, was the imperialist rage, and *Goodbye, Mr. Chips* cornered the huge prewar market on sentiment. Later in the year, *Gone with the Wind* was released in a land far more willing to enjoy its war epics on the movie screen than on the battlefields of Europe.

As the year warmed, hundreds of ballplayers meandered into Florida for spring training. Ted Williams was an attraction at Sarasota. The Boston press corps was ready for him even before he arrived. On March 3 Gerry Moore of the *Globe* headlined a comparison that, having been initiated by Bobby Doerr's awed father in 1937 and having reverberated around Minneapolis for most of 1938, became a baseball standby, a saloon controversy, and an albatross around Ted's neck: "WILLIAMS IS MOST TALKED-OF ROOKIE SINCE

DIMAGGIO." The writers covering the Red Sox remembered Williams; his brief appearance in 1938 had whetted their appetites. The lad was pure fodder in a press-hungry town. Any player who came into spring training for the Red Sox without self-protective savvy or a natural reticence was vulnerable to the press gang.

When writers spoke to Williams in spring training of 1939 they confronted a dervish. He fidgeted, he gestured, he joked, and his verbal responses were either tangential or monologic. He was rarely careful of tongue or gesture; he was by turns motor-mouthed and abrupt. His outward exuberance was one symptom of a mercurial attention span. Williams never could get a good read on the impression he made upon others, especially writers. If he was too good a hitter for the Red Sox to ignore, he was too good a subject for the press to coddle.

Harold Kaese of the *Globe* was aware that the writers were training their sights on Williams. They would set him up when they needed a story; and, moreover, they would enjoy the sport of it. He could be provoked, ridiculed, insulted into good copy. Kaese cautioned him early on that his relations with the press could make or break him in Boston. Although the conversation was intended as a warning, Williams interpreted it as a threat and remembered it that way years later in his autobiography. The fine distinctions between warnings and threats are sometimes difficult for the most keen observer to perceive; they were almost always lost on Williams. He listened to Kaese, stored the information, and mentally killed the messenger. Williams never got on well with Kaese, though Kaese knew more about Williams's hitting than anyone and would defend him as often as he sandbagged him.

But not even Kaese's threat—as Williams saw it—could diminish his natural exuberance that spring. He couldn't have dreamed up a better year than the one he'd had at Minneapolis, and he was glad to be in Florida. The summer on the West Coast had been no picnic. His parents' marriage was coming apart, and he was too old to witness it with the same awkward embarrassment that had served him in his youth. Mother May was no less militant in her service for the Salvation Army, Father Sam was a bit more negligent in attending to the beliefs of Mother May, and brother Dan was exceptionally diligent at dismantling the family car to sell its parts for spare change.

Williams couldn't wait to leave and, in fact, must have known as he departed that he had seen the last of his Utah Street home.

On the day Williams was supposed to have arrived with Bobby Doerr and his wife from California by train, the Sox were told that their impetuous rookie had, a few days before, decided to drive his new car across the country—mostly to wind down from a trying winter in San Diego, and possibly to keep the automobile out of the hands of his parts-ravenous younger brother, Danny.

Joe Cronin resisted panic: "If Williams isn't piled up somewhere in a Georgia ditch, he should arrive sometime tomorrow." Forty-eight hours late, Williams showed up, looking, says Cronin, "like shit." He had lost two days en route in New Orleans when he checked into a local hospital with a soaring fever and flu symptoms. It was diagnosed as an upper-respiratory virus, a misery that would plague him again and again during cooler weather. He wasn't well yet, but he was out there shagging and swinging. Jimmie Foxx, edging toward the end of his career but still a powerful man, drunk or sober, did what Williams was reputed to have suggested that he do last spring training: he devoted a few minutes to watching *him* swing. Foxx's verdict: "The kid's a hitter."

Cronin had it all figured out: "One of our problems last year was that we couldn't take our ballpark on the road. Williams hits the long ball. He's apt to hit four or five home runs in Yankee Stadium alone." His diagnosis proved right and wrong. Williams would hit brilliantly on the road throughout his career; the stats prove it. But Cronin put his finger on a virus that would pretty much determine the next four decades of Red Sox history. The ball club, for a curious amalgam of reasons that only changed slightly over the years, wilted on the road.

Baseball is a finely tuned game. A step or two of slowness at enough defensive positions can throw a team into a tailspin in large ballparks; a pitching staff designed for an oddly shaped field can seem like a poor fit in another; a lineup ballasted for a short fence in one field can founder when the fences lengthen. Whatever the case, the Red Sox came into most towns around the league just looking for the next train out. The Yankees, perhaps because their ball clubs were better designed for all aspects of the game, arrived in the league's cities like the traveling company of the Metropolitan Opera: they simply assumed that no local company could outsing them.

The most ominous talk of spring training in the early stages of 1939 was word from St. Pete and the Yankees' camp that Lou Gehrig was in some kind of trouble. Under the headline "IRON MAN LOU AIN'T WHAT HE USED TO BE," the *Globe*'s Gerry Moore wrote, "Seldom have we seen Gehrig look so bad as he did in yesterday's contest. Not only did he give the how-do-you-do to two successive ground balls during a four-run splurge by the Bees in the seventh, but at all other times in the field and in running he looked slow and uncertain." Jimmie Foxx was shocked when he ran into Gehrig: "He looks 45 years old."

Williams coming in must have thought he felt as bad as Gehrig going out. He simply couldn't shake his upper-respiratory virus during most of spring training, but he made the time eventful nonetheless. Toward the end of the spring tour the teams began to inch their way up the southern coast. Williams played in a game against the Atlanta Crackers on April Fool's Day and got his first dose of major league discipline. He tripled early in the game but popped up with men on base late in the game. He threw such a tantrum that Cronin pulled him from the game and sent Fabian Gaffke into right. (Johnny Sturm recalls an even better performance in Minneapolis when he and Ted played in the American Association. Williams drove one into the teeth of the wind that looked like a sure homer over the short fence at Nicollet Field. But when the wind pulled it back in for a fly-ball out Williams geared down from his home-run trot and began kicking the bag at second as if he'd been betrayed by the gods. He took these things personally.)

Cronin had no intention of letting the effects of Williams's tantrum linger. He started him the next day and, as Gerry Moore tells it, "Ted Williams, the glorious screwball, celebrated his return to the Red Sox lineup by belting a well-smacked homer that accounted for the first run of the contest." The Red Sox pennant hopes were soaring this spring—on paper they looked tough—and Cronin looked forward to a late series of spring-training games with the powerful Cincinnati Reds to gauge his team in full battle regalia. This "should give us a line on the pennant and on Williams." Depending on how his remark is read, the fates of the Red Sox and Williams are either linked or separate. Inadvertently, Cronin set the parameters for a debate that would linger for twenty years.

The Red Sox lost the first game 7–4 and got involved in an absurd donnybrook, an 18–18 tie in a tropical-wind-swept game in Florence, South Carolina, in which the game was suspended because the wind blew so many balls out of the park fair and foul that neither team could supply any more baseballs. In game one of the series Williams hit a towering drive 450 feet over the fence in right center. But before game two he checked in with a fever so high and a throat so sore that the Red Sox trainer, Win Green, scurried off to Greensboro, North Carolina, to buy Williams a hat and a tie. He told Ted in no uncertain terms that he couldn't show up in Boston at the tail end of spring without protection for his head and neck. The tie was one of the few Williams ever owned.

The Red Sox season was scheduled to begin on April 19 at Yankee Stadium, but rain all along the eastern seaboard delayed the opener a day. Manager Joe McCarthy of the Yankees kept to his original rotation. He did not want to set everyone back so he bumped Lefty Gomez from the first spot and started his big right-handed fireballer, Red Ruffing, for the game on April 20. Ten future Hall of Famers were in uniform for this game, and nine of them started: Lou Gehrig, Bill Dickey, Red Ruffing, Joe DiMaggio, Lefty Grove, Jimmie Foxx, Bobby Doerr, Joe Cronin, and Ted Williams. Only Lefty Gomez missed the action. When Williams stressed, as he later did, the high quality of baseball just before the war, he was not just talking through his new hat.

Williams batted sixth in this powerful Red Sox order. On his first trip to the plate in the second inning, Ruffing blew it by him. Williams never was surprised at a pitcher's good stuff; he always assumed a good hitter feeds on mistakes or good guesses. When Red Sox pitcher Jack Wilson looked at Williams returning to the bat rack after facing Ruffing, he gave him the business: "What's the league look like to ya' now, Bush?" Williams responded: "If he puts it in there again, I'm riding it out." The cat-and-mouse game had begun. Would Ruffing challenge him? Would he come back with heat or could he finesse him? Having gotten him out once, Ruffing would probably try again hard and up. That wouldn't be a dumb thing to do early in the game and year. So Williams was already zoning.

In the fourth inning, after DiMaggio made a wonderful shoestring catch of Jim Tabor's sinking liner, Williams homed in on a Ruffing fastball and kissed it on the sweet spot of the Joe Cronin–model bat he had been using since spring training. The ball crashed off the stadium wall in right center for a double and Ted Williams's first major league hit. As he pulled into second base, Ted was thrilled. Yankees second baseman Joe Gordon, whom Williams knew from the Coast League in 1937, asked if he was nervous. "Boy, am I—nervous as hell." Ruffing got Williams two more times that day and beat the Sox and Lefty Grove 2–0. But Williams had crushed a ball at Yankee Stadium off one of the best pitchers in the league. He savored the moment.

Williams had another thrill on that day, though he couldn't put it in perspective quite yet. Playing first base for the Yankees was an aching and neurologically racked Lou Gehrig. Gehrig tapped two harmless double-play balls on the day but also managed one savage liner to right that was speared by the rookie Williams. This would be the only play Williams ever made on Gehrig because it was the only official league game in which they both appeared. When the Yanks and Sox were scheduled to play next, in Boston, the entire series was rained out. Soon after, on May 2, Gehrig simply stopped playing after 2,130 consecutive games. The first major league game Williams played—indeed, the first official major league game he ever *saw*— would be the only game in which he played with Lou Gehrig.

The Red Sox returned to Boston for their home opener on April 21, and Williams singled in a 9–2 win over the A's. His hit, coinciden- tally, was off Cotton Pippen, the very same pitcher who struck him out in his first at-bat for the San Diego Padres in 1936. Life for Williams in Boston really began two days later, on April 23, when the *Globe* headlined on its front page: "TED WILLIAMS RENEWS FEATS OF BABE RUTH." His "mammoth" homer against the A's off a Luther Thomas fastball soared into the right-center-field seats in the first inning, but that hit only crowded the rest of his line in the box score. He went 4 for 5 on the day, including two singles and a double off the left-center-field wall. Typically, the Sox lost 12–8 as their pitching and defense collapsed.

The hucksters were a beat ahead. In the paper that day was a photo of Ted with his box of Wheaties, captioned "Watch That Boy Wil- liams." And Victor O. Jones's column in the *Globe* put a finger on the heart of baseball idolatry in the late '30s, with an even slier finger pointing at the agony of European politics: "Ted is lucky to come along in a baseball age that worships at the shrine of power, pure, unadulterated power." Jones pointed out that on a raw, ugly, damp day, with the Sox well out of the game, the bulk of the crowd stayed in the park to see Ted try to go 5 for 5 in the ninth. He scorched a liner to left that hung up just long enough for his only recorded out.

The following day Williams left 11 men on base as the Sox lost to the Senators 10-9. He also crumpled under the Boston spring chill, recycling the virus he picked up en route to spring training. He was in bed yet again with a sore throat and a fever. So was half the Red Sox squad. In his May 2 column Victor O. Jones had the audacity to blame it all on Williams, which must be a new low in microbe reporting: "Ted Williams ought to realize he's got the responsibilities that go with membership on a pennant-challenging ball club and stay out of bed even if it means wearing a hat in New England's spring. That grippe of his has now spread to half the ball club and comes at a very bad time."

This was the same day the Yankees played a game in Detroit and won it by the lopsided score of 22-2. That, however, was not the distinctive feature of the game—Lou Gehrig's benching himself was. He decided to do so after a miserable day at the plate and in the field the game before. Gehrig thus ended his record consecutive-game streak. His year so far had been a sorry one, with only four hits for a .143 average and a single run batted in. "Despite my slump," he said, "the fans never got on me." That June Gehrig headed to Minnesota for a battery of tests at the Mayo Clinic to "find out what's sapping my strength."

In the next series for Detroit at Briggs Stadium, the Red Sox blew into town and a new legend was born just after an old one faded. Those who witnessed Williams's performance at Briggs Stadium on May 4 are still astonished by it, including Williams himself. Before the game, Williams entered the park with Tommy Carey. "You know, Ted, I once saw Jim Bottomly put one on the roof." "Tommy, you're full of shit. Nobody can put one up there."

Williams felt good that day. On his first at-bat off Roxie Lawson he hit one foul on the roof and then lined to center; in the fourth, with Detroit up 4-0 and with Cronin on first, Williams worked the count to 3-2. A power hitter can sit on the fastball with pretty good odds in this situation. If he guesses wrong, so be it. Ted guessed hard and down the middle. He guessed right, punishing the next pitch with a blast that landed atop the roof of the third-tier press box added a few years earlier. Only Gehrig and Sunny Jim Bottomly were known to have equaled that feat.

In the fifth inning, with the score tied 4-4, the reliever, rookie Bob Harris, pecked and nibbled and found himself down in the count 3-0 to Williams. Catcher Rudy York got on Williams and told him the cripple was coming down Broadway—why not see if he could hit it? Cronin had the same idea, and the Red Sox bench flashed him the hit sign. Williams let York know he was hacking, but York figured the show was worth it.

York set up for a low fastball over the heart of the plate. When a catcher doesn't know a hitter well he usually begins by setting him up low. For most hitters, upstairs in the wheelhouse provides the best cut. For Williams it was lower, waist to thigh, but his slightly upper-cut swing could launch the very low strike well, especially out in front of him on the inside. Harris put it down and in (too far inside for York's tastes), and Williams uncoiled, smoking the pitch on an arrow-line trajectory never more than a few feet from the foul line. The ball cleared the roof of Briggs Stadium and hit the wall of a taxi garage on Trumbull Avenue. Never—not even when there were only two tiers in right field—had anyone put it completely out of the park. Williams's blast was one of those electric moments that shape a legend. As he rounded the bases, Billy Rogell at third for the Tigers just shook his head: "Hey, what the hell you been eating?"

The Detroit fans were both stunned and thrilled, and the *Globe* dispatch reported home that the reaction was the "greatest ovation we have ever heard a visiting athlete receive here." Williams couldn't contain himself after the game. He first tried the "aw, shucks" routine and then just savored the feat: "That's about as good a drive as I can hit." Not only had he done what he'd said was impossible—reach the roof—but he had sailed one completely over it.

While Williams was talking to reporters in the visitors' clubhouse, a message came from Hank Greenberg of the Tigers—would Williams come out early for batting practice the next day and give him a few tips? It turned out that Greenberg had bet some of the Red Sox before the game that their slugging rookie would not hit over .320 for the year. He also left word via his messenger to those on the Boston squad who had taken up his bet that he was ready to welch on it. It is hard to imagine a finer or better-natured tribute from a great player, and Williams was one happy Red Sox rightfielder that day.

In the next game of that same Detroit series, Williams had the honor of facing the extraordinary Bobo Newsom, about whom he had heard so much from Rogers Hornsby in spring training for Minneapolis the year before. Boston won the game, but Newsom took Williams to the cleaners, striking the kid out three times. Williams later wrote about the experience in a magazine article: "First game against him I fanned three times on nine pitches. I watched his windmill windup, his arms, legs, and butt going in all directions, and nearly laughed myself to death. But I also forgot to watch the ball. I had to learn to control myself while facing Bobo, and, once I did, I found I could hit him."

After the Detroit series, the Red Sox faltered on the road, as usual, and Williams couldn't buy a base hit. He faded to .235 by May 18, though he did win one for the Sox with a three-run home run in the 10th inning at St. Louis on May 9. Cronin recalled: "We got all good pitchers—Hudlin and Newsom and Harder, Rowe and Trout and Lyons. They handled the kid pretty good, and he told me, 'Don't worry. I'm not. I'll catch up to those pitchers once I've had a look at them. I can hit 'em, Joe, I'll show you.'" He would, in short enough order, but not just then. The Sox returned to Fenway and it made little difference to Williams; his power output all but ceased. Jim Tabor, the other rookie, brought up late the previous year, was outshining and outhitting Williams by a whopping margin at .330. The first time Williams faced the great Bob Feller he came away muttering that the minor leagues never showed him anything like this. Feller collared him, 0 for 4. Cronin gave some thought to putting Red Nonnenkamp in right, but couldn't bring himself to do it just yet.

The season was beginning to hit its pace—well over a hundred games to go and all the kinks pretty much worked out from the spring. News from Europe was increasingly tense, as it had been ever since the Austrian Anschluss and the Czechoslovakian invasion of 1938. Prime Minister Chamberlain of Great Britain told Hitler that any move against Poland meant war, and this time he would hold to his word. America got a brief taste of the trauma of European affairs near her borders when the refugee ship *St. Louis*, filled with middle-class Jews escaping Germany, was refused admission to Caribbean ports. It became a floating symbol of worldwide alienation and abandonment. Meanwhile, Charles Lindbergh, the great American aviator, had just been declared persona non grata in England for his soft attitude toward Hitler's aggressive postures. The English asked him to pack his bags and return to the United States. "He is controlled by forces more sinister than himself," said Chamberlain. Roosevelt agreed. This would set off a major propaganda battle between the isolationist Lindbergh and the interventionist Roosevelt for the hearts and minds of Americans.

Decoration Day 1939, a holiday designed for honoring the nation's past military actions, arrived with opinion sharply divided about its future involvements. The Red Sox were playing well enough to hang in the race five games behind the surging Yankees, who were at Fenway for the traditional jam-packed holiday doubleheader. Williams came alive with two tremendous clouts as the Sox split the games, and the headlines were again flowing in his favor: "INCOMPARABLE TITANIC TED WILLIAMS." In the first game he came up against Red Ruffing just after Joe Cronin served one over the infamous Fenway left-field wall in the first inning. This never made a pitcher happy, though Ruffing could tell himself that routine fly balls, in the best of all worlds, ought to stay inside the park. Williams, at least, would have to hit a real blow to clear the wall in straightaway right, then over 400 feet from the plate.

Ruffing gave the matter some thought. At Yankee Stadium in the season's opener Williams hit a fastball off the wall in right against him. What now? In Fenway Ruffing had more room; he would challenge Williams again. And again Williams tied into a fastball over the plate and drove it over the fence, 75 feet back into the open bleachers in right field, a blow he still considers the single hardest ball he ever hit.

Early in June, Williams got his first hit ever off Bob Feller, a triple in a 10–2 loss to the Indians. Feller had decent luck with Williams in 1939—Ted hit only .257 off him—but he never felt he could pitch to Williams successfully. Feller thought it through. "You see, he could just hit everything, and he could pick up my ball real well. I tried breaking stuff with him mostly on the key pitches. Sure, I threw hard stuff to him as well. But for an out pitch I'd try to curve him low and inside. The pitch had to be perfect. You know, he wouldn't even swing at a strike he didn't like when there were two strikes on him. That's what he was like at the plate. Of course, he shortened up. There weren't all that many strikes he couldn't hit when the count reached two strikes. It had to be right there—low and in to tie up his wrists or low and away to freeze him—and no pitcher could do that all the time. Yeah, he could hit me—after a while in the league I just did what I could with him and went after the next guy."

Because of its legendary, folkloric history and its byzantine rules, baseball is a game that can go from the sublime to the ridiculous in the blink of an eye. On June 10, 1939, the sport got its Valhalla: Honus Wagner, Grover Alexander, Tris Speaker, Nap Lajoie, George Sisler, Walter Johnson, Eddie Collins, Babe Ruth, Connie Mack, Cy Young, and Ty Cobb showed up at Cooperstown, New York, for the dedication of the Hall of Fame and its first induction ceremony. The larger-than-life photo of the group (with a late-arriving Cobb missing) now graces the walls of the Hall's museum.

But on the flip side of that glorious day, the commissioner of baseball, Kenesaw Mountain Landis, worked himself into a stew about the rigging of standard-manufacture baseball gloves. His office pronounced an edict banning the addition of leather strips between the glove's fingers. It is hard to imagine in the present age, when an outfielder can put a contraption on his arm suitable for jai alai, that Landis was upset because some players were actually using wide laces or actual leather patches between the thumb and forefinger of the glove. *The Sporting News* soon produced a picture of exhibit A, Hank Greenberg's first baseman's mitt, with a leather strip and extra laces serving as a supplemental web. Ring Lardner had a go at a mock description of the unfair advantage Hank had with his particular piece of equipment: "three lengths of barbed wire; four corner and two side pockets; fish net, rod, and trowel; a small sled; library of classics; a compact anti-aircraft gun; a change of clothes; and a pocket comb."

About this time the Red Sox began a presummer fade. After Detroit swept four games at Fenway in mid-June, Boston trailed the Yanks by 11½ games and the season looked dim. Williams was hovering in the .280 range at the plate, but he didn't feel right. He told Johnny Orlando, who ran the Boston clubhouse, that he might have been better off playing another year in the minors. He was thinking of the short porch at Nicollet Field in Minneapolis, of some of the friends he made hunting and fishing nearby in smaller Minnesota hamlets, and of a girl he met in 1938, Doris Soule, whom he had not seen regularly for a long while. Orlando predicted Williams would still hit .335 with 35 home runs and 150 runs batted in. Williams bet him his car he wouldn't. Ted won the bet—just barely—at season's end, but Orlando would have refused the car anyway had he won. He figured the bet was just a motivator.

In late June Williams began a three-week surge during which he hit .458. He began with a 4-for-4 day—a triple, double, and two singles—as Lefty Grove beat the Senators 3-0 on June 26. His fellow rookie, Jim Tabor, having such a wonderful year so far, was suspended that day for the second time during the season. "Training infraction," the papers so tactfully put it, which is what the baseball-writing code meant by drunk as a skunk in the hotel lounge. Tabor couldn't get off the sauce; it was a problem that plagued him all his baseball life and too much of his mortal one. He died young.

By July, Williams was pushing toward the .300 mark, and his run production was way up; he was tied, in fact, with Hank Greenberg for the league lead in runs batted in with 61. In one of those patented Boston barrages, the Red Sox beat Connie Mack's A's 17-1 and 18-12 in a July 4 doubleheader. Williams hit one out on the day and took over the league lead in runs batted in, but Jim Tabor, temporarily dried out and chastened, went on a different sort of binge, hitting three home runs in the second game of the day to go along with one he hit in the first game. Two of the homers in the second game were grand slams, and with another run batted in that game Tabor accounted for half of Boston's 18 runs. With Doerr, Cronin, Foxx, and Tabor surrounding him in the lineup, Ted Williams had some real protection on that 1939 team.

Just before the All-Star Game, for which Williams was not picked, he cracked the .300 barrier and his runs-batted-in total still led the league. The Red Sox were hot. In eight days they moved from 13½ games out of first to 6½ out, primarily by sweeping a five-game series at Fenway, including two doubleheaders, with the New York Yankees.

Jimmie Foxx—aging, drinking, and fumbling baseballs at third and
first—was still bashing the baseball at a .358 clip. Williams said he
was the best right-handed hitter he ever saw—then added, "well,
Foxx and DiMaggio." Foxx's strength left a lasting impression on the
rookie Williams:

> That Foxx. I remember when I was just a kid in my first year in
> 1939. We were playing in Chicago and the wind is blowin' a
> 90-mile-an-hour gale toward the plate. He hit a homer that day
> right into the teeth of it up into the upper deck. What power! As he
> crossed the plate he stuck out that meaty hand to me and said "Go
> ahead, Kid, you can do it." There I was, chilled to the bone, long
> and lean, and I almost fell over when he gripped my palm. Was he
> strong!

When league play resumed after the All-Star Game won by the
American League 3–1 at Yankee Stadium—the Red Sox were unbeatable. Their ninth straight win, a 6–5 victory over Cleveland and
Bobby Feller, brought them to within 5½ games of first. By July 16
their winning streak was at 12 but the Yanks maintained their lead
with some devastating baseball of their own, aided by hot hitting from
Joe DiMaggio, batting well over .400 after his return to the lineup
following an early-season leg injury.

But the pattern for the Red Sox as the season progressed was not a
happy one. They had a difficult time putting together sequences of
wins, despite the fact that their everyday players—those garnering
over 400 at-bats for the season—would average out at .320 for the
whole year, and despite Williams's steady increment of home runs
and runs batted in. Late in July, Williams had his rookie average up
to .323, with 16 home runs and 86 runs batted in, and Jimmie Foxx
had his veteran average up to .363, with 25 home runs and 81 runs
batted in, but the Sox were still eight games out of first. Things had
gotten to the point that Cronin even brought in the redoubtable Foxx
to pitch a game early in August when the Sox were losing 10–1 to
Detroit. He got the side out, fanning Pinky Higgins and getting Pete
Fox and Birdie Tebbetts on grounders, which was more than the rest
of the Red Sox relief corps could usually boast. Foxx had now played
every position on the field in the majors.

At this time, the first inklings of Boston's plans for next year at

Fenway began taking shape. Management wanted to move in the right-field fence to accommodate the productive swing of Ted Williams. The right-field power alley at Fenway ranged from 402 feet to 420 feet. In his July 3 column Hy Hurwitz dubbed this area "Williamsburg" and hinted that Red Sox management planned to bring it to a more reachable 380 feet, making Fenway Park the "House that Ted rebuilt."

While Williams was trying his best to put together a creditable rookie season—and doing a fine job—his family's troubles traveled 3,000 miles across the country to catch up with him on his sacred plot of ground, the batter's box. News from San Diego reached its low point. Sam Williams was walking. He had had it with Salvation May and was ready to leave her to the streets of San Diego and to leave his younger son, Danny, to whatever fate his increasingly delinquent nature had in store for him. There was nothing Williams could do, but the events nagged at him. Bobby Doerr recalls that Williams would not talk to anyone about his family, but to this day he remembers the pained expression that would come over Ted's face in the Red Sox clubhouse while he was reading letters from home.

Williams was allowing the strain to get to him. He had severe lapses on the field. In a game against the A's on August 9 he failed to run out a pop fly and was almost thrown out when it fell in for a hit. Cronin pulled him from the game after the play and put in Lou Finney. Management and the Boston press knew about the crisis in San Diego, but Cronin only said offhandedly that, "whatever his problems, he looks like he's thinking only about himself. There's a whole team out there and a whole game." The part-time Red Sox catcher Gene Desautels, who was Ted's friend in San Diego, tried to say something to him in the clubhouse, but Ted responded gruffly and even suggested, only half kidding, that they settle the matter with their fists. Gerry Moore of the *Globe* tried to key the fans into Williams's woes, but decorum allowed him scant mention of the situation and only titillated the reading public with "some outside circumstances of a private nature that do not permit printing here."

The benching sobered Williams enough that he snapped out of his lethargy and hit the cover off the ball for the next several days. This was always a pattern. He would fade at the plate or lose concentration, and something external would focus him again. In an August 17 profile in *The Sporting News*, reporter Jack Maloney asked Williams,

"I suppose you'll go home and receive the plaudits of San Diego?" Ted replied, "No, I don't think that will be my program." Maloney assumed that love had entered into the picture, but love was only part of the program. Simply avoiding the sheer awfulness of San Diego might have been just as appealing to Williams as spending time with Doris Soule in Princeton, Minnesota.

Williams hit the first grand-slam home run of his career (he would hit 16 more) on August 19 at Griffith Stadium against Pete Appleton of the Senators. He hit it in the ninth to win the game, 8–6. A few days later he hit one that cleared the fence in Sportsman's Park in St. Louis and reappeared off Grand Avenue. Jimmie Foxx also hit one out, the seventh time during the season that both had homered in the same game. It presented pitchers an ominous prospect: "WILLIAMS RIVALS FOXX IN LONG-DISTANCE CLOUTS" read the *Globe* banner on the game. But the *Globe* had a more shocking banner that day on its front page: "HITLER AND STALIN SIGN NON-AGGRESSION PACT." This shook the Western world to its core. Its effect on European politics, American politics, and the Allied preparations for war was immeasurable and set off a torrid debate about the status of our own Neutrality Act of 1937. Hitler was clearly protecting one flank as he prepared to move on Poland, and England would have to decide, and quickly, who was going to pay the piper when Hitler did so.

During the last months of the 1939 season, as Europe inched toward all-out war, Williams steadily added to his league-leading runs-batted-in figure; he hit his second grand slam of the month on August 29 against Cleveland. Cronin was willing enough to wrap up his prize rookie's season then and there: "Whew! The Kid has lived up to his advance notice. I guess that's so even if he doesn't drive in another run for the rest of the year." Even some management hijinx were in order: Tom Yawkey and team secretary Phil Troy were eating in their suite at the Lake Shore in Cleveland right above Williams's room. They called to him from their open window, and when the Kid stuck his head out to answer, Yawkey, a kid himself at heart, let go with a pitcher of water. A drenched Williams screamed so loud the entire hotel was roused.

In a crazy doubleheader at Fenway on September 3, with a large Boston crowd there to see the Yanks, now making a mockery of the American League pennant race, the lead in the second game kept changing until the Yankees, trying to conclude the game before curfew, began intentionally striking out to protect a two-run lead. When George Selkirk was thrown out by 30 feet stealing home, the fans rioted in disgust, heaving seat cushions, beer bottles, and hot dogs onto the field. The umps forfeited the game to New York, but the decision was overturned a few days later when the league office rescheduled the game and told both squads to start from scratch. But the stats for the game, including Williams's two home runs and four runs batted in, remained on the books. In yet another brilliant late-season burst of hitting during a September 10 doubleheader in Philadelphia, Williams went 5 for 7 with two more home runs and another three runs batted in, his total soaring to 131.

With September came the full horror of war in Europe. The course that had begun with the rise of national socialism in Germany, perhaps even the settlement of World War I at Versailles, reached its inevitable destination as Hitler moved into Poland, and France and England declared war. For the time being the United States would spend its energies and its resources figuring ways to finesse the arms embargo dictated by its neutral status and help England in her desperate and lonely struggle against Hitler. France would make her one feeble effort against the German lines (the German blitzkrieg, of course, was avoiding immobile positions), and England would send an army to Dunkirk whose major accomplishment would be getting back from Dunkirk to British soil.

In America positions on the war began to harden early. President Roosevelt expressed his shock at the Luftwaffe's wanton bombing of towns and villages in Poland. The legendary British war correspondent Sir Philip Gibbs saw Hitler's brutal advance as the harbinger of a conflict he could name but not yet fully comprehend: "filth without glory." Charles Lindbergh went public on the radio begging for restraint, for suppression of judgment, for a quieting of rhetoric: "If we enter this war for democracy abroad, we may end up losing democracy here at home."

The season wound down as the war heated up in Europe. Joe DiMaggio's dream for a .400 season pretty much came to grief on September 13 against Cleveland when his nemesis, Mel Harder, hung the collar on him, 0 for 5, and plummeted his average to .394; the next day Bobo Newsom of Detroit dried him out 0 for 4, dropping him down to .390. DiMaggio would end the year at .381, and the Yankees would crush the Cincinnati Reds in the World Series in four games, with their own great rookie, Charlie Keller, leading the way at .438 with three home runs.

The Red Sox, despite their tremendous team power, finished 12 games behind the Yankees for second place in the American League, a position they occupied the year before and would occupy again for two of the next three years. Williams's final line for the season was impressive: a .327 average, 31 home runs, and 145 runs batted in. He hit 17 of his home runs on the road and 14 beyond the distant reaches of Fenway's fences in center and right. His road average for the year was .301 and at Fenway a healthy .353. For most of the year Williams owned the Philadelphia A's, hitting .432 at Shibe Park and .490 against them at Fenway. He was no slouch at St. Louis either, hitting an even .400 there in 11 games. He hit four home runs both in Sportsman's Park in St. Louis and Briggs Stadium in Detroit—his best home-run parks on the road. Williams's bottomless pit for the year was the home of the Washington Senators, Griffith Stadium. Ted came to the plate 38 times there and got two hits, though one of them was his first grand-slam home run.

Part of the reason this season meant so much to Williams was the fire in his eyes at the end of it. Rarely had any rookie displayed such run-production power so late. Pitchers, rather than hitters, tend to do better the third and fourth time around the league in August and September. But in the last three months of the season, Williams batted .349 in 93 games, with 21 home runs and 87 runs batted in. That's a great year in and of itself, as the Red Sox manager, Joe Cronin, pointed out at season's end.

Harold Kaese remembered telling Williams late in the 1939 season that he was having a pretty good year for a 20-year-old. Ted responded, with some embarrassment, that he was actually 21. His birthday was in August, but since he had begun playing ball he celebrated it in October—he just didn't relish the distraction during the season: "He thought of everything," Kaese recalled, "even when he was a kid." Williams went off to celebrate his birthday belatedly in Minneapolis at the King Cole Hotel. He would hunt and fish that winter in Minnesota, and he and his girlfriend, Doris Soule, would see if the cold clear air could filter out memories and miseries of San Diego. He was a major leaguer and had finally sworn off trundling home for winter batting practice in North Park.

◊ 4 ◊

"Williamsburg" 1940

TED WILLIAMS TOOK A BREAK from his Minnesota winter vacation and returned to Boston in January to have his tonsils removed. His bouts with illness the year before had worn him down in spring training and at the beginning of the season. This year he would give viruses less to shoot at. Hy Hurwitz asked him if he planned to wear a tuxedo at the February 1 Baseball Writers Dinner in Boston. "Nah, that's not me," Williams replied. But he reconsidered and gave himself a touch of class; he showed up in a rented tux to receive the Tim Murnane Award as the most valuable player on the Boston club for 1939. He looked like an uncomfortable kid with enough crawl space around his collar to catch drafts.

Williams's remarks at the dinner were brief: "Thank God I ain't got any notes. This is really the greatest and happiest honor I've ever achieved in my short baseball career." Later he told the milling writers: "That stuff about breaking up the Yankees gets me sick. Give us a pitcher and a catcher and we'll break up those Yankees. They're not as tough as a lot of people think. Why, we beat them more than they beat us last year. And, say, I hit more home runs off them than against any other club."

The Sox were ready to go, and Eddie Collins, general manager, was having none of the backbiting that characterized press reports at the time Williams was agonizing over his parents' separation the previous season: "They talk about Teddy Williams being a headache—well, I wish I had 15 or 20 headaches like him." Boston's press was ready to ease off on the sniping and gear up for the hyping; they

warmed up for spring training by cranking out the colorful descrip-
tions of Williams: "Baby Babe," "The Big Wallop of Fenway's
Fusiliers," "Toothpick Ted," "Fresh as Wet Paint." As for Williams,
he planned to stay in the East for much of February, visit his aunts in
New York, and then return to Boston for the long train trip to
Sarasota with several local Boston players. "We're one big happy
family," he told reporters as he boarded the train. This was a subject,
by default if not by experience, about which Ted Williams claimed a
kind of wry expertise.

As was so often the case during the Williams era, the Red Sox
looked superb before spring training; 1940 seemed especially golden.
The farm system was cultivating excellent prospects and championship teams. Scranton, Canton, and Danville won pennants in 1939.
Moreover, had the Sox played their cards right, they could have had
Pee Wee Reese from Louisville and Dom DiMaggio, who hit .360
and was Most Valuable Player in the Coast League, on the squad at
the same time. But Cronin, though his aging bones ached at short,
put the kibosh on the young and eager Reese. The party line was that
Yawkey had to sell Reese to the Dodgers to get $35,000 in cash to
buy Dom DiMaggio from the Seals, but the truth is that Cronin,
Boston's playing manager, wanted little of Reese's grit and speed and
even less of his raw youth haunting him during the fading days of his
career. He convinced Tom Yawkey to let the young shortstop go. The
Red Sox always found it difficult to separate the personal from the
personnel. That was "the real virus in the Boston organization," as
David Halberstam put it. Shortly after the Reese decision the Red Sox
canned their superb farm director, Bill Evan. He was ready to leave;
the Reese dealings disturbed him deeply.

However nice it might have been for the Red Sox to go into the
1940s with Reese in the infield teamed with Bobby Doerr, the club
still looked good. There were a couple of fine pitchers to support the
aging Lefty Grove: Mickey Harris was up for his rookie year and Tex
Hughson was being groomed for 1941. Tom Yawkey and Evan were
going about their business with care and efficiency, which was more
than could be said for other clubs of that era, who conducted much
of their shady minor-league business like pirates.

The Detroit Tigers, for example, were at that time in danger of
losing their entire minor league support structure. Kenesaw Mountain

Landis, just before spring training, had come down on the Tigers like Alaric the Visigoth, releasing by fiat 91 minor league players from contracts (of a sort) with the parent club. Landis ruled that Detroit had entered into collusion with minor league owners to stockpile talent. The Tigers claimed that $500,000 in development money was down the drain, and Landis shot back that he wanted fair procedures for developing ballplayers rather than back-door deals shrouded in secrecy. The commissioner proposed an intricate waiver and compensation system for the minors to handle the process of players rising through league ranks. Much of his plan would encourage the open affiliation system that the Yanks and Red Sox were then building, though it would also set the scene for the kind of serfdom that plagued baseball in the courts during later disputes of the 1940s and 1950s, especially during the fledgling Mexican League player raids. These same problems would resurface during the free-agent controversies of the 1960s and 1970s.

Before spring training, *The Sporting News* polled members of the Baseball Writers Association for a major league All-Star team, and Ted Williams was the only rookie from 1939 named to the squad. He would take his shots this year at a fence moved in 20 feet in the right-field power alley. Moreover, he would play in left this year, with the excellent fielding Dom DiMaggio penciled in for the tougher sun field at Fenway and Doc Cramer still patrolling center.

As spring training unwound in 1940, Disney's *Pinocchio* and the superb Depression film *Grapes of Wrath*, with Henry Fonda, opened across the country. In March, Joe Louis took out one of his Bums of the Month, Johnny Paycheck, with a right to the chin at 44 seconds of round two. The ref, Art Donovan, and Benny Leonard, working Paycheck's corner, rushed to the fighter, who was in cuckoo land. Donovan didn't even bother to count. Leonard had to pick up his Paycheck before Johnny could pick up his.

World war affected America in strange ways. A nation divided during the Depression by the politics of want now began to configure its differences over the politics of hate. The organized isolationist movement in America, led by Charles Lindbergh, and the growing movement of Nazi Bund groups all over the East Coast made strange but provocative bedfellows in trying to forge public opinion against entering the war on the Allied side. In an unusually blunt legal confrontation, federal authorities in New York even charged one fascist goon with attempting to overthrow the government in order to set up, in the stark words of the indictment, "a Jew-baiting dictatorship in America." The case eventually collapsed, but, ironically, a black was selected as the first prospective juror.

While the issue of engagement simmered, the forces of science raged. It was during these same springtime days that physicists at Columbia University's 1,550-ton cyclotron announced the successful isolation of U-235, the uranium substance necessary for nuclear fission. It would take the bulk of the war for scientists to figure out just how to dispose U-235 in an atomic bomb, but the solution would end one troubling epoch in world history and begin another.

In Europe by spring of 1940, the Nazis entered Scandinavia and moved into Holland and Belgium and would soon push to France and force British armies out of Europe at Dunkirk. Churchill took over the office of prime minister in England from an exhausted and discredited Neville Chamberlain. Roosevelt, calling Nazi Germany an "enemy" (clearly challenging our own Neutrality Act of 1937), asked Congress for $1 billion for, among other things, the construction of 50,000 airplanes, the new weapons of choice for modern warfare. The tough-minded and feisty political columnist Dorothy Thompson, on the rampage against fascism for years, advocated that we simply declare war on Germany and have done with it. The newspapers in Boston, responding to Thompson's forthrightness, featured open-column citizens' responses on this matter for weeks to come. America did not exactly bury its collective head in the sand on the issue of world war before Pearl Harbor. Active and opposing positions were tenaciously held and forcefully debated by the people and the nation's leaders.

For Ted Williams, prospects for his year began rosy. He had admired Charles Lindbergh when he was a lad, and his politics before Pearl Harbor were right about where Lindbergh's were: keep out of the war and keep Ted Williams in a baseball uniform. Williams had managed to forget his family's troubles (or so he thought) for the winter; he was well; and he had traveled around the league several times getting to know the pitchers and gauging the ball parks.

His mouth watered at the prospect of a cheerier shot at the right-field fences in Fenway, now a mere 380 feet away instead of a monstrous 400 plus feet. Ted was ready.

Williams played in a manner to which all around him were growing accustomed. He would crush the ball one day, but his sense of righteousness and perfectionism would get in the way of the natural order of things the next. When he felt good at the plate he thought he should rip the ball every time, and he threw a fit when he felt cheated of his due. Late in a spring training game against the minor league Atlanta Crackers, at a time when he was still moping about a previous at-bat, he let a short fly drop between the fence and foul line without giving it much of an effort. The crowd let him have it. Williams's peeved reaction merely made it worse; this was a pattern that would be repeated on all too many occasions. He picked up the foul ball, turned, and heaved it over the fence through a fourth-story window across the street. Cronin later fined him $50. More chagrined than despondent, Williams made Cronin a deal, his best effort of a forgettable day: "Okay, I'll pay you $50 for every one I throw out, and you pay me $50 for every one I hit out." If Cronin had taken the deal, would the inside-the-park homer Ted hit the next day against the Cards in St. Pete have counted? Twenty-four hours later, he hit another against the Cards 500 feet into the trees beyond their outfield fence.

Grantland Rice took in the Boston games with St. Louis and called Williams the "King of the Sophomores." He said the league had two of the best second-year men he could ever recall: Williams and Charlie Keller of the Yanks. Then, in what must be one of the first uses of a now-overused word, he pointed out that "anyone who comes along good enough to outhit, outfield, and outthrow DiMaggio will have to be a *super-star*." (Italics added.) He was giving Williams a tall order; but, Rice continued, "Cobb, Ruth, Speaker, and others have dropped out of the parade. The game must have replacements to fill these big gaps—and the game usually gets them."

Baseball writers have plenty of time on their hands during the lazy days of spring training. They can speculate, as did Grantland Rice, or they can sidle up to future immortals and just listen to the chatter that goes on before, during, and after games. Things are far less tense when losses count for little and when spring batting averages have about as much significance for regulars as their golf scores. Williams was fun to hang around in those days. He had not yet entirely soured on the writers, and his incessant banter, most of it reserved for his Red Sox teammates, was good copy. One extremely windy day in late March in Sarasota, he and rookie lefty Mickey Harris were going after each other about the distant fence in right, over 460 feet away. Ted said he could put one out easy with the wind blowing the way it was. "But you're not even playing today," said Harris, "and I'm pitching. Why do I gotta listen to you talk about how far you're goin' to hit 'em when you're on the bench?" "Maybe I oughta be pitchin' today," Williams shot back. "Hell, there's a guy out there I pitched against in high school—he couldn't get a loud foul offa me." Harris asked, "Who, who did you pitch against?" "Graham. Jack Graham," said Ted. "Jeez," said Harris, "he can hit." "Nah, I could handle him. Maybe I better pitch again and show you a thing or two," Williams taunted. "You stick to hitting, meathead," said Harris, "I'll get the outs." "Dunno, dunno," returned Williams, "maybe I'd better pitch. You seem a little shaky."

The season neared. As the Red Sox made their way by train north for the opener, Williams sought out the advice of veteran Moe Berg. Berg caught for the White Sox and the Indians during the 1920s and 1930s and later became a linguist and intelligence officer for the United States Army during World War II. He was with Boston, though not on the active roster, in 1940. Williams wanted to know everything about the great left-handed hitters; Gehrig in his prime, Ruth, Chuck Klein. Berg interrupted Ted's endless stream of questions with wedged-in answers. "Gehrig could wait and wait—he took it right out of your glove. Ruth had no weaknesses. He had a good eye, and that means he laid off pitches like you, Ted. If you want to know the type of hitter you most resemble, I'd say it was Shoeless Joe Jackson. He was a little stiffer than you at the plate. You're better than all of them when it comes to wrists." Among his other talents, Berg was a bit of a psychologist. What better way to prime a young hitter for a possible pennant-contending ball club?

Cleveland's Bobby Feller opened his 1940 season with a no-hitter against Chicago, and on April 16 Boston's Lefty Grove had to settle for a shutout in his opening-day 1-0 win over Washington in Griffith Stadium. Grove not only won the game but *won* the game—his single produced the only run. Williams got a couple hits but stirred the fans and his own mates by a play in the field. Cronin could barely contain himself: "I've been telling him for a year that the game is played all over the field as much as at the plate. Ted made the defensive move of the day in left. Just great." He lunged for a smashed line drive to deep left by Gee Walker, and the ball nicked his glove. But he picked it up and in one motion rifled a long strike to Doerr at second to nab Walker by five feet. Cronin said he had been working with Williams on quickness, on getting an angle on balls, cutting them off, and releasing the throw with dispatch and accuracy. Their work paid off early, and the manager was as openly happy with Williams's throw as he ever was with any of Williams's hits.

Still unused to the eastern chill, Williams had a bit of trouble getting unwound at the plate in the early days of the season. In colder weather, he lacked feeling in his fingers; he felt tight; and, most of all, he had it in his head that he wanted warmth, that he would swing better and feel better when it came. Indeed, in early May, when the weather heated up, Williams began to stroke the ball well. The Red Sox were in first place, thanks to a miserable 4–11 start by the Yankees. Williams's average soared to .364 even though he had hit few home runs. Tom Yawkey was so happy with his club that he suited up himself after games and had Eddie Doherty, Sox publicist, toss him fat ones as he hacked away in the ballpark he owned. The trick for anyone pitching to him was to put the ball on his bat. Yawkey did not take kindly to looking foolish.

At mid-May the Sox were 2½ games in front with a 17–6 record. Pennant fever swept Boston early. The Yankees were playing poorly, and Gehrig's departure was taking its toll; Detroit was playing with a veteran squad in the best sense and an old one in the worst; the White Sox lacked power; the Indians were riddled with dissension that would soon escalate into almost full-scale mutiny against their manager, Ossie Vitt. The question was whether Boston could win, weak as they were at catcher and slow as they were up the middle at short.

With the fences moved in at Fenway and the team in obvious position to contend for the pennant, Williams in late May began to press for home runs. In fact, he was hitting over .360, and no one was complaining yet about his lack of power. But it was on his mind. He knew what he expected and transferred that thought to fans, writers, and teammates. He began muttering to reporters and players that he was underpaid at $12,500 a year, that he was not getting protection in the lineup, a thinly veiled suggestion that Foxx and Cronin were over the hill. He needed quality pitches for home runs even if he could hit junk for an average.

With Williams rarely was any expression of behavior random, but just as rarely did it represent what was nominally at issue. He was a man with agendas hidden at times even from himself. Salary whining in 1940 had little to do with him as a player and much to do with the pressures put on him in San Diego: he felt that he had responsibilities for his mother and younger brother. Williams would never just talk about this with the press; instead, he would mumble, in the presence of writers, about his paltry earnings, the expectations, real or imagined, for him to hit the long ball on a punch-and-judy hitter's salary, and the price of tea in China.

When Williams moped, no one could miss it. His moods were exaggerated. Cronin watched him in left and thought all his work in spring training was going to seed. In a Detroit game Ted played one of Rudy York's long drives as if he were hunting for gophers. Lefty Grove, pitching the game, absolutely hated it when his fielders screwed up, and he made his feelings known in the clubhouse. Cronin did something radical. He benched Williams and put Finney in left for a game, telling reporters, "My decision is the result of a lot of incidents recently where the Kid has shown once again that he is thinking about nothing else but hitting. All great players are team players."

Williams got right back in the lineup the next day and rode one out of the park. A few days later, May 26, the *Globe* sports banner read "TED LOCATES WILLIAMSBURG," in reference to the first home run he polled into the new bullpen area in front of the bleachers. He hit it off Yankees reliever Johnny Murphy. Williams, set adrift for so much of his early life without anything resembling parental attention, usually responded well to an ultimatum if it came from the right source. But his first reaction was to dig himself deeper in a hole. It is a salient characteristic of his life and his career that he groped for a response to his own moods that would supplant self-pity with productive anger and irritation. Then he could snap back. More important, he could focus and concentrate, what he always felt he needed to do as a hitter.

For the jammed Decoration Day games at Yankee Stadium on May 30, before 82,437 fans, the Red Sox were sailing. They took a split in the doubleheader, but their outfield was stroking the ball at a combined average of nearly .380, and Jimmie Foxx was still ripping his home runs, 11 so far on the year. Avuncular *Globe* columnist Victor O. Jones now thought it about time to kick in with a belated open letter to Williams about life in the big leagues:

> Dear Ted ... Twenty-one is pretty young, and this sure is a mighty tough world if a kid of 21, particularly a sensitive kid like you, can't get in the dumps occasionally. But whether you like it or not, you are a public character and, as such, you've got to stand the gaff. You can't afford to thumb your nose at the public, turn into a loner, and let the world go hang. You're a great kid, a great ballplayer, with maybe 20 years of major league ball ahead of you. Don't go and spoil it all.

A few days later, the *Globe* printed a picture of a gloomy Williams with a beaming, happy Cronin; the caption read, "Cheer Up, Ted, You're Still Outhitting the Boss by 145 Points." Indeed he was, .354 to .209, but the image of Ted as the beleaguered star sank in. Johnny Orlando, the clubhouse man for the Red Sox for the whole of Williams's career, would always claim that the Kid got a bad rap. He was approachable and sensitive if the terms were right.

> It ain't that he don't want to be friendly. It's just that he hates front runners. He don't like people who run up and make a big fuss over him when he's done something good. Now take me. I never shook his hand once after he hit a home run. Never once. He don't need it then. It's after he goes 0 for 5 that I talk to him. That's when he needs it, not when he's doin' good. But a lot of people don't understand that.

This may have been fine for Johnny Orlando, but few sportswriters over the years, hailing from Boston or anywhere, experienced much sense of Williams's need for a bit of a buck-up after an 0-for-5 day. More likely, the writers would steer clear of Ted, for good reason, or sandbag him for the mere sport of it.

To put all of these matters in perspective, Victor O. Jones's column appeared on the same day that all of Great Britain and millions of her supporters in the United States were tremendously buoyed by news of the successful evacuation of the 350,000-strong British Expeditionary Force at Dunkirk. Churchill's somber tones filled the American airwaves: "We are brought back from the jaws of death. . . . we shall fight on the seas and oceans, . . . we shall fight on the beaches, we shall fight on the landing grounds, we shall fight in the fields and in the streets, we shall fight in the hills; we shall never surrender." On that same June 4 the U.S. Congress passed a billion-dollar tax hike for defense. The future Allies of the Atlantic corridor were readying for the long haul.

The Red Sox continued to lead the league through mid-June, around the time of one of the stranger occurrences in baseball history. With Cleveland breathing down Boston's neck in the pennant race, a delegation of Indians met with the team's president, Alva Bradley, for the express purpose of dumping their manager, Oscar Vitt. They claimed that Vitt was relentless in bad-mouthing his ballplayers in public, that he would say vile things in front of friend and foe alike. The players complained that it was getting way out of hand. After a bad outing by Feller, Vitt screamed for anyone within three city blocks to hear: "He's supposed to be my ace! Look at him. I'm supposed to win with him?" As for Mel Harder, the manager complained that "a man with his salary ought to be able to win one for me."

After the Indians management promised that the public humiliations would stop and that team meetings and grievance procedures would be de rigueur (there was an unspoken understanding that Vitt was on the way out), the players agreed to release the following cosigned statement on June 16: "We the undersigned publicly declare to withdraw all statements referring to the resignation of Oscar Vitt. We feel this action is for the betterment of the Cleveland baseball club." Roy Weatherly, who hated Vitt with a particular passion, was the only Cleveland player who refused to sign. He stormed out of the meeting.

At about this time, with a deeply troubled Cleveland ball club still nagging at their heels and with Detroit nearby, the Red Sox dropped two to the lowly St. Louis Browns. The next day, June 21, Oscar Vitt's Indians moved into first as the Red Sox arrived in Cleveland for an early-season showdown. Boston, as usual, collapsed on the road. Worse, Williams and Doc Cramer collided going after a fly to left center on June 23, and Ted ended up in the hospital with a mild concussion. He was kept under observation a few days, no doubt happy to read in *The Sporting News* at the end of the week that "Dom DiMaggio played a gorgeous left field while Ted was out."

Williams continued to worry about his power. He had hit eight home runs and driven in 37 runs by the end of June, even though his average was hovering in the .330s. These stats were not satisfactory to him nor, in his mind, to anyone. He was taking it out on the writers, treating them to his clubhouse rumblings, whether they said anything to him or not: "Hey, what stinks? Something stinks? Oh, no wonder— you. That shit you wrote last night. . . ." It was just a matter of time before the scribes turned on him with a vengeance. The bellyaching and whining were getting on their nerves, on Williams's teammates' nerves, and certainly on Cronin's nerves.

Williams heard only what he wanted to hear; that was characteristic of him and plagued him for his entire baseball life. For reasons that had to do with embarrassment and sensitivity, the lone taunt from a crowd or the single sentence in a newspaper article could claim his unwavering and, subsequently, undying attention. Writers tried to prop him up, to focus him, but it never did much good because he seemed to want to remain irritated. On July 3 the *Globe's* Melville Webb gave it a try: "There are some Fenway fans who boo Ted Williams. But when these boys start into action there is a drowning burst of cheers from the rank and file. Boston's fans are still fair-minded." The fair-minded weren't the ones who primed Williams's pump. He admitted in his autobiography that he had special antennae out for the one jeer in a chorus of cheers. He thrived on antagonism, as much as that very antagonism seemed to sap his soul, to challenge his basically decent nature. In one sense he knew that what Harold Kaese later said was true—"fans boo him because they are sick and tired of cheering him"—but he hated the very sound of derision; it played too centrally on insecurities about public exposure he had borne since his San Diego youth.

Williams's performance didn't help his spirits much at the 1940 All-Star Game, with his getting a couple of hitless at-bats as the National League won 4–0 on Max West's three-run homer in the first inning. When the season resumed, the rookie Dom DiMaggio was stealing most of the thunder in the press. He had been filling in for the injured Lou Finney in right and would not be dislodged for the rest of the year. On July 15 Hy Hurwitz, who was a curious sort of charitable nemesis to Williams for 20 years, wrote that when Finney came back Cronin might well bench Williams. In an odd phrasing that was the newspaperman's way of saying in the 1940s that Ted was a hostile bastard in the clubhouse, Hurwitz wrote: "Hitting is Ted's life. When he isn't hitting he just can't live normally."

The power issue kept nagging at him. Every time Williams looked at a Boston writer he thought of the expectations upon him with the fence having been moved and the bullpen area set up as a target in Fenway's right field. Hurwitz's article screwed right into his soul. And Williams did what he almost always did—he proceeded to lash nine hits in his next 16 at-bats. Boston edged again toward first, hovered, and then began losing ground rapidly when Williams's bat cooled again. Foxx was limping with a bad spike wound, Finney was disabled, and, heaven forbid, the team was on the road. Things were breaking up for the 1940 Red Sox, and they never did bring the pieces back together.

On July 21, the Indians beat Boston twice and Williams had just about had it. He told Harry Grayson, a Cleveland writer hanging around his locker in the visitors' clubhouse, about when he was in New York and invited his uncle, John Smith, a fireman in Yonkers, to a Yankees game. Later he returned to visit the fire station. As a kid in San Diego, he had often hung out at the station where Elmer Hill served. It was a quiet day in Yonkers, and everyone was lounging in the sun and playing cards. "Hell, you can live like this and retire with a pension. Here I am hitting .340 and everybody's all over me. Maybe I shoulda been a fireman." Had he left it there, the incident may have been harmless enough—in a sense it remained harmless enough—but Williams added his usual refrain that the Sox were getting him this year for chicken feed at $12,500. Grayson printed the whole conversation.

These were times before players had public relations firms to screen their offhand remarks or to put what is now called a beneficial spin on them. Ken Keltner of the Indians was razzed all year—one of his worst, by the way, as a major leaguer—for an incident that was

reported during the off-season. After literally winning the shirt off a
friend's back at a bowling match, he joked that he got paid so little
playing ball he ought to apply for unemployment insurance during
the winter. His friends, as a gag, got him the forms and he filled them
out and processed them. The story leaked, and during these tag-end
days of the Depression Keltner took heat all season long for his greedy
chicanery in diverting the welfare sluice into his own pockets. Surely
the opportunity was inviting, and one could hardly expect Keltner to
escape scot-free. He didn't. The fans and rival players gave it to him
hard.

Woe came to Williams in a similar manner from the stands and
from the rival benches around the league. In Chicago, Jimmy Dykes,
a playing manager for the White Sox who could shout commands to
the Pacific Fleet without a megaphone, began to let Williams have it
about the fireman story. Dykes was a one-man show—whistles,
alarms, sirens: "Fireman! Fireman! *Save my child!*" Even Williams
had to laugh, though there were other taunts about his salary and his
tepid year in the power department that didn't strike him as one bit
funny.

The Red Sox spent the rest of July losing, even though Williams
put a couple of home runs in his power column on July 26 at friendly
Sportsman's Park in St. Louis. In early August he got hot at the plate,
and in mid-August he started hitting a few out—but not before
another outburst and the worst controversy yet in his brief career.
The Sox were traveling to New York for a big doubleheader on
Sunday, August 13. Williams was in a foul mood and hurting to boot.
He told Cronin that he had a sore back. Cronin said he would rest
him, but then Jimmie Foxx checked in with his sad story. He had to
leave the club to attend to his four-year-old son in Philly, who was
having his tonsils removed.

Cronin was getting edgy. He had his doubts about the will of this
team, and mentioned to a writer, as if Williams's sore back were
marginal, "the team trainer will look at him." Cronin was ever so
subtly implying that, with Foxx on parental sick call, he was less ready
than he might have been to take Ted's word on the condition of his
back. Williams was furious. He began ranting to a writer he didn't
much like in the first place, Austen "Duke" Lake, of the *Boston
Evening American*. Lake sensed two things: first, the sportswriting

code of the day told him he ought to try to turn Williams off; and, second, if he couldn't calm his man down, he had a hell of a story.

The tirade was a Williams classic. Arms and torso got into the act. He spoke and flailed at the same time. Everyone and everything were indicted as co-conspirators: fans, press, management, teammates, Boston's streets, its climate, its trees. Anyone who has ever witnessed such an explosive verbal tirade knows that the issues that come to the fore are not necessarily the only ones of import. This is what made a Williams exchange with writers so volatile and inflammatory. Each of his responses harbored dozens of others. As he fulminated about one thing, another would rise in his gorge. Such was his way of inflicting maximum damage with his insults, calling up multiple targets, painting the corners with the same brush he might use for the open spaces.

Lake heard it all—none of it pleasant and little of it in language fit to print. The charges were the same as those simmering all year: the fans are an outrage; Boston is a hellhole; the writers expect home runs on every swing; his salary is chickenshit; he wants out and has asked Cronin and Yawkey to trade him. Lake kept telling him to calm down, that he surely didn't want all this on the record. The Boston press, no matter what Williams had been saying publicly, had been soft-pedalling his complaints all year long because they knew he could hit like hell and thought he was still just a kid. But Williams got louder and more abusive: "Hell, yes. This is on the record, dammit." Lake shrugged, wet the tip of his pencil, and let fly with an article that hit the streets like Hitler's Luftwaffe: "Ted Williams is a grown man with the mind of a juvenile."

Before the dust settled, Williams's ravings produced responses from every baseball writer up and down the Atlantic Coast and into America's heartland. That week's *Sporting News* headlined the story. Jack Miley of the *New York Post* got off a typical zinger: "If his noodle swells another inch, Master Ted Williams won't be able to get his hat on with a shoehorn." Dave Egan, "the Colonel," the writer Ted Williams hated most in Boston, took the most offended tone of all in the *Record*. Egan didn't know much about baseball, but he was perhaps the most contentious writer in town on the subject. He used to love to inflame the local fans by setting forth outrageous suggestions and then inviting letters of response to the paper. This was the equivalent of what is now known as shock radio or shock television. Egan was a Harvard-educated lawyer, but in the ridiculous-looking photo accompanying his column he sported a Confederate hat, with mustaches and sideburns. What Egan couldn't get out of his craw concerning the Austen Lake interview was the insult to Boston: "Williams is the prize heel ever to wear a Boston uniform." Egan would have liked to run the young man out of town on the evening freight train.

The Red Sox damage-control brigade took the day off on this story. Tom Yawkey, from his semipermanent suite at the Pierre Hotel, heard the account on the radio broadcast of the Yankees doubleheader. He was not a happy sportsman. Cronin was already raw on the subject when Williams hooked up with Lake. When Yawkey spoke to the press he put Williams out on point and let him take the arrows: "His dealing with the writers is his business. Bad language, not hustling on the field is ours. I feel sorry for him. He had the writers and the fans, practically the whole world, at his feet. Now he is tossing it all away, and he is the only loser." Yawkey said he had spoken to Williams about his tirades against the press: "When it gets so a person seems out of step with the whole world, it is high time a person take stock of himself to see if he isn't the one to blame."

Cronin took with one hand and gave back a little with the other: "He's always popping off. You don't pay attention to him, do you? My lookout is that he hustles in the field. He's been doing that lately, no?" Cronin had already gotten to Williams privately and asked him point blank about the trade talk business, and Williams denied it. But Cronin couldn't imagine Lake made it up entirely. Ed Barrow of the Yankees, claiming to be speaking off the record, said to writers on Sunday: "So he wants to come to the Yankees, huh? Why, a pop-off like that wouldn't last two minutes with McCarthy." It turned out Barrow was wrong about McCarthy, though for a host of reasons he might have been right about New York.

What worried Cronin most were the hostile remarks about Boston. What were the fans going to say about Williams's harangue against the very topographical features of the city? Ted shot back: "I'll tell you what. I'll hit .400 on the next home stand and they'll forget about it." When asked by New York's writers whether Austen Lake had quoted him correctly, Williams sucked it up and gave the response that had no doubt crossed his mind at the time: "I still say Boston is a lousy town, and I expected the fellow who wrote it would put it strongly."

Williams's teammates were particularly galled about his muling and puling on the salary issue because he had griped all year to those making little more than he but far senior to him. "Crazy" was a word bandied about in the clubhouse. The salary structure for rookies and second-year players was fairly standard and fairly low all around the league. Yawkey had not been cheap. He had invested $3,131,526 in the Red Sox since acquiring the team in 1934, and he was carrying a substantial payroll in those days of over $300,000. He ran $65,870 into the loss column for 1940 when the final figures were in. As for Williams, he was on the up side of the downside, and most of his mates thought he should consider himself fortunate.

There was, however, a lighter side to all this, and some of the Red Sox had a hard time taking Williams too seriously. Joe Heving, relief pitcher, put the matter in a way that proved the very point he made: "If I only had his talent and he my brain." Rookie Jim Tabor, who had his problems with management and with demon rum, tried to put Ted's bellyaching in perspective: "You should have heard him in Minneapolis to really appreciate him." And a crusty old Boston writer tried to warn him in the clubhouse. "You see western movies?" the old scribe began. "Well, you got to take the jeers with the cheers. A cowboy star is in a good movie, and he's a hero. He's in a stinker, and he's a bum actor. Ya' catch my drift?" "Yeah," said Ted, "but you ever see that Hoot Gibson? He's always great!"

Amidst all the controversy, Williams still had to play the double-header. The Red Sox were less ready than he. The baseball seemed to float up to the plate with Austen Lake's—or better, Dave Egan's—portrait on it, and Williams belted one out during Boston's two pastings by the Yanks, 9–1 and 19–8. In the next few days, he hit four home runs, a response to the power failure charge he felt hanging over him most of the season. Hitting for Williams was a favored stepchild of incitement.

The next day Jimmie Foxx was back in town from Philadelphia and his son's tonsillectomy. Reporters asked him about the incident, knowing that Williams deeply admired Foxx: "If you want a frank statement, I'll give it to you. Teddy is a spoiled boy. How long it will take him to grow up remains to be seen. But he'll have to grow up the hard way now." Foxx said that all the world was before him, and now he had a host of antagonists on every front. Williams later wrote in his autobiography that "Foxx never bad-mouthed anybody," so his remarks on this occasion revealed how delicate Williams's position was.

Williams complained that the Red Sox rarely rallied around him, though, for his part, he never truly understood the devastating effect his scattershot reactions had on those who, presumably, should have come to his defense. A more temperate Williams recognized that overreaction was simply part of his nature, but those who might, under different circumstances, mount the barricades to defend Williams against his enemies often found themselves included in his list of enemies. His tactics were not endearing, and he was right to think of himself as out there most of the time with little advice and even less protection.

By Monday's game, the Yankees took their turn getting on Williams's case. Even though he hit another ball out of the park for his 17th of the year, Lefty Gomez went crazy on the bench with the fireman bit, which Williams thought would have been laid to rest with the juicier Lake interview so fresh on the wires. But no: Gomez had his sirens and fireman's whistles, making it hard for Williams to get set at the plate. The ump, Red Ormsby, having a hard time suppressing his own laughter, warned Gomez time and again. Finally, he threw him out of the game, though Lefty was far from his scheduled niche in the pitching rotation and had the day off anyway. Maybe these antics helped. Williams smiled noticeably when Gomez got the heave. It was, after all, funny. More important, it was in fun, what the game was supposedly all about. Later in the year, the people at the Hall-of-Fame town of Cooperstown, in the spirit of fun, named Williams honorary fire chief. He was delighted.

By the time the Red Sox returned home to Fenway, Austen Lake was ready to marshall the troops against Williams. He had tried to protect him during the infamous interview—if it could be called that—and now figured that his own efforts to save Williams's skin had themselves been belittled by Williams's imperviousness to warnings: "You've sat sullen and aloof in locker rooms and hotels. Often you've looked lazy and careless on fly balls. Occasionally you've snarled things back at the bleacherites. You've taken the attitude, sometimes, that you're bigger than the game." It would seem that the Fenway fans would have been loaded for bear. But they weren't; Boston fans were that contrary. During the home stand, the fans reacted to Williams with something resembling pure baseball emotion—they responded to his performance on the field. And he was not sulking. At the plate, he hit .420 over 14 games and made a series of excellent plays in the field, refining the art of playing the left-field wall at Fenway so that he could master the caroms with the skill of a Willy Mosconi.

But he also swore off tipping his hat on any home run he might happen to park in the bleachers at Fenway. He had no wish to deprive the fans—actually he didn't think much about the fans—but he did not want writers in the press box to get the idea he cared enough about them or their abusive art to acknowledge what he imagined to be *their* contempt of his power. This was his petulant way of telling the writers that he had just done what they said he hadn't been doing, but that he did not attach the same significance to it as they.

Williams went 3 for 3 in a game on August 24; they were all singles, so there was no need to tip the hat at all. But he might have tipped it for other reasons. He delighted those at the park and, no doubt, himself when Cronin had him come in to pitch two innings in the Tigers' 12–1 shellacking of the Red Sox and their beleaguered relief corps. He hadn't pitched in a game since his gopher-ball debut in San Diego back in 1936. Williams got the side out, including Pinky Higgins and Hank Greenberg, the latter on a pop-up, but he gave up a run on three hits. He got his biggest kick fanning Rudy York, not altogether the most difficult thing in the world to do but not simply there for the taking either. Williams had the support of the fans for this stint, and the message was clear: if fan support is what he really wanted, it was all his. But Williams was never certain that the veneration of that fickle species, *homo fanaticus*, was what he really wanted. His truer struggle was with the press, a struggle for his psychic balance and whatever relation that balance might hold to his hitting prowess.

The Tigers were now clinging to the top spot in the pennant race, but the Yankees were not dead yet—they would make a final move and then fade. Cleveland was right in there, though the team's hostility to Vitt was brewing again. Boston would settle in fourth place for the rest of the year. Yawkey had resigned himself to another mediocre season, and his good nature took over again in regard to Williams. The two hunters spent an afternoon after a day game in late August shooting pigeons for sport in Fenway Park. Hy Hurwitz was so disgusted he tipped off the Humane Society, and Williams, on the way to Philadelphia and then Washington, would face another barrage from outraged Bostonians when the team returned. This time Yawkey thought it best to keep his profile low, even lower than usual.

Ted may have thought a few dead pigeons were to be his next crisis during a doubleheader on September 2 with the Senators, but Lefty Grove, who lost the first game 1-0 in 13 innings, blew a gasket in the clubhouse when he heard Williams boasting to writers about the big triple he hit off Sid Hudson in the second game. Lefty was touchy, and the sound of Williams's voice set him off. "Nothing in 13 innings and he's talking about 'wham, bam, did ya' see me hit that one?'" The players were uneasy, and another spark could have set the whole clubhouse aflame. Jimmie Foxx later told Harold Kaese, who kept it off the record for then: "I think that marked the day Williams was lost."

In the last weeks of the pennant race, Cleveland was tenaciously holding on to their place, at the top of the heap one day and near it the next, but they were barely holding on to their sanity. The players insisted yet again on a team meeting with the club's president, Alva Bradley. They were near mutiny. Reporters got to Ossie Vitt, the manager who was the source of all the trouble, and he told them the Indians were having a "pep rally." This was, by a long shot, the most refined euphemism of the year. Cleveland tried to claw their unhappy way to a pennant, but the Tigers held on and sewed it up by beating the Indians and Bobby Feller 2-0 in Cleveland on September 27. The Indians' fans pelted their own team with garbage for what they considered a woeful display by all parties in the midst of a pennant drive. By then the Yankees had sneaked by the Indians into second place. In the National League, Cincinnati was 11 games in front and coasting.

All that was left for the Red Sox was to play out the season. They did so in typical fashion, with an incredible burst of run-scoring energy while they were also floundering 9½ games out of first. On

September 24, Jimmie Foxx hit his 500th home run, one of four by the Sox in the sixth inning against the A's. On September 27 the Red Sox, free from the pressure of the pennant and the concern of any but a few Fenway diehards, punched out the Senators 24-4. In a season-ending doubleheader, Ted went 6 for 8 to boost his average to .344. Coincidentally, he would go 6 for 8 in a season-ending doubleheader in Philadelphia the very next year, his .406 season, to boost his average under much more trying conditions.

Williams hit nine home runs at Fenway with the fences moved in, five fewer than he had in his rookie year with the fences at a Herculean distance. On the road he hit 14, three fewer. His batting average all year long was remarkably consistent. He had a strong run early, from April 27 to June 2, when he hit .429, giving him a cushion to sit on all year. At the All-Star break he was hitting .3445 and at season's end he was hitting .3440. He hit .348 on the road and .340 at home. For the second year in a row his highest road average, .381, was against the Philadelphia A's at Shibe Park; and his highest combined average for the year, .370, was against the Tigers. His most home runs in any one stadium was four at Yankee Stadium. Even at his favorite park, Briggs Stadium in Detroit, Ted hit only one home run. Williams had everything going for him but what he wanted most this year—his power stroke.

After the World Series, won in seven games by the Cincinnati Reds, William headed again to Minneapolis to visit Doris Soule and to hunt and fish in the wilds. The off-season rumor mill went to work. *The Sporting News* ran a story about a White Sox trade even-up: John Rigney for Ted Williams. Boston needed pitching and Rigney was quality. This rumor was the first of many over the years involving Williams and his lure as trade bait, but this one had a special symmetry that no one could have guessed at the time. Had it taken place, the White Sox and Red Sox would have exchanged not only two stars but two controversies almost identical in nature. In 1941, Rigney would be the only player in the majors involved in what the papers called a draft-dodging attempt, Rigney claiming he was the sole support of his mother. In 1942 Williams would find himself in the same pickle and under the same public scrutiny for changing his draft classification with the claim that his mother was dependent upon his support.

There was another *Sporting News* item of interest reported the following week, the week of the national elections in which Roosevelt defeated Wendell Willkie to gain his third term in office. Larry MacPhail of the Dodgers proposed a new scheme for postseason play, a series of interleague playoffs, in addition to the World Series, in which each team occupying the same spot in each league's respective standings would play a seven-game series. Not only would the playoffs provide revenue, argued MacPhail, but they would also provide a measure of team-by-team quality in both leagues. No one was buying his scheme at the time, and a different model of postseason play would have to wait more than a quarter century for its debut in 1969.

◇ 5 ◇

The Last .400
1941

TED WILLIAMS: WHEREABOUTS UNKNOWN. The Boston brass in February had no idea where their tempestuous leftfielder was at the start of spring training. Cronin had last heard from Ted a few weeks earlier, just before he disappeared into the woods of Minnesota to hunt wolves. Rumors were floating around camp at Sarasota that Williams had shot a huge wolf, the biggest seen in those parts for years. Already the Florida bench jockeys were retuning from the 1940 chant of "Fireman, save my child" to "Who's Afraid of the Big Bad Wolf?"

The big press story of spring 1941 in the world of sports was the switch of the noted sportswriter Bill Cunningham from the *New York Post* to the *Boston Herald*. At $26,000 per year Cunningham was the highest-paid sportswriter in the business and wealthier than the bulk of the players he covered. Williams liked him and disliked him by turns. Cunningham could be a pompous windbag, though on the subject of Ted Williams he was usually fair-minded. Indeed, his columns early in Williams's career were among the most colorful and supportive, and in the spring of 1942, during the draft-dodging crisis surrounding Williams, Cunningham would really kick in on Ted's behalf.

One never knew what Cunningham had on tap for the day's brew. His columns were often about current events, world history, and politics. He was a Scripps-Howard right-winger with tough-minded opinions that he wrapped in ornate literary and historical allusions. He had been an isolationist on war but had just come around to full

85

support of the interventionist position, arguing that war was inevitable and Hitler had gone too far. He was convinced that the Germans were committing atrocities, even against their own citizens, and that these would soon come to light. Cunningham turned out to be right on a matter that many of his countrymen refused even to contemplate before our entry into the war, and, indeed, during it.

He wrote later that spring: "Where civilization is laid aside like a tailcoat and the exquisitely organized job of mass murder takes over, the call is for tough guys, no matter how they look or talk or dance in off-hours, who will make tough, merciless soldiers in a new and tougher kind of fighting. If we're in it, let's go." At the time, Hitler was moving into Yugoslavia, Greece, and readying for a spectacular paratroop invasion of Crete and a second-front blitzkrieg invasion of his own putative ally, the Soviet Union. Bill Cunningham devoted over half his columns to the political events of the year. He used the sports pages to tell readers what to think about almost everything— about war, peace, life, liberty, and the pursuit of happiness. His first column for the *Herald* during spring training was about how a whole town in Maine pitched in to rebuild a family's burned-up house. The article was a thinly veiled allegory about our obligations in wartime, and to read him in 1941, as fans did all season long, is to appreciate something of the richness of a print culture in sports that has virtually disappeared from the scene today. Red Smith was the last great writing voice of this magnitude.

Driving in from Minnesota, Williams finally arrived in Sarasota a week late. Contrary to rumor, he had not bagged a big bad wolf and didn't have wolves on his mind; rather, he talked about one huge cow he almost smashed as it ambled along the roadside. A frontal hit would have saved him the agony of dealing with the Boston press in Sarasota, which was already on him: "There was a 'lost, strayed, or stolen' sign tacked over the gateway of Teddy Williams's locker at the Red Sox Payne Field training quarters today." When Johnny Orlando brought a New York writer by for a profile, Williams heard but one sentence: "Guess you feel pretty good getting your name in the headlines." Ted stared hard at the writer, spun on his heel in contempt, and headed toward the batting cage, muttering, "It's my turn to hit, and my favorite actor is Buck Jones." The interview was over.

At least one Boston fan, however, a generic A. Rooter, who supposedly wrote to the *Globe*, was quick to come to Ted's defense: "Boston may or may not win a pennant, but every player will do his share. When rumors go around claiming that Ted Williams is this and that, what does it do to the Kid and to the club? It destroys the morale and spark of both. I say let the Kid lead his own life. A. Rooter."

Williams was prepared to be a better man in 1941 than he had been in 1940, and one of the ways he so prepared was to add a little heft to his playing weight; he weighed in at 185 pounds, up from 172 pounds at season's end in 1940. He was thinking distance. It was always on Williams's mind to change something in spring training. He did not always know exactly what, and he ended up changing almost nothing, but he always came with a notion of a new start for a new season. This year he wanted his home-run production up and up early to satisfy himself, mainly, and to keep those whom he considered journalistic jackals off his back. He would also have his girlfriend, Doris Soule, on hand this year to soothe him after the ball games. She would work as a cashier in Boston's Parker House Hotel.

To arrive at Payne Field for Williams was to come to a place well named. Tom Meany, who had been writing interesting guest columns for the *Globe* on important baseball issues, took time out to insult and stroke the Boston bad boy in the same brief sentence: "The misanthropic Ted Williams is still on the rise." It would have made more sense to say "scriptophobic." Williams liked the general run of mankind; it was just the genus *sportswriter* that he distrusted. Spring training was not his favorite time of year, and it became less and less his favorite the more he realized how the press lay in wait for him. If the writers weren't on him for something he had done the year before, they were on him for the pace at which he readied himself for the year coming up. He always wanted to train on his own schedule, and only much later in his career did he begin to get his wish.

Before Williams had arrived in Sarasota, Tom Meany had other things on his mind. He took the time in the dead days prior to spring training to take the pulse of a sport that made its claim as a national pastime. In a *Globe* column he raised an issue that would soon change the face of baseball. Meany had been watching some integrated teams play ball in the Cuban Winter League, and he knew that "some Negro ball players couldn't miss in the majors if it wasn't for baseball's Jim Crow law. Others couldn't make it if they were as Nordic as one of Hitler's dream children." Meany went on to make a crucial point about the effect of discrimination on attitudes that, in turn, become the basis for further discrimination: "Too many Negro ballplayers take the game as a joke because they feel that for them there is no future in it. You can't blame them for not taking in all seriousness a game which doesn't give them a fair shake."

The issue of discrimination was coming to something of a head in America because of the laws governing the burgeoning defense industry and the armed forces. President Roosevelt saw a potential crisis at hand, and he set his Justice Department to work on new governmental regulations that would become the basis for antidiscriminatory legislation in the postwar period. In sports, Jim Crowism was beginning to prove an embarrassment. A story breaking that spring in Annapolis revealed the social state of America on the eve of world war. The Harvard lacrosse team showed up for a game against the United States midshipmen but were told that they could not suit up a black team member, Lucien Alexis. Harvard coach Richard Snibbe filed a notarized statement: "There can be no doubt that Rear Admiral Russell Wilson repeatedly said that it would be impossible to play Alexis against the Academy and that if Harvard insisted, the Academy would forfeit the game."

Fresh from the Minnesota woods, Williams probably missed all of this and a good deal more during a war-torn spring. He merely wanted to do what he always wanted to do—get a bat and hit. Ted told the swarm of writers at the batting cage that his legs were strong this year from winter hunting, but his hands were soft. That's what he was there to work on in the spring. He wanted to hit as much as he could to develop calluses and harden the skin on his hands. If over the years his teammates had any consistent complaint about him, it centered on his unappeasable appetite for taking extra cuts on his own time or on theirs. In his heart of hearts he was still on the sandlots bullying and blustering his pals for the chance to get an extra swing or two.

Williams grabbed his bats and whirled them overhead. In a jiff he'd be in the box, hogging time. He would hound anyone on the field whose arm was attached to his shoulder to pitch to him. Local kids, with some kind of an in with the club, would shag in the outfield. Williams's voice took over. Batting practice was not solemn—Ted would loosen up with swings, trying first to line a few where they were pitched. Then, warmed up, he began creating situations, naming a late inning, a park, a quality pitcher, putting imaginary runners on base, demanding a pitch worthy of the circumstances.

If the batting-practice pitcher was a member of the Red Sox staff or a rookie trying to be so, he had to thread the needle. Williams wanted the ball near the plate and he wanted tough pitches. To waste his time with bad balls in batting practice infuriated him, but to set them right down the middle was just as useless. Some of the younger Red Sox pitchers, such as Joe Dobson, up with Boston in 1941, claimed to have learned their craft by throwing to Williams in batting practice. He scared the bejesus out of them and made them think about where their pitches were going. The crack of Williams's bat was unforgettable, but the scorn in his voice if a pitcher let up was even worse.

The best part of the coverage of Williams was always in spring and always with an indirect ear turned toward the chatter on the field. Williams joked with Mike Ryba about their days in the American Association. Ryba struck him out three times in one game—"You were an out I could always count on," he said. The players joked about Williams's offer to give Ryba a lift to his hotel after the game. Ryba was a bit suspicious. "That's just the kind of guy I am," said Williams, perhaps recalling the salvoes of the San Diego Salvation Army. "I return good for evil." Then Ted grilled him about how he pitched him that day and why. There is no such thing as a free ride.

Spring training moved apace. Lefty Grove cut a finger on his pitching hand severely when, as a gag, he and some other Red Sox were trying to attach a firecracker under the hood of Williams's spanking new Buick. The joke obviously backfired. It seemed that either Williams caused his own trouble with Grove or the fates interceded and caused it for him. Two days later, on March 19, Williams hurt himself with no help from Grove or anyone else. He injured his instep, near his ankle, sliding into second base on a hit-and-run play against Newark of the International League. He had been hobbling on an already-bum foot, first feeling a slight twinge going for a fly in a game on March 15 against the Reds. The Red Sox

brass were concerned and used their famous family connection to get
him immediate help. Dr. L. E. Sorrell, Mrs. Yawkey's brother-in-law
and a radiologist in Birmingham, had the foot x-rayed in Norwood
Hospital. The results were not encouraging. Ted had a very slight
fracture, more like a chip, of a small bone near the ankle instep on his
right foot. Cronin sent him to Boston, where team physician Dr. T. K.
Richards told him he might be out for six weeks. "Bullshit—I'll be
back in two," Williams stormed. The pain was less a concern to
Williams than the noticeable catch or twinge whenever he pivoted on
the foot at the plate or on the field.

Ted's was not the only spring-training foot in the news. Hank
Greenberg, at $50,000 per year the highest-paid player in the game,
was just drafted for service in the new lottery system devised by the
government. His number was near the top. Greenberg's and the
Tigers' first impulse was to get a letter from the doctor, Carl
Kroovand. Diagnosis: flat feet. The newspapers picked up the explanation, in language typical of the 1940s but awkward, if not offensive,
now: "He suffers from *pes valgus*, or fallen arch, not *pes planus*, or
congenital flat foot. The latter is debilitating, the former is not. Fallen
arches are predominant among Negroes and Hebrews."

In a few weeks, with Hitler on a spring rampage, Greenberg would
waive his medical excuse and join the tank corps at $21 a month, the
first prominent ballplayer to bag the season for the war effort. Detroit
fans were frantic, writing to their congressmen that Greenberg ought
to have an exemption based on his role in buttressing the United
States economy. Anyone earning $50,000 a year must be an essential
employee. But Greenberg was a man of honor in terrible times. The
same could not be said for all ballplayers in the early 1940s or all
baseball executives, some of whom, such as Larry MacPhail of the
Dodgers, a hero from World War I, were doing everything they
possibly could to reconfigure the draft system to salvage major league
ball in case of all-out war.

With Williams hobbling and out of uniform and unavailable for
controversy, the Red Sox turned to another colorful presence: their
third baseman, Jim Tabor, apparently enjoying one of his recurrent
and heavy benders. There were murmurings among the writers:
"Anything that is unusual always is a mystery when one is with the
Red Sox. We writers get whatever comes to mind from the boys

higher up, and the stories do not always agree." On March 24, the
Red Sox let the cat out of the bag; they announced Tabor's "rustica-
tion," easily explicable as code for drying him out. When Tabor
returned to camp a few days later for a boat ride to Cuba with the
club he staggered off the ship a total mess: "mal de mer," or seasick-
ness, was the club's little official joke as they listed his condition for
the press. Cronin, speaking off the record to writers traveling with the
club, said wryly, "I wonder what type of medicine he took for his 'mal
de mer'?"

Clearly, the Red Sox were ready for one of their seasons. Williams
was uncertain for the opener, but he was thinking long range. On the
last swing north he took a side trip to Louisville to discuss exact
specifications for a custom-made bat. When he was in the American
Association with Minnesota he used to listen to Johnny Sturm and
Pee Wee Reese, both of Louisville, talking about how they had
learned from the craftsman at Hillerich & Bradsby the cleverest ways
to cork bats. But Ted settled for natural specifications. He had been
using a Cronin model and wanted a similar bat with its handle a little
thinner: more whip, more power. From Louisville he headed to
Boston. When he showed up a pack of writers met him at the train
station, eager to know about his foot. All they could get was a shrug
and an invite: "Right now I'm hungry. If any of you guys haven't had
dinner, you're welcome to come over to the hotel and join me."

The *Globe* printed a state-of-the-union poem on the Red Sox
submitted by a reader before the season even started; it is worth citing
because it provides a sense of what the Boston fan was like for much
of what Williams himself called the great age of baseball history. Joe
Cronin seemed to be the focus of this fan's ire, but any one of a
number of precedent and subsequent Sox managers might do just as
well. Tom, of course, is Yawkey; Moe is Berg; Jim is Tabor; and Casey
is Stengel of the Boston Bees in the National League.

Ode to the Red Sox
by K.P.

Listen my friends and I shall bark
The sad, sad story of Fenway Park.
It cost three million and then some more,
To learn that Tom would never get sore.

We have a manager as managers go
And you'll all agree that he ought to go.
He can't handle pitchers at home or away
And afield he gums up every play.

A word about our so-called hurlers.
They ought to have their hair in curlers.
They've worn a path from the pen to the box
And the showers are always flooded like locks.

"I wish I had a catcher," said Joe.
"Here I am and only forty," said Moe.
Ted hates Boston, just hear his wail.
Jim is always kicking the ball.

Well, I s'pose you'll just have to take 'em.
Anyway as long as Tom will stake 'em.
But as for me—I have a plan.
Just stick with Casey like a "regular" fan.

By the time of the season opener on April 15, Williams was not ready to take the field, but he was able to pinch hit, which he did with stunning success—his line shot to right put the winning run in place for a 7–6 win over the Senators. He was anxious: "I never wanted to play every one of the 154 games more in my life. Now it looks as if I'll have to be a pinch hitter for a while. There's nothing wrong with my eye."

Later, and with considerable hindsight, Williams took a more strategic view. He claimed that his limited playing time early in the year helped him by easing him through the cold opening days of the season when he had trouble getting loose and keeping warm. The dugout was a cozier place than the outfield. The one time in these early days he tried to rush the process he aggravated his delicate foot. Pete Fox was out with an abscessed tooth on April 22 and Williams talked Cronin into starting him for the game. He singled and doubled, but he also turned his ankle chasing down Cecil Travis's fly in the sixth. He was out again.

When Williams finally resumed full-time play in left field on

April 29, he began in a way very different from the previous year. He undid the top button of his flannels and rocketed one of John Gorsica's pitches about 425 feet to right in Detroit. A few days later he tied into one of John Rigney's deliveries in Chicago and hit it over the double-decked seats in right. Melville Webb of the *Globe* did the honors: "The homer was one of the longest Williams or anyone else ever hit at Comiskey Park. The front of the right-field stands is about 360 feet from the plate. The roof of the upper deck in right field is easily 400 feet from the batter's box. Williams's drive was a lift far above the top of the upper grandstand roof, which in turn must be 70 feet above the playing field. When it landed on the roof the ball bounded at least 50 feet in the air, and then disappeared to parts unknown."

Williams continued to hit a ton through May. For the entire month he averaged .436, the best month of this phenomenal season and the third-best of his career (exceeded only by his .460 in June of 1948 and by his .440 in July of 1957). But for the last half of the month, from May 17 to June 1, he hit .536, a spurt that gave him a needed cushion going into what turned out to be an exceedingly hot and exhausting summer. His late-May run carried him into June and produced the highest 30-day sequence during his record year, May 17 to June 17, a nifty month's work at .477 with 52 hits and ten home runs.

During these very games Williams was matching the early course of Joe DiMaggio's famous 56-game hitting streak on a day-to-day basis. Both DiMaggio and Williams began streaks on May 15. Ted's lasted for 23 games until June 8, his longest consecutive-game effort in his major league career. During that sequence, Williams outhit DiMaggio .487 to .368, and, though he would go hitless eight times in all during the course of DiMaggio's streak ending on July 17, he still outhit DiMaggio for the span of those record 56 games, .412 to .408.

Williams took the collar in both games of a doubleheader against the White Sox on June 8, Ted Lyons and Thornton Lee shutting him down. Dan Daniel, on the sports desk for the *New York World Telegram* and *The Sporting News*, caught up with Williams, and he was still revved up despite his poor day at the plate. He went into the games on June 8 hitting .431 for the year, so he had little angst about his brief dip in performance: "Say, you should have seen Grove and Lyons fight it out for ten innings. It was the greatest exhibition of pitching I ever hope to see. Certainly Feller is tops. But you should have watched those two old-timers maneuvering, outwitting hitters, making their heads do for them what their arms used to do. It was beautiful. I became so engrossed watching the game, I guess I just forgot to hit."

Daniel probably wrote half of these words himself, but the sentiment was accurate enough. Williams had a special respect for Lyons, and it didn't hurt to be nice to Grove either, since Lefty was all over him most of the time for one thing or another. Williams hit Lyons pretty well in his rookie year but soon learned that Lyons was one of the few pitchers who really knew what the art of pitching was all about. He never could pick up exactly what Lyons was doing to get him out as consistently as he did, but he knew it must have been subtle and it must have been the product of experience: "Lyons was tough and got tougher the more you faced him, because he'd learn about you by playing those little pitcher-batter thinking games, and he'd usually outthink you."

Ted Williams was riding high as summer came in, and an incident in a Detroit doubleheader on June 17 revealed his spirits. In the opening game he hit his 13th home run of the year. Right field at Briggs Stadium always looked to him like heaven's gate. Yet in the first inning of the second game he did what he did only as an afterthought in batting practice—he squared around for a perfectly styled bunt attempt. And he did so against Johnny Gorsica, a pitcher he had already touched for two home runs so far that season. The entire Detroit defense froze for a moment, and then everyone in the park collapsed in laughter as Ted jabbed at the ball, missed it entirely, and tried to put the breaks on his loping legs already three steps out of the box on their way to first. Baseball bathos, the "biggest laugh of the day," the papers howled. No one laughed harder than Williams, who even took Gorsica's next pitch, which nicked him on the thigh, without complaint. A bunt single, after all, would have been a greater blow to Gorsica's dignity than another Briggs Stadium home run.

There was little of the rancor left in Williams from 1940, and his dealings with the press and the Boston organization were as good as they would ever get. For a June 19, 1941, *Sporting News* profile by

Carl T. Felkner, Williams sounded as though he were an irrepressible kid: "Hitting is the biggest thing in my life. And the thing I like next best is to hunt ducks." These were special days for Williams; he never could exactly recapture them after the war.

On the other hand, things were getting nastier and nastier in Europe during these weeks. Hitler was invading Crete, and the British, having held their air space in the last summer's Battle of Britain, now were trying to retain control of the Atlantic, buoyed tremendously by their dramatic tracking and sinking of the German flagship *Bismarck* on May 27. On June 22 the Germans attacked across the Russian border with 150 fully armed divisions; and the United States was readying for huge lend-lease expenditures on behalf of the Allied cause. News photos of the Russian invasion began to tell a story almost beyond comprehension. One printed on the *Boston Globe*'s front page revealed a Dantesque heap of civilian bodies piled up in what appeared to be a forest near a road sign outside the city of Lwów. German censors released the photo with a caption claiming that Russian secret police had butchered masses of people before the invasion of the city. "Nevertheless," said the *Globe* version, "reports of mass civilian executions by German forces in Russia, Rumania, and Yugoslavia have been filtering to the West." However brutal Stalin's secret police might have been, it was hard to know what purposes would have been served by murdering heaps of Russian citizens in the woods before the Germans were to attack the city.

In America, Orson Welles's *Citizen Kane* opened in New York; Whirlaway won the triple crown; and Joe Louis came back from the dead to haunt the cocky Billy Conn in the 13th round of their championship fight on June 18. A young Ronald Reagan and Jane Wyman were named Hollywood's most blissfully married pair. Ted Williams kept driving the baseball at a .400 clip, and major league baseball enjoyed one of its most scintillating seasons ever: DiMaggio's streak captured daily headlines across the country, and the intense pennant race in the National League between the Brooklyn Dodgers and the St. Louis Cardinals kept people on the edges of their seats.

The war had not in any significant way affected the game yet— Hank Greenberg was the only major player to have been drafted into army fatigues. But it would soon enough, and in ways not even reported until many years later. An intriguing baseball story was silently brewing that June, set in a fold of time that might have changed baseball history if "might haves" determined the course of events. The St. Louis Browns, off to one of their typically miserable starts, changed managers from Fred Haney to Luke Sewell the first week of June. This was part of a much more significant projected change. A deal was then afoot, already worked out in its preliminary stages, to move the Browns to Los Angeles. Don Barnes, club president, along with a major stockholder, Harry Arthur, President of Franchon and Marco Amusement Company, had negotiated with several California businessmen about the possibility of a move. The other American League owners were in the know and had given a tentative green light, though transportation arrangements were proving difficult.

The Browns would purchase the Los Angeles Angels from the Cubs' owner, Philip Wrigley. The Angels would move to Long Beach and the Browns would play in the Angels' ballpark. Strictly speaking, the Browns were only under an obligation to compensate the Pacific Coast League up to $5,000 and the Angels up to a preset formula for damages. But the deal became more elaborate when the St. Louis Cardinals and their president, Sam Breadon, agreed to pay the Browns $250,000 for leaving all of St. Louis to the more successful National League resident of the city.

The only rub in the deal was the worry in 1941 that the airline flights over the Rockies could put an entire franchise at risk. It had not been a good year for transcontinental travel; several passenger flights had already crashed in mountainous terrain, including Eastern's Silver Sleeper flight with the famous aviator, indeed the airline's president, Eddie Rickenbacker, on it. (Rickenbacker survived, barely.) Team owners were aghast at the thought of a whole team going down on a swing to the West Coast. So over the next several months, continuing on after the 1941 season, all American League clubs were involved in secret negotiations with TWA over the safety of travel plans and schedules. Later in the year, the airlines and the team owners were on the verge of a deal. Split flights would leave the Chicago hub on off-days with the team members on different planes arriving at slightly staggered hours. Baseball officials and the airline met one Saturday and agreed to finish up at a breakfast meeting the next day.

The date for that projected Sunday meeting was December 7, 1941. Needless to say, Pearl Harbor took precedence over the St. Louis Browns. With the threat of a West Coast invasion very real in those bleak months, no move could be contemplated and the deal was off. After the war, the Browns scrapped the idea and turned their thoughts in the direction of Baltimore.

With the season edging toward the halfway mark and with Williams hitting .407, the Boston press corps began to sing of the last great Boston star to hit .400, Hugh Duffy, who hit .438 in 1894. Duffy, still with the Red Sox organization, thought Williams had a good chance. He spoke with Hy Hurwitz about his own effort in 1894 and told him that his teammates wanted him to bag the season with two weeks to go so that he could insure his remarkably high average, then around .430. Ed Delahanty of Philadelphia was then within shooting range. Delahanty ended up hitting .407 that year, and two of his teammates, Sam Thompson and Billy Hamilton, also broke the barrier, both hitting .404. Why so many .400 hitters? The mound had just been officially moved farther from the plate, to 60 feet, 6 inches. Pitchers were throwing up dying swans.

Duffy wasn't about to sit it out at the end of the year. "Hell, no. I played." He even added a few points. The still-voluble Duffy figured Williams wouldn't match his .438 high, but he told Hurwitz that he might well match the modern-day record at .420—more precisely, George Sisler's .41979 in 1922 and Cobb's .41962 in 1911. Babe Ruth passed through Boston early in July and concurred: "When I first saw Ted Williams swing a bat I knew he would be one of the best. He's loose and easy, with a great pair of wrists. Just a natural. Williams ought to be one of the first hitters in years to pass .400."

Before Williams, with the imprimatur of Duffy and Ruth, could make a run at the fabled .400—last achieved in 1930 when Bill Terry hit .401 for the Giants—the majors took a few days off for the All-Star Game on July 8 at Detroit's Briggs Stadium. With DiMaggio in the middle of his streak and Williams at .405, the atmosphere was festive. Bobby Feller was going against Whit Wyatt of the Dodgers, who had pitched against Williams in the American Association in 1938. The

previous year the American League suffered a 4–0 loss to the Na-
tionals, and the players wanted revenge. But by the ninth inning of
this year's game it didn't look like they were going to get it.

Led by Arky Vaughan's two home runs, the National League took
a 5–1 lead into the eighth. Ted Williams's double in the fourth had
put the only notch in the American League's gun. Dominic DiMaggio of the Red Sox got another run for the Americans in the bottom
of the eighth when he singled in his brother Joe, who had doubled. In
the ninth the American League needed three runs and the National
League needed three outs. The American League managed to load
the bases with one out against the Chicago Cubs' right-hander
Claude Passeau, a great pitcher but a classic nervous wreck on the
mound. Keltner got a lucky infield hit, Joe Gordon a bona fide one,
and Travis walked. Joe DiMaggio and Williams were next.

Joe took his time getting set, staring out at Passeau. Despite the
little beads of sweat running down his brow, Passeau did not blink. He
got DiMaggio to top a grounder to Eddie Miller at short. Miller
grabbed it, pivoted, and tossed to Billy Herman, who got the force at
second but was tangled up on the slightly wide throw as Cecil Travis
came barreling down on him from first. DiMaggio beat the poor relay
to Frank McCormick at the bag. A run was in, two were out, and two
were on base.

Williams came to bat, and the place was a madhouse. Passeau had
gotten him the previous inning on a vicious inside strike that Williams thought was inside by a measure too much. Umpire Babe
Pinelli made the call that set Williams's teeth on edge: strike three.
J. G. Taylor Spink, the dean of sportswriters and a fixture on his
beloved *Sporting News*, got Williams to recall the scene shortly after
the game.

> When I got up to the plate, all the National League team except
> the outfielders ganged up with Passeau on the mound and I figured
> they were discussing how they would pitch to me. So I turned my
> back to them and talked to Pinelli. I asked him where that third
> strike was and he said right at the knees. I told him I thought it was
> low, but he wouldn't agree.
>
> Then I stood back and sort of gave myself a fight talk. I said
> "Listen, you lug. He outguessed you last time and you got caught
> with your bat on your shoulder for a called third strike. You were

swinging late when you fouled one off, too. Let's swing, and swing a little earlier this time, and see if we can connect."

Passeau pitched to me pretty careful. I did foul another one off, but he pitched two balls, so I was ahead of him—had him in the hole and the next one would be in there. I was cocked when he let go. And soon there it was—a fast one, chest high. I swung and I got the fat of my bat on it and away it sailed. I knew as soon as it was hit that it might go all the way, but I wasn't sure whether it would clear the roof until I saw it hit the front of that third deck up there in the sky.

The key for Williams had been not to let Passeau get ahead in the count. Williams knew he had good stuff and could get his breaking pitches right on the handle of the bat. So he inched up a bit in the box to get the bat out before Passeau's ball took its severest break. If Passeau had gotten another strike without being too fancy, he would have been in the driver's seat. But when he came in just above the waist Williams put all of his young whippet body into it, and the shot he hit simply soared. Even years later, in a *Collier's* magazine profile, Kyle Crichton was writing of the home run as an event that transcended its time, "a wallop which for altitude, violence, and timeliness has never been bettered by Babe Ruth, Lou Gehrig, Shoeless Joe Jackson, or anybody in the history of the world."

Meanwhile, Enos "Country" Slaughter ambled from his position in right to pick up the ricocheted ball (he kept it as a trophy) as Williams was jack-rabbiting around the bases. His home-run trot was pure exuberance, and the American Leaguers were hardly less restrained. As Gerry Moore put it in his column: "Hardened veterans and more publicized stars like Joe DiMaggio, Bob Feller, Joe Cronin, and Jimmie Foxx were suddenly transformed into boyish hero worshippers while curly-headed Ted slowly trotted his triumphant four, in familiar stoop-shouldered fashion, around the bases." Feller was even showered and in street clothes after his early stint in the game, but ran on the field leaping in tribute to a ballplayer who had just created and enjoyed a moment that would become legendary. Detroit's manager Del Baker planted a huge kiss on the Kid's face. In the clubhouse the writers wanted to know if they saw what they thought they saw. "Kiss him?" echoed Baker. "You're damned right I kissed him."

Claude Passeau was the classic victim. He told the writers in the clubhouse: "The instant it left my hand I knew I was a dead duck." He claimed it would have been a fly-ball out in some parks but then said the "American League baseball seems to travel farther. You can get a good grip on it, but it seems to travel farther." Nary a writer in the room pointed out the obvious: it certainly does when Williams hits it.

Williams stayed a long while at the park to savor the home run, and when he finally left the clubhouse to catch a cab to his room at the Hotel Cadillac there was none to be had. A man driving with a young boy stopped and gave him a lift. Ted kept quiet most of the way and finally could contain himself no longer. "Say, I'm Ted Williams. Did you know the American League won the ball game today?" The driver and his son looked blank: "Nope. Don't follow baseball." Just Ted's luck. But he reveled in the story and told it with appreciative glee.

When the season resumed the Red Sox were in Detroit. Rain postponed their first game, but Williams talked a few players into taking batting practice anyway when the skies cleared. They would all pitch for each other. His old Pacific Coast League manager, Frank Shellenback, was at the park, and Williams was dying for the chance to hit his famous spitball, which Shellenback tossed up for the White Sox of 1918 and briefly for the Black Sox of 1919. Frank was still in his early 40s, and Williams was, after all, a protégé of sorts. Sure, he'd deliver him a batch of wet ones. Williams watched a few slither up, still with wicked movement on them: "Hell, they can *keep* that pitch outlawed," he said, and then proceeded to belt half a dozen into the stands.

In the Detroit game on July 12, Williams reinjured his bad ankle hustling like a raw rookie on the field a day after Cronin spoke to him, unfortunately within earshot of a couple of writers, about some lax outfield play while Lefty Grove was on the mound trying to win his 300th game. Lefty had been at it for a while—stalled at 299—and was getting edgy. There was no way Ted was going to get caught in a row with Grove or anyone else if he could help it. Things were going too well this year. His injury kept him out of a few games and then in some for pinch hitting only. It was during this period, in which his average dipped under .400, that Joe DiMaggio went 0 for 4 on a damp night in Cleveland, July 17, and ended his streak at 56 games. But by this time the Yankees were moving out toward a runaway pennant drive, and the Red Sox were preparing to nestle a good margin behind into third place for the rest of the year. In contrast, the torrid Dodgers-Cardinals pennant drive in the National League would last until the final days of a tension-packed season.

Williams was back in the Red Sox lineup in left on July 22, and on July 25 his two-run homer helped Lefty Grove sew up a sloppy but glorious 300th win, 10-6 over the Indians. Jimmie Foxx's two-run triple also was a key blow and an important one for a long friendship: Foxx's error on a ground ball in Grove's previous start against the White Sox lost his old teammate that ball game. Grove and Foxx broke in together with the Philadelphia A's in 1925 and joined the Red Sox within two years of each other in 1934 and 1936, respectively. Now they were ready to party in Boston. But one long and lanky leftfielder on the squad hitting .400 dressed and split without registering the time and place for the team celebration. Williams was still smarting a bit from Cronin's unintentional public rebuke a couple of weeks back. Moreover, he just did not make it a habit of hanging out with teammates after games.

No one said much publicly, but Jim Tabor, who could carouse with the best of them, made some noise at the party about Williams being too good to socialize with his teammates. Jack Wilson, a pitcher on the squad who lived to get a rise out of Ted, mentioned Tabor's comment. A few days later, after stewing for a while, Williams confronted Tabor in the trainer's room and called him a rotten son of a bitch. Tabor must have thought he had fallen through some kind of drunken sinkhole. He hadn't the slightest idea what Williams was talking about. Ted, who had kept the matter brewing internally, wasn't exactly clear himself about the nature of his beef, and the two started sputtering at each other. There was a bit more incoherent blubbering and a bump or two and the whole fiasco was over. Aside from a half-joking tussle with Gene Desautels in 1940, this was his only near-fight with a teammate, though there were a few who would surely have loved to grace their season by flattening Williams with a cast-iron pan.

Little of this seemed to faze Williams in 1941. By the end of July he was back at .410, and through August and September the *Globe* began running a daily feature comparing the averages of Bill Terry in 1930, his .401 year, and Ted Williams in 1941. At this time in his great season, Terry had 127 more at-bats than Williams and was hitting .393. He benefited from a rule then in effect (as it was from 1926 through 1938) that any fly ball that advanced a runner—to second, third, or home—counted as a sacrifice fly. Williams might have hit .430 in 1941 with that rule still in effect. To relax before his final push, Williams went tuna fishing with a friend, William Huddleson, off Newport and caught a 375-pound monster—1941 was a career year in more ways than one.

The .400 hitters' log on August 5 showed Bill Terry raising his average to .404 with a 5-for-6 day; Williams was at .408. The next day, Williams managed but one base hit in a doubleheader against the Yanks at Fenway and fell below Terry, only to rise above him again the next day by going 3 for 4 with a home run against the Yanks. In an almost complete contrast to the season before, Williams was now feeling so good that even Boston delighted him. An urban ingrate the year before, he became an angel of mercy in 1941. In Victor O. Jones's August 7 column, he described a letter he had received from a Mrs. Dennis Callahan of Watertown, Massachusetts. She told him of writing to Williams and asking him to visit her brother, a fan of his, in a Boston hospital. Not only did Williams drop by, but he stopped in the gift shop on the way up and bought the chap a box of candy. This flabbergasted Jones. Could this be the man who in 1940 treated Boston as if the city suffered from bubonic plague? He chose to devote nearly the entire column to the story.

The Yankees were so far ahead at this time in the pennant race that Cronin could almost imagine them earning enough credits to take the pennant in 1942 as well. At least that is what he seemed to imply when he told Gerry Moore of the *Globe* that the war meant another pennant for New York. Before the United States actually entered the war it was very difficult to keep one's priorities straight: "As soon as this campaign closes, you're likely to read every day about some young major leaguer marching off to the Army and heaven knows when they'll be back. The strangest thing, and hardly encouraging for the rest of us, is that the Yanks don't figure to lose a single player to the Army next year." Cronin was right that the Yanks would remain virtually untouched until 1943. What he didn't know was how close Uncle Sam would come to touching Ted Williams in January 1942.

Williams remained hot through mid-August, hitting .479 from the time he returned to pinch hit on July 20, after his second ankle injury of the season, to August 13. He reached a high of .414 on August 21 and would struggle to hold those 14 points for the rest of the season; Bill Terry was at .407 on August 21, 1930. In late August Lefty Grove tore a muscle in his back during a Detroit game and called it a career at an even 300 wins. On September 1, Williams warmed up for the last month's run at .400 by hitting three out of the park during a doubleheader at Fenway against the Senators. That gave him 34 for the year and the league lead. His home run in game two off Red Anderson was one of the longest he ever hit in Fenway, a monster shot deep into the bleachers of the grandstand in right. On the way out of the park the writer Fred Barry heard a couple of fans arguing: "Yeah, yeah, Williams is hitting way over his head, that's all I gotta say." "And over everybody else's head, too," continued the other fan.

On September 2 the Boston police picked up Billy Kane, 14, who was wandering the streets near Fenway Park. He told them he had hitched down from South Brewer, Maine, 250 miles away, just to see Williams play. But the Red Sox had an off-day. Williams was friendly with several cops in the local precinct—he even went fishing with a couple of them and occasionally joined them and their wives for home-cooked meals. So they called Williams. He'd gone skeet-shooting that day early in the morning and had already undressed for bed; but he got dressed and made a visit to police headquarters. The slightly confused but delighted kid ended up with a box-seat ticket to the next day's Yankees game as a guest of Mr. Williams (he had expected to sit on a wooden crate somewhere in the cheap section; what did he know about "box" seats?) and a discourse on hitting from the master himself.

With Williams hitting the ball tremendously hard in these last weeks of the season—he was not only sustaining his average but powerfully ripping the ball—visiting teams coming into Fenway were beginning to shift their defenses to the right more and more. The short left field and Williams's almost total disinclination to hit in that direction precipitated a strategy for which Lou Boudreau was not given full credit until 1946. But Cleveland, with Boudreau at shortstop and not yet managing in 1941, pulled a shift on September 18. Umpire Eddie Rommel was asked by writers after the game whether a team could rotate its infield as dramatically as Cleveland did. As Gerry Moore reported, "Umpire Eddie Rommel disclosed yesterday that it would be illegal for the right fielder to stand in foul territory if the unprecedented idea should ever strike him."

In the second game of a doubleheader against Washington on September 24, when Williams was tiring and struggling to keep over .400, he beat out a grounder deep at second off a rookie pitcher, Dick Mulligan, with Jimmy Bloodworth playing more like a short right field than a normal second base. Umpire Bill Grieve made the eyelash call, and the Griffith Stadium fans thought Grieve had Williams's .400 season in mind more than the bang-bang play at first. Years later during the 1957 season when he was going for another .400 year, Williams ran to first base as if he were wearing snowshoes. He often figured that even his modified speed of 1941 would have pushed him over in 1957.

Williams, who studied pitchers so rigorously, also later pointed out how much of a nuisance it was for him to face rookies brought up for the first time late in the season without any idea what they threw: "Remember 1941, when I hit over .400? For many months I was going along as smooth as you please, and suddenly in the last month my average tailed off and actually dropped below .400 [author's note: .3995, to be exact]. The main reason was that I was swinging against a lot of new birds up for late-season tryouts."

Williams was hitting .401 as the Red Sox detrained in Philadelphia for the final series of the year. He was dead tired but insisted on going out to Shibe Park on his off-day, September 26, because he was worried about the shadows at this time of year and wanted to get acclimated. It was bad enough facing pitchers he had never seen, but it would be even worse if he had to adjust to treacherous shadows. On September 27 he doubled in the fourth off the A's Roger Wolff to keep his average technically at .400. He could have bagged Sunday's doubleheader but refused. Years later he put it succinctly to Maxwell Stiels of the *Globe*: "I figure a man's a .400 hitter, or he isn't."

Bill Terry played during the season-ending game in 1930 but went in at .403, with a couple of percentage points leeway (he needed them—he went 0 for 3 against the Phils). Williams, at .3995, was already on the downside of .400 by .0005 points. Johnny Orlando remembers taking a long walk with Williams before the game. Since 1938, when Orlando took him to the bus station on the way out of the Red Sox spring training camp, the two had gotten on well. Williams said right out that he wanted to hit .400 more than he had ever wanted anything, and he'd be the "most disappointed guy in the world if he didn't make it." He was nervous, but not too nervous to make Orlando stop with him for a scoop at every ice cream store in a five-mile radius.

In the first game Williams looked at Dick Fowler, a Toronto farmhand just called up, for the first time. Connie Mack told his pitchers that they could do whatever they had to do to get Williams out, but they had to throw strikes. He would not abide the chintziness of semi-intentional bases on balls. Mack must have made Fowler nervous. His first two pitches were not within hitting range. The rookie took a look at Mr. Mack's scowling face and grooved a 2-0 pitch that Williams drilled past a helpless Bob Johnson at first base. In the fourth inning, Williams took one of Fowler's deliveries high and far over the fence in right center. Porter Vaughan relieved in the sixth, and Williams singled off the lefty into right field. He came up again in the seventh and singled again. In the eighth, with the Sox winning handily, he reached on an error at second base.

Now at .404 he could play in game two, go hitless in five at-bats, and still hit .3995, exactly where he began the day and technically at .400 for the year. The four hits in the first game were a tonic. Williams played loose and went up to the plate hacking. A rookie, Fred Caligiuri, was on the mound, and this was one of but seven games he pitched in the majors. Williams had little difficulty hitting him. In the second inning he smashed one between the first and second basemen for a hit; in the fourth, he ripped a drive off the public-address speaker for a ground-rule double. On his last at-bat of a glorious year, Williams flied out to Elmer Valo in left field.

The topography of Williams's great season was fairly even. He was on his game for almost the entire schedule. Only from April 30 to May 24 and from July 12 to July 25 was he ever below .400 for the year, though his unrounded figure on September 27 dipped unofficially below. His highest monthly average, .436, was in May; his lowest, .372, was in June. At home in Fenway he hit .428 and on the road, .380. His highest average at any one ballpark was .485, at Yankee Stadium; and his highest average at Fenway against any one team was .484 versus Washington. His lowest average on the road, .281, was against those same Senators at Griffith Stadium. Home and away combined, his highest average, .471, was against the Yankees; his lowest, .377, was against the White Sox. His home-run production increased at Fenway to 19, with 18 hit on the road, seven of those at Sportsman's Park in St. Louis.

Regarding Williams's exploits against the Yankees in 1941, Yankees catcher Bill Dickey later told Grantland Rice that he had never seen anything like it: "The man was a hundred percent poison. He waited so long that I swear I caught some of the balls he hit. He's got eyes like a hawk. No weaknesses at all." Dickey had seen some great American League hitters, but he hadn't seen any .400-year men. The last American League hitter to reach .400 was Harry Heilmann of Detroit, who hit .403 in 1923. Three players managed to reach the magic average on more than one occasion. Ty Cobb and Rogers Hornsby did so three times and George Sisler twice. Joe Jackson was the only .400-club member to make it in his rookie year, turning .408 in 1911, the same year Cobb hit .420. Cobb was the luckiest of the .400 hitters: he didn't reach .400 in 1922 until the league president, Ban Johnson, credited him with another hit. John Kieran, the *Times* writer and official scorer, admitted that he had relied on another spectator's version of a Cobb at-bat in a late-season game and had credited the second baseman with an error. Kieran had moved out of the unprotected press box during a drizzle and had been bamboozled by a Cobb hater.

No other .400 hitter in the American League had Williams's power. He finished the year with 37 home runs, 120 runs batted in, and a .735 slugging average. Only the National League's Rogers Hornsby could boast similar numbers, with his extraordinary five-year average of .402 from 1921–1925 with over 2,600 at-bats to his credit. He hit 144 home runs during those years, including 42 in his triple-crown year of 1922, when he hit .401. In his other triple-crown year, 1925, Hornsby hit .403 with 39 home runs. Someone had put some juice into the baseball during those remarkable hitting years of the early 1920s. Hornsby, by the way, was the man who told Williams in Minneapolis that there was more to baseball than hitting. With stats such as his there scarcely needed to be much more.

The Yankees won the series in 1941, aided by the infamous Mickey Owen passed-ball incident of game four at Ebbets Field. In an October *Sporting News* poll, fans voted Williams the most valuable player in the American League by 55 percent to 26 percent over DiMaggio, with other votes going to regional favorites such as Cecil Travis of Washington for his career year of .359 or to Bobby Feller for his standard year of 25 wins. In November the baseball writers took the real Most Valuable Player vote and elected DiMaggio. They might have expected Williams to groan in despair. He most certainly didn't. Even today he thinks DiMaggio's hitting streak is the greatest record in the game. His reason is pure, vintage Williams: there is nothing harder in the world than hitting a baseball consistently for base hits—base hits of any caliber. That DiMaggio was a power hitter made the record all the more exceptional in Williams's eyes. And that he did it during the boiling dog days of summer for so many straight games remains for Williams a wonder. His admiration for DiMaggio's streak and for Joe's value to the Yankees was genuine— and the genuine in Williams was always an easy read. He never was Mr. Subtle.

After the 1941 World Series, Williams and Jimmie Foxx barnstormed as part of a public-relations deal that gained the players some extra spending money before year's end. The tour ended in Los Angeles, and Williams briefly swung through San Diego before heading back to his favored Minnesota hunting grounds. He would soon be the only .400 hitter in the history of baseball who had to figure out what to do about the draft. That sorry saga awaited him in 1942.

◇ 6 ◇

Draft Bait
1942

THE NATION WAS AT WAR early in 1942. The Pacific Fleet under Admiral Nimitz mounted its first attack in Japanese waters at the Marshall and Gilbert islands at the beginning of February. Nearly $5,000,000 in war relief tumbled into coffers in the Boston area. Newspapers chose hope over experience—"Corregidor's Armies Destroy Jap Invading Force"—when something like the opposite was true. By mid-March General MacArthur would be declaiming his famous words about the Philippines from his retreat point in Australia: "I shall return." And in May General Wainwright's forces on the Bataan peninsula in the Philippines were devastated, leading to the infamous Bataan Death March.

The *Boston Globe* did its bit to buoy the spirits of a nation at war. It held up to public humiliation on its front page citizens such as Irving Kemler of Revere, arraigned for trying to bribe his way out of the draft by offering $500 to a member of the local examining board. At the same time the *Globe* took pride in its feisty syndicated columnist Dorothy Thompson, who in early February punched out a woman in a New York nightclub frequented by entertainers and writers (many of them Jews) for shouting out "Heil Hitler" on the dance floor.

With thousands of troops billeted at bases around the world, the machinery for wartime communication was barely in place, and families were at a loss to unravel the complicated censorship rules in effect. The *Globe* parodied the kinds of correspondence allowed from the staging areas of war by offering a form letter making it easier for everyone.

My (*dear, darling, dearest*) (*father, mother, sweetheart*), I am (*sick well, sober, weary, footsore*) and hope you are (*the same, sober, thinking of me*). How is [are] (*mother, dad, the kids, the maid*)?

I have sent (*money, allotment*) and trust this will keep you in the mode to which I have accustomed you.

your (*son, husband, sweetheart*)

In early 1942 the *Saturday Evening Post* ran a feature story on Ted Williams modestly titled, "I Wanna Be an Immortal." Williams declared: "So I think I'm one helluva hitter? Well, all I'm asking is, suppose I stop thinking it, then who do you suggest is going to?" The recipe for Cooperstown for Williams was part talent, part diligence, and part self-confidence. He stinted on none of the ingredients.

In January rumors began floating around Boston that Williams was draft bait after a reclassification following Pearl Harbor. He had registered in Minneapolis and carried a 3-A classification as sole supporter of his mother. But under wartime conditions he, like hundreds of thousands of others, got his 1-A notice. So the question that remained was *when*, not *whether*. The Hall of Fame, in Williams's case, would have to wait for Hitler and Tojo to desist in their dirty work. *The Sporting News* ran a cartoon of Williams as sharpshooter in full fatigues standing in Fenway and shooting a rifle. The caption read: "If Uncle Sam gives Ted a uniform th' guy'll certainly be dressed to kill." The subtext of all this was that one adventurous day when Williams and Tom Yawkey stayed late at the ballpark to pick off pigeons with their .22 caliber rifles.

The inroads made on baseball by the war were beginning to take significant shape, mostly in the minors, and *The Sporting News* in the spring of 1942 began to run features such as "In the Service," "In Step with Uncle Sam," and "Taking a Swing in the Navy" to keep tabs on what would have been thriving rosters all over the country. In the majors, the Tigers would contribute the most to the war, about $500,000 worth of baseball talent, including Hank Greenberg, Birdie Tebbetts, Fred Hutchinson, Billy Hitchcock, and Pat Mullin.

The major leagues were debating various measures to aid the war effort. Larry MacPhail's notion of a percentage on gate receipts was turned down, but the allotment of night games was increased to 14 per club to discourage the labor force from playing afternoon hooky;

two All-Star games were voted in, the receipts of the second to go to the service organizations; voluntary deductions from players' salaries for war bonds were authorized by the ball clubs; and all military personnel could attend ball games for free.

These matters were not without precedent. Baseball had shortened its 1918 season because of America's entry into World War I, and, indeed, the "play or fight" controversy over reduced revenues affected the 1918 World Series between the Red Sox and the Cubs. The shortened season limited Series shares; when the players learned of the reductions they struck the fifth game of the Series until the commissioner, Ban Johnson, arrived to settle differences right on the spot.

In February Casey Stengel of the Boston Braves spoke with Grant-land Rice for a profile in the *Globe* titled "Best Philosopher in Baseball." Casey had no problem with continuing the season in the midst of world war: "Baseball is a great American game that will last a long time after we've mopped up the Germans and the Japs, who will finish far lower than the Phillies and the Browns ever dropped in their worst years." Stengel grew speculative: "The average human mind can handle only so much trouble and brooding. It needs some form of release now and then. The entertainment and amusement baseball brings to millions will be badly needed. And this can in no way interfere with war work of any sort." The Boston Braves' president, Bob Quinn, chipped in his warning words: "Baseball and sports in general will do their utmost toward the war effort. But there is bound to be lots of criticism directed at them. It will be in the nature of putting the 'finger' on certain people and demanding to know, 'where is your uniform?' "

All this war talk must have made Williams a little nervous. He sent telegrams to Boston that he would not appear at the Baseball Writers Dinner in early February, and that his trophy as the team's Most Valuable Player should be sent to his aunts in Mount Vernon, New York. What no one else knew yet was that he had appealed to a special presidential commission hearing to be reclassified 3-A. Williams, in fact, had a legitimate story to tell, but he hadn't told it yet and, as it turned out, he couldn't tell it fast enough. The storm that would break on this one would be a deluge.

Hy Hurwitz, who had just enlisted as a marine, wrote in the *Globe* that Williams was service bound: "Eddie Collins, Red Sox G.M., reports that Ted Williams will telephone him the instant he receives his notice to report for induction into the Army, which may come any day for Williams hasn't a chance of being deferred." Some of the Sox had already enlisted or been called: Emerson Dickman, Mickey Harris, Al Flair, Earl Johnson, and Larry Powell. Joe Cronin assumed the same: "To replace Greenberg, Williams, or Feller just isn't possible overnight. Ted was destined to be one of the greatest out-fielders of all time, as his last year's record plainly attests, and the big task of the coming season will be to find someone who can at least make an attempt to fill his shoes." He told Jim Tabor to begin shagging flies for a possible move to left.

By the middle of February the Red Sox told the increasingly curious Boston press corps that they had lost contact with Williams. He was in the woods somewhere. Management now knew about his reclassification efforts but kept them mum. With Williams's name still on the team roster, the writers were beginning to suspect something was up. A *Globe* reporter made contact with Williams in Princeton, Minnesota, on February 20. Ted told him, in an artful use of the passive voice, that his 1-A classification had been appealed for him. What did this mean, exactly?

In late February all the Boston papers carried the startling news that Williams's draft status had changed to exempt. To comprehend the collective howl from the newspaper offices to the streets of Boston is to understand something of the atmosphere in the country at the time. America was still reeling from the near destruction of its Pacific Fleet battleships at Pearl Harbor and fearing the impending annihilation of its armies in the Philippines. The day before the Williams draft story hit the headlines, February 26, the *Globe* sports section ran a photo story on the sons of owners of National Hockey League teams who were in the armed services. The feature ran under the caption, "The Bosses' Sons." Across from that story was a photo of Hy Hurwitz in his marine uniform, writing from his barracks at basic training. Hurwitz, a pint-sized scrapper who would turn into a major Williams nemesis, was doing his bit; he would end up seeing vicious action at Tarawa and Saipan, while The Big Man was willing to sit it out.

It was in that atmosphere that the Williams draft reclassification story hit the streets. The early-morning *Globe* on February 27 rang out: "TED WILLIAMS GETS DRAFT DEFERMENT." By the late edition that afternoon, someone had reached Williams in Minneapolis at the King Cole Hotel. He was already distraught about the turn of events. The headline blared: "I HAD NOTHING TO DO WITH DRAFT DEAL—WILLIAMS"; the subhead continued: "I just made a routine report. The appeal did not come from me."

Boston was aghast. Since the beginning of the appeal procedure, only eleven classifications had been overruled in all of Massachusetts. Even fewer had been overruled in Minnesota. In his *Herald* column a couple days after digesting the story, Bill Cunningham recalled the furor over Jack Dempsey's failure to register for the draft during World War I: "It looks as if the sports world may see another crucifixion. God help any American youth dependent upon good will and public applause when the crowd begins to find its voice and hurl that yellow word, 'slacker.'" His advice to Williams, whatever the circumstances of his reclassification, was to enlist. After all, "plenty of sons making $16.50 a week and turning $10 of it over to also-dependent mothers have been taken, and are being taken. That's what gives the case its bite."

Cunningham made what case he could for mitigating circumstances: "The boy, from all accounts, doesn't come from a normal home. He's done what he could to help it, while realizing that it was wiser for him to stay out of it. That's the real secret of why he winters in Minnesota. A lot of us have known that, and a lot of us have felt that we could explain a lot of things if we could only tell that whole story. But how far does privilege go in that sort of matter, especially when the victim of such a situation is fiercely sensitive about it?"

Cunningham then recalled a colleague's (Harold Kaese's) comment, " 'But what can you expect of a boy who doesn't care enough about his own mother to go home and see her in the off-season?' This turned Williams into a wildcat. His mother he'd made his major responsibility. He apparently figured that if one sportswriter was his enemy, they all were, so he gave it to all of them."

Finally, on March 5, Bill Cunningham threw down the gauntlet: "He'd better have a challenge-proof excuse, if he wants to hold his head up among men for the rest of his days." Williams figured he did. On March 6 he announced by telephone that he would keep his 3-A classification because he attained it absolutely by the book.

Though the appeal may not have come from him in so many words, Williams surely put himself in a position to have it processed. Late in 1941 he had been setting up annuities for his mother from his baseball salary—projected out in a big jump at $30,000 per year—and he had also borrowed $5,000 from the Red Sox against that salary to remodel his mother's Utah Street house in San Diego. After his 1-A reclassification following Pearl Harbor and a scheduled date for a physical in January, he began to rethink all of this. Who was going to pay on the annuities or pay the $5,000 advance on the remodeling if the Red Sox decided he had no salary? He, quite rightly, wanted to know what the 1-A status meant in terms of financial arrangements already made.

Williams spoke to a friend who told him to consult an attorney, who, in one of the finer ironies of this whole mess, had just been drafted himself. The attorney contacted a man by the name of Wendell Rogers, a Selective Service advisor. Rogers filled out the forms and took it before the local appeal board. A few days later, the appeal was rejected 5-0. With a bit of a disingenuous spin, Williams wrote in his autobiography that his advisor (not naming Rogers) "got mad," as if he, Williams, were the model of equanimity in the whole proceeding. But the appeal did not end there. John Fabre, a friend of Rogers at the board, went to Colonel J. E. Nelson, the state director of Selective Service in Minnesota. Only he or Herbert W. Estrem, the governmental appeal agent for Minneapolis Draft Board Number 6, could make a further appeal. Having lost on his own steam, Williams would have to let someone else power his case from here on.

Estrem thought that the focus of this case had been distorted, that May Williams, her health, and her ability to support herself was the proper center. Affidavits on these matters had already been solicited and filed earlier in November. Estrem took the case to the presidential board established by the director of the Selective Service, General Hershey, whose name would chill potential draftees up through the time of the Vietnam war. Estrem defended his action as largely self-motivated: "Williams's part has been overemphasized and my own understated. It should be stressed that he consented to the appeal. I think the word 'request' is too strong although technically he did request it." For Williams's part, he knew, or sensed, or was told to go into a phase of tactical silence. His passivity was the saving grace surrounding the appeal; Williams portrayed himself by phone to the

Red Sox front office and to the Boston newspapers as a baffled witness to the appeal procedures. Action seemed to generate of its own volition. A little over three weeks later, in mid-January, President Roosevelt, or whatever rubber stamp employed to sign his name in his stead, passed favorably on Williams's reclassification to 3-A. Fate had a yen for .400 hitters.

The notion of officials rushing at breakneck speed to serve as the proper conduits for appeal procedures rang a little false. That was the part that made the entire business strange. Who but the influential elicit such meticulous attention from a bureaucracy? But Williams made a decision. The letter of the law would will out.

Boston's management heard loud repercussions echoing over the horizon from all of this. Joe Cronin tried to set in motion a new course of action for Williams. He contacted Mickey Cochrane, former Detroit catcher serving at the Great Lakes naval base in charge of athletics, who set up a special tour for Williams on March 5. Cochrane had him ready for launch but then pushed the wrong torpedo button. He told Williams that Americans would boo the hell out of him if he played this year. The wrong images flashed across Williams's screen. Boos he well knew, but back came those three annuities for his mother and that contractor hammering on the porch. It was no go. He was playing ball and that was the end of it.

Williams released a statement through the Red Sox front office: "While deferred from the draft in a 3-A classification, I made certain financial commitments. I must carry through with them. Therefore, despite a strong urge to enter the service now, I have decided to play ball with the Red Sox this summer. That will enable me to fulfill my obligation to my family and make everything right all around." He then got in his car, drove to Princeton, Minnesota, to say goodbye to Doris, gassed up, and headed to Sarasota. They may have been preparing to lynch him in Boston, but when he stopped to cash a check in Nashville, Tennessee, no one knew or cared that he was Ted Williams or that Ted Williams was a name that carried any weight: "Sorry, young fella, you could sign it Babe Ruth and we wouldn't cash it."

For their part, Boston's management, as so often was the case, had clammed up until the crisis broke and then, with poor planning and poor coordination, fed the press mixed signals. First there was equivocation; Cronin played dumb: "To show you what little knowledge I had during the past month on Ted's status, I actually sent a letter to him addressed to Fort Snelling, Minnesota, at the end of January thinking Ted was already inducted." Next, he sashayed over to Ted's side: "There's another side to this case. I'm certain his is a most worthy case and that Ted wouldn't hesitate an instant about jumping into the Army when and if he is called. If Uncle Sam says fight, he'll fight. Since he has said play ball, Ted has a right to play. There's a chance that Ted can be put on the spot without any justice in this thing."

Behind the scenes the Red Sox brass were doing a two-step, trying to buttress Williams's legal position while undercutting his ethical one. They had an almost-frantic fear about fan reaction to the crisis and were energetic in their efforts to get Williams enlisted in the navy. Tom Yawkey made a personal call to Williams and told him to go see Mickey Cochrane again. Ted said he was "dazed" by it all, and, besides, the reclassification decision had already been made. He wanted support, not in this instance for his tirades or fits of temper but for his legal position. And it was in large part the public waffling by the Red Sox during these days that bred in him a resentment that he carried into his autobiography more than 20 years later, almost begging for a different response, "some common meeting ground to head these things off before they got worse, which they always did."

Jimmie Foxx, who had visited Ted at home in San Diego during their West Coast barnstorming tour in October 1941, knew full well the dicey situation, with Sam Williams gone and with Danny struggling to stay afloat in his own life: "I'll certainly vouch for him." Other members of the team were in Boston and taking phone calls. The Red Sox had told Jim Tabor to shag flies, even in the middle of January, because Williams might not play in 1942, and when Tabor was contacted by the papers he shot back: "Hell, Roosevelt saw me shag flies for one day in left, and he gave Williams a deferment from the draft." Johnny Peacock, a reserve Red Sox catcher, recognized immediately that every Ted Williams story has both a warp and a woof, not merely what happened but how it was represented: "It's up to you press boys to make sure Williams gets a fair shake on this issue."

The first reaction from the big guns of the Boston press, those

Williams detested as well as those for whom he had either a grudging respect or outright admiration, was tentative. Harold Kaese, whose relationship with Williams was strained when he purportedly threatened that the press could make or break him in 1939, saw trouble on the horizon: "The first reaction from all sides yesterday seemed to be 'Wait'll he comes to bat—wow! Boy, they'll just ride him out of the league.'" This was the biggest news in Boston since Harold Frazee sold Babe Ruth to the Yankees, and the press vultures were hungry for carrion.

Kaese was still on his case the next day, arguing that perception takes precedence over cause, and that Williams was naive to forget this or react so diffidently to it. Willy-nilly, Williams would "squirm in agony under the accusing stare of the American public." Kaese continued:

> The case seems black. A youth, healthy and highly paid, is transferred from 3-A to 1-A by his local draft board. He is on the verge of being inducted into the Army, like thousands of other young men, like poor young men and rich young men, like Hank Greenberg, like Cecil Travis, like Hugh Mulcahy. The case goes to Washington. There is a delay. Those with sensitive ears hear strings being pulled. An ominous silence envelops the youth.
> There is suspicion. There is contempt. There is hatred.

A "Man on the Street" feature in the *Globe* captured the fan reaction, swaying about 2 to 1 against Williams: "Not fair to Hank Greenberg, Bob Feller, and others"; "I am in the draft and have a mother and a child to support. I know someone will take care of them if I'm called"; "If that's the opinion in Washington, it's okay with me." Fortunately, Williams was not without press support, and some writers were doing better for him than the Red Sox public relations office. The oracular Bill Cunningham took the tempered road. In his column headlined, "TED WILLIAMS'S BOOK STILL OPEN," Cunningham wrote that America is still a country of laws and "this is a matter between Williams and his draft board. It is unfair for an outsider, unfamiliar with all the intimate facts, to pass judgment."

Within the next couple of days the story became investigative. The Boston writers were dying to drop revealing hints about the disconcerting funnel of Williams's San Diego life—the resources sunk into the family by Ted and drained by brother Danny—but the code among them just didn't allow for anything of this nature in the 1940s. Jerry Nason wrote in the *Globe*: "There aren't a half-dozen people in the game of baseball who know the story." He then dredged up the old Jack Dempsey draft-dodging case from World War I and, in one of those moves that make people wonder why a matter was ever raised in the first place, claimed it was unparallel: Dempsey never registered for the draft, and he was actually indicted. He won his case on technical grounds. Nason was on a roll; next he told the story of Benny McCoy of the A's who signed for a $45,000 bonus as a free agent in 1940 and then appealed for a deferment as sole source of support for his mother, brother, and sister. The same president's board that decided on Williams's case granted him the deferment. Of course, as Nason was quick to point out, America wasn't then at war.

With spring training on the immediate horizon, many worried what would happen with Ted in uniform, though the Philadelphia A's owner and manager, the venerable Connie Mack, a veteran of the Spanish-American War, offered to trade the William Penn statue atop City Hall in Philadelphia for Williams if the Red Sox didn't want him for 1942. Few were without an opinion on the Williams affair, and few were sparing of advice. The *Globe*'s Victor O. Jones, who had an annoying habit of writing Williams open letters, sought a compromise on the family money issue. What one hand giveth, the other taketh: "If you went off to the war and your mother was left destitute thereby, I wouldn't have a shred of respect for you. If, on the other hand, provision could be made for your mother without your playing baseball, why wouldn't this be a good compromise?"

Bill Cunningham had something of the same idea: "If I had Yawkey's millions, I'd guarantee to pay his mother what Williams has been sending her for as long as he's in the service, and that if anything happened to him, I'd pay her in a lump sum whatever he figures he can save out of this extra year's salary. Then if Williams didn't enlist, I'd fire him. I wouldn't even bother to sell him, for I'd want no money that came out of that sort of property." On the day Williams was scheduled to arrive in Sarasota, Cunningham dispatched another item that might have been meant for Williams's eyes and ears: "Sgt. Hank Greenberg, the former 100 percent ball player is now 100 percent soldier . . . a player who was the American League's most valuable when he heard his country's call."

Even Williams's business manager, James A. Silin, got into the act, worried over such developments as the cancellation of a $4,000 Quaker Oats endorsement. Silin telegrammed his client, advising him to enlist on his own, and then thoughtfully made the telegram available to the papers: "Your baseball career as well as your patriotism and your future happiness for many years to come are at stake. If you enlist, you will gladden the hearts and stir the Americanism of thousands of kids to whom you have been and should always remain an idol. Don't let those kids down, Teddy. If you accept deferment from the army, you will ruin the greatest baseball career of all time." After the war Williams changed business managers.

Eddie Collins, Cronin, and Yawkey did not want Williams to show up at Sarasota the first week in March. They continued begging him to enlist, but he was adamantly against it and told reporters by telephone hookup: "The quickest route to a solution of this whole matter is to earn some big dough this year, then just as soon as I lay down my bat in September or October, I'm in the Navy. And quick, too. I certainly do not feel that I have committed any crime or done anything dishonest; and if I wasn't sincere I wouldn't be picking what is not going to be any bed of roses."

The Red Sox were unhappy with this message. The notion of Williams attending to the indecency of world war as soon as he straightened out his cash-flow problems had little appeal to Yawkey. From his New York offices, he released a counterstatement: "His decision in all likelihood will affect not only his entire baseball career, but his life as well." At this time Williams was taking as much grief for falling back on his legal position as he was for crying poor. All one had to do in March 1942 was consider the fervor in this country for digging us out of the hole into which we had fallen. Even the comic strips set a context for the Williams decision. On March 9 Superman addressed a joint session of the United States Congress, and told of his readiness to enlist:

> This modern plague has crushed one peace-loving nation after another—Austria, Poland, Czechoslovakia, France. It has warred

against Ethiopia, China . . . and now it menaces the stronghold of Democracy—our beloved America. But we will battle the menacing hordes until they are smashed completely and finally so that once again decency and humanity will be restored throughout the world! Like every other patriotic American, I want to aid in the downfall of these Fascist vultures.

When the Red Sox began arriving the second week in March, tension was high. They were all receiving letters. Tony Lupien showed Kaese an unsigned handwritten note from a fan: "While you play, some men fight to make it a free country." Mail call for Williams was voluminous on March 10, with one envelope containing nothing but two yellow sheets of paper.

Williams showed up on March 10. "Hi, Meat," was Joe Cronin's casual greeting. Ted was not silent. He had been in cold storage in the Midwest and now was dying to get his story out. Like the ancient mariner, he stoppeth one of three and repeated his saga detail-for-detail: "Honest to God! I didn't pay anybody a single cent." The older players began grumbling at once about their animated left-fielder: "Christ, he's still just a kid, listen to him!"

In a long and necessary press conference that very day, March 10, Williams faced the public and stayed until all the questions were asked. He claimed that the president of the American League, William Harridge, called him before he left Minnesota and approved of his decision: "I may be called on the carpet for telling all this, but I'm going to be honest with you. Mr. Harridge tried to get me on the phone Friday. I didn't get his message and that's why I stayed longer than I expected to in Minneapolis—just to talk to him."

It was clearly galling to Williams even then that his support was coming from the league office and not the Red Sox: "Mr. Harridge told me to keep my chin up. He told me to conduct myself as I did last year. Mr. Harridge said that he thought if I did that everybody will be pulling for me in the end." In Williams's very tone was the kind of pleasure he took from those who offered the protection he always felt he lacked, whether at home as a child or in professional sports. If not Yawkey, Collins, or Cronin from the Red Sox, then Harridge from the American League.

Williams laid it out, insofar as he could bear talking about the details of his life. He admitted the finances behind his decision. He would lose the benefits of three annuities in addition to salary: "That's big money for me. I'll tell you frankly what I've done with the money I've made in three years in the big leagues. I spent more than I made my first year. I split even the next year. Last year I managed to save a little, but it's still not enough to take care of my mother, and won't be until I can take care of things this year. Sure, this is the toughest decision I've ever made in my life. But I've made it and I intend to go through with it. I'm on my own. I know it."

Williams played in his first game on March 12, and the worries from the front office were titanic. But a polite 800 fans showed up in Sarasota, and when Ted pinch hit late in the game—maybe Cronin figured the crowd had thinned out—nothing much happened. The fans clapped. Spring training did much to dampen the controversy that blared before it. By March 24, the conservative and patriotic Bill Cunningham put his own lid on the story and then reserved the right to open it for another peep come the regular season: "Just whatever became of the 'Ted Williams case'? It's dead as a doornail down here. Has it likewise died in the northern end, or has it only died down? Or does it wait perhaps until the California cracker hits those big-city ballparks where those waiting to fire can really see the white of his eyes?"

In a game at Tampa late in March, 2,000 soldiers showed up, most of them from McDill Field, where Hank Greenberg was now a sergeant in the tank corps. The soldiers gave Williams a huge, boisterous ovation: "Stay where you are, Ted. We got enough soldiers." Williams was feeling pretty good, and the strain was easing. After the Tampa game he returned to Sarasota and skipped another road game just to hit with half the squad at the complex. No one could stay in the cage long with Williams hovering. Eddie Pellagrini gave up without a struggle and wandered over to Bill Cunningham: "Jeez, I can't hit with that guy pushing me. I like to concentrate up there, but he keeps crowding you. He keeps saying, 'You've had enough, haven't you? Let me get up there and swing.'" Over the years the Boston press did what it could to foment bad relations between Williams and his teammates, but they had a hard time. He may have been a lone wolf, but he was likeable. His nature was essentially good, and his inclinations generous. What his teammates did not like was the embarrassment that came with his more exaggerated antics, or with his hogging time at the batting cage.

But Williams even made his batting-practice greediness fun. Pitcher Andy Karl was throwing to him, and Ted would chatter about each pitch. "Where was that? A little outside? Caught the corner?" Karl wanted out at 12:30 when the scheduled practice was over, so Williams turned toward Pellagrini: "You pitch, and then I'll throw to you. Come on!" A reluctant Pellagrini shrugged at Cunningham, then said, "All right, but me first," Williams motioned to a local black kid to shag for them. When the kid fell chasing a Pellagrini blast, Williams turned around at the mound and mocked Joe Cronin's voice: "For crying out loud, that Williams in left—he cost us another game." A half hour later Pellagrini begged off. "Aw, a few more," begged Williams. Cunningham stored a phrase for his column, one that Williams later picked up as his own refrain in a series for *Sports Illustrated* in the 1960s: "I think the young man goes a little mad out there, but hitting is his whole life."

The Red Sox completed spring training and began their swing home for an exhibition series with the Boston Braves, a yearly ritual, the second week of April. Williams told reporters that the letters he'd been receiving were running 60-40 for him. Those against were mostly from out of state: "If a middle-aged man boos me, I just feel sorry for him because I think he ought to know better. But if the kids, even though I realize they may be ignorant of the facts, start to get on me, I'm afraid that may prove a little too tough to take."

Under a photo of Fenway and its fans, the *Globe* printed a sly caption: "Williams (deferred) of the Red Sox faces Boston fandom tomorrow for the first time since the No. 1 batter of the majors became the center of a stormy 'should he–shouldn't he' debate. Your verdict, ladies and gentlemen? Safe at home." Safe at home, indeed. The phrase is double-edged—read innocently, it refers to the comforts of Fenway; read sardonically, it is a wartime insult.

For a timely image of the first exhibition game, which the Braves won 7-5, the *Globe* sports cartoonist Gene Mack drew a mean-looking Hulking Hun on the pitcher's mound and a minuscule batter at the plate with 1942 SEASON written on his back. The sentiment could be construed as general, unless a particular leftfielder for the Red Sox took it as specific. Boston fans were more generous. They

gave Williams a robust cheer on his third at-bat when he singled off
Johnny Sain. Ted was in pretty good spirits even with his rabbit ears
well tuned: "Yeah, everyone was for me except a couple of kids in the
left-field stands and a guy out in right. I could hear them. That fellow
in right had a bullhorn for a voice and those kids in left gave it to me
all through the game." One of the kids riding him in left screamed
that he had two brothers serving with U.S. forces in Australia. Williams shrugged: "There'll be people like that. They feel pretty bitter."

For those fans who expressed appreciation for his talents, Williams
supplied a first-inning three-run homer on opening day, April 14,
against the A's. He hit a Phil Marchildon waist-high fastball into the
second row of the bleachers in right behind the Sox pen. For the
opening set against the A's Williams hit .600, with nine runs batted
in and two home runs. His spirits were up, and so were the nation's
the next day, April 18. The headlines read: "TOKYO BOMBED," and
for the first time in the war long-range B-25 bombers from America's
carrier fleet penetrated Japan's surprised aerial defenses and retal-
iated in small measure on the empire's home islands. The *Globe*
afternoon headline said it all: "REMEMBER PEARL HARBOR."

For the second series of the year, the Red Sox trained to New York,
where 50,000, including 2,000 soldiers, packed Yankee Stadium.
Williams was cheered. It turned out that writers such as Grantland
Rice were absolutely right about baseball in wartime America. The
nation, even its trainees and fighting forces, delighted in the image of
normalcy and energy displayed on the ball field. It was a tonic, not an
outrage, that the season continued and that the finer players were still
on the field. The draft timetable would take care of itself as the
contours of the war became clearer. Williams, for one, had already
told *Globe* writer Gerry Moore that he intended to enlist the moment
the season ended.

During the Yankee series in New York, Bill Cunningham wrote a
column on that peculiar creature—the baseball fan. He was trying to
put the frenzy around Williams in some sort of perspective by
suggesting that there is an inherent irreverence in the fan, an urge to
harass that is seemingly licensed by the purchase of a ticket. The
issue is not simply one of decency and sensibility; it is part economic
and part psychological. Cheering and its antitype, booing, are a
purchased release. And spectator sports, from the time of the Greeks

and Romans, serve a social role. Witnesses are judges; opinions are a kind of law.

Cunningham sat in the stands anonymously during the Yankee series and listened to the talk. He centered on one rabid fan who was all over DiMaggio, the great DiMaggio, whom Williams was convinced never heard it much from the New York fans: "Here comes DiMaggio again, and the guy cut loose like a fire whistle: 'That's the g-r-r-r-r-eat, magnificent, hell-for-breakfast Joe DiMaggio.'" "And what've you got against him?" asked Cunningham, not telling the fan he was a writer. "'Nothing. Except the big bum—Booooh!, ya' big bum, you couldn't hit a basketball—except the bum holding out for all that dough. Stank up the World Series, ya' big bum, and $38,000 is not good enough? Ya' big bum. Look at him—he hasn't even smelled the ball all day."

This creature, wrote Cunningham, may seem a monster, but a ball game is a kind of hole in time where Dr. Jekyll all too often becomes Mr. Hyde. The psychology of the fan is, by definition, an abnormal psychology. In this case, little of the man's harangue was truly personal. Some fans get a huge kick out of jumping all over a player with far greater skills than they and making far more money. Even so tempestuous a ballplayer as Williams was surprised again and again when he would meet the friendliest and warmest people who, with not the least embarrassment, would tell him how they loved to scream at him from the left-field seats at Fenway.

As the season moved through May, Bobby Doerr, hitting .467, carried the Red Sox, with Boston fighting it out with the Yanks for first place. Williams was holding steady at around .300, but, more important, he was playing relaxed. Harold Kaese listened to Ted and Dominic DiMaggio on the dugout steps watching the Indians' Jeff Heath taking his cuts during batting practice. Williams: "He's a good hitter, a mighty good hitter." DiMaggio: "Ted, you think everybody's a good hitter. I never saw anybody see so much good in hitters as you do." Williams: "Aw, g'wan." DiMaggio: "That's right. Remember the other day when York fell out of the box and hit a pop fly. What did you say?" Williams: "I don't remember." DiMaggio: "You said, 'Maybe he looked bad on that pitch, but I still think that guy's a great hitter.'" Williams: "Yeah, and I still do."

The Sporting News in the beginning of May ran a feature on a one-armed player by the name of Pete Gray, for Three Rivers of the Canadian-American League. This seemed to be a hint that the majors better start looking for 4-Fs to continue their seasons through the war. Pete Gray would play for the Memphis Chicks in 1943 and then finally make it up to the majors for the St. Louis Browns in 1945. It was at this very time that the blood of those not yet drafted began to stir for good reason. General MacArthur announced to the world that our naval forces on May 8 had dealt a devastating blow to the Japanese at the Battle of Coral Sea, off New Guinea, sinking or badly damaging a significant proportion of Japan's fleet. Advertisements were now running daily in the newspapers: "If you are itching to be in the thick of the fight, and you'd like to slip those Japs and Nazis a man-sized dose of their own medicine, then here's your chance to do something about it."

Williams was doing some heavy thinking on the matter as the Red Sox headed west and hoped that their road trip would not be accompanied by a typical spring swoon. Typically, they swooned. The plaintive lilt of the yearly refrain—"What's the matter with the Red Sox?"—began early in 1942. Williams was not hitting with particular authority, and he was worried about going into Cleveland, a part of the country from which he had been receiving the most savage letters about his draft status, though an army major by the name of Culligan, working for the service's public relations office, was telling Cleveland sports broadcasters that Williams had just requested reclassification to 1-A. Melville Webb made the sardonic point that "most of the fans who are trying to disconcert Williams are making pretty good money in local defense factories."

Williams did something emphatic in Cleveland: he hit one out in the ninth inning for his ninth home run of the year on May 21 to ensure a Red Sox win, and the next day, after the team swung back into Boston, he enlisted in the armed forces of the United States. The rumors in Cleveland had been correct. On May 17 he had officially requested reclassification. On May 22 Williams signed up for the navy aviation program—perhaps prompted by nostalgic memories of the naval aerial operations around San Diego, or perhaps by the daily ads for fliers in the newspapers all around the country. He took his physical, administered by Lieutenant Frank R. Philbrook, and passed, as it were, with flying colors. His vision, 20-10, was merely very good, despite reports that it was supernatural. (He had been bothered by mild eyestrain in his right eye ever since he injured it as a kid when he and his brother were hitting hazelnuts with a broomstick.) Actually, his hearing was better than his eyesight. Lieutenant Philbrook whispered, "Can you hear me?" "Hell," said Williams. "If he only knew I could hear a heckler at Fenway in the 40th row, he'd know my ears were okay."

Williams was then sworn in by Lieutenant Commander Thomas A. Collins at the Flight Selection Board at 150 Causeway St., in Boston. His scores on the three-hour placement exam were high for aptitude, though he made no claims to special mathematical skills beyond basic high school level. Math threatened to be the bugbear of his aviation training, but he was as dogged with the numbers as he was with the bat. A young Johnny Pesky, who was in training with Williams, remembered that he really ground it out: "he was always near the top of the training class."

Williams's decision had been brewing for some time. Two days before he made it he wrote to tell his mother. Her finances and health were the center of the reclassification storm, and he owed that much to her. He had been thinking about the matter seriously since April 29, when the Red Sox publicist, Ed Doherty, introduced him to navy Lieutenant Robert "Whitey" Fuller, former Dartmouth sports publicist. Fuller wanted to take Williams on a tour of the V-5 naval flight-training program. On May 6, with the Red Sox facing an off-day before a trip to Philly, Fuller drove Ted to the Squantum Base. He loved the navy fighter planes and filled out an application for the program on the spot. He would begin classes while he continued to play ball.

His action was a tonic for his hitting eye. By June 1 he had upped his average to .333 and was leading the league in home runs with 15 and in runs batted in with 56. There was something a little surreal about the course of life these days, and the course of the baseball season in particular. The enormity of the war was such that the season seemed to be shutting down in stages, even though few were leaving just yet. But the nature of the news had by this time pretty much convinced everyone that the struggle ahead was unique. It was at this time in June that the West began receiving unconfirmed reports that the Nazis were systematically "murdering entire families" in eastern Europe. To separate these reports from typical war propaganda was a difficult thing, but there were some, at least, who credited them, though the horror and full details were ghastly and confused. One correspondent, Leland Stowe, reported Nazi plans for a massive experiment in Russia that would entail the transporting of entire populations to concentration camps for purposes of slave labor and possible medical experimentation. It sounded like science fiction to contemporary audiences but turned out, in its rudiments, to be frighteningly true.

In a more visible theater of war, the United States Navy won another massive battle in the Pacific at Midway Island on June 4. The Japanese Navy lost half of its fleet. This, along with the decisive victory in the Coral Sea, set in motion the eventual strategy of island hopping that tightened the noose on the Japanese venture in the Pacific. Williams was proud to be in naval aviation during these times—he could pick up any newspaper and read long accounts of the exploits of the navy marine pilots at Midway. The contributions of those pilots, many of whom would be instructing Williams, were stellar and courageous. One of the officers at Midway, Lieutenant Colonel Walter Sweeney, commented: "I can't get over those marine fliers, many of them just out of flying school. Their courage and fortitude under savage fire was simply amazing."

The Red Sox were in second place and had fallen 9½ games behind the Yanks by mid-June, though Williams had inched his average up to .344. He took some abuse from the Fenway fans on Sunday, June 14, during a Tiger doubleheader, when he misplayed Bill Hitchcock's liner into a double. One fan near the dugout gave him particular grief and Williams wanted a piece of him: "Yeah, I mean you," he growled as he glared and pointed at the culprit. His patriotism won him precious little leeway from this Red Sox fan, who preferred a fielded ball to navy wings in the middle of a pennant race.

At month's end Williams was producing with consistent power and the Red Sox were making a run at the Yankees. They had reduced the Yankee lead to three games by July 1, winning 21 of 26, but that day at Fenway Williams went into an unaccountable fit. At the plate he took feeble and intentionally useless swings; on the bases he jogged when he ought to have dashed; in the field he loafed after balls; between innings he made peculiar, though obviously hostile, gestures at fans. Cronin benched him in the second game that day and put Pete Fox in left.

This is one of the few times that Williams's petulance was purely a matter of immature self-pity. He could not account for fans and the press acting toward him in the same fickle way they usually did. After all, he had done what everyone originally expected of him: he enlisted. But the tension on this matter, especially after the season began, was mostly internal. Williams was the one who felt better about himself for enlisting, and he couldn't understand why his own opinion didn't carry the day at every moment of the day. To an extent, most everyone was pleased that he enlisted—and said so—but that didn't mean they loved the way he hawked flies or cut off ground balls in the outfield. For Williams's part, he had heard just one too many shouts of "Hey, Williams, why don't you give Dom DiMaggio half your salary? He does half your job out there!" He blew up.

Cronin took Williams to the woodshed and fined him $250. Williams calmed down in short enough order, taking full blame, after a fashion. "I deserved to be put out of the park. I'm just thickheaded enough and screwy enough and childish enough to let those wolves in left field get under my skin. Some day I'm going to take 25 pounds of hamburger out there and invite those wolves to come down and enjoy it. I'm not really sore. I was just kind of unconscious. I was all set to take three strikes right down the groove just to show them 'what the hell.' Then I thought I'd drive some fouls into the left-field stand and knock some teeth out." It's difficult to know whether Williams was more dangerous infuriated or contrite.

Having come to apologize, Williams wound it all out: "They say what's the matter with Williams. What the hell. I'm leading the league in home runs, in runs batted in, in runs scored, in bases on balls. What do they want?" In this case, they wanted him to run out a pop fly. But fans are forgiving if they are not taunted or insulted with poor play. Williams came back from this little contretemps swinging. At the break for the All-Star Game on July 6, he had taken over the league lead in batting at .351, with 18 home runs and 80 runs batted in.

A night game at the Polo Grounds was the venue for the first of two 1942 All-Star games. All revenues over $100,000 for the first game and the full kitty the next night in Cleveland were slated for the service organizations. But the weather kept attendance down in New York, and the night was almost a debacle. The game was pushed back to a 7:20 P.M. start by rain, and then Mayor La Guardia refused to lift the 9:30 blackout time. There was scant time for ceremony, though the American League scarcely needed much time or ceremony. Lou Boudreau and Rudy York hit home runs in the first inning to build a 3–0 lead that lasted until Mickey Owen homered for the Nationals. The final score: 3–1. Williams got a single in the third.

The most notable moment of the game for Williams came before it started and before the weather almost postponed it. Later he told Jimmy Piersall that this was the single best team he ever saw—with DiMaggio, Dickey, York, Henrich, Keller, and, modestly, himself supplying the punch. National Leaguers, Ted recalled, "lined the dugout steps just to watch us take batting practice." The next evening in Cleveland a collection of service ballplayers could watch the American League stars hit in batting practice and during the game. All-Star Game Two featured the winners of All-Star Game One against such in-service stars as Bob Feller, Johnny Rigney, Pat Mullin, Johnny Sturm, Benny McCoy, Cecil Travis, and Ben Chapman. Williams drew walks in all but one at-bat, a big triple in the seventh to drive in Phil Rizzuto, and scored a couple of runs in the game, won handily by the American League, 5–0.

When the season resumed, Williams worked out a deal with the navy to begin taking courses for his training program. This was no snap regimen. For four hours three nights a week he showed up at Mechanic Arts High in Boston to study navigation, physics, and mathematics. The classes were cycled to accommodate waves of recruits, so he was able to abandon them for road trips and pick up with a new cadre of students where he had left off when he returned. He was working his tail off. "Advanced math? I never had any of that. These birds will call me meathead—like they do in the left-field bleachers."

The Red Sox run at the pennant took a nosedive after a bad home stand and western road trip. They had fallen to 11 games out by July 21, but Williams kept steady at .356. A few days later a quiet but historic event took place for baseball. Larry MacPhail of the Dodgers released a statement—seemingly out of the blue—that the Negro leagues might well be raided in the near future by the majors: "There is no understanding against black players in the majors." MacPhail had gotten wind of a secret tryout conducted by the Pittsburgh Pirates that day, July 28, for three black ballplayers, including a youngster named Roy Campanella. After the war MacPhail ended up doing what he could to confirm the very opposite of what he had said for public consumption before the war: he would encourage the league's silent efforts to impede integration. His natural enemy at that time would be Branch Rickey, who had been thinking about introducing blacks to the majors but who knew that St. Louis, where he was with the Cards, would be a poor place to try.

Satchel Paige, freelancing for about $37,500 a year in 1942, responded to rumors that the Pirates would begin trying out black ballplayers: "Might as well be honest. Nice words won't K.O. Jim Crow in this country." Paige claimed the truth of the matter was that blacks on ball teams would present a host of nearly insurmountable racial problems in the major cities of the country. He knew, as did other blacks, the well of prejudice that existed throughout the land. A few months earlier in Kansas City the bulk of a white audience walked out of a Paul Robeson concert when the singer complained from the stage about the paucity of blacks in the audience. Soon thereafter Robeson's hotel reservations were canceled at Santa Fe, New Mexico, a fitting response, supposedly, to his public complaints.

As the season headed into its final phases, the Red Sox were too far out for the run to be in any way interesting. But naval trainee Ted Williams looked to have a shot at his first triple crown. An August 14 cartoon in the *Globe* had Williams flying in the cockpit of a baseball bat with three targets on the horizon: the batting title, the home-run lead, and the runs-batted-in lead. Local scribes figured Williams had taken himself out of the Most Valuable Player competition by alienating the writers, even though Joe Gordon of the Yanks was having a career year on a pennant winner. Jerry Nason wrote that Williams couldn't get three votes from the Boston press because the last run the Red Sox made at the pennant was stunted by his blowup in July: "The Sox, a brisk, sharp, fighting ball team right up to the moment of Williams's blowup, . . . flopped all over the park and all over the league after that."

America in August got its first look at the Lou Gehrig film biography, *Pride of the Yankees,* right about the time American land forces in the Pacific launched their first major battles, in the Solomon Islands near Tulagi, and soon at Guadalcanal. After a week of savage hand-to-hand fighting, the marines claimed their first victories of the war on land. In the European theater, a kind of trial run for a sea-land invasion of Nazi-held territory took place on August 19, when 1,000 commandos landed near Dieppe with aerial and naval support. They held positions for nine hours and then, as planned, evacuated by sea.

Also in August, Williams's girlfriend, Doris Soule, appeared with Ted on a front-page photo in the *Globe* with a ring on her finger, a way of announcing marriage plans without actually doing so. Like so many in wartime America, the fighting men and home-front women were seizing the day. It made sense, in its way, to deny danger by courting desire. And it made life seem somehow continuous and connected to carry on and marry on in the face of long absences. Williams would do so near the completion of his own flight training program in 1944, at a time when he thought it likely he would be shipped out for overseas service. But this was still 1942. The Red Sox had a pennant to continue losing.

The Yanks fairly well coasted to their second straight American League pennant, as the St. Louis Cards and Brooklyn Dodgers once again clawed right to the last week of the year for the laurels. The National League teams changed places in 1942, with the Cards taking what they lost the year before to the Dodgers. St. Louis won the Series in five tough games, each played closer than the final imbalanced result seemed to suggest.

Williams had an exceptional year in a season that only looked good for the Red Sox for a couple of weeks around the All-Star break. His numbers were glorious: .356, 36 home runs, and 137 runs batted in: the Triple Crown. In one of those freak statistics that, if it measures anything, measures the remarkable consistency of Williams as a hitter, Williams hit .356 on the road in 1942 and .356 at home, with an identical number of at-bats and hits. His power on the road registered higher—20 home runs to 16, and 77 runs batted in to 68. He hit his best against St. Louis, averaging .471 at Sportsman's Park and .439 against the Browns at Fenway. In four years his combined average at Sportsman's was a robust .423, with 17 home runs.

The balloting for the Most Valuable Player in the American League was closer this November than it had been the last, but Williams still pulled in fewer votes than he might have had he been placed higher on the ballots by those voting baseball writers who so detested him. Joe Gordon of the Yanks took the honor with 270 total points to Williams's 249. Gordon was first on 12 of 24 ballots; Williams, on 9 of 24. Each had 8 second-place votes. Williams was a touch disingenuous about the vote, but he eased into dead realism before his obligatory remarks concluded: "I was glad Gordon got it. I really think he kept the Yankees up there. Yeah, I wanted it, but I knew I wasn't going to get it and got it out of my mind. I just put the award out of my thoughts. There is a bigger game to think about now."

That November Williams was officially activated as a naval cadet. He began with a course of studies at Amherst College's Civilian Pilot Training program. At Amherst with Williams were Johnny Pesky, Jerry Coleman, and Johnny Sain. The program was no piece of cake, and the classes on the ground were tougher than anything in the air. Those who washed out, and many did under the rigorous program, were subject to 1-A classification and a redrafting into the infantry. Williams liked his training so much he considered another career change—first a train engineer in 1938, then a fireman in 1940, and now a career naval flier in 1942: "If I can make a success of flying, I'd just as soon stay in the service—provided I could get a month off once in a while to go hunting."

◇ 7 ◇

Interlude
1943-1945

THE 1943 BASEBALL SEASON WAS conceived and played under very different conditions from those of the year before. In February the draft exemption for married men disappeared, and there was little reason for anyone without a physical disability to remain exempt from the draft or remain reticent about enlisting. Baseball may have been considered an essential home-front diversion, but its players were most decidedly not considered essential wartime employees. Joe DiMaggio was among the first to enlist after the phasing out of the marriage exemption in February, and this exemplary move by an exemplary ball player was played to the hilt in the newspapers. DiMaggio was stationed in Monterey, near his San Francisco home. *The Sporting News* for that week featured a photograph of DiMaggio's locker with number 5 hanging on a hook, and near it a uniform with 6 on the back. Put together, they exhibited his record hitting streak of 1941. Above the locker was the caption "Closed for the Duration."

For those who remained on the major league rosters, many things would be different. There were cutbacks in spring training, and the travel circuits around the league were reduced. Among the many suggestions for wartime baseball that were considered seriously was a proposal by Cubs' general manager James T. Gallagher to draft from a pool of all deferred players in order to distribute available talent evenly around the leagues. This struck other owners as a dangerous precedent—even if there were gaping holes in club rosters—that would, under other circumstances, have been downright embarrassing.

As the list of inductions and enlistments grew, teams began coming up with all sorts of ideas, including drafting Latin American ballplayers and reactivating retired ballplayers. Fans in Boston made a pitch for signing Hugh Duffy, who had hit .438 for the Red Sox in 1894, though Hugh said he wouldn't know what to do with the huge gloves the players used in 1943—"they looked like your grandmother could sit in them and knit."

The war during the spring and summer of 1943 was turning in the Allies' favor, and the country relished a stream of fresh news reports to bolster spirits. While the campaign of greatest significance—namely, D-Day—was in secret preparation, campaigns of substantial significance were headlined daily in the newspapers: North Africa was in Allied hands; and invasion forces were making Sicilian and Italian beachheads in the European theater; United States marine and infantry forces continued their grueling series of island sieges in the Pacific.

Early in the 1943 season Ted Williams was in Chapel Hill, North Carolina, for preflight training. His only baseball action that season came when he showed up at Fenway Park in Boston and in a Red Sox uniform—with the Red Sox already way out of the pennant race—for a charity ball game. Babe Ruth managed and even pinch hit for the North Carolina Pre-Flight Cloudbusters against the Boston Braves. This was the only time these two great left-handed hitters were photographed together wearing baseball uniforms. Ruth flied out weakly to right in the game; Williams hit a massive 425-foot home run to lead the service team over the Braves 9–8. Ruth and Williams took their charity show on the road for another game in Yankee Stadium on July 28, with Ruth drawing a walk as a pinch hitter and Williams singling. Proceeds from the game—$35,000—were donated to the war effort.

The Red Sox were a sorry lot in 1943, protected from the cellar of the American League only by the more inept and woeful Philadelphia A's, who lost 105 games. The only soul in the lineup to hit .300, even with Bobby Doerr at second, was the manager, Joe Cronin, mostly in a pinch-hitting role. The Yanks took the pennant again, but this time they reversed their World Series loss to the Cards in 1942 and won in five games.

Williams finished his preflight training in North Carolina in September of 1943 and headed on to Kokomo, Indiana, for 100-hour basic flight training at Bunker Hill Naval Air Station. The commanding officer, Captain D. D. Gurley, told the few baseball writers checking up on Williams that he was so good a pilot he fulfilled requirements for his course two weeks early, which gave him a little time to play ball for the base team at Freeman Field. Williams trained at Bunker Hill with the best, Captain Dixie Kiefer, hero of the marine fighter pilots at Midway.

On December 6, 1943, Williams left for Pensacola, Florida, for intermediate training. One of his fellow trainees at Bronson Field was the Boston football star Frank Maznicki, who told Williams that he used to go to Fenway to boo the hell out of him in left field: "I guess I was one of those bleacher wolves who chewed on that raw meat you used to toss us." Williams said, "How could that be? You're a wonderful man." If it hadn't become clear to Ted just yet, it surely would by the end of his career: human nature changes in the outfield seats.

At Pensacola there were two routes available for a trainee: fighter-pilot training or flight-instructor training. For some the desirable—but reckless—choice was fighter training. For the more technical and deliberate—for the sane, most would say—the better option was flight-instructor training, a rounded and detailed program. Williams took the flight-instruction route. Though he would have occasion in the next war, the Korean, to fly a jet fighter by the seat of his pants in one extraordinary adventure, he was not by nature an aerial cowboy. He liked to practice the art of flying the same way he practiced the art of hitting—technically.

The new year, 1944, brought another assessment of wartime baseball. Stocking the teams were 157 draft exemptees and enough others of various stripes to mount a schedule. Many were still subject to the draft or awaiting orders. Boston, for example, would lose Tex Hughson to the navy after his 18th win in August and Bobby Doerr in September during the heat of the pennant race. On the other hand, Detroit would gain themselves a July gift when the first of the bonus babies, Dick Wakefield, was released from the navy soon enough to hit .359

and 12 home runs for the surging Tigers. Wakefield reenlisted for
another hitch after the 1944 season and played some ball with
Williams while stationed in Hawaii during 1945. His headiness over
his 1944 performance slickered him into a sucker bet with Williams
about how each would do after the war. Williams knew what had
apparently escaped Wakefield's attention: the quality pitchers were
coming back in 1946. Williams would get the better of the bet.

Most of the war news in 1944 was genuinely good, with the
Germans folding badly on their Eastern front, in Italy, in North
Africa, and even in Germany, subjected to massive daylight bombing
of Berlin by U.S. Liberators and Flying Fortresses. A nationally
syndicated newspaper series on the Bataan Death March sustained
the necessary rage to fuel the difficult run of island sieges against
Japanese strongholds that comprised America's Pacific strategy. The
detailed information on the treatment of surrendered forces in the
Philippines early in the war played no little role in framing the
propaganda policy that facilitated dropping the atomic bomb on
Hiroshima and Nagasaki the next year, 1945.

With the odds great that Williams would see active service in
1944, he did what so many other men in the armed forces did—he
married his girl. There was a wartime sociology of marriage, and
Williams was one of its participants. Later, his wife would say he was
one of its victims, but that was another matter. On May 4, 1944, Ted
Williams and Doris Soule were married in Pensacola, Florida. June
6 of that year brought D-Day in Europe, and the mood in the
country from then on was one of gradually building relief. But
Williams still assumed he was headed for the Pacific theater.

With the war entering its final phase in fall of 1944, the home-
front fans had a wonderfully tight four-team pennant race to cherish,
with the Yanks, Browns, Tigers, and Red Sox all in the thick of it in
September. But Boston faded woefully at season's end to close 12
games behind the Browns, who clinched with a dramatic October 1
win over the Yankees as the challenging Tigers lost to Washington. In
the all–St. Louis World Series that followed, the Cards took the
honors over the Browns four games to two.

The Red Sox plunge at the end salted an open sore. Even the
wartime hiatus couldn't put an end to the controversy surrounding
the Red Sox as a ball team. Jimmie Foxx, writing for the service

magazine *Yank,* tore into Joe Cronin for consistently mishandling Boston pitchers over the years. Foxx claimed Boston was the kiss of death for pitchers and that Dennis Galehouse, Jim Bagby, and Joe Heving all became better, or at least more effective, after leaving the team. Cronin lost the club pennants by butchering his staff year after year, Foxx claimed. This gave the Boston press and fans something to mull over for the rest of the war years, and, in a broader sense, for seasons after. A recurrent question for over two decades—"What's the Matter with the Red Sox?"—had many answers for many years: pitching, baserunning, fielding, managing, management, and, though he wasn't even there then, Ted Williams.

There was one more baseball event that passed virtually unnoticed in December 1944 that would end up having direct bearing on postwar ball and an even more far-reaching bearing on the history of the game in the 1960s and 1970s. At the annual minor league meeting in Buffalo, New York, on December 14, two Mexican businessmen, Ernesto Calderon and Frank Montes, made a strong pitch for affiliate status for Mexican League baseball. They wished to set up a system for developing and selling players. The American minor leagues turned their request down flat. Hence, the Mexican League would go it alone after the war, except for a few famous instances of raiding the major leagues for talent. The chain of events that followed formed the basis upon which individual players would challenge baseball's reserve system in the courts. When the major leagues tried to fend off the Mexican challenge by barring players who signed from returning, a number of players, including Danny Gardella of the Giants, sued. Gardella almost won, though he settled before a decision was rendered. Had he pursued the case further, the subsequent labor-relations battles between players and teams over the reserve clause and free agency might have taken a different course.

With 1945 came a powerful sense that wartime baseball was rounding to a close. The general manager of the Cubs, James Gallagher, had prepared a report on ballplayers during the war. Nearly 5,000 men from the rosters of the minor and major leagues had served their country. In 1941, 5,298 players were in organized ball; in 1944, that figure was reduced to a bare-bones 1,753 with only 12 of 44 separate minor leagues in action; in 1945, 3,576 former minor leaguers were in the services, as were 1,188 who had, at some time, played in the majors.

When the Red Sox opened spring training for this last interlude season they were only several hours from home in Pleasantville, New Jersey. Patton was leading his armies into the Saar Valley as a prelude to crossing the Rhine; *Murder, My Sweet,* with Dick Powell, and *National Velvet,* with the young Elizabeth Taylor, opened in New York; and some ballplayers of the wrong color for the major leagues were getting attention. On April 16 in Boston, just before the season opened and a few days after the death of President Roosevelt, several Negro league ballplayers—Jackie Robinson, of the Kansas City Monarchs; outfielder Sam Jethroe, of the Cleveland Buckeyes; and second baseman Marvin Miller, of the Philadelphia Stars—tried out for the Boston Red Sox at Fenway, with the field closed to press observers. This was an open tryout day, originally scheduled on April 12 but postponed because of Roosevelt's death.

The tryout had been arranged by Boston city councilman Isadore Muchnick and Wendell Smith, *Pittsburgh Courier* sports editor, and it proceeded with a certain cool efficiency. The Red Sox were especially impressed with Robinson but simply didn't know what to do with him. Their affiliate minor league teams were predominantly in the south, and, even in much less controversial circumstances, Boston management did not exactly rise to the dare. The Red Sox were more adept at sweeping dirt under the carpet than at cleaning up an unaccountable mess in baseball. So they gave the three black players application forms and left it at that. Red Sox scout Larry Woodall told Wendell Smith openly that he would sign Robinson if he had any idea where to dispatch him in the farm system. Meanwhile, the three players went to get a bite to eat on Tremont Street and joked about the application forms: "Don't call us, we'll call you."

Despite their indecision on the tryout, the Red Sox handled the matter with civility compared to the behavior of the Brooklyn Dodgers, the team that would eventually break the color line. Two weeks earlier, on April 7, the Dodgers had tried out Terris McDuffie, a pitcher, and Dave "Showboat" Thomas, a first baseman. But they did so only after threats by Nate Low, sports editor of the *Daily Worker,* and Joe Bostic, sports editor of the Harlem paper *People's Voice,* to invoke the Quinn-Ives antidiscrimination bill on behalf of black ballplayers. Branch Rickey had ideas of his own on this matter, but he hated strong-arm tactics. He said that only the Dodgers' seventh-place finish in 1944 made them immediately susceptible to community-group pressure, to which Low replied: "I know these guys are better than those you have on your team and could help you win."

Rickey had lunch with Low and Bostic and told them, "I'm more for your cause than anybody else you know, but you are making a mistake using force, dictating in this manner." He gave the ballplayers a tryout at the team's West Point Field House, but he brought out his nay-sayers, Durocher and Charlie Dressen. Showboat Thomas, said Rickey, "couldn't hit a breaking pitch with a bull fiddle," and McDuffie's arm was dying a slow death. This was a no go before it started, and Rickey hammered the last nail in the coffin: "Any ballplayer who came into camp and used the methods these people have used, demanding an immediate trial without any recommendation or scouting whatever, would have been ushered to the door immediately. However, because of the unusual circumstances, I acceded to their wishes and granted the tryout."

The season began in 1945 at the same time Allied troops were sweeping through Europe and beginning to discover the true gravity of the Nazi Holocaust. Nordhausen was liberated on April 15, with starving and racoon-eyed slave laborers horrifying Allied observers. Belsen was liberated on April 20, and the scenes of death and decaying corpses just got worse. In the Pacific theater, the death of Ernie Pyle on April 18 in Okinawa sent the country into another tailspin just after the death of President Roosevelt. Pyle was the soul and voice of the fighting man in World War II, and the news of his death was the closest thing to national anguish that the war produced on the home front.

Ted Williams was still stateside in Pensacola in April, and he remained there until June 6, after 13 months of service, part of it as a flight instructor. He claimed that his stint at Pensacola made him twice the flier he might have been. "You learn most teaching others." He had the same attitude about hitting a baseball; he taught all comers whether or not his pupils wished to learn. Baseball nostalgia had by then set in for Williams, but he was also feeling deep financial resentment about his military stint. An army magazine writer, Lieutenant J. G. Furman Bisher of the Pensacola Air Station, got

Williams to talk about his career hiatus, and the account was picked up by *The Sporting News.*

> It's a damned shame, but it's no more than is happening to anybody else's career. Sometimes I feel that fellows like Bob Feller and me have suffered most, career-wise. We were just before hitting the big dough for a sustained period and now we have had the very heart taken out of our baseball lives. On the other hand, Hank Greenberg and players his age had a chance to lay away a nest egg. I'm not complaining, though. This war is tough on everyone. I've still got two arms, two legs, and I'm healthy. For that I'm thankful, and I know I'm lucky.

Williams had put on some weight since his 1942 playing days, and he intended to carry it with him for more power once his career resumed. He was also singing a different tune about his future as a navy flier: "Flying is all right in wartime, and I like it, but when I get out of this uniform I'm never going to fly again." He was transferred to Jacksonville, Florida, for the last phase of his training, a ten-week operational program where he set base gunnery records for aerial fire. If the war had lasted long enough for him, he was prepared to pick off everything in the Pacific Ocean that moved.

The war ended before Williams's trained eye took aim at anything. He was still stateside in San Francisco through July and much of August. Howard Hughes was building his "Spruce Goose"; a B-25 bomber crashed into the 78th floor of the Empire State Building on July 28, killing 13; the army air corps unveiled its first jet fighter on August 1, a 550-mph marvel; and on August 4 a one-legged and war-ravaged pitcher, Bert Shepard, hurled part of a ball game for the Senators against the Red Sox, giving up three hits and a run in five innings in a losing effort. Two days later, the United States dropped an atomic bomb on Hiroshima, the final result of the war-long Manhattan Project, which in a test explosion two weeks earlier in New Mexico had stunned scientists by completely vaporizing a deserted observation platform. It did much worse in Hiroshima and, three days later, in Nagasaki.

On August 14, the *Boston Globe* ran a cartoon of Uncle Sam holding up the Statue of Liberty's raised arm with the caption: "And still champion . . ." With the war all but ceremonially over in both theaters, Ted Williams shipped out to Hawaii on August 18. Hank Greenberg had been back in his Tiger uniform since July, banging home runs as if he had never left for military service. Bobby Feller, also back from active duty, pitched a game against the Red Sox on September 5 at Fenway, losing 2–1 to a Boston team hopelessly ensconced in the second division.

At season's end in October, Hector Racine, president of the Montreal ball club in the International League, signed Jackie Robinson to a professional baseball contract. Tom Baird, co-owner of an all-black ball club, the Kansas City Monarchs, protested the signing as a violation of a verbal contract he had with Robinson, but on October 25 he said he would not get in the way of Jackie's path toward the majors. Branch Rickey downplayed the move because he did not wish, just yet anyway, to precipitate trouble with a host of major league teams that he knew opposed it. He covered his bet on Robinson and at the same time tried to pacify the leagues: "He is not now major league stuff and there is not a single Negro player in this country who could qualify for the National or American leagues." Rickey knew otherwise.

While discussing his tenure at St. Louis with the Cards, where blacks were not even permitted in parts of Sportsman's Park, Rickey was asked why he was developing Robinson: "I saw Negro clubs playing here at Ebbets Field. I watched them. I decided that something would have to be done about the Negro player in relationship to the major leagues. I want to win." The president of the National Association of Minor Leagues, W. G. Bramham, a southerner, was crudely disdainful of Rickey: "Whenever I hear a white man, whether he be from the North, South, East, or West, broadcasting what a Moses he is to the Negro race, right then I know the latter needs a bodyguard." Branch Rickey had a nice comeback, with a real historical twist to it: "Well, the time is ripe, and if any players from certain parts of the country feel the need to boycott teams with colored men on the roster, I am sure they will have a few other thoughts on the matter after a year or two working in the cotton mills."

◊ 8 ◊

The Real Thing
1946

TED WILLIAMS WAS DISCHARGED from the inactive list of the Marine Corps as a 2nd lieutenant on January 12, 1946, at Camp Miramar, California. In his tour on Hawaii, he had qualified for carrier landings but never saw active combat. From Camp Miramar he headed home with Doris to San Diego, where he relaxed, fishing on the Salton Sea and at San Diego's Lake Otay. Marine life had put about 20 extra pounds on him, and he began playing handball to shed a few of them before spring training. Everyone seemed eager for the homecoming year. A few months before, Hy Hurwitz did a profile on Johnny Pesky, stationed at an air base near Pearl Harbor. Pesky's service mates said Pesky chattered about "baseball and Ted Williams in his sleep."

Stars and athletes got back into the swing of things with everyone else in a big way in 1946. A sidebar piece in the February 9 *Boston Globe* was titled "Actresses Are Eating Again," with postwar fashions designed for a little more meat on the same bones. "Going fast on curves," the article continued, meant "good-bye to the silhouette." The exemplar of all this was the starlet Dagmar, a mid-'40s harbinger of Marilyn Monroe and Jayne Mansfield.

Postwar America was a lively place all the way around. A war hero from Boston, one John Fitzgerald Kennedy, readied to run for the 11th Congressional District; and a famous Boston politician, flamboyant Mayor James Curley, was convicted in the spring for mail fraud in a war-related bribery scheme. Curley would end up serving five months of a 6-18 month hitch before President Truman commuted his sentence. Meanwhile, tens of thousands of returning vets filled the burgeoning college campuses and flooded the mortgage home loan offices under the generous terms of the GI Bill. Many brought overseas brides. On February 4, the first vanguard of 456 brides arrived on the S.S. *Argentina* from England; 11,568 more new wives and newly minted dependents would arrive by the end of the month, with 30,000 more to follow.

That spring in Nuremberg, the Allies began settling accounts with the most prominent of the captured Nazis while still trying to absorb the enormity of civilian slaughter in Europe. In March Winston Churchill came to the United States for a visit. In the inconspicuous town of Fulton, Missouri, he told his audience that an Iron Curtain was descending over eastern Europe. The phrase and its political resonance would dictate western policy for the next several decades.

One of the first things President Truman had to do in the new year was put restraints on both labor and industry, restraining one from inflationary wage demands after the controls of the war and the other from exploitative price demands. Many of the ball clubs, having gotten rid of their mediocre wartime talent, were unleashing bigger bucks for their returning vets. The payroll of the majors was over $4,000,000, a seemingly enormous sum then, though now it seems just about enough to keep José Canseco in sliding pads. That spring the New York Yankees wanted a heftier $2.50 for a box seat, but Hank Greenberg had a better idea for beating the cost of living. Already the highest-paid player in baseball at $60,000 a year, Greenberg settled in for security on the home front by marrying Carol Gimbel of the famous department store family.

It was around this time that the more labor-conscious players were interested in forming a union, the American Baseball Guild, under the direction of Robert Murphy, a former Labor Relations Board examiner. Their idea was salary arbitration, an idea whose time would come, but in 1946 it simply chilled the owners. Many players were warmer to it, even more so when they realized that team ownership was less a rich man's hobby than a corporate dream. Del Webb, the speculative adventurer who purchased the Yankees on June 19, 1946, said just this of his acquisition: "The majors are now a battle of business giants. The rich man's plaything idea is out."

Webb had some startling notions, one of which was to put a price tag on Joe DiMaggio and see who came sniffing around. Mel Allen recalls the time he ran into Webb's partner, Dan Topping, and Tom Yawkey at Toots Shor's talking over a Williams-for-DiMaggio deal shortly after Webb purchased the Yanks. He thought they must have been kidding because neither made any attempt to change the subject when he joined them. He called the Yankee games on radio, after all, and Yawkey ought to have been cautious. But Yawkey truly admired Allen and genuinely wanted his reaction. Was this a crazy notion? Apparently, it wasn't. By season's end the Yankees were even considering a Joe DiMaggio–Mickey Vernon trade with the Senators. DiMaggio seemed to be playing a little long in the tooth in 1946, and this might be the right time. As for the Sox, Yawkey thought he could get DiMaggio plus Aaron Robinson or maybe another prospect, Larry "Yogi" Berra, for Williams. But what kind of sweetener was that squat little leftfielder? Yawkey turned to Mel Allen, wondering out loud: "Can I do this? Naw, the fans in Boston would hand me my scalp." Nothing more happened until the story leaked to the press around World Series time.

Berra to this day has no idea he was ever trade bait for Williams, though he and Williams chattered at each other incessantly over the course of their careers. Berra always begged Williams to take him fishing. For Williams's part, he loves to tell the story of riding on a train with Yogi through the Hudson River Valley after the war and sighting a tugboat flying a skull and crossbones. Williams guessed it was probably some company insignia from during the war; Yogi looked at it, and, thinking of his time in sick bay in the navy, said: "That's an *iodine* ship."

With the beginning of the year, Ted Williams had a new business manager, Fred Corcoran, who represented the Professional Golfers Association as well. Williams had gotten rid of his former business manager, James Silin, because of bad feelings surrounding his draft reclassification in 1942. Corcoran set him up with a run of renewed endorsements and with other personal investments, mostly in the rod-and-tackle business. This time Williams's choice proved to be a wise one; Fred Corcoran became a friend and confidant, another of those many father figures in Williams's life.

In February, Babe Ruth's smiling face appeared in an ad displayed all over the country. But rather than plugging cereal or fishing equipment, as Williams was doing, Ruth was boasting about the medicinal value of Raleigh cigarettes: "Now! Medical Science Offers *Proof Positive!* No other leading cigarette is safer to smoke," declared Ruth, baseball immortal. Not immortal enough, however: in 11 months he would undergo surgery for throat cancer, and in two years he would be dead.

The second week in February Ted Williams and his wife began the cross-country drive to Sarasota. Williams had signed his 1946 contract early, as usual, with a boost of $10,000 over his 1942 salary of $30,000. This would make it easy to kick into his mother's annuity funds again. A March 7 cartoon in *The Sporting News* said it all for this postwar spring: many of the great stars were depicted arriving— Williams, DiMaggio, Henrich—with the sorriest-looking excuse for a down-and-out ballplayer imaginable, labeled "WAR-TIME BASE-BALL," slouching off the field with a look of deep chagrin for ever having appeared there in the first place.

Williams looked and felt rusty in his first days at Sarasota, but he claimed he would unlimber and start ripping in short-enough order. He even dragooned a local high school kid to throw him batting practice the day he arrived when everyone else had already left the field. Hy Hurwitz, who thought Williams pretty much a blowhard, listened when Ted talked hitting: "There's only one thing you can count on Williams living up to. He'll always hit the ball. He'll say a million other things and won't live up to them, but when he talks about hitting the ball, you can always count on it."

Later that spring Ted spoke to Grantland Rice about the wartime hiatus and his hitting. Williams said he would have to get a line on the new pitchers—that would be a problem—but that he still believed he was the best hitter in the business: "I could have led the league in 1939, but I didn't think I was that good. A big mistake. Now I have kidded myself into thinking I am the greatest hitter in baseball. Maybe the greatest of all time. Maybe I'm not. But that's my target." He looked Rice in the eye: "Suppose I'm wrong? Then what? I'll still keep thinking I'm the best. They can't arrest me for that."

"Kidded myself" is only the mask of humility. Williams always recognized that hitting is technical on the one hand and psychological on the other. *Could've, would've, should've* are intangibles. They

Ted Williams shows up for publicity photos on June 26, 1936, after signing with the San Diego Padres. He is sporting a cap and jersey of one of the local teams he played for. *(San Diego Historical Society, Union-Tribune Collection)*

A young, 17-year-old Williams at Lane Field shortly after signing with the San Diego Padres in 1936. *(San Diego Historical Society, Union-Tribune Collection)*

Williams standing with Eddie Collins (wearing hat), general manager of the Red Sox, and Bill Lane, president of the Padres. Ted has just signed with the Red Sox after the winter baseball meetings in 1937. *(San Diego Historical Society, Union-Tribune Collection)*

Williams with Donie Bush, manager of the Minneapolis Millers, during spring training of 1938, after the Red Sox optioned Ted out to Minneapolis. *(Star Tribune, Minneapolis–St. Paul)*

First-ever photo of Ted Williams in a Boston uniform—spring training, March 1938. *(Boston Globe Photo)*

WILLIAMS OF RED SOX IS BEST HITTER

The most sensationally consistent hitter in big league baseball is a gangling, 22-year-old outfielder named Ted Williams of the Red Sox (see front cover). With most of the season behind him, Williams' hefty .400 plus average is almost certain insurance that he will ease into the American League batting title.

Williams is a great hitter for three reasons: eyes, wrists and forearms. He has what ballplayers call "camera eyes" which allow him to focus on a pitched ball as it zooms down its 60-ft. path from the pitcher's hand, accurately judge its intended path across the plate, and reach for it. He even claims he can see the ball and bat meet. The rest of his formula is never to stop swinging. On and off the field he constantly wields a bat to keep the spring in his powerful wrists. Even when he is in the outfield he sometimes keeps waving his arms in a batting arc. And, more than most other great batters, he keeps his body out of his swing, puts all his drive into his forearms.

Here on these pages are high-speed pictures taken by Gjon Mili which show the great co-ordination of these factors, the split-second release of power which enables Ted to hit safely four out of every ten times he comes to bat.

REPETITIVE-FLASH PICTURE SHOWS TED REACHING FOR A HIGH ONE, HITTING IT

This extraordinary sequence of photos originally appeared in *Life* magazine, September 1, 1941. *(Gjon Mili, Life magazine © Time Warner, Inc.)*

(Opposite page, bottom) Williams during 1941, his .406 season. *(National Baseball Library, Cooperstown, N.Y.)*

Williams swinging a rolled-up newspaper in his hotel room. This photo was reproduced from the June 19, 1941, issue of *The Sporting News. (Jules Pierlow,* The Sporting News*)*

Williams and Jimmie Foxx in 1941. *(National Baseball Library, Cooperstown, N.Y.)*

Visiting San Diego after his .406 season, Ted is pictured with his mother, May Williams (right), and his aunt Alice Williams. *(San Diego Historical Society, Photograph Collection)*

Williams enrolls in a naval flight training program in May 1942. *(Wide World Photos)*

count only insofar as a ballplayer feels them to count. That's why he behaved as he did even during batting practice. When he swaggered out of the cage asking Dom DiMaggio or Johnny Pesky for the thousandth time if he was the greatest hitter that ever lived and responding "Damn right" even before their obligatory "Sure, sure, Ted," it was not so much a matter of arrogance as it was a kind of Williams mantra.

Williams had not been near a batting cage for a long while, and he had not played nearly as many games in the service as other major leaguers on other bases. Williams had barnstormed most often in 1943, playing in more than 40 games; in 1944 he played half that many; and in 1945 just seven for the marines and for the American League All-Stars in Pearl Harbor. During the winter he had been offered a deal to play ten exhibition games in the Caribbean for $1,000 an appearance, but when Tom Yawkey heard about the offer to a cash-hungry Williams he paid him the same $10,000 not to play. The last thing Yawkey wanted was his prize player to get beaned somewhere in the tropics.

So when spring training began Ted Williams was sound and taking his cuts in Florida. Though he had lost some prime years to the war he was young enough to work out the kinks early. Veterans such as Greenberg and DiMaggio might find the long season of 1946 a bit tougher. In early March the *Globe* ran a Gene Mack cartoon of Williams, under palm trees near his beloved batting cage, accompanied by the following ditty:

News is all bad in Manchuria,
  Guess they'll oust Franco in Spain,
Strikes from Podunk to Peoria,
  Everything's wrong as the rain.

Wonder how's things in Dakota,
  I wouldn't know about that,
But everything's normal in Sota,
  Where Teddy is swinging his bat!

While kibitzing with reporters, some of whom he had not seen for years, Williams mentioned that he was specially motivated this season. A cocky Dick Wakefield had bet him $1,000 in Hawaii, where both were on duty, that Williams wouldn't match his 1942 home-run total of 37, and that Wakefield would match Williams's batting average on a handicap ratio of 5:4. That is, if Williams hit .500, Wakefield could win by hitting .400.

The two ballplayers had a good deal of time to kill in Hawaii; they also made subsidiary bets on an intricately handicapped home-run and runs-batted-in competition. When the commissioner's office got wind of these shenanigans, Happy Chandler spoke to Williams and Wakefield in order to put a public stop to their wager; the betting talk wasn't good for baseball. The commissioner's order turned out to be a godsend for Wakefield: he would have lost every row and every column of his betting card with Williams in 1946.

The first stories circulating in spring training had Williams trying to duck out of the team hotel and live with his wife. But Doris was already on her way to Boston when the story broke, trying to rent a house with a yard big enough for the couple's 75-pound German shepherd, Slugger. They ended up with a roomy apartment in Brighton. Ted would, indeed, live in the team hotel at Sarasota, and would, indeed, indulge the Red Sox front office and live with a roommate, Charlie Wagner, on the road. Would they get along? "Sure," said Williams, "if Charlie doesn't get temperamental." And what of Mrs. Williams? Did she like baseball? Did she understand her husband's nature? "I think baseball's a grand game," she said when reached in Boston, "but only when Ted's hitting." Her voice had the ring of genuine experience behind it.

During the early days of spring training, Williams was generally getting on better with everyone, and everyone was saying the marine experience had matured him. Williams later discounted such notions: "I'm always nice enough in the spring, until I read what those shitheads write about me." In 1946 the Red Sox, principally at Williams's and Dom DiMaggio's urging, barred writers from the locker room 15 minutes before and after games. DiMaggio said that the postgame time was an especially vulnerable period. It was when the players most regretted popping off, which was exactly what the writers liked about it.

There was little the Boston press corps could do about the new policy except fulminate, though the ban cut the afternoon writers off at their very lifeline. The morning paper folks could huff and puff over their typewriters; the afternoon guys had to get on the phone with tight deadlines right after ball games. But Yawkey was not an owner who sought wonderful press relations, nor did he think the press could hurt the Red Sox at the gate, so the pleas of the newspapermen fell on largely deaf ears.

The entire issue resembled the attitude Bill Terry used to take toward the press when he managed the Giants, and Terry remained convinced the resentment toward him by writers kept him out of the Hall of Fame for years. A Minneapolis sportswriter, George Barton, had written on the subject when Williams played in that city in 1938, complaining that Terry did the public a "disservice by closing his team off from the press and reporting only on the action taking place on the field."

Now, in 1946, Harold Kaese of the *Globe*, who simply despised the 15-minute rule, let the Red Sox have it broadside. Kaese began chanting the yearly refrain—"What's the matter with the Red Sox?"—earlier than usual this year, that is, before the season even began, though Boston would come up with a decidedly different answer for 1946. Kaese pointed out an alarming fact in a feature article on the Red Sox in the *Saturday Evening Post*, one that managed to insult an entire team. Not one of Joe Cronin's 11 Red Sox ball clubs had held first place in the American League after June 19 in any season: "That a team with the resources of the Red Sox should have such feeble recuperative power is hard to believe. It is explained not only by the Red Sox tendency to fold up, but by the ability of the Yankees to stay in front once they got there."

Kaese's piece was sheer murder: the Red Sox torture their pitching staffs, ignore percentages, let players loaf and malinger, display wanton favoritism, and are wretched assessors of talent. "Cronin," wrote Kaese, "doesn't know a ballplayer from a singing Cossack." Yawkey is "a bemused example of inherited wealth," Eddie Collins is a "bookend," and even "Fenway's pigeons are bums."

Cronin was legitimately upset at Kaese's attack and suggested mercenary reasons for his writing it, as if professional writers would shudder at such a charge: "Why did Harold write it? I suppose he got a thousand bucks for it." Yawkey said that Kaese had a right to speak his mind, and that he still felt about him the way he always had, a response that was wonderfully equivocal. Williams supplied a hedge and a challenge: "Well, maybe Cronin's got a few faults, but it would be great to make Kaese eat those words." When the subject was other than himself Williams was more relaxed, but he still expressed the almost vengeful joy of forcing writers to eat their words, a feast for some and a famine for others.

The Red Sox could ponder Kaese's comments all year long during the 15 minutes before and after their ball games. Of course, there were other things to ponder. It was not long before one of the bigger baseball stories of the decade began to break. Rumors circulated that the Mexican League was on a sustained raiding party in Florida and Cuba. Bobby Feller, always the consummate businessman and self-negotiator, had been approached by Mexican League director Jorge Pasquel, whose clever scheme was to purchase talent with the league's money and then distribute the players to various teams. Feller heard figures totaling $300,000 for three years for a jump to the Mexican League. Pasquel was after the likes of Ted Williams and Hank Greenberg as well, though so far his pickings had been slim: Danny Gardella, the body-building pretty boy of the Giants; and Mickey Owen, at the sagging end of his career.

Jorge Pasquel was a character right out of the Old West. He was worth between 30 and 50 million dollars, with a flair to match his bankroll. He toted his own six-shooters, as much for necessity's sake as for show; some of his teams played in real hellholes. In 1945 Pasquel traveled in the United States to visit his uncle at the Mayo Clinic in Rochester, Minnesota. On the way back to Mexico he stopped in St. Louis and took in a game between the Cards and the Pirates. A friend at the ball park told him he was lucky—he could see Marty Marion play his first game at shortstop since ending a holdout for a contract worth $12,500. Pasquel said he'd double that salary for a player of Marion's caliber for his Mexican League. His friend told him that the Cards held the rights to Marion under the reserve clause: the player can only negotiate with the team he happens to play for. Pasquel couldn't believe it—this was "funny business" for America.

Jorge Pasquel took a closer look at the personal ledger sheets of the major league stars. No one had been raking it in and those in the services had not been building up much of a cash reserve during the

war years. The major league owners were frightened of inflation and
the players saw dollar signs in each other's eyes. In March, Jorge
dispatched his brother, Bernardo Pasquel, to talk to Ted Williams in
Sarasota. Joe Cronin tried to head off the encounter, but Williams,
partly in fun and partly in earnest, said, "Where is the fellow? Get
me an interpreter." Cronin sent over Johnny Orlando to pose as
interpreter, but Pasquel didn't fall for that stunt. Later, he cornered
Williams in the hotel lobby and spoke to him for a few minutes,
promising short fences, prevailing winds, and nearly $500,000 for a
three-year contract. Williams asked, "Have you got Feller?" "Porqué
no?" responded Pasquel, which wasn't exactly an answer. "Well, if
you've got Feller," says Williams, "that's reason enough for me to
stay in the American League."

Pasquel kept at it. He invited Ted and Doris to Mexico for a visit,
even offering to put $250,000 down on the table as a bond against
Williams's salary. "That's bush league," said Williams, speaking the
literal truth while intending the metaphoric insult. Pasquel walked
away, undeterred: a few minutes later he offered Johnny Pesky
$45,000 per year with a $10,000 advance.

On March 30, Jorge Pasquel nabbed his biggest prize of the spring.
He signed Vern Stephens of the St. Louis Browns to a five-year
contract with Veracruz, with enough up-front money to put more
than his yearly Brown's salary in the bank as a postwar bonus.
Stephens could do what only a few shortstops could do—hit around
.300 and with power. For three years running during the war he hit
more than 20 home runs, and when the Red Sox got him in 1948 he
would do even better. Pasquel was getting a quality player. But in the
next few weeks the saga of Vern Stephens would have enough intrigue
to rival the best postwar espionage movies.

Early in April the majors began wheeling the heavy artillery into
place. Commissioner Happy Chandler claimed that attorneys for
organized baseball were considering the option of banning for life
any jumpers to the Mexican League. This upset Jorge Pasquel even
more than the reserve clause did. So he offered Chandler $50,000
plus all living expenses to chuck American baseball and become
commissioner of the Mexican League. "How can he banish a free
people?" Jorge asked. "The United States is a free country. A man is
free to work where he wants." Pasquel's interests at this point were not

exactly constitutional, but the question was raised precisely this way in the reserve clause and free agency battles of the 1960s and 1970s.

At about this time, Vern Stephens arrived in Veracruz, went out to the ball park, took one look at the conditions under which he would have to play—"Hell, it's like an armed concentration camp down here"—and, on April 5, started to back out of the deal. He got in touch with Charley DeWitt, the St. Louis Browns' traveling secretary, who made arrangements with friends in Monterrey for Stephens to jump the Veracruz club and head to San Antonio. Stephens's father, posing as a St. Louis newspaperman, helped spirit his son out of the country.

When Pasquel discovered that his star had flown the coop, he contacted him by phone and told him he intended to sue. Stephens pondered the historical relations between Mexico and the United States, considered his legal position, and rendered an appropriate response: "So what? I didn't get the $17,500 I asked from the Browns, but I'm sure happy to be back. Pasquel can have his money—I don't want it." But Pasquel was by now livid. He tried plan B: he offered Bill Roberts of the *Houston Press* an intermediary's fee of $5,000 to talk Stephens into returning to Veracruz.

Nothing worked. Two days later, Pasquel encountered more problems. Mickey Owen threatened to desert the Mexican League. Pasquel threatened to sue him for $100,000. Owen demurred for a while and then jumped anyway later in the season, claiming that during ball games Pasquel was making tactical decisions for the team Owen managed. And the man had six-shooters to back him up. Happy Chandler, more furious at Pasquel than at the renegade ball players, said the majors would gladly pick up the legal tab for Stephens and Owen.

By now Pasquel had contacted friends in the Mexican government who were putting pressure on the U.S. State Department. Baseball, which had so successfully skirted its constitutional vulnerability on the basis of interstate commerce, was now vulnerable on the matter of diplomatic relations. The Mexican League shenanigans would get even more ridiculous later in the season when for a moment Pasquel thought he had Stan Musial's name on a contract, until he looked more closely and realized that Stan had forgotten how to spell his last name: the fake signature was *Musiel*.

The second week in April, the Red Sox swung up the coast from spring training and settled into Boston for the traditional exhibition set with the Braves. Williams belted two out of the park on April 12 in an 11–5 Red Sox win. He seemed to carry his few extra postwar pounds with gusto. When the season opened on April 16, at Griffith Stadium in the nation's capital, Williams hit a tremendous home run, one of the legendary drives of his career. With two outs and no one on in the top of the third, he tied into a 3-2 pitch served up by Roger Wolff and hit it 12 rows into the center-field bleachers, about 460 feet from home plate. Harry Truman was on hand to get a look—if he could see that far.

Another ballplayer, a minor leaguer for Montreal, got off to a good start in his opening game. Jackie Robinson hit a three-run homer and three singles and had two stolen bases before a packed house of 25,000 fans in Jersey City. The Montreal clubhouse was jubilant after the game, and Robinson was pleased by his performance and by their reaction: "One thing I cared about was that my teammates backed me up. There wasn't any riding out there, but if there was I wouldn't have minded as my team was behind me. They've been great." If the Dodgers could make their black recruitment scheme work, they had a couple of other prospects on the line: Don Newcombe and Roy Campanella were part of the regular pitching-rotation battery for the Nashua (New Hampshire) Dodgers of the New England League in 1946.

Boston began the season hot, and took a 6–1 record into Fenway for a midweek series with the Yankees that packed the stadium. As if to prove that baseball's returning stars were mortal, Williams hit into three double plays in the game on April 24 and DiMaggio went 0 for 6. But the Red Sox continued to smash their way through the season. Williams enjoyed a run of nine games at the beginning of May that saw him hit four home runs and stroke .545. He hit a bit of a glitch in Yankee Stadium for a couple of games, including one on May 11 in which he heard a sound that had grown into a dim memory from prewar days: a boo. He took a third strike that he thought was away from the plate. In left between innings he kicked a divot or two and then worked himself into a lather, kicking at the turf in left as if he were plowing it for seeding. The next moment he entirely lost Heeney Majeski's pop in the sun, and the Yankee fans let him have it, partly in derision and partly in delight.

Jerry Nason, commenting on the sort of vile remarks to which

Williams was so regularly subjected around the league and in Fenway, wondered why he didn't climb into the stands and crack heads with a bat: "The ordinary ballplayer, in the throes of a peeve either at himself or his umpirical majesty, may indulge in dropkicking divots from the ball field without inspiring fruity remarks from the stands. But not Ted the Kid."

Williams's average receded from its empyrean heights, but the Red Sox continued to surge. And then in another nine-game sequence early in June, Williams hit .559 with six home runs; one of them, a shot in the second game of a doubleheader at Fenway against the Tigers, was by all accounts the longest, if not the hardest, he ever hit in his home park. The day was June 9, and one Red Sox fan remembers it particularly well. His name was Joseph A. Boucher, a construction engineer from Albany, who took in an occasional Fenway game. He was deep in the right-field bleachers, dubbed the "light artillery target area" by the local press, when Williams leaned into a Fred Hutchinson fastball. Boucher tried to gauge the ball and catch it with his straw hat. No such luck. Williams's ball blew a hole in the hat and landed another 12 rows up, a full 34 rows from the fence. This was the fourth tape-measure home run of the year for Williams. Those few extra pounds of beefcake he carried back with him from the service were taking their toll on American League pitching.

By June 11 the Sox were at 41-9 and 10 games ahead of the Yankees. They had already produced winning streaks of 15 and 12 games. "A hero a day" is the way the papers began reporting the games. There was nary a soul in Boston wondering out loud this year what was the matter with the Red Sox, though the team was known to hit some grievous midsummer swoons. But perhaps not this year. Boston had some real balance, powered by Williams, Rudy York, and Doerr, sped by Pesky and Dominic DiMaggio, steadied by the veteran Pinky Higgins at third, and sustained by a genuine pitching staff led by Tex Hughson, Boo Ferriss, Mickey Harris, and Joe Dobson.

At midseason the Red Sox placed eight men on the American League All-Star Team. Williams had been on a power tear, with 23 home runs for the season, and he did not disappoint in the All-Star Game, which was played at Fenway. The American League walked away with the win 12-0, and Williams had the best All-Star Game of his life, with four hits on the day. He hit one out against Kirby Higbe in the fourth, then singled off Ewell "the Whip" Blackwell (known around the National League as "Death on Vacation") in the fifth and seventh. When Williams came to the plate in the eighth, he faced Rip Sewell, the Pirate pitcher who broke in with Detroit in the early 1930s and had played for Pittsburgh since the late 1930s. In 1941 he hurt his toe and changed his motion, developing a new pitch for his new look: an eephus ball, a "nuthin' " name for a "nuthin' " pitch. The etymology is actually more precise: "eephus-eiphus-ophus" is a crap-shooting phrase for the high lob of the dice.

Vern Stephens blooped a single off the pitch before Williams got his chance in the inning. Sewell was determined to live or die by the eephus. The hometown Boston fans were getting a huge kick out of the challenge. Williams fouled off the first eephus behind him. The second was outside. Sewell then fired a conventional straight ball for a strike. On the next pitch Williams crept up, taking Bill Dickey's advice on how to hit the thing. He inched toward the front of the batter's box and measured the upward arc of his swing with the by-now downward arc of the ball. Smash. Almost solely on steam provided by the force of his swing, Williams hit a tremendously high shot 380 feet into the bullpen. Umpire Larry Goetz knew full well Williams was out of the box when he hit it but said nothing: "We're not really playing for blood."

The game was broadcast all over the country, and several friends and a host of curious kids on Utah Street in San Diego were trying to get May Williams to take an interest in her son's play. Sewell's blooper was a sight to behold, and the announcers on the radio were getting their listeners all worked up over the absurdity of the pitch. The mood on Williams's street was festive already, and when everyone heard the home-run call from the radio on the porch, the screaming and laughing confused May. She had a bit of a time grasping the mirth and joy about the particular pitch Williams hit. "It's a blooper pitch, a balloon," said the kids. "Ted hit a balloon? That's very good. He's a wonderful boy."

After the All-Star break the Red Sox and Williams picked up where they had left off. In the first game of a doubleheader against the Indians at Fenway on July 14, Williams hit three home runs, drove in eight runs, and sewed up an 11–10 win for Boston. Lou Boudreau, playing manager of the Indians, went 5 for 5 in the first game and didn't like to contribute that much to his own cause and still lose. In the second game, Williams began by doubling down the line, and Boudreau had had enough. The next time Williams appeared at the plate Boudreau set a Cleveland alignment that placed second-baseman Meyer about 40 feet into the outfield and about 10 feet off the foul line. Boudreau moved from short to a deep second, and third baseman Keltner played just on the right-field side of second base. Two outfielders played right. And it worked, to the extent that Cleveland's pitchers gave Williams anything to hit. He walked a couple of times and grounded out for the rest of the game.

This game has been recorded as the first time that a truly pronounced shift was employed for Williams, but something like it had occurred on September 18, 1941, against the Indians. Actually, there was a dramatic Williams shift employed in Boston on April 23, 1926. But that shift was for Cy Williams of the Phils. The *Boston Globe* for that date had on its sports page an amusing Gene Mack cartoon of the Braves' weird alignment for Cy Williams. Three infielders were on the right side, with the third baseman playing short and the shortstop behind the bag to the right of second. All three outfielders spread from left center to the foul line in right. Everyone in the cartoon had a slightly bewildered look on his face.

Not all teams in the American League put the shift on Williams in the manner Boudreau used it, but Cleveland's policy inaugurated a modified Williams defense everywhere. For the first few games it hardly seemed to matter. Williams hit .526 at Fenway from July 14 through the end of the home stand 11 games later. From then on, the shift and its modifications began to bother him. Oddly, his home-run production suffered more dramatically than his batting average. He was hitting .353 before Boudreau's shift, and his average from July 14 to the end of the season was still healthy at .329. But he had 26 home runs on July 14 and hit only 12 more the rest of the year. It is difficult to generalize from a few months. Williams bullied the shift, and he admitted to trying to drive balls through the stacked alignment. Trying to hit the ball harder resulted in hitting it less hard. There was a subtle difference between the effect of anger—which usually sharpened his concentration—and the effect of pressing—which invariably disturbed the precision of his timing. Williams himself thought this was precisely the case, and he eventually did much better against the shift by ignoring it rather than by trying to smash through it.

Purely by coincidence, a baseball statistician was working on a Williams spread sheet right around the time of the shift. He was trying to figure out where Ted hit the ball and how. John Chamberlain, working on a profile of Williams for *Life*, got his hands on the raw data. The breakdown revealed that only 10 percent of his hits so far in 1946 were to left, a healthier 29 percent were to center, and 61 percent were to right. But the key to these numbers lay elsewhere. Of Williams's hits to left, 60 percent were grounded through the infield; of his hits to center and right, 72 percent were in the air. Williams's power swing, as the bicycle brigade that used to follow him around San Diego knew, put balls on an upward trajectory. Bunching infielders was not likely to make that much of a statistical difference, and the outfielders played him to pull anyway.

The significant spot Boudreau's shift plugged was the line drive right down the foul stripe over the first baseman's head. That was a favorite Williams spot. So what was he going to do about all this? Ty Cobb and Paul Waner advised him to alter his stroke and hit to left. But Williams was resistant. The position he took was sensible: "I'm not going to tamper with my style just to hit a few extra singles to left. I've spent too many years learning how to pull the ball to right to take chances. If I change style now I might lose my power to right. I'll keep swinging away even if they put the catcher out in right field. If I smack the ball over the fence they'll have a hard time fielding it." This was essentially what Babe Ruth said in Cleveland one day, with Mel Harder on the mound, when the Indians pulled a kind of shift on him. "Hell, I got five singles to left and the fans booed." John Lardner once asked Ruth what he thought of the suggestion that Williams ought to hit more to left: "Bullshit." Lardner was kind enough to translate: "Like all sluggers, he preferred to hit where his power was."

The only calculated move Williams made to handle the shift was to step back just a bit from the plate so that he might pull the ball less. He would have preferred not even doing this, but he recognized that it would open up the field for him. This was a tactic he developed into a fine art two years later, in 1948. Toward the end of his career his bat speed slowed just enough—a split second—to take care of making him a better all-fields hitter naturally.

Shift or no, on July 21 Williams hit for the cycle for the first time in his career in the second game of a doubleheader against the

Browns at Fenway. For the day he went 7 for 9, jacked his average up to .365 and his home-run total to 27. And then he plunged for almost four weeks, hitting just over .200 for that sustained spell, though he added five home runs. The Red Sox, with a balanced and proficient ball club, had no difficulty holding onto first during Williams's dry spell; in fact, it was a coast to the pennant marred only by a seeming reluctance to clinch mathematically when the time was ripe.

Early in August Williams decided to take a nip of the hair of the dog that bit him. He agreed to do a column, under the header "TED WILLIAMS SAYS . . . ," for $1,550 a week for the *Globe* during the rest of the season and, the fates willing, the Boston World Series. He told John Chamberlain, who was in the midst of the *Life* magazine profile, that the column was a pain in the ass, though he didn't have to work much at it. For the most part, Williams played Mr. Nice Guy. He stroked his friends and foes alike, claiming that he intended "nothing controversial. I've had enough problems in the last two weeks trying to get base hits against screwy defenses."

A rival columnist, the great sportswriter Red Smith, was doing much better work with the pen right around that time. He wrote a syndicated piece on August 5 that tracked Jackie Robinson's first season. There was a real poignancy to some of Smith's stories. For example, he wrote of Robinson traveling alone to the ballpark in Baltimore because he was forced to stay in a segregated hotel. But whatever their prejudices, the Baltimore fans could not restrain themselves when they saw the man play: they gave Robinson a standing ovation after it took nearly the whole Baltimore squad to put the tag on him in a simple run-down. In a game at Syracuse, the first-base umpire was livid enough to threaten to empty the Syracuse dugout if the taunts didn't stop, but Robinson told him sotto voce to leave it alone. Branch Rickey had warned him about abuse coming from rivals and focused him, instead, on the support from his own Montreal club. That was tactically right; the baseball color line had to be broken by expanding a wedge from the apex, not the base.

For his column on August 12, Williams provided a little insight into what life was like for the off-duty ballplayer. On an off-day after a Yankee series in New York, Williams, Cronin, and Johnny Pesky took in a Dodgers-Giants game at the Polo Grounds. Williams began joking with a fan in the dugout seats about the short right-field porch:

"So, Williams, you'd like to hit here, huh? Or maybe you wanna go to Mexico. Listen, I can cut you a deal. Maybe $250,000 a year. For 25 percent I'll arrange it. Send you right to Mexico. A mansion you can live in—ten rooms. With a pool. How's that, Williams, huh? And you don't even have to eat down there. Just breathe in the air."

In spite of himself, Williams was enjoying the column, which was talked out in spurts and crafted by the *Globe* sports desk into something resembling stream-of-consciousness prose. On occasion he delivered up technical bits about the game that revealed a thing or two about the way he approached hitting. His column on August 17 addressed on-the-field chatter. During a pitching change late in one of the games in a recent series at Yankee Stadium, Williams asked ump Cal Hubbard about an earlier at-bat: "What was that 3-2 pitch I squibbed to second in the first inning?" Hubbard: "Hell, Ted, I don't remember." As a hitter, Williams obviously wanted to register the pitch for his internal memory; as an ump, Hubbard forgot the pitch because he never had to call it.

Williams, who would talk to the foul lines on a ball field whether or not they answered back, marveled at DiMaggio: "Now I know why they call DiMaggio the Sphinx. He played left because of his sore arm today and we passed each other sixteen times going to our positions between innings. I heard one sound out of him all day long, a grunt after he flied out to Wally Moses 420 feet away in center." Apparently Ted managed to get a few more words out of DiMaggio before the game. In a column for August 19, he recalled how he cornered DiMaggio and Keller at the Stadium on this trip and asked them to think hard about whether they actually saw the ball hit their bats. Williams had a theory that hitters, for the most part, only imagined seeing the bat and ball at the moment of impact. Both agreed, but DiMaggio jokingly pulled rank: "Well, maybe I've seen it hit the bat a few more times than you said you did. But then I've been playing a few more years."

The Red Sox were well ahead in the pennant race, and excitement came from unexpected sources. Cleveland was back in town for a series, and during the game on August 26 the Indians moved into their Williams shift, with Keltner deserting his position at third to take up on the port side of second base. A dwarf jumped out of his seat along the third-base dugout, grabbed Pinky Higgins's glove—the players still left their gloves on the field in foul territory when their team was at bat—and took up a position at third, ready for whatever Williams might do. Everyone in the park was convulsed, and even the Fenway security personnel were gentle in removing this small surprise supplement to Cleveland's defense.

The next day, August 27, Williams was at the center of an event much less funny. He was cut off—so he said—while driving in Holliston; his car was badly smacked up and Doris was moderately shaken. Fortunately, Williams's friend and neighbor, John Blake—a state policeman—was with him. The incident received no controversial play. Having a cop in the car did wonders for his version of the accident, though after four years of legal tangles the courts eventually saw it otherwise.

Williams needed a lift. The shift and a reconvened slump were getting him down in late August and early September. He was even writing in his column about having one sixty-fourth of an inch shaved off his bat handle for a snappier swing. In frustration, he even bunted for a base hit in a game against the A's at Fenway after umpire Bill Summers told him to give it a try. But Williams was wary of such an approach to the shift. He was Ted Williams, not Rabbit Maranville. Later in the A's series Williams hit a line shot into the teeth of a fierce wind, and Elmer Valo grabbed it just before it left the park in deepest right center near the bullpen. Williams threw a tantrum and flung his glove to the ground in left when those he so charitably called the "New England buzzards" got to him the next inning. On his at-bat in the sixth he topped one to the shift-infested right side of the diamond and didn't even run the ball out. The whole park let go with another salvo of boos. Joe Cronin made a point of saying that he intended to do nothing—a big fat nothing—to Williams: "He's been struggling. Give him a break."

When the Red Sox arrived for a series in Washington, Bobo Newsom walked over to the Red Sox clubhouse and told Williams, as only he could, that he had to calm down on the field. Newsom was a plain-speaking character, and he delighted in Williams. Ted wasn't about to take his advice, but he loved listening to Newsom's talk: "You're as big as Ruth. The fans react to every move you make, every gesture." Williams came back: "Bullshit. When the day comes when I can't hit them home runs, they'll skin me alive." Bobo thought about this a minute, and simply agreed, as if Williams was getting huffy about the disposition of atoms in the universe: "Well, that's baseball," said Bobo, "don't forget it." Newsom then made his point: "Ted, it looks like you're unhappy out there. Everybody knows it. That's when they go after you."

The Red Sox began losing ball games consistently in the first weeks of September, but they were so far ahead the pennant was less the issue than the quality of play, the edge necessary to go into the Series on an upswing. Cleveland's Bobby Feller didn't help any—he shut Boston down for their sixth loss in a row. Feller was driven by a public feud with the Red Sox over a barnstorming tour he organized for postseason play. The idea was to help the ballplayers recoup some wartime losses by earning a bit extra after the season and the Series. He wanted Williams to play as a draw to the promotion and offered him $10,000 to do so. Yawkey had the same attitude toward Feller's scheme as he had at the beginning of the year to Williams's playing in the Caribbean. He didn't want his star hurt. So he said he would kick in the $10,000 to keep Williams hunting or fishing somewhere after the season. Feller responded that he would cut other Red Sox players from his squad, those whom Yawkey would not even consider paying to default.

Feller's tactic was to drive a wedge between management and players, and if it happened at World Series time so much the better. Williams wasn't touching this one with one of his snazzy fishing poles: "Let Bobby talk. No comment." Feller did plenty of talking for the rest of his career about baseball's labor relations. He was a savvy and shrewd promoter of himself and he thought more than most about the financial model under which players were held as chattel by ball clubs largely protected from the checks of interstate commerce under some shaky legal precedents. The scales fell off Feller's eyes in the postwar years, and he was a nuisance to baseball owners right through the Senate antitrust hearings in the 1950s.

On September 13, Williams met with another variation on the shift. Lou Boudreau was, in modern parlance, trying to mess with his head. The Red Sox were playing at Old League Park in Cleveland, and Boudreau figured that the short right-field fence, 290 feet in the corner, would prove so tempting to Williams that the Indians could play no one in left field, a more distant 375 feet, at all. So in yet another version of the shift, the Indians' leftfielder, Pat Seerey, played 20 feet on the grass behind third and 15 feet from the foul line. Centerfielder Felix Mankiewicz was way over in right center and deep. In the first inning, Williams took one look at this defense and changed his shift theory. Forget the right-field porch. He pasted one off Red Embree on the line to left center. The ball rolled to the wall 400 feet away and came to a rest in a gutter near the fence. Mankiewicz pursued it, relayed to a beaten Boudreau, who had run out about 300 feet himself as Keltner scampered to third for the throw. But Williams flew right by the bag—as Hy Hurwitz put it, he looked like a cross between Jesse Owens and Man o' War—and touched the plate before Boudreau could do much of anything with the retrieved ball.

This inside-the-park home run was sweet in so many ways. It beat the shift, won a tense 1-0 game for Tex Hughson, and clinched the pennant for the Red Sox, their first since 1918, the year of Ted Williams's birth. Unfortunately, the postgame celebration was not a simple matter. Boston won their game before Joe DiMaggio's 24th home run of the year beat Detroit a couple of hours later to resolve the mathematics of the pennant race. By then the players were scattered. Williams, of course, could scatter with the best of them. In an interview with Pulitzer Prize–winning journalist Russell Owen, he had put it point-blank: "When I look at a guy all day and am working with him, hell, I don't want to look at his mug all night, do I? When I'm on the field I'm one of the team."

Yawkey wanted all the Red Sox rounded up for a celebration before he opened even one bottle of champagne at the Statler Hotel in Cleveland, and traveling secretary Tom Dowd was dispatched to gather the loose marbles. He found Tex Hughson after four hours, but Johnny Pesky was out with some old navy buddies and Ted Williams was tying fishing flies with a friend in Cleveland named Bill Whyte. Dowd saw trouble on the horizon so he made up a story that Williams was visiting a war vet in a local hospital. The *Globe* headline the next day was "TED DUCKS PARTY TO VISIT DYING VET."

When that cover was blown, Williams had to take it on the chin from his most grievous enemy, Dave the Colonel Egan of the *Boston Record*: "Williams is for Ted Williams and Ted Williams alone." This would be yet another crisis in a horrendous relationship with this heavy-drinking, Harvard-educated lawyer turned sensationalistic writer. Egan used Williams for copy fodder and was merciless as an insult artist, except on matters of Williams's private life, where Egan's legal training surprisingly infused his writing with something resembling discretion. But on the ball field, Williams was fair game for the clever Colonel, who, later in the '40s, began calling Williams "the inventor of the automatic choke." He was a tough customer, though he spread his venom with a kind of democratic zeal. Once Egan offered homage to the local gods in his column when Casey Stengel, managing the Braves in Boston, was hit by a taxicab.

The issue of Williams as a team player haunted him from his early days when Lefty Grove had an occasional opinion on the matter. But, generally, the Red Sox had few complaints with him on the field. He gave it his best, which, at times, could be startlingly good and almost always savvy. As for the best he could give the team, that was generated from the intensely focused contest between himself and every pitcher he faced. Baseball is a game in which teamwork can influence some aspects of any given at-bat but, in truth, not *that* many. A home run starts out as inherently personal; it's for the team when the runs it produces go up on the scoreboard. Williams was later to put this starkly: "Who up there in the press box can judge whether a man hits home runs as a tribute to his wife, for his own ego, in memory of his mother, for his salary, for God, or for his team?"

By late September Williams was fading in his contest with Mickey Vernon of the Senators for the batting title and with Hank Greenberg for the home-run title, though his all-around performance and that of the Red Sox made him the American League's Most Valuable Player when the vote was taken after the season. But now the press hounds were on him. He was so tired after the long season and the wartime hiatus that he kept his own counsel and just tried to rest for the World Series. This was a big week in sports, highlighted by the great National League pennant race and the brilliant Rocky Graziano–Tony Zale fight before 30,000 at Yankee Stadium on September 27. In the sixth, Zale's savage right to the stomach and left hook to the chin put Graziano down for the count. They would fight again. As for the pennant race, the Red Sox still had no idea who they were going to play. The Cardinals and the Dodgers were in another of their almost-patented pennant finales, clawing and scratching at each other until the last day of the season, when they both lost, forcing a best-of-three playoff, the prospect of which, according to Red Smith, was so exciting that it might make an anticlimax of the World Series.

For an already listless Red Sox ball team this was not good news. But a generous collection of American Leaguers agreed to play three games with Boston to keep them sharp. The conglomerate squad would split the revenues for the games at Fenway, and the Red Sox would play for a prorated share of their yearly salary. Everybody had an angle in postwar America.

The playoffs began on the very day the Nuremberg tribunal declared several key Nazis of the German Reich—Göring, Ribbentrop, Streicher, Speer, and Hess—guilty of "crimes against humanity." St. Louis took the first game, beating the Dodgers and Ralph Branca 4–2. In the tune-up series at Fenway, Williams leaned into a spinning curve by Mickey Haefner and took it on the elbow in the nippy fall weather. His bone was badly bruised but not damaged beyond that. The Cards dispatched the Dodgers in short-enough order in game two, beating them 8–4 in a gloom-drenched Ebbets Field. Boston, with Williams taking whirlpool treatment for his elbow, ended up winning two of three from the American League All-Stars.

The World Series was set to go when the story broke about the possible Williams-for-DiMaggio trade, rekindled from the meeting between Dan Topping and Tom Yawkey earlier in the year. This became a hot topic at the wrong time. Boston fans had the image of DiMaggio shooting for Fenway's Green Monster in left field on their minds when the St. Louis Cardinals ought to have been a higher priority. Yankee fans were a bit more subdued about the image of Williams aiming at the Stadium's short right-field barrier designed for Ruth. Williams had his own opinion, as one might guess, on these matters, though he, too, would have done better to concentrate on the Cardinals. He pointed out that, as power hitters, he and DiMaggio received a better selection of pitches to hit in their home parks because of the distant power fields in each. Pitchers figured the park could take up a little slack. Williams's argument seemed at least worth making. Perhaps he would have terrorized the right-field porch at the Stadium and Joe the wall at Fenway. And perhaps both would have gotten just that much less to hit from pitchers around the league.

At any rate, the deal had broken down on both sides, the Yankees not willing to give too much and the Red Sox, in their way, timid about taking too little. But the story of the deal resurfaced in the October 5 *Globe* with a bizarre first-page account of a torch singer, Betty Sharp, who claimed to be looking for an apartment in Boston because she was getting married to Joe DiMaggio: "I could have told you two weeks ago that Joe would be playing for the Red Sox." It turned out that Betty herself, whom DiMaggio admitted to dating twice, had placed a call to Joe that afternoon to tell him about the breaking story. DiMaggio made his own contacts with the press: "Why is she doing this? I hardly know her." Need he have really asked? By her own shrewd, if unscrupulous, doing, Betty Sharp had gotten her name all over the Boston, New York, and San Francisco papers.

The Boston Red Sox had not been playing especially well for the last month. Williams was upset at the trade rumors, telling his teammates that he would skip to Mexico rather than live in New York. There were other live trades on the rumor agenda: Hal Newhouser and Dick Wakefield of Detroit for Williams. Williams had hit .474 with six home runs in Briggs Stadium on the year, and a Detroit trade was viable for Williams but less so for Yawkey and the Red Sox. Nonetheless, Yawkey would not directly deny the rumors, dodging the question with the equivocal "I wouldn't dignify these matters with comment."

Harold Kaese, who had blasted the Sox as losers before the season began, couldn't say much about his springtime charges with Boston readying for the Series, so he turned full cannon on Williams and all the trade talk: Yawkey must come out and stop these rumors. This was not the time for the Red Sox to submit their lineup to the scrutiny of trades. Didn't the Red Sox management understand even the basics of emotional readiness? Besides, the Yanks didn't really want Williams—"He ain't a money player"—and he couldn't hit in the Stadium (a paltry .147 in 1946). Kaese apparently forgot that for the past five seasons Williams had averaged .316 at Yankee Stadium.

The St. Louis Cardinals preferred that the controversy swirl around the Red Sox. They prepared for this World Series with extraordinary diligence. Knowing that if they scrambled to win the pennant they would be facing Boston, the Cardinals dispatched scouts early to track the Sox through most of September. They thought they could win by playing their usual speed game. More important, they thought they could outsmart Ted Williams. The trick was not to beat him with the percentage pitch but the percentage guess. If the distinction seemed a fine one, the scouts put it to the Cardinal staff this way: Williams can hit anything—so don't try to throw the right pitch, try to throw the unusual pitch. Take chances; pitch to his power; throw breaking stuff whatever the count. Williams was very much a guess hitter and the Card pitchers were told not to set or fall into patterns that he could guess consistently. Harry "the Cat" Brecheen turned this suggestion into a fine art.

The Series opened on a Sunday in St. Louis with the Red Sox winning 3-2 on Rudy York's home run in the 10th inning. Cards manager Eddie Dyer put a shift on Williams that left Marty Marion at short but moved Whitey Kurowski all the way from third to deep second. Red Schoendienst shifted to a wide first, and Musial hugged the foul line. With this alignment Ted whipped a line drive over Kurowski for a single. In his column Williams wryly noted that "I singled to right over the third baseman's head." Stan Musial, who had a terrific year at .365, went 1 for 5 on the day with a double.

On Monday the Sox were shut down 3-0 by Harry the Cat. Brecheen pitched a four hitter and got Williams four times. Musial didn't do any better—he also took the collar, 0 for 4. Williams commented in his column: "Brecheen's pitches look nice to hit at, but when you try to hit him the ball just isn't where you think it's going to be." Williams went on to make a point he had made often: the pitcher always has the advantage over a hitter who hasn't seen him regularly. That is the nature of the game. Perhaps for this reason Williams tried to use the odds against Brecheen and punch the ball to left to beat the shift. But as Red Schoendienst so charitably put it to reporters, "he looked pitiful." This is something Williams already knew in a general, if not specific, way. He argued about it with Joe Cronin during the regular season. Going to left only looks good when it works. Ted Williams did not generally pick up his paycheck by looking bad at the plate. It was a matter of pride as well as power.

Back in Fenway on October 9, the Red Sox coasted to a 4-0 win on the strength of Rudy York's three-run homer in the first. Williams got a base hit on a bunt toward the vacated third-base area, but the Cards were willing to let him take that piddling junk all Series long if he wanted it. Williams said he laid the ball down because the wind was blowing in and he just wanted to let the Cards know he had some options. Red Smith was eloquent on Williams's bunt: "The Kid's bunt was bigger than York's home run. Thirty-four thousand, five hundred witnesses gave off the same quaint animal cries that must have been heard at the bonfires of witches in Salem when Williams, whose mission in life is to hit baseballs across Suffolk county, pushed a small, safe roller past third base."

After the game, Joe Cronin, stung by the talk in the papers that he was the one who most wanted Williams off the Sox roster for the next season, issued a statement on behalf of the Red Sox that Ted Williams would most decidedly play in Boston next year. His team was up 2-1 in the Series and he wanted no more flak from the press. But in the next game he got all the flak he could handle from St. Louis, who blew the Red Sox away 12-3 on four-hit performances by Enos Slaughter, Joe Garagiola, and Whitey Kurowski. Williams got a base hit and Musial doubled; neither was burning up this Series. Joe Garagiola got off the best line of the day when he commented on Williams throwing out a man at the plate: "Williams was the best pitcher on the Red Sox today."

Boston went up by a game, winning the next one 6-3 when Pinky Higgins's double in the seventh broke up a tie. Williams singled in the first, driving in his first and only run of the Series. He was quiet for the rest of the game, though the fans screamed wildly for him, heartened by the vote of confidence, if it can be called that, given him by the Red Sox brass. Williams was not without perspective on his performance or on himself. He wrote in his *Globe* column: "I said I would let my bat do the talking, and it's tongue-tied."

In St. Louis the Red Sox ran into a stone wall named Harry Brecheen again. He beat them 4-1. Williams came up with little on the day but a meaningless ninth-inning single. Harold Kaese was merciless: "As matters stand, Ted Williams is an enormous bust." Kaese seemed to have the greatest of stakes in all this. His long article on the Red Sox before the season made him persona non grata for most of the campaign, and now—damned if he wasn't scapegoating Williams for a collapse that could well be turned around in one game. It was almost as if Kaese were trying to salvage some dignity for a bit of preseason backbiting that had gone sour.

Williams, on the other hand, was ready to extend some credit to Brecheen: "Brecheen is one of the smartest pitchers I've ever faced. You don't know what spot he's going to throw to." Eddie Dyer and his bevy of Cardinal scouts had been thinking about just this for weeks. They must have loved Williams's column on game six because what he describes is precisely what Dyer's staff had been instructed to do: be unpredictable. Brecheen had now allowed just two runs in 36⅔ World Series innings pitched.

The seventh game of the 1946 Series was a classic. In the top of the eighth inning, Eddie Dyer brought in Brecheen to close out the game. But he got himself in trouble, running the count to 3–1 against Dom DiMaggio. Figuring Brecheen would not challenge him with a fastball, DiMaggio looked for a breaking pitch and got one on the outside part of the plate. He drilled it for a run-scoring double. But he pulled up lame at second base and was unable to play center field in the bottom half of the inning.

In the last of the eighth, with Enos Slaughter on first, Harry Walker drove one to left center. Slaughter never stopped running as Leon Culberson, who had replaced DiMaggio, relayed to Pesky and Pesky, with just a slight hesitation, relayed to Roy Partee at the plate. The flying Slaughter had already checked in with the winning run when Pesky's throw arrived. St. Louis won 4–3.

Pesky was upset at game's end, but then shook it off: "Oh, hell. It just happened, that's all." Williams flied out four times in the game. He sat silently by his locker for half an hour and left the park. Later, Grantland Rice, a writer Williams admired greatly, spent some time consoling him; he wrote, "Heck, he's just a great big kid with an inferiority complex." This was the only piece of jargon about his mental health Williams ever repeated without scorn, perhaps because Rice had said it or perhaps because it was pat enough to dodge all the implications attendant upon it.

To put things in perspective, the postseason playoffs in 1946 had begun on the day 12 high-ranking Nazis were condemned to death by the Nuremberg tribunal; the World Series ended a day before 11 of them were hanged. The 12th, Field Marshal Hermann Göring, committed suicide on October 16, a few hours before he was to be executed. One maniacal Red Sox fan claimed that Göring was probably more distraught over Ted Williams's Series average than

over his own conviction for war crimes. The fan could well understand the motivation for suicide.

Before the close of 1946, baseball would give itself another black
eye, but it would keep the blow private. At the winter baseball
meeting Larry MacPhail, chairman of the policy committee for the
major leagues, prepared a full report, affirmed by all major league
clubs, that concluded: "However well-intentioned, the use of Negro
players would hazard all the physical properties of baseball." Branch
Rickey accounted it one of his most shameful days that he attended
that meeting without protesting publicly. He had not made a final
decision yet on whether to bring Jackie Robinson up from the minors,
and he did not want to play all his cards—indeed, any of them—too
soon.

The report was handed out, read, affirmed, and collected because
MacPhail claimed that any wider distribution might prove embarrassing to Happy Chandler, the commissioner. Rickey felt the reason
for spiriting away the report was clear. Later, when the time was ripe,
he would blow MacPhail's cover. More important, he would invite
Robinson to spring training and boost this great talent to the majors
in 1947.

◇ 9 ◇
Triple Crown Redux
1947

IN 1947, THE YEAR OF THE MARSHALL PLAN, the famous refugee ship *Exodus*, and the sound barrier—Chuck Yeager broke it in a Bell X-1 experimental plane—baseball was cherished more than ever in America. Attendance records were set all around the leagues in 1946, and advance sales in 1947 were stupendous. The World Champion St. Louis Cardinals sold out their season boxes in early spring. Del Webb's Yankees were thriving, playing in a spiffed-up Yankee Stadium with lights. The Red Sox, also with a newly lighted ball park, were reporting unprecedented advance-ticket sales. A Gallup Poll later that year profiled postwar America and determined that the average male liked brunettes and baseball (in that order) more than anything else; the average female liked clean-shaven men and marriage; 96 percent of Americans believed in God; 76 percent in an afterlife; and a startling 80 percent in sex education in high school.

Whatever Americans believed about race relations in 1947, it became clearer and clearer during spring training that the Brooklyn Dodgers were going to have to make a decision on the status of their rookie, Jackie Robinson, whose play in Montreal had been brilliant. That decision would be gratifying to many fans and players and disturbing to others. But for now the talk of the circuit was, as usual, about money. Partially because of money, Hank Greenberg was waived out of the American League on January 11 and sold to Pittsburgh. Though he hit 44 home runs and drove in 127 runs in 1946, his age, 36, and his salary, in the stratospheric 60 thousands,

168

worried the Tigers. It seemed to worry the Pittsburgh Pirates less; they were ready to pay $80,000 for Greenberg's services.

Ted Williams signed early in 1947 for a figure approaching $70,000. And Bob Feller worked out a complicated contract that would serve as a model for the future. He took a base pay of $55,000 with attendance clauses; another $7,500 if attendance reached 700,000; and $7,500 more for every 100,000 fans over 700,000. Feller also incorporated himself as Ro-Fel, generating $60,000 beyond his salary in endorsements, talks, books, and radio deals. Harold Kaese suggested Williams do the same, calling himself Te-Wil. Williams already had agreed to do an interview with Feller on one of Ro-Fel's radio deals in the Midwest, and in return Feller agreed to pitch to Williams—that is, throw him balls somewhat near the strike zone—unless first base was open and other runners were in scoring position.

Later in the spring, Red Smith wrote a piece on the major leagues as big business, in which the standards for performance and reimbursement were changing rapidly. His scenario for 1947 has become all too close to the truth now: "Contract negotiations will be complicated next winter by players holding out for $30,000 on the grounds that in 1947 they batted .197, served as scoutmaster of a Scarsdale Boy Scout troop, appeared on the Bing Crosby program, addressed 23 luncheon clubs, played a split week at the Roxy, and did a striptease on a table at the Stadium Club."

Some general managers and owners had objections to the spiraling baseball salaries in what passed for a competitive market, but Eddie Collins spoke for the high rollers.

> It is about time that such club executives as Sam Breadon [Cardinals], Clark Griffith [Senators], and Herb Pennock [Phillies] mind their own business and allow Tom Yawkey and myself to run our affairs and those of the Red Sox our own way. I'm sick and tired of those bleats of Pennock, Breadon, and Griffith that salary boosts threaten to shake the structure of the major leagues.

Collins went on to point out that the Red Sox drew 1,500,000 at Fenway and 2,000,000 on the road in 1946. They had a payroll commensurate with their sense of value returned—nearly $500,000 for the entire team: "Any member of the Red Sox is entitled to as much as he can show he's worth."

What particularly griped Collins was that Breadon was trying to keep the lid on a salary increment for Stan Musial, who hit .365 in 1946. Breadon's opening ploy was an anemic $14,500 a year. Musial wanted $30,000, and Breadon wouldn't hear of it. But he was having a hard time convincing Musial with Greenberg raking in $80,000 and Williams, $70,000. Moreover, Pittsburgh was ready to offer Musial what he wanted and more if the Cards would sell them his contract for a quarter of a million dollars. The Cardinals refused Pittsburgh, but they did end up paying Musial $28,000 for 1947.

That Eddie Collins was clearly ticked by all this became apparent when he wouldn't let the issue die. The Red Sox loss to the Cards in the World Series of 1946 didn't help matters any. Collins got to rambling on, and he finally sputtered, "Musial couldn't hold Williams's glove." Eddie wasn't paying proper attention to his baseball clichés: Williams's glove was the one piece of paraphernalia that Musial could easily carry.

Collins's feud with Breadon provided the baseball writers with a speculative contest they would enjoy for the next decade and a half. Who was the better ballplayer, Williams or Musial? *The Sporting News* posed the question to readers and to baseball writers. One fan wrote in that "Musial not only can carry Williams's glove, but it would be better for the Red Sox if he *were* carrying it." Another reminded Eddie Collins that "in his palmiest days, he couldn't carry Larry Lajoie's glove." The general run of opinion was that Williams was the better hitter and Musial a better all-around player. This would not have clashed terribly with Williams's lifelong ambition to be the best hitter that ever lived. He never said anything about baserunning or fly hawking.

Ted Williams was still off fishing the opening day of spring training, but he was heading in. When asked about the Williams versus Musial debate in *The Sporting News* and in papers around the country he said of Eddie Collins's position on the matter, "I've at least got the right guy on my side—the one who writes my ticket." The tension around World Series time in 1946 had eased and the Red Sox wanted to begin the year, insofar as Williams allowed them, standing behind him rather than dangling him every other day as trade bait. Moreover, Collins and Cronin felt that Williams's late-season slump in 1946 had more to do with his general weariness after the wartime hiatus than with his stubbornness against the shift imposed by Lou Boudreau of the Indians after the All-Star break. The brass intended to keep him fresh and frisky this year by cutting down the rigors of spring training. Williams approved, but he later thought that the Red Sox had set a pattern for him here that they soon enough violated.

Williams arrived in camp on March 1 at a trim 195 pounds, and, with Paul Waner in attendance, immediately took some cuts. Waner had been invited for the express purpose of talking to Williams about hitting to left field. Joe Cronin publicly said Williams should hit the way he wanted but privately tried to talk him into breaking the shift by going to left more often. Williams did not want to talk about it much in 1946, and in his characteristic manner would stifle Cronin with an offhand, "Sure, I'll give it a try, sport." He rarely did, except as a measure of diversion for the host of writers who somehow thought they had programmed him to try. In his own defense, Williams said he actually thought about stroking to left until he got up to the plate, but when he saw all those bodies bunched around the right side he just wanted to drive the hell out of the ball.

Paul Waner picked up a bat during the session with Williams and asked for a volunteer to toss a few up to him. With every pitch he called the location and sprayed line drives in the area pegged, whether or not the pitch was zoned for him to do so. Players began to gather around the cage. Waner's accuracy was astounding. Williams admired what he saw, but he had some philosophical differences with singles hitters and expressed them. Waner's swing, for instance, was level to the plate at contact or even down at a slight angle when chopping balls to left. The very look of such a swing did not impress Williams, who felt that the natural power swing was angled slightly up. Williams's target was the bottom half of the ball on a swing. When he did get on top of the ball with his uppercut swing the overspin was wicked. Infielders hated a hard Williams shot on the ground, but Williams liked them no more himself. He recalled a remark of Babe Ruth's when writers asked him why he didn't just try to ground them through open spaces in the infield: "They don't pay to see me hit ground balls."

Williams claimed in 1947 what he had not fully articulated in 1946: "I can hit to left field. But when they try to make me do it, I just don't want to do it." Like so many of Williams's remarks, this one sounds petulant, but there are technicalities behind it. He knew all of the ramifications of altering his stance and swinging to hit to left; in the long run, that was not where his psychological advantage over a pitcher or his good to the team resided. There were legions in Boston who argued otherwise, who pointed out that variety was the spice of life and that Williams would be a more effective ballplayer if he would spray to all fields, if he would move around in the box, if he would break out of his locked-in habits, or if he would swing every once in a while at a bad pitch—especially with men on base. Williams's point was always more emphatic: there was a price to pay for doing all this, and over time that price would be exacted against the effectiveness and precision of his natural, disciplined strategies at the plate. His petulance was simply a brash and brusque expression of the rules of his art.

But the Boston baseball writers had it in their minds this year, and Williams encouraged them to some extent with conciliatory and accommodating comments, that at least on a few occasions he was going to beat the shift with left-field hitting. So every slash and cut to the left side by Williams during spring training was noted and written about. The writers even brought in human interest as an ally. On March 15, the *Globe* featured a story about one Billy Fitzpatrick, 15, arrested in Sarasota when he ran away from home to watch Williams play. Billy said, "Williams was my hero until the World Series. But Ted disappointed me then. He didn't hit to left field. That wasn't teamwork in my book." Williams doubled to left field that day against the Yankees in an exhibition game and chuckled when the writers made a much bigger deal of it than he ever would.

The coverage of Williams approached the ridiculous. As Harold Kaese put it: "When the Red Sox play a practice game the first question is: Did Williams hit to left? The second question is: Did the Red Sox win?" After Williams tripled to left against the Phils in another March game, the papers announced that he could do it if he really tried. The next day Williams ran into Hank Greenberg at the Pirates' camp. Hank insisted that he not change his style at the plate. Williams had heard that same advice at the beginning of his career from Lefty O'Doul, at his first spring training from Jimmie Foxx, with the Minneapolis Millers from Rogers Hornsby, and now from Greenberg. Paul Waner and Ty Cobb told him otherwise, and Hornsby, just to be his old prickly self, changed his tune in 1947 for no other reason than that Williams was just as bullheaded as ever: "He reminds me of a boxer who is a 'head-hunter' and tries constantly for a knockout when he could win one decision after another with a succession of body punches."

There was some relief from all this during a Red Sox exhibition game on April 2 in Dallas. Before the game the management of the minor league Dallas Rebels okayed a preplanned routine. Williams came to bat in the first and the entire Dallas team, except for the pitcher and catcher, made a mad dash for the right-field bleachers, climbed over the waist-high wooden fence, and lined up in defensive positions along the first row of seats. Williams just shook his head with amusement.

At about the same time in early April, while the Brooklyn Dodgers' brass were taking a close look at Jackie Robinson, still nominally on the Montreal Royals' roster, big trouble brewed for the Dodgers' manager, Leo Durocher. In a column he was writing during spring training with the help of the Dodgers' traveling secretary, Harold Parott, Durocher mentioned, supposedly as a throwaway item, that he spotted Yankees executive Larry MacPhail lunching in Cuba with gamblers so shady that they made Mafia types in Las Vegas look like mah-jongg players: "If I saw types like that in the Brooklyn park, I'd have them thrown out."

When MacPhail read this little bit of spring training gossip he was livid: "I was eating with Hector Racine, the president of the Dodgers' Montreal farm club." MacPhail made it known in no uncertain terms that Durocher would have a hard time distinguishing gamblers he saw in a Cuban watering hole from those he had up for drinks in his hotel room. Apparently Leo had blundered, but perhaps not so accidentally. MacPhail and the Dodgers had been on the outs ever since he had moved to the Yanks; besides, there were bad feelings about aborted or stillborn managerial changes at the time, and Durocher felt betrayed.

Durocher knew that his own association with less-than-church-going types in New York, in Las Vegas, and in Cuba was an agenda issue for the National League office—indeed, for the commissioner's office. On the infamous Durocher theory that nice guys finish last,

Leo was out to get the jump on anyone who might sandbag him. MacPhail seemed a likely candidate. But Durocher ended up in deeper trouble on this one. The problem, as most soon saw it, was that Durocher did indeed recognize the face of MacPhail's primary luncheon companion, but he just assumed that the familiar face belonged to one of his own gambling acquaintances. Durocher was prone to such an error.

Branch Rickey, who first confirmed the story in the papers because it had the imprimatur of the club's traveling secretary, now backed away from it with dispatch. Durocher, apparently, had made a mistake, a bad one. On April 9, Happy Chandler came down on Durocher with the full force of the commissioner's office. He suspended him for the season, citing conduct generally detrimental to the game, including a host of "unpleasant incidents" culminating in the slander against MacPhail. Chandler's office conspired to keep the charges unspecified. Baseball would be hurt less if names were not named. But the commissioner had a dossier on Durocher that looked as bad as it smelled.

In an admonitory gesture, again not protested by Rickey because Durocher and Parott had put the Dodgers in a vulnerable position, the commissioner's office slapped Parott with a $500 fine for his part in writing Durocher's column. He even slapped a $2,000 general fine on the Dodgers and Yankees for making hay of this issue in public. Chandler thought the whole matter distasteful and its public airing a disgrace.

Two lines of baseball history intersected on this date, April 9: Rickey informed Durocher that he was a goner for the year and that Burt Shotton would take his place; and at the same meeting, the Dodgers, with Durocher still kicking and fighting about his own fate, made the final decision to place Jackie Robinson on the Dodgers' roster for 1947. Durocher kept mumbling "What for? What for?" throughout, but his plea had nothing to do with the Robinson decision. He just couldn't focus on anything during the meeting but his suspension.

Larry MacPhail took about three weeks to think about the events surrounding Durocher's suspension—including the bad blood between him and Leo because of some broken promises—and then began to feel that he had placed the straw on the camel's back. Moreover, he wasn't too fond of the idea of the commissioner as a martinet. He appealed to Chandler to let up on Durocher or to name the specific charges. Chandler wasn't buying. In a special seven-hour meeting he told MacPhail that stirring these things up again would be detrimental to baseball. Upon the threat of his own banishment, MacPhail backed off.

Known around the league as the "Stalin of Swat," MacPhail was also raising some hackles on his own team. He fined a few, including none other than Joe DiMaggio, for refusing to hang around for a photo session after an early-season game. So many fans wrote in to the Yankees offering to pay DiMaggio's $100 fine that the Clipper said he could retire if he put all the offers into a trust fund. MacPhail was at the time also deducting train fares from the salaries of his players if they refused to fly on the team's air charter. Many were none too keen on leaving the ground and even less keen on salary deductions for what they considered a sensible decision.

Durocher had by then all but given up trying to get his suspension lifted. Few extended him sympathy. His baseball career was as enemy-ridden as that of his early rival in baseball, Ty Cobb, whose mantle for orneriness Durocher had inherited. Indeed, the story was told of a raw Durocher playing second in his rookie year for the Yanks when an aging Ty Cobb played for the A's. As Cobb motored around second base trying to go to third on a teammate's single, Leo jutted out his hip at him. The glancing blow set Cobb enough out of sync so that the throw got him. Cobb glowered at Durocher: "Do that again, you shit, and I'll cut your legs off." The rookie shouted back: "You'll cut nobody's legs off. You're a goddamn bluff. Come in high and I'll jam the ball down your goddamn throat."

In the midst of all the gambling and suspension talk, the days of the wrenching Black Sox scandal of 1919 came up, and Ty Cobb, who had been tracked down by reporters because they knew what he thought of Durocher, told a story about the shame of suspension and the fate of Shoeless Joe Jackson, working in a state liquor dispensary in Greenville, South Carolina. Cobb made a special trip to visit him, which Ted Williams always wished to do and never did. Shoeless Joe saw Cobb walk in but did not acknowledge him. "Don't you know me, Joe? I came by especially to say hello." Jackson said, "You know I know you. But I wasn't sure you wanted to speak to me. Lot of them don't."

The Dodgers were in Cuba on April 9 when Durocher began his

suspension and Jackie Robinson began his stint as the first black ballplayer in the modern major leagues. The simple first sentence of Harold Kaese's column on the signing—"The Brooklyn Dodgers today purchased the contract of Jackie Roosevelt Robinson from the Montreal Royals"—masked the more complex and cynical gist of his piece. Kaese was convinced that Rickey signed Robinson because he feared losing the gate revenues that the irascible Durocher could generate. In other words, Kaese reduced the years of delicate work on the Robinson signing to a gimmick, a freak show. Robinson could ponder these matters and others from a segregated hotel in Cuba; the Dodgers could not register him at the Hotel National in Havana where the team was staying. He could also contemplate his major league minimum salary for 1947: $5,000.

A week later the season opened. Ted Williams singled in his first at-bat to drive in the first Red Sox run of the year. The Sox took the opener at Fenway against the Senators, 7–6. Jackie Robinson had the collar placed on him in Brooklyn's opener and reacted with an almost obligatory rookie awe: "Jeez, these guys can pitch." A few days later, by April 20, Robinson was hitting .429. The entertainer Bill Robinson called him Ty Cobb in Technicolor.

Still early in the year, on April 25, the Yankees honored a dying Babe Ruth before 58,339 at the Stadium. Ruth would say what America then felt and many in America still feel: "The only real game in the world is baseball." On his way to the field the Babe had stopped by the umpires' dressing room; they were his contemporaries. Bill Summers described how Ruth passed by with the commissioner and kicked at the door: "We opened slowly, as an umpire will, and there he was." His voice rasped, "Hello, you blind lugs. Only a few of us left, kid." Summers said he was near tears: "We loved it [the needling] from him, and we were kind of weak and shaky with our 'Hello, Babe.' You must know why."

The Red Sox traveled a bit lighter on the inspirational road the same April 25. Rudy York fell asleep in bed at Boston's Hotel Myles Standish with a cigarette dangling from his hand. With smoke billowing from his room, he awoke in time to flee down to the street below. His bad habit had cleared the building. No one was hurt, but the big man took some merciless ribbing. The 1940-vintage gag of Ted Williams as fireman was briefly revived for the comical York. After a slow start on the year, the Red Sox had little else to kid about.

But then Williams gave them a show in St. Louis, where Boston was still news from the previous year's World Series, and where the Williams-Musial controversy brewed with special gusto. The Browns, not known for turning away droves at the gate, were surprised at an overflow crowd for a Sunday doubleheader on May 4. The center-field bleachers were closed, as usual, to provide a better hitting background. But the crowd kept pressing for more comfortable seating space in the bleachers and mockingly sought Williams's assistance when he took his position in left. He gestured that he wasn't the right person to see about this problem and then gestured a bit more graphically when the screams for his assistance turned to insults about his upbringing and personal hygiene. His response was met with a volley of soda-pop bottles.

The St. Louis management hustled to take the barriers down and let the bleacher crowd spread out. After a one-day break for everybody to cool off, Williams came back on Tuesday and began his season in earnest, tying the ball game with a home run in the ninth and winning it 6–5 with a three-run homer in the 11th over the screen behind the pavilion and out onto Grand Avenue. He then ran up his home-run total six more notches to 11 within the next two weeks. By May 20 he was hitting .337, compensating for a sluggish start. Then the bottom dropped out. For the next three weeks he hit .214.

The local writers were all over Williams about his refusal to go to left, claiming he had already lost 12 sure hits because he insisted on driving balls to right field. For good measure, the theorists of the press box claimed he was taking too many hittable pitches just off the plate on the outside. He was being walked, the general opinion ran, a disproportionate number of times, and it had to do with his waiting even longer for a pitch in his zone to drive over the fence and nullify the shift. Of the advice he read every day early in the season—that he try moving farther from the plate, that he go after the outside pitch, that he try the contact swing—Williams had this to say: "I get all that sort of advice from newspapermen who can't hit, from pitchers, and from .250 hitters. I'm not changing my position at the plate."

During his slump Williams lost the headlines to a revived Joe DiMaggio, who was ripping again in 1947 the way he did before the war, and to some sparkling rookies: Jackie Robinson of the Dodgers and Ralph Kiner, the phenomenal home-run hitter of the Pirates. To check Williams's stats for 1947 is to gain a real sense of how the teams around the league were developing a double-tiered defense for him. In addition to swinging the bulk of their players around to the right side of the field, managers were clearly instructing pitchers to keep the ball away, so far away that Williams's already high percentage of walks increased. He was getting just a couple of official at-bats in many of his games, and he was getting ticked off: "Frankly, I don't think I'm that good a hitter that they should walk me every time I come to the plate." Williams did remember that the strategy was not altogether new. Before the war Luke Sewell, manager of the Browns, used to hold up four fingers to his pitcher while Ted was still in the on-deck circle.

Partly in frustration, Ted Williams did something on May 13 he had never done before. He took two outside pitches to left at Fenway and put them out of the park over the Green Monster during a 19–6 win over Chicago. The writers joked that the White Sox forgot to put the left-field shift on for Williams. That morning Williams had been to the hospital to visit a kid, Glenn Brann, who at the time didn't know that his legs had been amputated after a horrible accident. Glenn asked Williams to hit one, and he said he'd give it a shot. In spring training he had visited a kid in a hospital in Chattanooga and promised a home run because the fence was so noticeably short. He ended up hitting one out about 485 feet to right. Williams took his own goodwill to heart: "Maybe I should visit the hospital every day."

In the National League, Jackie Robinson's presence in the majors met its major racial test in early May when several St. Louis Cardinals players threatened to strike on the basis of Robinson's occupying a spot on the Dodgers' roster. They wanted the right to determine with whom they would play, as if baseball's general exemption from the interstate commerce clause of the Constitution made the season a social event. Cardinals president Sam Breadon worked frantically with Ford Frick, president of the National League, to block the move.

Cardinals players were convinced that some of the Dodgers would stick with them—Pee Wee Reese was rumored to be the most likely. Originally, the Cards were going to strike alone in Brooklyn, but now they had in mind a symbolic one-day strike by players around the league. Frick was highly successful in conveying to Breadon the stark message that anyone involved in such a scheme would face immediate suspension. Breadon was to tell his players that the press would crucify them and that Frick's position was simple: Robinson plays, and that's that. Frick said he would fold the league rather than take Robinson's name off the Dodger roster: "This is the United States of America and one citizen has as much right to play as another."

Later in August the Cardinals' reaction to Jackie Robinson took a different form. Robinson was spiked by Enos Slaughter on the base path heading toward first. Jackie insisted that Slaughter had plenty of the bag if he wanted it; Slaughter insisted that he ran with his head down and didn't see Robinson's foot: "Nope, not on purpose. I just didn't do it on purpose." Cardinal manager Eddie Dyer said he had warned his men about causing trouble ever since their threatened strike. "This just happens in baseball, and he's going to have to get used to it."

As the season unfolded in the American League, the Red Sox were holding close enough to first place that things were pretty calm in Boston. When the Barnum & Bailey Circus arrived in town Harold Kaese did a piece in which he imagined the famous ape Gargantua taking in a game in the left-field seats at Fenway. Kaese set the scene so that Williams, facing the typical barrage of insults, finally looked toward the stands, ambled closer to the foul line, and turned what was usually directed at him against his antagonist: "Why, you big 600-pound gorilla!" Kaese went on to recall how a Boston writer told Williams of a Temple University research project that concluded that razzing and booing were a largely postwar phenomena. "Hell," said Williams, "what were they doing prewar? Asking me for a date?"

Things livened up a bit for the Red Sox in mid-May when Boston obtained the garrulous and amusing veteran catcher Birdie Tebbetts from the Tigers. Williams remembered that Tebbetts had once hit him on the back of the head throwing the ball back to the pitcher— "one less thing to worry about," Williams said. For his part, Tebbetts told the local writers that Williams had it easy compared to Rudy York, who was virtually ridden out of Detroit by fan hostility. Now the buzzards were after Wakefield. Tebbetts said he was booed after the war just for coming up to the plate to pinch hit. "The fans didn't even remember who I was," he complained, "but that was reason enough for them."

Boston began to win a few games in June and was creeping up

near first place. So far everyone's play had been mediocre, and first place was less an honor than a temporary default. On June 13, the league-leading White Sox lost to Boston before 34,510 in the first night game ever at Fenway. Ted Williams got a couple of singles in the 5–3 win. Two days later the Red Sox zoned into range within one game of first, and they celebrated by signing Walt Dropo, a minor league prospect out of the University of Connecticut. Another night game on June 18 proved a special sort of endurance test for the local fans—the Red Sox took 15 innings to win a ball game 6–5 against the Browns. In a town not known for its frolicking after-hours life, the El was jammed with night voyagers and celebrants until 2:00 A.M. The *Globe* sports desk was besieged until dawn with calls from irate wives wanting to know whether their husbands were lying about the extra-inning game the night before. A lot of folks were late for work, but, then again, the Red Sox were now a half game out of first and would tie the Yanks for first after their next win.

Williams began to jack his average up toward the .300 mark by the last week in June. At the beginning of that week, on June 24, Sugar Ray Robinson's fight with Jimmy Doyle achieved unwanted notoriety when Doyle did not survive a postbout operation for brain damage. Robinson was questioned by the coroner because ring officials suspected he and his handlers knew that Doyle was unfit. Doyle seemed to leave the ring one way after every fight: unconscious. This time he left it brain-dead.

Through July 1947 Williams surged, but the Red Sox faded. Matters were made no easier when the Yankees went on a 19-game winning streak, which fairly put away the pennant. The only real excitement in the American League these days took place in Cleveland. On July 5 the Indians called up Larry Doby from Newark. He was the first black ballplayer to crack the circuit. Doby pinch hit against Chicago's Earl Harrist and struck out. The next day he started the ball game and singled for his first major league hit. A couple of weeks after the All-Star break, the St. Louis Browns brought up two black ballplayers, Henry Thompson and Willard Brown, for their major league debuts in Boston. Brown played and got two hits. And later in the year, on August 26, the Dodgers brought up another black ballplayer, a pitcher named Dan Bankhead, who got pounded around and knocked out of the box in his first start, an eventual 16-4 loss to Pittsburgh, but who also hit a home run 375 feet into the left-field seats. Of the 24,000 on hand in Ebbets Field for the occasion, 9,000 were black.

To gain some sense of what things were like around the country at the time blacks began breaking into the majors, a story from Ahoskie, North Carolina, that began as pathetically local and emerged as painfully national is instructive. At a civic drawing organized by the local Kiwanis club a green Cadillac was the grand prize. Singing at the event was Leslie Long of the Carmen Cavallero Band, who was also on hand to select the lucky ticket. But when she did so she saw consternation on the faces of the local Kiwanians. A black man, Harvey Jones, had the winning stub. Miss Long was told quickly to draw again because her first draw was a mistake. In disgust, she refused.

Nonetheless, Mr. Jones was given back his $1 ticket (and the dollar he spent to buy it) and told that since he couldn't come to the dance where the prize would be awarded, he couldn't have the car. The Kiwanians drew again and awarded the prize to a local white dentist: "We tried to do the fair thing," said Rupert Massey, president of the chapter. In the next few days the story got out, and the chapter received so much outraged mail from across the country that it had to dig in and award an additional $3,200 Cadillac to Jones. The fair thing, so very loosely defined, ended up costing these charitable Kiwanians double.

Meanwhile, the baseball season hit its midpoint with the July 8 All-Star Game, at Wrigley Field. Williams got his revenge, of sorts, against Harry the Cat Brecheen of the Cards by singling sharply to right and doubling down the line. The National League did not employ the shift at Wrigley Field, and he had a bit more of right field to shoot at. He had seen Brecheen enough during the World Series to begin to gauge him but was half a season too late. When the season resumed after the break, the Red Sox were playing truer to form—their usual form—than the year before. On July 18 they lost a donnybrook to St. Louis 9-8, as Williams went 5 for 5 with two home runs. He raised his average to .323, but Red Sox fans took one look at this box score and moaned, "Ain't it always the case? Williams goes

5 for 5 and we lose." He had picked up 39 points on his average in three weeks, most of them against the Browns, hitting .638 in his recent rampage against St. Louis pitching.

Jeff Heath, with the Browns in 1947 before moving along to the Boston Braves, considered Williams's performance against St. Louis: "I thought he hit .750 against us. He wore us out, and the reason was that our pitchers wanted to throw to him. They wouldn't walk him, like other sensible pitchers. They kept thinking they'd found his weakness. If he took a swing and missed, the pitcher would say, 'Ah, now I got it. I know how to pitch to him.' The next time Ted batted the pitcher would throw the same pitch, but this time Williams would hit it out of the park, or, if the pitcher was lucky, against a fence. St. Louis pitchers couldn't believe that anyone could hit like Williams. They sure were dead game." On the year Williams would hit .500 at Sportsman's Park and .458 against the Browns in Fenway.

On August 28 a curious game took place at Fenway. Steve O'Neill of the Tigers went out to the mound in the third inning to remove his starting pitcher, Hal Newhouser, after he had given up five runs and seven hits to the Red Sox in an eventual 13–3 loss. Newhouser wouldn't give O'Neill the ball. The two wrestled halfway to the dugout, O'Neill with a bear hug on his pitcher, trying to pull him off the field. Manager and pitcher had already gone way past the point of public humiliation when Newhouser relented and left on his own steam. Later, the Tiger ace claimed he was just about to put the lid on the Red Sox: "I was bearing down." For his display, the Tigers fined Hal $250, but there was something about that kind of grit that had its appeal.

Williams was still hitting well in September, but he had one tough day against the A's on September 5 at Shibe Park. He was 0 for 4 when he came up for his last at-bat; he took a futile cut at a pitch, missed, and headed back toward the dugout in disgust. But the ump followed him to the batter's circle and whispered, "Jeez, Ted, it's only strike two." An embarrassed Williams, who so rarely lost concentration at the plate, turned red but dutifully returned to the batter's box. He hit the next ball over the wall in right off Russ Christopher for his 28th homer of the year. His reprieve turned into his atonement.

Although the Red Sox finished up the season in third place, 14 games behind the Yankees, Williams won his second Triple Crown, hitting .343 with 32 home runs and 114 runs batted in. He fed mostly on St. Louis pitching, hitting a combined .476 with 11 home runs away and at home. In his favorite park, Briggs Stadium, he tailed off a bit in 1947 to bring his six-year average to .352, below his Shibe Park average of .354. So far in his career he had hit 23 home runs in Sportsman's Park, 21 in Shibe Park, and 20 in Briggs Stadium.

Yet Williams again lost the Most Valuable Player balloting to Joe DiMaggio by a mere point. He was gracious about it again, as he was when he lost in 1941. This time, however, he felt he deserved the award. In 1941, despite his own .406 year, he genuinely thought DiMaggio was the most valuable player in the league. In 1947 he felt he was. He felt no better when he later found out that *Globe* writer Melville Webb hadn't even placed Williams in the top ten for Most Valuable Player. A tenth-place vote would have pushed him over the top in the balloting. For Webb, needless to say, Williams had little but contempt.

In the National League, Harry Walker hit .363. The young Ralph Kiner, with a spurt of eight home runs in four September games, caught Johnny Mize for a share of the home run title—they both finished with 51. An ailing but expert Babe Ruth said of their slugging race: "Hell, they're putting a whole rabbit in that ball these days."

The wonderful Dodgers-Yankees World Series, highlighted by Lavagetto's hit with two out in the ninth to break up Bill Bevens's no-hitter and Al Gionfriddo's spectacular grab of DiMaggio's prodigious drive to left at the Stadium, was won by the Yanks in seven memorable games. Williams was at the World Series when he ran into Ty Cobb, who had taken it upon himself to write Williams a two-page letter on the art of spray hitting. Williams answered Cobb in a way that could silence a geophysicist, let alone an old-time ball player: "Yeah, yeah, fine, but the arc and sweep of my swing should not vary more than 15 degrees from the direction of the pitch." Cobb complained to Harold Kaese: "Will they ever go back to the old game, when one run meant something? Midgets hit home runs now. Williams sticks to one swing and never changes. Spring training is commercialized. Ah, but who am I to find fault?"

The off-season was eventful for Williams in a personal way; his wife, Doris, was pregnant. And the winter was eventful for the Red Sox in a public way; Joe McCarthy, the legendary genius of the New

York Yankees, was going to manage Boston for 1948. He had health problems and a penchant for the bottle, but Yawkey was convinced the Red Sox needed a touch of his genius to go along with the slam-bang trade they had made with the Browns, getting Vern Stephens at short, and two front-line pitchers, Jack Kramer and Ellis Kinder, for what turned out to be mere chicken feed. This would be a competitive Boston team, and now they had a field manager that knew how to win with discipline and fundamental baseball. How would Williams react to this? McCarthy tried early on to take the burden off of his leftfielder and place it squarely on his own shoulders: "A manager who can't get along with a .400 hitter ought to have his head examined."

◇ 10 ◇
Daddy-O
1948

WHAT SORT OF A FAMILY MAN was Ted Williams? This question hounded Williams early in 1948 at a time when the release of the Kinsey report from the University of Indiana suggested that distinctions between the public and the private were even dicier than they once seemed. Doris Williams was pregnant in Princeton, Minnesota, the home of her grandparents. Williams had already signed his contract with the Red Sox by phone in January with no difficulty—that's the way he liked it—and he planned to head for the Everglades for a little fishing before the birth of his child. Doris would travel to Boston in preparation for delivery, not expected for several weeks. Williams dispatched a telegram to the hosts of the annual Baseball Writers Dinner in Boston, telling them that he did not plan to be in town, but was deeply grateful for the award they intended to give him as the team's most valuable player. The telegram was not read at the dinner, part of the pique silently expressed by the writers who felt, first, that Williams should have shown up, and second, that he had no business being in Florida when his wife was on the verge of delivering a child in Boston.

The February 2 edition of the *Boston Globe*—still brimming with news of the assassination of Mahatma Gandhi two days earlier in India—found room on its first page for a photo of a beaming Williams deplaning in Boston early on Sunday morning, January 30. Unfortunately, his daughter, Barbara Joyce, had been delivered on the previous Wednesday, earlier than expected. Williams claimed he was snook fishing in the Everglades, and by the time he made it to Miami the Sunday flight arrival was the best he could do. He couldn't even be located until late Wednesday, many hours after Doris delivered.

The Boston dailies were in a feeding frenzy. It was as if Ted Williams had committed a crime verging on infanticide, and Harold Kaese in the *Globe* ran a public-opinion sampling—parenting by mob condemnation—in which Williams came up on the short side by a 2–1 margin. Kaese even wondered if Williams felt about his wife the way he felt about his teammates, and he later defended his viciousness by a piece in *Sport* magazine, "Why We Pick on Ted Williams": "In Boston, a man does not qualify as a baseball writer until he has psychoanalyzed Ted Williams."

Ted Williams, already public enemy number one for an extended series of misdemeanors, now added desertion to his criminal ledger. In New York, Paul Gallico chastised his man—"You are not a nice fellow, Brother Williams"—though, surprisingly, the flamboyant Dave Egan of the *Boston Record* came to Williams's defense: "This is all simply an attempt to put Williams in the grease." Williams did what he almost always did when faced with an abusive barrage; he became truculent and strident: "To hell with public opinion. It's my baby and it's my life. My personal life is nobody's business but my own."

Williams had reason to say this often enough over the course of his career, and he had every reason to believe it on general principles. The Boston writers had known for a long time that his marriage was no more than cordial and that he did some gallivanting. The gossip mill in Boston churned the rumors privately, but a press code of honor kept them out of the dailies. On this occasion, however, innuendos about his fitness, or lack thereof, for family life reflected on his conduct concerning not only his new daughter but also his patient wife. Writers were making that point sub rosa while readers got only what might be called the Everglades fish story.

In Boston, Doris had been staying in Brighton with the family of John J. Buckley, a friend of Ted's. She was then at the Richardson House of Boston, a lying-in hospital, and Williams was headed there. The newsmen seemed prepared to follow: "No pictures there, boys, I don't care what you think." Williams softened by afternoon, and the papers ran a picture of the Kid looking at his kid through the glass nursery window. "Won't the flash bulbs hurt her eyes?" he fussed.

But the pride and natural warmth of a new parent took over: "She's a little on the light side like me. They tell me she has a temper, too. I wonder where she got that?"

Because Williams was in town unexpectedly, he wandered over to the Sportsman's Show with his friend Herb Welch to join the ex-heavyweight champ Jack Sharkey. When asked about the rifle given him as a present by the baseball writers, Williams cackled: "When I get a chance, I'll show the boys how much I appreciate it." He began fly casting with Sharkey on a stage set up for an exhibition; then he got involved in earnest. The trick was to hit a target 80 feet away. Williams cast in 2 of 8 and Sharkey, 4 of 8. This was the first of a series of matches and return matches. Williams loved it. He would improve over the years, claiming to be the greatest fisherman in the world until someone told him that honor belonged to Jesus Christ.

While in Boston Williams couldn't shake the sly comments and charges that were hovering all too near the center of his marriage under the rubric of fit fatherhood. Nothing shot his gauge toward the red zone more quickly than speculations in the papers about his personal life. If one writer happened to suggest the least little something untoward, Williams turned his wrath on the whole fraternity. Jerry Nason of the *Globe* pointed out that Williams's private life really was no one's business, but it was tough for a writer who had written or implied nothing personal about him to bear the brunt for those who had: "Naturally, you do not run around oozing with affection for somebody who considers you a so-and-so without even the courtesy of finding out whether you are or not." Even so, "What Ted does in his spare time off the ball field is none of my business, and what I do with mine is no affair of his." Nason assumed that Williams's usual refrain—"Go fuck yourself"—was rather an intrusion into a writer's private life.

In the wider baseball world in the spring of 1948, Branch Rickey made an unforgettable speech on racial prejudice in the major leagues at Wilberforce University, a black school in Ohio. For the first time he publicly revealed the story of Larry MacPhail and the highly classified Policy Committee Report of the Major Leagues that recommended against signing black ballplayers after the war. Rickey felt that his silent participation at the secret presentation of this report was the lowest moment of his career and his least courageous action.

But he assuaged himself with the knowledge that by then he had authorized a budget for scouting black ballplayers and intended to go ahead with his program in spite of the filed secret report: "I believe that racial extractions and color hues and forms of worship become secondary to what men can do. The denial of equality of opportunity any time is not understandable to me."

MacPhail, in semiretirement from baseball, responded almost incoherently to Rickey's charge that his committee buried the document. Yes, the document was distributed, collected, and safely filed, but so what? The leagues always acted in private. Rickey was a double-crosser, according to MacPhail. He seemed to agree with the other club officials not to pursue the signing of black players, and then he proceeded to use the time to get a leg up on everyone else by hiring the best one in the business, Jackie Robinson. Besides, he sandbagged the Kansas City Monarchs on Robinson's contract and then paid his new star peanuts in 1947. About the only note of truth in MacPhail's harangue was Rickey's legendary cheapness.

When spring training began on March 1—at about the time the famous streamlined, cyclops-headlighted Tucker automobile debuted for its short, troubled life—Ted Williams drove to Sarasota in his Buick. He arrived in time to take batting practice, with McCarthy having put in an almost unheard-of three-fair-balls rule to speed up the hitting cycles and avoid cage hogging, a trick Williams had developed over the years to a fine art. McCarthy also eliminated the ritual batting-practice bunt. When the writers tried to get a rise out of Williams on the new system, he looked them square in the eye and said: "No bunts? Great!"

Rumors persisted all through spring training that the Red Sox were having a difficult time warming to McCarthy, and that only Williams could talk to him with ease. A *Time* magazine piece hinted that his respectful address, "Mr. McCarthy," might have been impudence, but this simply was not Williams's way, and even the Boston writers came to Williams's defense on this one. McCarthy had the good sense from the beginning to treat Williams as if he were a consummate professional, a rational, reasonable, and controlled adult. And Williams, for his part, responded to McCarthy in kind. It was a matter of pride for both of them to get along. Each thought the other the best at what he did in baseball. Moreover, the two shared a reaction to the press: "If somebody misquotes me, I'm not going to help him do it again," said McCarthy. Williams's position was usually less precise and more explosive but carried the same import.

Williams got an early start north on April 8 when the Red Sox decided to send him to Boston by train because what he thought was stomach flu, contracted in New Orleans, might have been appendicitis. He and coach Paul Schreiber took the Crescent Limited out of New Orleans. Remembering Stan Musial's difficult early season in 1947 trying to nurse a delicate appendix, Williams said he would have his removed immediately if necessary. But by the time the train pulled into Boston Williams was fine; minor food poisoning replaced appendicitis or stomach flu as the diagnosis.

In an oddly scheduled opening-day doubleheader against the Philadelphia A's, in which the Red Sox lost both ends, Williams batted in the nightcap against 24-year-old Lou Brissie, whose left leg was virtually held together by an aluminum brace because of a war injury. On December 7, 1944, in the Appennine Mountains near Florence, Italy, he and 11 other soldiers of the 351st Infantry were shelled by the Germans. Twenty-one shell fragments shattered his left leg. He needed 23 operations and 40 blood transfusions to save it.

On a 3-2 pitch, Williams lined a rocket right at Brissie, and the ball caromed off his left knee. Brissie went down as if felled by an ax. Williams was beside himself at first base after running out the play; he kicked the bag in disgust and remorse. But five minutes later Brissie stood up and tenderly took some warm-up pitches, saying to Williams: "For Chrissakes, Williams, *pull* the damn ball!" Brissie stayed in the game but stopped for X-rays at the hospital on his way back to the hotel. He was fine. Williams was so shaken by the episode that in his autobiography he placed it two years earlier than it actually occurred—in 1946 instead of 1948.

The Red Sox couldn't buy a win early in the season, but their losses were spicy. On April 24, Mel Allen was calling the 7–2 Yankee win over Boston for WINS radio when the lines from the Stadium got crossed with phone lines. One caller was so frustrated with Allen's announcing over his phone line that he let out with a resounding, "What the fuck? . . ." The Red Sox might well have asked the same question about the opening games of the season, but not over the airwaves. The station immediately cut power until the lines were uncrossed.

These were also the early days of television in America, and on

April 29 the radio stations broadcasting the Red Sox and Braves games in Boston received the rights gratis from the ball clubs to contract broadcasts from any television station willing to screen a game. On June 15, WBZ televised a Braves game to Boston-area viewers within a radius of 40 miles. At this time the teams thought television an advertising gimmick to get fans out to the ballpark, and if the radio stations were willing to do the setup, why shouldn't they collect what minuscule revenues fell to them by the by? The Gillette Company pursued the same tactic in the early days of television broadcasting. The company used its extensive radio advertising contracts to leverage rights for television broadcasts of the World Series, beginning on a modified national basis that year along the eastern seaboard.

The potential of television, tried unsuccessfully for broadcasting baseball before the war, was seen as limited in 1948, but a hint as to its future could have been gleaned from the May 18 telecast of a New York Giants game from the Polo Grounds. Local taverns owned most of the sets, and the bars of Jersey City were exploding with patrons for the major league game that Saturday night while the Giants' minor league affiliate, the Jersey City Giants, played to almost no one in their home park. This would be the model of things to come.

The Red Sox were coming alive in early May after a rough start. Williams followed a 3-for-3 day against the Yanks on May 1 with a game the next day in which he homered, tripled, and drove in five runs. In addition, he had one of the best defensive days of his life, making two difficult catches in left and holding two carom shots off the wall to harmless singles. Williams had the older fans joking about his outfield play as even flashier than the extraordinary feats of Tris Speaker, who owned center for the Sox early in the century. The story went around that Speaker wasn't much of an outfielder until he got to Boston and Cy Young began hitting him fungoes. Young was the best fungo hitter who ever lived and got an enormous kick out of placing them just inches beyond Speaker's reach on swing after swing. Speaker became so fed up he began gauging everything he could— foot position, bat speed, sound—in order to get a better jump. It worked, and Cy Young had a little less to laugh about as a fungo hitter and a little more to gloat about as a pitcher with Speaker roving center field for him.

With the Sox on the warpath, their catcher, Birdie Tebbetts, acquired the year before from the Tigers, tried to fire them up even more. He blocked the approach of a Tiger rookie, George Vico, on a play at the plate on May 6 at Fenway, and the kid came up swinging. But Tebbetts hadn't removed his mask yet and Vico took a punch at heavy metal. Both players began rolling on the ground before ump Red Jones collared them and personally escorted the combatants to the clubhouse runway. All three disappeared for a moment through the dugout when Jones reappeared from the runway alone screaming for the cops. Tebbetts and Vico were scrapping again. "Help!" cried Jones, "They're killing each other." The cops took it from there, with the league office chiming in with $100 fines a couple of days later.

Meanwhile, Williams continued to stroke; his average was at .411 by May 12. On that day he received a photo, sent by a fan, of his picture on a huge billboard in Shanghai with incomprehensible ideograms and a local brand of cigarette. It was a sure bet his business manager, Fred Corcoran, would be on the line to China about this one. But as May wore on Williams slumped at a time Boston was having trouble, as usual, winning on the road. The team was floundering in seventh place. Williams's shift nemesis, Lou Boudreau of Cleveland, was burning up the league at .430, and Williams was down 40 points—down, that is, until a game in Cleveland on May 21 when he mauled the Indians' shift with a home run and three singles, gaining back half the points he had lost on his average over the past couple of weeks.

By June the Red Sox fell 9½ games behind Cleveland, and Ted Williams finally acceded to suggestions that he go to left more consistently against the shift. Indeed, 9 of his last 15 hits had been to left or left center, forcing the shift to sag counterclockwise. On June 16 the Indians took off their shift against Williams for the first time since they had installed it in 1946. Williams promptly went 4 for 4, leading the Red Sox to a 7–4 win with a home run, two doubles, and a single off Bob Feller, the three extra-base hits all to left. His average was at .408, and Boston, sweeping the Indians with another win, 8–6, seemed poised for a move. In their next series Boston steamrolled the Tigers, with Williams stroking at a lofty pace, 12 hits in his last 15 at-bats.

While the Red Sox were on their western swing, Babe Ruth,

looking very frail, traveled to New Haven to present a copy of his book, *The Babe Ruth Story*, to the captain of the Yale baseball team on the college's legendary field. The awed young ballplayer accepting the book from the Babe was George Bush. Williams all the while remained pistol hot. By June 24, after hitting two out of the park in the second game of a doubleheader against the White Sox, his average was up to .417 and the Red Sox were closing in quickly on the first-place Indians. When Roger Birtwell of the *Globe* asked Williams why he was suddenly hitting to left he answered tartly: "Because they're pitching me outside." His average for the month of June cashed in at .460, his highest monthly average ever during his career.

In late June, about the time the Berlin airlift began in Europe, the Red Sox were on a streak that saw them winning 17 of 22 games. They had halved Cleveland's lead and were 5½ out, where they hovered until the All-Star break. In the American League's 5–2 win that year, Williams only pinch hit (a walk) because he had torn some rib cartilage in a friendly goof-off wrestling match with Sam Mele on a train ride. McCarthy was furious and Mele's position on the team was forever weakened; he was traded early in 1949 to Washington. After the All-Star break, the rib injury did not respond well, and Williams sat for two weeks, a period during which the Red Sox managed to win 10 of 11 games. The predictable talk began: The club played better without their great star. He faded in the clutch. He ruined the Red Sox chances in 1947 because he wouldn't hit to left. He was ruining them this year because he was hitting to left. He lost his power. He walked too often. He didn't tip his cap. He called people "Sport."

When Williams returned to the lineup in late July, the Red Sox had tied for the league lead, coming back from a deficit of 11½ games on May 30. Their 13-game winning streak was stopped by a decisive 13–0 loss to the Tigers on July 28, but the race was tighter than a C-clamp, with four teams separated by one game on August 1: the surprising Philadelphia A's, the Indians, the Yanks, and the Red Sox. Manager Joe McCarthy was getting pennant fever in a way he grew to expect from those years directing the New York Yankees. And he was not to be deprived. In a game against Cleveland on August 2, McCarthy charged the plate after Lou Boudreau slid under catcher

Matt Batts's tag for a run. He kicked the dirt hysterically when the ump, Summers, told him Batts hadn't gotten his glove down for the tag. Then he turned to Batts and chewed him out. In full view of everyone in the park, McCarthy kicked his catcher in the butt as he berated him: "Next time take him out."

Later McCarthy said he hadn't kicked Batts for Batts's sake but for the umpire's benefit so Summers would get it in his head that Batts wouldn't dare miss such a tag again. This was ingenious in a way that escaped the humanitarian impulses of those who witnessed it, but McCarthy was impatient with Boston's writers, who wanted to know why he humiliated his rookie catcher. He didn't wish to take the time to explain that protests on particular calls have in view other potential calls down the road. His antics might never pay off, but just possibly the umpire might assume on the next close play that Batts got the tag down because he wanted no part of McCarthy's swift foot.

On August 16, 1948, the baseball world and the fiery pennant race in the American League paused for a moment in honor of Babe Ruth, who had died of throat cancer at age 53. He lay in state at Yankee Stadium, and 50,000 fans came to view his body. His funeral drew another 100,000 along the cortege's route. He was the greatest figure ever in American sports, and his fans paid him proper homage.

Through the month of August, the Red Sox continued to play good ball and moved into first place on the 24th by beating Cleveland 9–8 at Fenway on Vern Stephens's clutch ninth-inning home run. Williams was not doing well. His ribs were killing him on every swing, and he couldn't drive the ball. But as September approached, things were not nearly as bad for Williams as they were for actor Robert Mitchum in Hollywood. Mitchum was arrested in a dawn raid on the Laurel Canyon home of Lila Reed. There were "reefers," as the police called them, all over the floor. When the cops asked him his occupation Mitchum was witty enough to judge the effect by the cause. He answered, "Former actor." For his reefer madness, Mitchum ended up doing a few months' time.

Amidst the struggle for the pennant in the American League, the citizens of Boston awoke on September 1 to find that the Red Sox and the Boston Braves were both in first place. And on September 6, with the Red Sox in Washington and the Braves at home, Boston experienced one of the most euphoric baseball days in the town's history.

Both teams won their doubleheaders, and it looked more and more like the first city Series ever. Dedicated fans began petitioning school boards to delay the scheduled opening of the semester because the kids were simply too excited to pay attention to anything not in the local sports pages.

With the *Globe* headline calling the shot—"HUB BASEBALL MAD"—Red Sox fans lined up all night in front of Fenway for tickets to the upcoming Yankee series on September 8, 9, and 10. This might be the make-or-break point. Boston took the first two, 10–6 and 9–4, but the Yanks averted disaster by winning the rubber game 11–6 on Joe DiMaggio's magnificent grand-slam home run into the center-field bleachers. With the Red Sox and Braves still in front in the American and National leagues, Grantland Rice offered the town a tribute to the teams and to their managers, Joe McCarthy and Billy Southworth.

> Here's to the Land of the Bean and the Cod,
> The Cabots and Lowells and also the scrod,
> To Lodge and to Saltonstall, wearing the shield,
> To Harvard's bright crimson that flames down the field.
> But greater than all in their new pennant bid,
> I give you McCarthy and Billy the Kid.
>
> The gay town of Boston is neck deep in glory.
> Its Bunker Hill party is now an old story.
> It looks to the past or it turns to the present
> And finds all the news is decidedly pleasant.
> But greater than all where the salt breezes blow,
> Here's the life for Southworth and Buffalo Joe.

The Red Sox were scrambling to hold on to a slim lead as September edged into its last weeks. Bobby Doerr was out with a leg injury, and the club was struggling, getting plenty of base hits from Williams but little power. He was physically worn, having played through the August heat in pain, and the wear was showing. On September 19 the Red Sox lost two to Detroit, and Williams hit his first home run in three weeks. And in a game that Feller called the most important he ever pitched, the Indians beat the Red Sox 5–2 on September 22 before 76,772 at Municipal Stadium to tie for the league lead. Two days later, the Yankees slipped into a tie with the Indians and the Red Sox for first. This race was incredible.

Williams tried to explain his low home-run production by citing a clipping a fan sent him about wind currents at Fenway being particularly brutal in the summer months this year. He said that he always took account of these things, and though he had no idea about the consistency of the wind patterns, he did think that he had been making conscious decisions not to hit into the wind more often than he could ever remember. This is precisely what made Williams so maddening to writers. A weather vane the Red Sox did not need; a run producer they did.

The Braves clinched the National League pennant on September 26 while the Yankees and Red Sox were alternating wins at Yankee Stadium. The Indians, meanwhile, slipped into first place. On September 28, the frustration was showing for the Red Sox and for Williams. The team lost 4–2 to the Senators, and Williams's bat almost skulled Earle Combs, coaching at first, when he heaved it up the line after striking out in the third against one of Ray Scarborough's low curves. Williams was angry before the game began, fuming at a story in the papers that he was out buying a brand-new red hunting outfit, the implication being that he was already thinking about leaving town for the wilds instead of readying to play in the World Series.

On the last day of September the Red Sox were still two games out of first, and only 4,998 fans showed up at Fenway for a game against the Senators. Red Sox fans seemed to have given up en masse. The town was then a one-team show: the Boston Braves. But it wasn't over yet. On October 1, Detroit scored three times in the ninth inning to beat Cleveland 5–3. Both the Red Sox and the Yanks were then one game out of first behind Cleveland. On October 2 Williams hit his 25th home run of the year in the first inning as the Sox coasted to a 5–1 win over the Yanks. The next day, Boston led the Yanks 5–2 in the fourth and the crowd at Fenway, now back up to a pennant-fevered 30,000, erupted in joy when the scoreboard operator posted four runs for Detroit in their game against the Indians. Boston ended up winning 10–5 and the Indians lost 7–1. The race was dead even yet again, and required a Monday playoff between the Red Sox and the Indians for the right to face the Boston Braves in the World Series.

Momentum and tension are funny things. The Red Sox had enough of the former to carry them to a tie for the American League pennant and too much of the latter to ease naturally into the Sunday playoff. The team was wrung out from the Yankee series, and everyone seemed to know it. McCarthy spoke to reporters as if he had already proved something. He said the last games of the season were unbelievable and that the Red Sox played brilliantly in the clutch when it counted. That was always the trademark of his former Yankee teams. But the one clutch game was yet to come, and McCarthy was speaking as if the war was over and the next battle not really of this world. He secured pride of place by beating the Yankees, and, in facing the Indians for one more telling game, he seemed tentative in a way that he had rarely been before.

The Red Sox approach to the playoff was oblique, statistical, and hunch ridden. McCarthy's first-line pitchers were arm weary—both Kinder and Mel Parnell were running on empty. Though McCarthy might possibly have wrung another start out of Parnell's arm, he chose to start Dennis Galehouse because he had had some luck against the Indians in the past. But on the other hand, Galehouse had not pitched consistently in the last few weeks. Even today Galehouse can't explain the choice. He didn't feel sharp, and he sensed that either McCarthy or others on the Red Sox staff were in their cups. Cleveland blasted the journeyman hard during the game. Lou Boudreau and Kenny Keltner did the bulk of the damage—two veteran hitters who knew how to hit in Fenway: don't aim at the wall, necessarily. On this occasion Boudreau made use of the right-field foul line and popped a two-run homer into the stands in a toss-up fair-foul call by the umpire. The Red Sox were never in the game after that. They scored in the sixth on a misjudged Williams pop fly and on Bobby Doerr's home run off Gene Bearden, but the final was an easy 8–3 win for Cleveland. Bearden for the Indians shut the Red Sox down with knucklers and nickel curves.

Somehow the mood in the Red Sox clubhouse was not as bleak as it might have been—or as it ought to have been—according to some of the town's baseball writers. The Sox as a whole left their energies where McCarthy left his, at Fenway against the Yankees. Even Ted

Williams was approachable after the game. Harold Kaese remembers milling in the locker room and hearing Williams stop a younger reporter: "What's the matter? Aren't you going to talk to me?" "I don't know if I dare," the writer answered. "Why? We've never had any arguments, have we?" "No, I don't know you well enough. But I've heard about your moods." "Oh, you have," said Williams with a smile that lit up the place, "Those damn things."

Kaese couldn't quite figure how the Sox lost the pennant. He wanted to lay it all at Williams's feet despite the man's .369 average. But most were little fish singles, Kaese charged, with no slugging percentage to speak of. It is true that Williams dipped in the second half of the season—from .392 at the All-Star break to .346 after, from 16 home runs in the first half to nine in the second, and from 72 runs batted in before the break to 55 after. On the other hand, Williams was a bright spot where the Red Sox needed it: on the road. In 1948 he hit .370 outside of Fenway and .368 at home, slightly better than 1942, when he hit .365 on the road and exactly the same at home. Once again, Sportsman's Park in St. Louis was a true haven for him. The ball park, combined with the Browns' pitching staff, earned Williams a .452 average in St. Louis to raise his seven-year career average there to .424. He had a great road year at Comiskey Park as well, hitting .483, and at Municipal Stadium, hitting .409. His worst effort for the season was at one of his favorite hitting parks, Briggs Stadium, where he managed only eight hits for a .216 average with one home run.

The 1948 World Series between the Indians and the Braves was the first to be beamed over a national—actually, seminational—television hookup into the taverns and homes of America, reaching over 466,000 sets and an estimated 7,771,000 viewers during East Coast and Midwest broadcasts. More than a hundred television monitors were set up on the Boston Commons to allow the locals to watch their Braves lose to Cleveland in six games. For the Yankees-Dodgers World Series in 1947, television broadcasts reached only the East Coast with 150,000 receivers and 3,000,000 viewers. From that time on, the wave of the future in baseball was intimately tied to television. Everything, in some way or another, was connected to media coverage and media marketing, from the structure of the minor leagues to league expansion to multiyear contracts.

◇ 11 ◇

Close but No Cigar
1949

TED WILLIAMS HAD LED THE American League in hitting for two years in a row, and his contract negotiations were a little slow for the first time in his career. Hugh Duffy, the ancient of days still working for the Sox, told Williams that he, too, had led the league two years in a row back in the 1890s and hadn't gotten a raise. Duffy's epic memory was fading a bit; he led the league only once. "Can you beat that?" the old-timer asked Williams. "I hope not," Williams replied, eager enough to try leading the league again, but in no way keen on forswearing raises.

Yawkey coughed up, finally, on February 24. Williams would log in for $85,000 in 1949 plus bonuses for the particular notch in the standings the Red Sox happened to occupy. At season's end they would once again just miss occupying the notch they most cherished. But these still were the Red Sox glory teams. Their fans loved them and suffered for them. And their owner, Tom Yawkey, joined in, though in the late 1940s he could afford to suffer a tad more easily. The commissioner of corporations in the state of Massachusetts forced the organization this year to make public its books. In only two of all the years Yawkey owned the team—since 1933—had it turned a significant profit: $55,296 in 1948, the season just ended, and $491,367 in 1946. Over the years Yawkey had laid out $3,826,526 for players.

If Williams's salary, which would edge toward $100,000 with bonuses, seemed high, the comparison to Hollywood's brightest stars bore about the same kind of results that it might in percentage terms today. In 1949, Humphrey Bogart topped the scales at $467,361; and Bette Davis, at $328,000, was the highest-paid actress. All this can be measured against the average annual wage of $3,000. Money ruled in postwar America. It no doubt ruled prewar America as well, but far fewer felt the glow of its availability.

On February 9 the U.S. Court of Appeals in New York ruled that Danny Gardella's $300,000 suit against major league baseball had grounds. A former fighter and bodybuilder, Gardella was the first ballplayer to jump to the Mexican League after the war and the first to feel the pinch of the ruling by the commissioner of baseball banning the return of renegade players as a penalty for having violated the reserve clause. Gardella's lawyers planned an assault against baseball by attacking the clause on two grounds, both of which had the leagues in a tizzy: illegal monopolies and the violation of federal laws applicable to interstate commerce (in that fees for baseball broadcasts constituted transaction of business across state lines).

Judge Jerome N. Frank said that the reserve clause was a kind of peonage. Commissioner Happy Chandler pointed out that if so, baseball's peons were certainly well paid. Gardella wasn't paid at all: that was his point. He jumped early and did not return under the umbrella of generosity extended by the leagues in 1946. As a player he never was great, toiling a couple of years for the Giants during the war. His most notorious baseball moment came earlier in the minors with Newark when he climbed out of a 12th-floor hotel window and hung from the ledge by his hands (attached to heavily muscled arms) while his roommate, Nap Reyes, was reading a fake suicide note placed on the bed. The emotional Reyes ran to the open window screaming in terror. Gardella was laughing so hard he could hardly pull himself up to safety.

Things were a bit different now. A less playful Gardella was out of work and eager to get back in baseball. The majors weren't buying. But his mouthpiece, Frederic A. Johnson, was a legal phenom. Later in the year, Johnson brought the majors to their collective knees. He petitioned the leagues, through the courts, to open their revenue books, insisting that the original reserve clause in 1880 had little bearing on the way it had been practiced over the decades. A mere five roster players per team were originally under baseball's protection. Johnson also threatened a full review of the minor league affiliate system and its jurisdiction by interstate commerce.

Johnson began by reciting from memory the names of 463 minor league teams in 63 leagues. The baseball representatives listened to this performance and decided almost immediately to pay off Gardella. Each team was rumored to have kicked in about $5,000 to soothe the former Giant and to keep the mnemonics freak Johnson from another court appearance like this one. The deal was worked out over several months and completed in 1950. Gardella was attached to the Cardinals organization and got only one more major league at-bat, in 1950, but he won his point in fighting the ban against ballplayers jumping to the Mexican League. Amnesty was generally granted that year by baseball in return for the dropping of other suits against the leagues by Sal Maglie, Max Lanier, Lou Klein, and Fred Martin for a combined total of $5,000,000.

As spring training of 1949 commenced, the Cold War continued to take shape and dominate the future of American life. The Berlin blockade was still on, though it would be over in May. The NATO Treaty was in the final stages of ratification. Strategic advances in aerial strike capabilities—the Lucky Lady B-50 bomber had just made the first nonstop flight around the world (with four midair refuelings)—inspired a defensively postured and hostile American foreign policy that would last through the next two decades. The Russians were perfecting their A-bomb. Tawdry red-scare accusations involving State Department figures Alger Hiss and Whittaker Chambers began to circulate in the spring and summer, conveniently boosting the reputation of an awkward young congressman from California, Richard Milhous Nixon. And Herbert A. Philbrook, a counterspy from the Boston area, began to sing publicly at the trial of 11 suspected communists.

In Boston that spring something known as pyramid clubs were all the rage. Like other schemes periodically sweeping the country, this one encouraged a string of donations from invited donors, each repeating the invitations and collections, so that accumulated funds would pyramid in a kind of commission system. The problem with such schemes was that the originators made out like bandits and those at the bottom of the pyramid (most everybody else) got taken when the demand exceeded the supply. Boston sociologists described this one as a "mass psychiatric bender."

The Red Sox wanted the pennant badly this season, and they were good enough to go after it. Hopes were no doubt buoyed by the news from the Yankees' camp: x-rays on Joe DiMaggio's heel revealed a bone spur with ligament damage. He was to go under the knife at Johns Hopkins and would be lost for the beginning months of the season. Meanwhile, at Sarasota, Ted Williams came with his yearly new idea: outfield warmups between innings. He told Hy Hurwitz, "Some day soon outfielders will have regular warmup throws between innings just like infielders do. Outfielders should have their arms loose just like infielders. Keeping runners from taking extra bases helps win ball games. That's one of the main jobs for an outfielder. It's tough to stand out in the field for eight innings and then be called upon to make a throw in the ninth." Johnny Sain of the Braves, listening to Williams talk, told Hurwitz that some outfielders found ways of doing just this. Dixie Walker used to toss the ball between innings with the Dodgers' bullpen regulars.

The Boston writers were trying a different tactic with Williams this year, and, by and large, they succeeded. Many chose to stay away from him entirely. Things had been so bitter at the beginning and at the end of the 1948 season that beat writers and columnists were simply writing their articles without taking what they thought was the needless humiliation of confronting Williams. Jerry Nason still hinted in the *Globe* that the Boston corps deserved some credit for resisting the provocation to go public with rumors of Williams's gallivanting.

> Without faking himself out of a job, a reporter can't interview a guy who refuses to converse. The average professional boxer will say, "I don't care what they write as long as they spell my name right!" The average ballplayer—heck, every ballplayer—wants only nice writeups. He hates your guts if you mention he made an error. Baseball writers owe baseball players nothing, because over the years they've made national heroes out of more than one who was illiterate, ill-tempered, ill-spoken, pampered, and profane. They've covered up more baseball sins than they ever have revealed, and sometimes did so at the expense of their own consciences as newspapermen.

On the very same day of Nason's almost-plaintive piece on the private side of the baseball hero, Williams played an exhibition game against the Jacksonville minor league team. The public side of heroism in sports—sheer talent—reflected itself in the impassioned words of Jacksonville's manager, Jack Aragon: "I've told my pitchers to pitch to him. The fans want to see him hit. I hope none of my players get killed." They were safe enough. Williams hit one 420 feet over the fence in right into a tree and scattered only the native wildlife.

Nason's column and Jack Aragon's remark highlight the balance in baseball between the nature of the volatile man and the nature of the great talent. The writers always knew that Williams was good copy on either count, and it would only be a matter of time, in this or any season, before they would be at their keyboards again, and Williams would be in the headlines again. They needed him; and, to the extent that his ego registered the responses of others, he wanted them.

A decade before, in 1939, the Red Sox missed a chance to keep Pee Wee Reese playing for their farm team in Louisville. This year a Red Sox scout got wind of a high school kid named Willie Mays playing in Birmingham, Alabama. He got in touch with Joe Cronin, who sent down a man from the Red Sox organization, but Boston passed on a possible $5,000 deal for signing Mays. He apparently wasn't Boston's "sort" of player. This is deliberately ambiguous language. It could mean Mays was too flashy and erratic. It could also mean Mays, like Jackie Robinson, was black.

The Red Sox moved north and Williams warmed up for the season opener by hitting three home runs against the Braves in a Hartford exhibition game. But the Philadelphia A's took them 3–2 in their first official game on the road. Williams got two singles off Lou Brissie, whose war-damaged knee he had almost crushed in the season opener of 1948. But what spiced the opening of the 1949 season was the irascible Leo Durocher, now managing the New York Giants. Leo got himself in a fight with a fan, one Fred Boysen, at the Polo Grounds, and Happy Chandler suspended him. But this one wasn't Leo's fault; he was provoked. Boysen was a shady character who couldn't resist nabbing a woman's purse near the police station where he went to file charges against Durocher. Needless to say, he was caught immediately and charged with felonious intent, which somewhat deflated the urgency of his case against Leo the Lip. Happy Chandler lifted Durocher's suspension.

The Red Sox were having their difficulties uncranking early in 1949, even though Williams and Vern Stephens were putting some good numbers on the boards. Frustration was mounting all around in a game against Detroit on May 24 when Williams took one of Dizzy Trout's fastballs down the middle for a called third strike and tossed his bat 75 feet in the air along the first-base line at Fenway. He was already unhappy at the second strike call on a slider, but Dizzy Trout said what really made him mad was coming back with a fastball down the middle. It froze him: "He didn't expect it. That's what got him mad."

Umpire Art Paparella turned his back to get more balls after the strike call and pretended, after his fashion, not to see the bat-throwing incident. But Detroit manager Red Rolfe was having none of it. He charged the field screaming at Paparella to do something. Paparella told Rolfe, "Hell, I only saw it come down. I didn't see him throw it." A perplexed Rolfe asked him: "Jeez, Art, where d'you think it came from, Mars? If one of my .200 hitters does this, he's outta the game. The league's gonna hear about this, Art, it's not right." Paparella knew that Rolfe had a point, but he knew two other things as well: Williams was not a .200 hitter, and baseball was a spectator sport. He pacified Rolfe with a final comment that invoked the decorum of the showdown: "He didn't say nuthin'. He just tossed the bat. Play ball!" The league office later entered the picture and fined Williams an admonitory $50.

This was the year of the injury. New York was leading the league with the walking wounded, and in late May the Red Sox lost Bobby Doerr with his chronic bad back. And then there was the bizarre event that took place at the Edgewater Beach Hotel in Chicago on June 15 after a Phillies-Cubs game. Eddie Waitkus, the Phils' first baseman, who had been traded from Chicago that year, received a note from a woman named Ruth Steinhagen, also registered at the hotel, that said "we are not acquainted, but I have something of importance to speak to you about. It's to your advantage to let me explain." It turned out to be less to his advantage than he might have wished. When Waitkus—who was hitting .306 that season, by the way—arrived at her hotel room after midnight, Steinhagen turned to her closet and told Waitkus that she had "a little something for you." Indeed she had. She swiveled with a .22 rifle in her arms and fired at Waitkus point-blank. Then she waited outside the room for the police.

Ruth Steinhagen had fixated on Waitkus when he played for the Cubs. Her room was a shrine of his photographs. His leaving town for the Phils was more than she could handle, though for the present she was forced to handle it as best she could while mopping floors at the Cook County Jail awaiting arraignment. As for Waitkus, he would require several operations to dislodge the bullet near his spine and to repair the damage done to his stomach cavity. But Ruth Steinhagen's schizophrenic passion could not keep Waitkus from resuming his career the following year, when he hit .284 and played in all 154 games plus the four ignominious Philly losses to the Yankees in the 1950 World Series.

June 28, 1949, marked one of baseball's historic moments. Joe DiMaggio, with no spring training, after weeks of misery from a painful bone spur operation, played for the first time all year in a series at Fenway Park. His performance was and still is a remarkable touchstone for pure baseball excellence. In the first game, he went 2 for 3 and homered as the Yankees won 5-4. The next day he hit two out of the park and chalked up five runs batted in as the Yankees, down 7-1, ended up winning the game 9-7. Ted Williams actually bunted himself on base in the second inning before Vern Stephens parked one during an early-inning spurt of runs that seemed insurmountable. But not in Fenway. In the fifth, DiMaggio drove one of Ellis Kinder's tentative pitches over the wall in left center, and in the seventh he bombed an Earl Johnson inside curve deep into the left-field screen. As the local *Globe* reporter described it, "DiMaggio hit one inside the nets in left; the other inside the city limits beyond the fence." DiMaggio, who had never been treated with veneration by the Red Sox fans, enjoyed a huge ovation after his second home run, despite the Red Sox debacle. The crowd reaction stunned and moved him.

The teams met again on June 30, and DiMaggio continued his rampage. He won the game on a three-run homer in the seventh off a Mel Parnell 3-2 fastball; the blast hit one of the steel towers in left. When a great hitter, fresh from a layoff but on fire with the eagerness and the thrill of resumption, gets as hot as DiMaggio now was, the only sane thing to do was to run for cover. With the power of Joe's revived bat stoking up runs, Vic Raschi pitched beautifully against Williams, collaring him 0 for 5 with vicious inside pitches at the toughest spots in Williams's hitting zone.

These games, marked by DiMaggio's amazing, virtually unrehearsed return to a championship lineup, pushed the Red Sox eight games out of first and sounded a low note for Boston in a season that would see the Sox surge around the All-Star break and through the second half of the year only to suffer a devastating blow again at season's end. When the talk resumed that week about the Williams-for-DiMaggio trade discussions back in 1946, Roger Birtwell of the *Globe* rubbed it in by pointing out that Tom Yawkey's big mistake was not merely failing to get Joe DiMaggio but failing to buy the Yankees when they were for sale that same year.

Things continued to plunge for the Red Sox. On July 4, the day after DiMaggio had batted in four more runs against the Senators, giving him 13 since his return, he hit another out against the Red Sox at Yankee Stadium. This gave him five home runs in five games against Boston. Worse, Williams hurt his ribs running into the fence in futile pursuit of DiMaggio's home run. The Red Sox had now lost 8 in a row and were 12 games out of first place. Joe McCarthy was in despair, and his condition was made no less grave by one of the weirdest plays of the season. Al Zarilla had lined a single to medium right with the bases loaded. Pesky, on third, thought rightfielder Cliff Mapes had a chance for the ball, so he held up. But Williams was flying from second, with that flapping motion of his, in the hopes of scoring on the liner. He had to put on his brakes when he saw Pesky hanging back at third to tag. Mapes had played the ball on the run, intending to come up throwing for a shot at Williams. But his throw reached the plate before Pesky. Berra took it like a first baseman for the force on the desperate and chagrined Pesky.

At the All-Star Game on July 12, the American League won in a slugfest, 11–7. Williams didn't get any hits but he made a tough backhand catch of a Don Newcombe liner to left, a game-winning play according to Williams's longtime nemesis and All-Star teammate Lou Boudreau. Joe DiMaggio, playing as an honorary choice, continued his amazing comeback from his heel injury by jolting a couple of hits. The National League pitcher who handled Williams was Larry Jansen, who got Ted with a perfect sequence of deliveries—two tough curves, which he fouled off, and then a fastball on the fists for a called third strike. Later that season Indians pitcher Jim Bagby, a friend of Williams from earlier Boston days, thought, "maybe that's the way to pitch him." He tried it, and, indeed, Williams fouled off two curves but then rocketed the inside fastball for a line-drive base hit. Bagby told Boudreau, "That is *not* the way to pitch him."

Williams got hot after the All-Star break, and so did the Red Sox. He hit .417 through to August and would hit .360 for the entire second half of the season, with 23 home runs from July 14 on. This was a far cry from his late-season stats in 1948. In August, the Sox put together a few winning streaks and a long hitting streak by Dom DiMaggio. They were creeping up on the Yankees, a team still staggered by injuries. Dominic's consecutive-game streak was up to 34 when he lined to his brother on his last at-bat on August 9 at Fenway; he ended up 22 short of Joe's record 56-game streak.

The next day at Fenway, Williams got himself in hot water yet again. He drove a ball to deep right center and coasted into second base, assuming he had an easy double. But he wasn't paying much attention in the outfield because Gene Woodling fumbled the ball and Rizzuto then couldn't handle the bad relay. Williams was rearranging his socks when he should have been scampering to third base. The Yanks won the game 3–2, and some of the Red Sox pointed out that they might have picked up that run from third.

The writers approached him, ever so carefully, about the play and got an earful: "Hell. DiMaggio did the same thing the other night. He gauged it off the wall as a single when he could have easily been in at second. But you can bet no one said anything about it. Me? Jeez, they gave it to me good." An agent provocateur, Dan Daniel of the *New York World Telegram*, tried to stir up DiMaggio by goading him with Williams's quote. DiMaggio took the bait, one of the few times in his career that he did so, perhaps because his heel was still smarting: "Williams is a crybaby. I didn't try for two on that play at Fenway because Williams knows how to play the ball off the wall better than anyone." In the past, DiMaggio was usually more circumspect on the subject of Williams. Clif Keane once asked him about Williams: "Williams? Greatest left-handed hitter I ever saw." "What about as a ballplayer?" Keane asked. DiMaggio simply repeated, "Greatest left-handed hitter I ever saw." Joe was a man of few words, some of them making their point by being the same words. "Thank you," said Keane.

The press war was on, and writers couldn't wait to get to Williams with the crybaby quote. But on the subject of other ballplayers, Williams had a built-in respect meter. He backed off. Then DiMaggio realized he'd been set up and toned himself down: "If I said it, I didn't mean it. Ted and I get along fine. Heck, I was chasing that one he hit the other day a mile. He really belted it."

By mid-August the Red Sox had won 19 of their last 23 and were three games out of first place. The locals were getting aroused and eager. Even the official scorers were getting into the act. Three times during a Yankee series the local scorers, having conspired on policy, recorded singles for Williams on ground balls bobbled in short right field by Jerry Coleman, playing only a nominal second base for the Yanks. The scorers' reasoning had a certain purity to it. Outfielders do not get charged with errors for bobbling grounders when the runner does not advance beyond first. And if teams are going to play four outfielders (even if one of them is more of a short fielder), then a grounder to the edge of the outfield is a single if the runner is not nabbed at first. If juggled, the pitcher takes the burden of a base hit rather than an error charged to a fielder. Scorers in other cities were less charitable to Williams on similar occasions. But the scorers in Boston were making a point.

The Yankees acquired Johnny Mize in late August for their stretch run, but Boston kept on coming. On August 26 the Red Sox took the White Sox in a doubleheader at Comiskey Park, with Williams hitting two home runs in the first game for 32 on the year, and with the flashy-fast Mel Parnell pitching brilliantly in the August heat: "MEL-TED," was the clever headline in the *Globe* as the Red Sox edged to within 1½ games of first place. On August 27 at Comiskey, Williams hit two more. He was red hot: .359 for the year, with 34 home runs and 135 runs batted in. The Yankees, on the other hand, were fading. On August 28 Tommy Henrich became the latest in a long list of casualties: He crashed into the wall at Comiskey and broke a small bone in his spine. Over the year, 71 injuries put the Yankee roster players out for an average of 15 games apiece. Only Phil Rizzuto played in every game. Even the team trainer was out in August with cracked ribs.

The Red Sox and Yanks were still scrapping for first place a week later during a series in New York. Reliever Joe Page held Boston off for a 5-2 Yankee win in the first game. The second game was rained out, and then the Sox, helped by a rare Johnny Pesky home run, coasted to a 7-1 win on September 9. And then came Black Sunday: the Red Sox moved on to Philadelphia and lost twice to the A's, 6-4

and 4–0, with Ferris Fain ringing hits all over Shibe Park, while the
Yankees won two from the Senators. This was a four-game swing late
in the season, and the Red Sox never truly recovered from it, though
a clutch winning streak in late September helped them claw back to
the top for a spell. But the dramatic turnabout on September 11 gave
them little breathing space. The rest of the struggle was intense, and
they had to go on the road for the pennant-clinching series with the
Yanks at year's end.

Harold Kaese was snide at the expense of the Red Sox and of Ted
Williams, who managed a scratch single in the A's doubleheader loss.
Some games, wrote Kaese, hitters have "one of those clutch days at
the plate." The reference was to Fain, but Fain had no reason to be
hitting in the clutch. For the Philadelphia A's, the phrase had no
meaning at this point in the season. But for the Red Sox it did. And
the sorry day in the box score belonged to Williams. Kaese finished
up: "The Red Sox are the best team in baseball. There is no logical
reason for its failure."

Dave Egan, as usual, was all over Williams, charging him with
jealousy over the home-run-hitting prowess of Vern Stephens. Egan
was always ready to stir previously muddied waters: "Defeat with him
starring is preferable to victory when he must stand in the shadow of
another." Jerry Nason chimed in the next day: "Should the Red Sox
blow this one it will be far more revolting to digest than all their
previous failures." Nason then filled his column with Red Sox miseries from the 1930s on: seven regulars over .300 in 1938 and no
pennant; six regulars over .308 in 1939 and no pennant; Foxx, Williams, Doerr, and Cronin hitting almost 100 homers combined in
1940 and no pennant; the still-bitter finale of 1948 and no pennant.
And this year, 1949, the Red Sox could not even make the claim that
their pitching was failing them. Both Parnell and Kinder were destined to win more than 20 games. "Screwy game, ain't it?" Nason
concluded.

Perhaps Boston needed comic relief for their final run, three games
out of first place in late September. Joe McCarthy unintentionally
provided it. In a game against Cleveland on September 20 at Fenway,
he protested to the umpires that Bob Lemon was pitching with a
dirty hat—that he had put grease on its bill. Lemon claimed the bill
was merely worn from tugging at it. The charge of loading up was
simply old hat. Lemon agreed to change caps and then lost the game

5-2. The next day during warmups he showed up in his uniform but wearing a brand-new gray fedora. Even McCarthy had a good laugh.

The Red Sox beat Cleveland again, 9-6, with Williams hitting his 41st home run of the year. Boston remained within two of the Yanks, while in the National League the Cards and Dodgers were fighting it out down to the wire, as they seemed to do every other year during the 1940s. As the season moved into the last week it was showdown time. The Red Sox had a handful of games with the Yankees—two in Fenway and three in New York. On September 24 Ellis Kinder won his 23rd game of the year against the Yanks, 3-0. On September 25 Parnell won his 25th, 4-1, with Williams hitting his final home run of the season, number 43.

The pennant would be decided by one rain-out make-up game in New York, a detour to Washington, and the final games of the season back at Yankee Stadium. On September 26, 67,434 jammed the Stadium to watch the Red Sox eke it out 7-6 after trailing most of the game. In a weird ninth inning, Dom DiMaggio ripped a line drive that tore the webbing out of Phil Rizzuto's glove to drive in the tying run. Bobby Doerr soon followed with a squeeze bunt with Pesky on third. Tommy Henrich, wearing a corset brace to protect a potentially serious back injury, fielded the bunt. His throw from first beat Pesky by a considerable margin, but umpire Bill Grieve claimed catcher Ralph Houk had not blocked the plate and made the tag. Houk went ape. Stengel screamed in semicomprehensible language that "blocking the plate is not one of Houk's weaknesses." Later, near the umpire's quarters under the stands, Yankee Cliff Mapes hinted within earshot of the crew that Grieve had a bet on the game. The league office fined him $200 for his indiscretion in the heat of the moment. Houk and Stengel were also fined for the vehemence of their protests. Pesky said he beat the tag and still insists that was the case, but Houk claimed Pesky would have had to have been a mole to score.

The Red Sox did not lose ground in Washington. They won 6-4 on September 27, their 11th win in a row; then lost 2-1 the next day as the Yanks beat the A's 7-5; and then beat the Senators 11-9 on September 30 while the Yankees were losing 4-1 to the A's. Boston came to New York with a one-game lead. Williams was slumping, with just a single for the whole Washington series, and DiMaggio was sicker than a dog.

The Yankees won the first game at the Stadium 5-4 on a day that

DiMaggio was honored in New York. His mother was in the crowd, but Joe needed the support of his brother Dominic's shoulder to even make it through the ceremonies. Johnny Lindell supplied the game winner this day, a deep home run toward the seats in left field over Williams's forlorn head. DiMaggio got a couple of hits in the middle of rallies on a day he should have been taking oxygen in a New York hospital.

The next day the Yankees held on to a 5-3 win and clinched the pennant while the Red Sox desperately tried to claw back into the game in the 9th inning. But Vic Raschi turned them back. Henrich's home run and Jerry Coleman's three-run double in the eighth—a bloop hit down the foul line that fell just out of Al Zarilla's desperate grasp—did the trick for the Yanks. Williams claimed that watching Coleman's bloop fall in for a hit was his worst memory in baseball; he has not been able to get it out of his mind for forty years. Williams went 0 for 2 off Raschi, while George Kell got two hits in his last ball game against Cleveland. Kell won the batting title from Williams by a few hundredths of a point. If watching Coleman's hit was a bleak memory, losing the title to Kell by a fraction couldn't have been much more pleasant for Williams.

"This team can give you a heart condition," said a Boston local in the next day's man-on-the-street poll in the *Globe*. He spoke for the entire Hub. In New York, on the other hand, Brooklyn and the Bronx were in heaven. The Dodgers had just clinched against the Cards as well, and Jackie Robinson took the National League batting title. In the World Series, the Yankees would put it all together in six games to beat the Dodgers on the superb pitching of Allie Reynolds and the surprise power, given his back injury, of Tommy Henrich.

The primary reason for the Red Sox demise in 1949 was their road record. It told the same old story: 61-16 at home; 35-42 on the road. If this weren't postmortem enough, Harold Kaese rode his favorite hobbyhorse into the sunset: Boston's failure, as a team, in the clutch. This time he trotted out the pinch hitters, who were an ignominious 3 for 46 in 1949. He had a point, but what was McCarthy to do? Kaese's answer was that he should have used Boo Ferriss, his good left-handed-hitting pitcher. Ferriss might have helped change a startling statistic—the 1949 Red Sox left 1,284 men on base during the season, a bit over eight runners per game. But Kaese was biting his tongue. What he really wanted to say he had already hinted a few days before: forget the pinch hitters, it was Ted Williams who could not put it together in crucial moments of crucial games. Bill Corum of the *New York Journal American* came right out and said it: "Williams is born to run second. You can't ever explain logically or scientifically why."

The Most Valuable Player voters saw it another way. The writers around the country voted for Williams at or near the top of the Most Valuable list almost overwhelmingly, an oddity in this or any year. He garnered 13 out of 24 first-place ballots, and he was no lower than fourth on anyone's ballot. Phil Rizzuto came in a distant second in the voting, and Joe Page was third. Despite the Red Sox failure at the end of the season, Williams had one of his premium years: a .343 average, 43 home runs, and 159 runs batted in. As usual, he hit well on the road, .337, and well at Fenway, .349. His career average on the road was now at .344 and at Fenway, .361. He hit .373 in Chicago and .371 in New York for his highest road averages and .429 against the Yankees in Fenway for his highest home average. He hit 20 home runs on the road in 1949 and unloaded for a hearty 23 in Fenway.

Writing for *The Sporting News*, Jimmy Powers summed it up: "One year it is Williams vs. DiMaggio; another year it is Williams vs. Musial; then it is Williams vs. Boudreau, or Henrich, or Feller. But always it is Williams up there, the leader in runs batted in, the leader in home runs, or total bases, or walks, or something. The others challenge and fall back. Williams is the greatest of our generation, and, long after we are all dead, future writers, thumbing through the records and looking at the newsreels, will wonder why some of us knocked him down." The figures surely back Powers up: in his last six full seasons, beginning in 1941, Williams had led the American League in slugging percentage all six times; in batting average, four times (and had come close the other two); in runs scored, five times; in runs batted in, three times; and in home runs, four times. On the horizon for the 1950s were two more challengers, Mickey Mantle and Willie Mays, but neither would string together numbers that matched these.

◇ 12 ◇

Elbowed Out
1950

THE SPRING OF 1950 WAS A season of intolerance. Joseph McCarthy—
the Wisconsin senator, not the Boston manager—began to work his
venom nationally with his persecution of Owen Lattimore and that
supposed "honeycomb" of communism that otherwise might be
called the State Department. Ingrid Bergman's movies were publicly
banned when the beautiful star gave birth to Roberto Rossellini's
child while still married to Peter Lindstrom. And Ted Williams had
a taste of taxicab intolerance in his beloved Boston. He showed up in
Boston in February to sign for over $90,000 plus bonus guarantees
and to do his stint fly-casting at the annual Sportsman's Show. The
town was abuzz about the recent Brinks heist, one that wouldn't be
solved until 1955, but the Red Sox were a rival topic of conversation
no matter what else was happening. When Williams took a cab ride
with writer Clif Keane to the Sportsman's Show, the cabbie got to
talking about politics, about the Brinks case, about the weather, and
about the Red Sox. Keane asked him what he thought of Williams.
Without any idea who the fellow was next to Keane—or who Keane
was, for that matter—the cabbie ranted on: "Yeah, the bum! Always
trying to hit homers; why doesn't he go for the single and win the ball
game?"

"There it goes again," Williams said to Keane. "Same old shit. If
I hit home runs, they yell for singles. When I try to hit to left, they yell
for home runs. Just what do these people want, anyway?" Matters
were not helped any when Vern Stephens, a player the local writers
had pegged as Williams's natural rival, wanted his segment of the

inflationary wage spiral from Tom Yawkey. Stephens, who had signing stories to tell ever since his ill-fated days with Veracruz in the
Mexican League, demanded $50,000 from the Red Sox on the
strength of his 1949 season. He held out for a brief spell in spring
training to get it: "Hell, I'm at least half as good as Williams."

Stephens's claim could be seen either as boastful or modest by half
a measure, depending on the way one looked at it. In 1949 he had hit
39 home runs and led the league in runs batted in with 159. And in
his two years with the Red Sox he had hit 68 home runs. According
to the Boston writers, Williams grew a little green around the gills at
Stephens's long-ball exploits, yet rarely had he seen such insulating
protection around him in the Red Sox lineup. Williams's own 43
home runs in 1949 were the most he ever hit; and he would have
more home runs, 25, by the time of his All-Star Game injury in 1950
than he had registered by that date in any other season.

While Stephens was trying to up his Red Sox ante, a more intriguing money story originated in the Pittsburgh Pirates organization. On
March 4 the Pirates signed Paul Pettit, 17, out of Lomita, California.
This was one of the strangest baseball deals ever. About six months
earlier, when Pettit was using up his high school amateur standing,
the Pirates worked out an arrangement with an agent, Fred Stephani,
who maneuvered for exclusive rights for Pettit when he graduated.
Since the Pirates were not allowed to sign the youth as an active high
schooler, they pretended that Stephani had the rights to market
Pettit's talent in any number of ways, perhaps even as an aspiring
movie star. Maybe, just maybe, the movie star route wouldn't pan
out, and Pettit might choose—just *choose*, mind you—to play a little
baseball. Lo and behold, when he was supposedly open for all bids
Stephani dealt Pettit to the Pirates for $200,000. The movie offers,
surprisingly, were slow in coming. The league office would have a
look at this one as a form of collusion.

Another big revenue story in baseball was the boom in televised
games and the potential effects of television on the 60 minor leagues
nationwide. In Los Angeles, for example, with televisions selling by
the thousands each month, and with KLAC televising Hollywood
Stars and Los Angeles Angels games, opening-day attendance was
down to a bare 6,000 at the Stars' Gilmore field. In the majors,
television coverage was just beginning to register in the till with big

bucks. Gilette was now paying $800,000 for World Series rights, up from $65,000 in 1947; and the All-Star Game this year would cost the razor company $50,000—up a bit from the first telecast in 1948, which cost $2,500. But revenue sharing was not exactly in yet. When the Philadelphia Phillies wanted a cut on the Dodgers television contract for games played in Ebbets Field, Branch Rickey called the Phils a bunch of socialists.

Williams appeared in Sarasota the first week in March and immediately took up his position near the clubhouse door keeping the writers out: "Not yet, you chowderheads, not yet!" Manager McCarthy was giving them all something to write about this spring. He was going to get his men in shape. The Red Sox had opened slowly the last two years, and this year McCarthy wanted his team ready for those cold spring games. The starting squad would play inning after inning in Florida and up the coast; in April they would think they were already half done with the season. Williams had a great deal of respect for McCarthy but much less for spring training. Nonetheless, he could joke about the rigors even the veterans were undergoing. When the brief holdout Vern Stephens showed up in camp and walked into the clubhouse in civvies, Williams muttered, "Ready to go nine?"

Meanwhile, the other Joe McCarthy, the junior senator from Wisconsin, continued lowering his misbegotten boom on the State Department. In these early days, McCarthy had not yet struck the fear of shame into the hearts of public officials in the way he would soon do; George Marshall, Harry Truman, and even Dwight Eisenhower responded to McCarthy with a full dose of hostility in the papers, calling him a menace. His Senate colleague from Maine, Margaret Chase Smith, was the most hostile. And she continued to berate McCarthy throughout his stint in the limelight, accusing him of riding with "the four horsemen of calumny—fear, ignorance, bigotry, and smear."

Ted Williams slumped his way through most of the spring, but he was in pretty good spirits despite his aversion to playing in so many games. When a writer in the clubhouse showed him a picture of the newfangled short flannels worn by this year's Hollywood Stars in the Pacific Coast League, Williams joked about his own way of wearing his pants low over his socks: "Maybe if I wore those shorts they wouldn't call the low strikes on me." The next day he actually did roll his pants higher—everything was calibrated in his world of base-ball—and Gene Mack drew a riotous cartoon in the *Globe* of Wil-liams wearing a pair of Hollywood Stars shorts down to his ankles. Like most ballplayers, Williams had a thing about the way he wore his uniform. His pants were just one part of an ensemble; his primary fussiness centered on his sweatshirt. Johnny Orlando had to air-dry them and nurse them for years. One of Williams's favorites lasted twelve seasons, patched and stitched but, after its fashion, still swing-ing.

As far as Joe McCarthy of the Red Sox was concerned, the season began and ended on opening day. He may have lasted a couple more months, but he never really recovered from the trauma of the season opener. He learned more this day about managing the Red Sox than he ever wished to know. The Yankees were in Fenway on April 18, and they had a rough time getting out of the blocks. When the afternoon edition of the *Globe* went into circulation, the headlines carried the early Boston lead: "Red Sox 9, Yankees 0." When the next morning's edition appeared, the score shocked those afternoon readers from the day before: Yankees 15, Red Sox 10. Casey Stengel had let all the pigeons loose for this one—he even batted his left-handed pinch hitters against Mel Parnell. But it was a fiery young rookie from Oakland, Billy Martin, who busted the game open with two hits in the same inning, the eighth, during which the Yanks scored nine runs. After that inning, Joe McCarthy looked as if he'd been mummi-fied.

But by May the Red Sox, if not McCarthy, recovered from their opening loss, carried by Walt Dropo, the big rookie just up from Louisville, and Ted Williams, who had rocketed seven home runs in 12 games and hit nearly .400 for the first two weeks. Then came a doubleheader at Fenway against Detroit on May 11. In the first game, Williams gave locals something to jeer about when he camped under Aaron Robinson's fly ball in the sixth and inexplicably dropped it. When he returned to the dugout at inning's end, the fans in the box seats let him have it. He waved in some indistinct way, not having found the full inspiration yet to mold his fingers into that universal gesture of contempt so familiar the world over. For the rest of the game, the fans' resentment grew, partly in direct proportion to Williams's belligerency. This was always the case. Even his grand slam home run in the eighth with the score 13-0 didn't help matters much. It only served to remind those who would boo Williams anyway that he hit his home runs when the Sox no longer needed them.

The second game was Williams's nightmare. Boston was winning 2-0 in the eighth, but the Tigers had loaded the bases, and Vic Wertz was at the plate. Williams did not figure that Wertz would try to hit toward left. He was paying less attention than he might have when a ground single through short off Wertz's bat ended up skidding through Ted's legs into deep left to clear the bases. That turned out to be the ball game—the Tigers eventually won 5-3. Boston fans had not seen the Red Sox lose a doubleheader at home since 1948. As Williams ran in from his position at inning's end, the onslaught was savage. He was enraged. So he bowed three times to various sections of the crowd at Fenway and flipped them all the bird. Before his turn at bat, he spit in the direction of the folks near the dugout.

The left-field regulars weren't about to be deprived of their fun, and they, too, let Williams have it when he moved to his position the next inning. Dick O'Connell, in charge of Fenway facilities, blamed much of the rowdiness and heckling on the excursions from Maine, New Hampshire, and Rhode Island coming into Fenway: "Every Sunday we get 40 busloads of fans from those areas. They all have reserved seats in the left-field stands. They're part of an excursion crew. Most of them are half liquored up after a couple of hours on what we call a rolling barroom. They don't need much of an excuse for goading Williams with insults. We're starting to eject the drunken hoodlums from the park."

Later, Williams let his frustrations out to the postgame writers: "I didn't mind the errors, but those goddamn fans; they can go fuck themselves and you can quote me in all the papers." The writers did, to a point, but they remained vague in print on the precise nature of the carnal act he recommended. Williams defended himself: "I played the ball. It took two good bounces and one bad one. The bad one ran the ball up my arm and in the air behind me." At this point, the Red Sox organization was far less interested in the trigonometry of the hop than in the trajectory of Williams's spittle. A public relations problem loomed, and, sure enough, Austen Lake of the

Herald, Williams's old nemesis from 1940, began it: "Williams removed himself from the ranks of decent sportsmen. Yesterday he was a little man, and in his ungovernable rage, a dirty little man." Harold Kaese made his point by recording, or pretending to do so, a conversation in the stands: Boy: "Why's Ted doing that?" Father: "He's mad. He's made two errors, the fans are booing him, and he can't take it." Boy: "But what does he mean when he does that?" Father: "Let's see if Dropo can hit one this inning, okay?"

Tom Yawkey did not relish Williams's unseemly outburst on the field. That night he was on the hooter to his left fielder and dictated the exact words of the apology—"Ted is sorry for his impulsive actions on the field yesterday and wishes to apologize to any and all whom he may have offended"—while Williams listened and seethed. The town's newspapers displayed the apology on the front pages the next day, and the fans at Fenway, perhaps imagining Williams's lips moving as Yawkey's voice squeaked, cheered themselves silly when Williams stepped to the plate. They hated him much less than they hounded him.

Manager Joe McCarthy was staying out of any row involving Williams these days because he was so down on the club and its front office generally that he would have felt any specific focus to be unfair. His solution was to retreat to drink. Jack Maloney of the *Boston Post* did a piece for *The Sporting News* that cut to the quick: The players couldn't stand McCarthy's vocal and undisguised criticism, and McCarthy couldn't stand the brand of baseball cultivated by Tom Yawkey's benevolent dictatorship. Joe Cashman of the *Record* saw an opening here and raised a charge that had always floated around the league, the Red Sox are a bunch of "overpaid prima donnas."

During the break between games of the Memorial Day double-header in Yankee Stadium on May 30, Williams felt the ball club coming apart and spoke to Jimmy Cannon of the *New York Post*. He hoped that the Sox would trade him, preferably to Detroit: "Boston's hostile and abusive baseball fanatics probably have succeeded in running Ted out of town." By then the Sox were back in Boston, and Hy Hurwitz called Williams at home. Doris said he was asleep, but Ted already primed her to label the trade talk "a lot of bunk," which loosely translated into, "Sure, I said it to Cannon, but I didn't say it to Yawkey." The next day, Williams said, "I wouldn't play for anybody but Yawkey," which translated loosely into, "I'm leaving Jimmy Cannon high and dry on this one."

The Red Sox had lost both ends of the doubleheader in New York, and the big city's writers were selling them down the river as a team filled with losers. Williams was point man for the attack. Dan Parker of the *Daily Mirror* wrote, "Possessed of more natural ability than any ballplayer of his era, Ted Williams could outhit Ruth if he had one tenth of the Babe's warmth and one twentieth of his competitive spirit." What warmth had to do with hitting escaped even the least technical of analysts. Someone who actually had to face Williams, Bob Feller, put in perspective what had always been the case for Williams: "The fans let him have it one day, and then cheer the next day when he pumps one out of the park." Feller was dead right. On June 2 at Fenway against Cleveland, Williams came to the plate in the second inning and hammered one over the right-field fence as the Red Sox eventually won 11-5. The fans were beside themselves in glee.

The Red Sox were still in the race, only four out in third place at the end of the first week in June. Williams was hot; he would hit .357 for the entire month of June, adding 12 home runs to his totals to give him 24 on the year a week before the All-Star break. In fact, Williams, Vern Stephens, Walt Dropo, and Bobby Doerr were all hitting at Fenway as if the park were a giant pinball machine. The St. Louis Browns made the mistake of coming into Boston for a two-game set on June 7 and 8. They left literally not knowing what hit them, losing games by scores of 20-4 and 29-4. The 49 runs and 51 hits amassed by the Red Sox were a major league record, surpassing the previous two-game record of 45 runs by the 1925 Pirates.

The Browns games came on the heels of a sweep of Cleveland, in which the Red Sox scored 11 runs twice and 17 runs once, and a split with Chicago, in which Boston scored 12 in a winning effort and 4 in a losing effort. So in seven games the Red Sox amassed 104 runs. Fenway was not the only place baseballs were flying. On June 18, Cleveland exploded for a 14-run inning in a 21-2 win over the A's. And on June 29, the Red Sox were back at it again with a 22-14 win over the Philadelphia A's in Shibe Park, with Williams hitting one home run and chalking up six runs batted in. For the year, all sorts of records were crumbled to dust, including 40 home runs on one day in the majors, and 11 home runs in one Tigers-Yankees game. Joe DiMaggio asked ruefully about the year, as he felt himself fading, "Could it be they use the old dead ball for me and the lively one for everyone else?" Later in the season, amidst charges of a juiced-up ball, a comparison was made with an old ball from 1912. When stripped down to its solid rubber core the 1912 ball bounced 12 inches from a height of three feet; the 1950 ball bounced 16 inches from the same height. Pitchers claimed they could feel the ears of the rabbit twitching in the cork center.

The Red Sox began a western swing around the middle of June, and therein lay a recurring sad tale. Joe McCarthy appeared about ready to bag it. The Boston writers had some sense of this and prepared the way with hostile stories about the team. Roger Birtwell of the *Globe* wrote of the train ride west: "Baseball's Country Club Set, the Boston Red Sox, were in Chicago today with a five-game losing streak, but it didn't seem to bother them at all. The Country Club boys, who receive half a million a season to play ball games, were relieved to escape from Detroit or Cleveland—two towns where the players are simply low-brow roughnecks. Besides, they play ball." Birtwell said the Red Sox could take some consolation in the fact that "they have a firm 4½-game lead over the fifth-place Senators."

After the Red Sox got beat in Chicago 3–1, with Williams taking the collar from Billy Pierce, who made him look bad in three clutch situations, Joe McCarthy threw in the towel: "I just feel weary," he said. Two days later it was for good: "When a man can't help a ball club any more, it's time to quit. I guess I'm just disgusted after three years of beating my brains out." Williams realized that his manager was hurting: "I'm awfully sorry to see him go, but perhaps it's the best thing because you could see it was killing him." A former Detroit manager and a longtime Ted Williams fan, Steve O'Neill, took over.

The change helped the Red Sox. They began playing good ball, though Williams was growing testier and testier. Birtwell wrote that he had a chip on his shoulder the size of Mt. Rushmore, and when asked about his bunt to beat the shift to begin a winning rally against St. Louis on June 25, Williams seemed irritated for irritation's sake: "When I retire in a year or two, I'll still be hitting .350. And I hope the writers are up in the press box with the temperature at 121

degrees—men die at 121 degrees." This was about as vicious a
coherent response to a question as Williams ever provided, though his
incoherent responses were, on occasion, much worse.

It was during this last week of June 1950 that the United States
found itself embroiled in another war. On June 27 North Korean
armies invaded South Korea. America had troops committed to the
fray almost immediately and was in trouble soon after that. By early
July the situation had reached a crisis, and the tactical questions of
how to react absorbed the government. President Truman sent in the
marines. With the ground troops increased, the question of tactical
air support grew critical. Plans were drawn to activate reserve forces
in highly skilled areas. Ted Williams, at nearly 32 years of age, was
a highly skilled pilot. He had no idea at this time, but his days as a
civilian were numbered.

Boston was in shooting distance of first place, 5½ out, when the
Yankees came to Fenway on July 1. Casey Stengel had the bright idea
of playing Joe DiMaggio at first base to extend his career. DiMaggio
was not a happy Clipper. He was decidedly nervous before the game,
during it, and even after when he thanked his lucky stars he wasn't
killed out there. Ted Williams didn't help matters when he saw Joe
on the field taking grounders: "Hey, Jolter, they come at you a lot
faster than they do in the outfield." In the game, DiMaggio had 13
chances at first and turned them all. But Tommy Henrich said
DiMaggio lost about ten pounds sweating it out. That was enough.
DiMaggio told Stengel he would think about playing a little first—
maybe—next spring training, but for the present he was the Yankee
centerfielder.

The war in Korea was taking desperate turns while the nation
paused for its Independence Day celebration and, soon after, the
baseball season paused for the All-Star Game. For Williams, the
game was fatal. At the break he was hitting .321 with 25 home runs
and 83 runs batted in. What went wrong perhaps should not have
gone wrong. Williams was on record from a few years back telling a
Life magazine reporter, "They'll never get me out of a game running
into a wall for a fly ball. I'll give it a damn good try, but you can bet
your life I'll never get killed. They don't pay off on fielding." But in
the first inning of the 1950 All-Star Game Ralph Kiner lined a drive
toward the Comiskey Park scoreboard, and Williams gauged it on the

dead run, crashing his left elbow into the wall as he held on to the ball. He did not leave the game. In fact, he played eight innings and singled in a run for an American League lead in the fifth, but the pain by then was intolerable. After a teeth-gritting strikeout against Larry Jansen in the eighth, he called it a day.

Ralph Kiner, whose blast drove Williams into the wall in the first, homered over the wall in the ninth inning off Art Houtteman of Detroit to tie the game at 3–3, and Red Schoendienst homered into the upper tier in the fourteenth for a 4–3 National League win. The *Boston Globe* headline of July 12 reversed the text and subtext of the game, putting the first inning before the 14th: "TED WILLIAMS' LEFT ARM BROKEN. Williams May Be Lost for Season." Dr. Ralph McCarthy of the Red Sox described the injury as an "impacted fracture of the radius," a common break when bracing against a fall, or, for that matter, bracing against a wall. The next day Williams went under the knife. Dr. Joseph H. Shortell, orthopedic surgeon at Sancta Maria Hospital in Cambridge, performed the surgery.

The American League's manager, Casey Stengel, was distraught. He took all the blame for the injury, telling the New York writers that he didn't check the wind properly or he would have repositioned Williams for Kiner. This was surely cutting it a bit fine for Casey, but he wanted to find a reason to take the blame. He admired Williams a great deal, and Ted's courage at once impressed Stengel and mortified him. How could he let the man play with a broken arm?

The surgery removed part of a chipped forearm bone jammed and impacted into a second bone at the elbow, and Williams could begin an exercise program only after an initial immobilization of his arm. At the same time, and still without causing Williams any anxiety, marine reservists were put on 10-day call-up. Williams was in the inactive reserve, but the nets were closing. During Red Sox home games, Williams spent some time in the dugout. He did not travel with the club, and he turned down, reluctantly, an invitation from those he called Fenway wolves in left field to sit with them during the ball games. He also passed on an invite from the Boston writers to join them in the press box. The Red Sox managed to hang in the pennant race during the early weeks of Williams's rehabilitation, lingering around seven games out. They did so because in mid-August 14 players on the roster (including pitcher Mickey McDermott) were batting over .300. Walt Dropo was hitting a ton with power, while Vern Stephens, Bobby Doerr, Johnny Pesky, Dom Di-Maggio, and especially Billy Goodman were also burning up the league. Goodman would end up winning the American League batting title in 1950 with a .354 average.

With the Red Sox 25-14 without Williams, and about to get even hotter for the stretch run, Roger Birtwell spoke for many in Boston in his column of August 18: "SOX DO BETTER WITH TED OUT, BUT O'NEILL MAY BE ANSWER." Birtwell had it both ways and used the occasion to raise other possibilities for the Sox. Perhaps Williams's market price was on the downward side. He was injury prone, 32 years old, slowing down, and high salaried. For all Birtwell knew, the elbow injury would affect his power. Williams was not in town to read this piece of encouraging commentary. He was on a fishing trip, partly to strengthen his arm and partly to allay boredom. But as soon as the writers got wind of his whereabouts rumors began to fly about his fitness. The purported strengthening of his arm got transformed by the rumor mill into the careless reinjuring of his arm casting a rod. No doubt this began as a snide insult and turned into a scoop for an enterprising reporter, but Boston was abuzz with the inglorious story that Williams had sacrificed his elbow for the lure of the Atlantic fishing lanes.

A day after the story about his new injury Williams was, in fact, back at Fenway taking fielding and some light hitting practice. He was in fine shape, and the arm was sounder than could be expected. The Yankees were closing in on the slumping Tigers and the Red Sox were only 4½ out on August 24. Williams might be back for the rest of the run, and with the Red Sox on a tear the town was again heated with pennant fever. But there was trouble ahead. Billy Goodman, who had moved to left to replace Williams, was hitting .361, and Johnny Pesky over .300 at third. O'Neill said he would have to sit Pesky and play Goodman at third when Williams got back. Some of the Red Sox grumbled about breaking up a winning combination.

The Tigers arrived at Fenway on August 25, and the Red Sox won 6-2 in front of 34,964 fans, edging close to first place; but they fell back again the following day with an 8-6 loss. The next game, against Cleveland, was a classic for the Red Sox. The Indians were ahead 12-1 with Bob Lemon on the mound. But Bob Lemon was soon off the mound during an eight-run Red Sox fourth. Bobby Feller came in to pitch in relief and gave up another four runs to help lose the game 15-14. Just another day at Fenway. By the end of August, the Red Sox had won 15 of their last 16 games, and they moved up behind the Yanks and Detroit, only 2½ games out.

After a series of rain-outs early in September, Ted Williams was nearing readiness for pinch-hitting duties. He would get his chance in the Yankee series. On September 7, Boston beat the Yanks 10-8 at Fenway, and Williams pinch hit and walked. Dropo put two out of the park for a total of 32 on the year. He had 136 runs batted in, and Vern Stephens followed at 133. Boston kept winning ball games, but so did the Yanks and Detroit. By September 12 the Red Sox moved within a game of first place and were heading to St. Louis to play a ball club they had beaten in 18 of their last 19 meetings. Williams was itching to start in a ball park where his career average was a robust .408 to that date. And he got his chance on September 15, the day after his pinch-hit run-producing double high off the screen in right center helped the Red Sox nail down a 6-3 win.

Williams's first full day back was glorious. He came to the plate six times and led the Red Sox to a 12-9 win with a three-run homer and three singles. His blast cleared the fence in right and landed on Grand Avenue, dispelling doubts about any permanent loss of power. His elbow might hurt—as, indeed, it did—but a ballplayer simply could not hit one that far with an impeded swing. The Red Sox had now won 24 of their last 27. Though there was plenty of backstairs talk about sitting Pesky down so Goodman could stay in the lineup upon Williams's return, O'Neill had to go with Williams. Pesky, who worshipped Williams, said: "I'd bench my mother if it helped us win the flag." Roger Birtwell of the *Globe* wondered how devastating the loss of Pesky's mother would be for the Red Sox.

Williams was rightfully miffed. Here was a man with a .353 lifetime average, who had led his league in slugging percentage for six seasons in a row, who played his heart out in the All-Star Game, who struggled to get back in shape after breaking his elbow, and who was now taking abuse from writers and teammates alike for having the audacity to don his Red Sox uniform. Jerry Nason wrote that the Sox of late had been cheering each other on and mobbing their mates at the plate when they hit one out, but "there were no such reception parties for Williams today. . . . Williams's return to the lineup isn't a popular move among some of the players."

The next few games were among the only times in his career that Williams did not respond to controversy with a hitting surge. In fact, he stopped hitting almost entirely, going only 2 for his next 17. O'Neill said he was way off on his timing, and Williams complained that his elbow hurt on the swing. On September 20, the Sox lost a doubleheader to the Indians and Williams got zapped on the day, striking out three times on poor cuts. Hank Greenberg, who was at the game, said that Williams was simply not ready to play: "At times he seems afraid to swing." But whatever might be said about Williams could go spades for the rest of the Red Sox outfield: the three of them—Williams, DiMaggio, and Zarilla—hit a combined .098 in that one week.

The Cleveland double loss was tough, though the Red Sox were still hanging in two games behind the Yankees when they lost two straight to New York at the Stadium on September 24, despite two home runs by Williams into the right-field porch. A few days later, the Sox lost a doubleheader against the Senators at Fenway, with Williams going 0 for 8 and dragging his average down to .309. This was one of the sorriest days of his career, made no cheerier when he read in the morning paper that his teammates in the clubhouse were treating him as if he played for the visiting ball club.

All that was left for Williams during the final swing was to try to reach 100 runs batted in for his abbreviated campaign. By his last game he needed six, and he made his run, going 4 for 5 and driving in three. The Red Sox won the ball game 7–3 to take third place, a consolation prize that seemed too much like so many others of the past. On this occasion they lost the pennant with a remarkable .302 team batting average for the season, the highest Boston team average during Williams's career. In the National League, the pennant went down to the wire with the Whiz Kid Phils beating the Dodgers 4–1 on a tenth-inning three-run homer by Dick Sisler. The heartbreak in Brooklyn was made worse by a play in the ninth. With no one out and Cal Abrams on third and Reese on first, Duke Snider came to the plate. The pennant was so close the Dodgers could taste it. Richie Ashburn, figuring the odds, kept creeping in from center field, and, sure enough, Snider lined a shot right at him. Abrams tried to tag and score, but the weak-armed Ashburn easily nailed him at the plate. The Dodgers couldn't convert, and Sisler did his work the next inning. This was Philadelphia's last hurrah. The Yankees dispatched them in four in the 1950 World Series.

Williams's injury-breached season was a curious one. For the first time in his career he hit under .300 on the road (.282), though he did manage .395 at Sportsman's Park in St. Louis, keeping his lifetime average there at .414, his highest for any park. At Fenway, Williams hit a steadier .356. But he was discouraged. It was not simply his injury; rather, it was a vaguely strained relation with a ball club that seemed to feel his return was an impediment to a pennant. To lose even the sense of what Williams meant to this club was to lose a vision of the club's competitiveness through the postwar era. The Red Sox would only come close to the pennant once more for the rest of Ted Williams's career, and his last decade in baseball, though filled with extraordinary moments, was rarely as intense as his first Williams was to play more for history in the service of what he called the science of hitting.

◇ 13 ◇

Boston Fade
1951

SPRING TRAINING IN 1951 BEGAN with the major league owners
ganging up to dump Happy Chandler from the commissioner's office,
with *Bedtime for Bonzo* making something of a chimp out of Ronald
Reagan, and with Mickey Mantle tearing up the Grapefruit League.
Willie Mays also broke in this year, but it was Mantle who captured
the imagination of the baseball world: Red Smith wrote that he hit
with tremendous power from either side of the plate "and runs like a
striped ape." The veterans ringed the batting cage to watch Mantle
hit. "Another *Oklahoma* on Broadway," said *The Sporting News.*

Mantle, however, was getting an early taste of what Ted Williams
went through in 1942, when he received a draft classification that
exempted him from service during the early months of World War II.
After the outbreak of war in Korea, Mantle's draft board in Tulsa
deemed him unfit twice, in 1950 and 1951, because of osteomyelitis.
Still, the writers were skeptical: "So Mantle has osteomyelitis. What's
the big deal? He doesn't have to *kick* anybody in Korea."

Meanwhile, Joe Williams of *Sport* magazine took up the brunt of
the annual spring attacks on Ted Williams in an article titled "Why
I Would Trade Ted Williams" (February 1951). The only solace
Williams took from pieces such as these was that, after all the bad
mouthing, the trades usually involved a club giving away its franchise
to get him. Why, he wondered, if he were such a drag on the pennant
chances of the Red Sox, would he be so valuable elsewhere? Yet Joe
Williams was loaded for bear: Williams was unresponsive to his
managers, he set a wretched tone for the whole club, he was a quitter.

226

Here are some choicer quotes: "The chances are Williams won't help you at all when you need help the most"; "The dimensions of his performance are heroic, but the effect isn't moving or genuine"; "Williams bulks large in the monstrous defeatist complex from which the Red Sox suffer."

Boston still wanted Williams's signature on the dotted line, though this year he took the same salary deal he accepted in 1950. The Sox paid him $90,000 plus ample bonuses. The major league owners, pretty much running a monopoly, had a way of keeping salaries, even high ones, in line by a rule that limited leapfrogging raises. No player could be raised above the highest-paid player in the league unless that raise appeared commensurate with a pattern of increments over the course of a career. The guideline was waived for free agents and traded players and could be appealed in other cases. The Cards, for example, appealed and won in 1951, leapfrogging Stan Musial from $50,000 to $85,000. What the owners did not want were runaway salary wars.

Williams was never a problem in this respect. He thought through his yearly requests in a way that would humble present-day players. For example, in the middle of winter he was not sure about his elbow; it didn't feel that well. He set his own standards clearly in his mind: He asked for what he brought the club on the basis of his previous season's performance. But he also asked that management understand his injury and not pencil him in for every spring-training game as McCarthy had done last year. Steve O'Neill told the writers that on his club the regulars would play: "Cobb and Ruth played during the spring. Why can't my guys?" Things began bad and looked even worse when Grantland Rice charged that the Red Sox were chasing a dream with a club of old-timers. Most of their lineup were over 30. Meanwhile, the team sent their trainer, Jack Fadden, down to Florida early to set up an exercise program for Williams.

On February 2 in Boston, during the writers' annual award dinner, 900 voices joined to sing a ditty on Williams's springtime woes.

I can't play in springtime ballgames
    Though they pay me ninety grand.
I'll go easy in the Southland,
    And go fishing like I planned.

Lou Boudreau appeared on the Red Sox roster this season and was

going to challenge for the shortstop job. O'Neill had seen enough of
Vern Stephens at short and wanted to move him and his bat to third
base. Pesky or Boudreau would play short. But Boudreau was more
than a shortstop; he was a future manager, and O'Neill knew it. The
Red Sox camp was on edge from the first. When Williams laid eyes
on Boudreau he got off a pretty good one: "Well, if it isn't a
Boudreau shift!"

China was fully in the Korean fray by spring and the see-saw
movement of large armies that characterized the conflict was taking
place around the famous 38th parallel. The greatest ally for the U.N.
forces was not so much tactical as medical: Chinese and North
Korean forces were falling by the thousands to dysentery. At home,
Sugar Ray Robinson took the middleweight crown from champ Jake
LaMotta in a legendary fight on February 14. Robinson won the title
when the fight was stopped in the 13th round. LaMotta by then was
a piece of hamburger. "I kept swingin', Jake kept standin'," said Sugar
Ray of the fight. LaMotta's wife, Viki, asked doctors if her husband
would ever look the same.

One of the best stories and worst scandals ever in college basketball
broke just before spring training in 1951. The national champs of
1950, the City College of New York, were shaving points on the
spread. All-American Edward Warner was among those working for
the fix man, Salvatore T. Sollazzo, who passed as a legitimate jewelry
dealer. Long Island University, with its nifty star, Sherman White,
was also in on the scheme with Sollazzo, shaving points at the NIT
Tournament. The whole scandal blew wide open when LIU bugged
out on Sollazzo and overwhelmed the point spread against Duquesne,
beating them 84–52 and taking the fix money anyway. The thought
of talking this over with some of Sollazzo's friends was more than the
Long Island players could bear, and they spilled their guts to the New
York D.A.'s office.

Ted Williams was in Sarasota by the opening of spring training,
and he took only easy swings in the batting cage. He told everyone
that his elbow was sore and stiff. Steve O'Neill had already penciled
him in for most of the team's exhibition games. Williams wanted to
set his pace, and O'Neill wanted to hurry it. Charges of malingering
and laziness were still hanging over the club from last season, and
they bothered the manager. O'Neill figured he could counter the
charge early by hounding Williams to play often. This was ill consid-

ered on O'Neill's part. Over the years he had expressed unabashed admiration for Williams; as manager of the Detroit Tigers he had argued that Williams was a better ballplayer than either Ruth or Cobb. The fact that O'Neill and Williams could circle each other without a direct confrontation was testimony to a past of great mutual respect.

Soon enough O'Neill came up with the notion of Williams playing in more games so that he might adjust his swing to hit to left. That would ease the strain on his elbow and beat the shift at the same time. He told the writers on March 6 that he was bringing Williams out to hit earlier than anyone else because it was not as windy then—it would help build his confidence if he didn't have to hit into the wind. It was clear that O'Neill was using the press to make his case and to goad Williams. The strain between the two had its subtle comic dimensions. O'Neill was decidedly uncomfortable in the unlikely role of martinet, and Williams was anything but a pain-sensitive shirker whose confidence would go to pieces if he had to hit into the wind. Besides, he felt he was rounding into excellent shape in his own way. He came into camp at 205 pounds and was down to the low 190s within a short period. He was exercising on a wire-and-pulley contraption under Fadden's supervision. He may not have wished to swing a bat relentlessly, as he had in past springs, but he was by no means unready.

On March 8, Grantland Rice asked Williams about when and how much he would play. He told Rice as simply as he could: "I felt that it was my arm that had been broken and I was the only one who knew when it hurt and when it didn't. After all, a guy can't do much with one arm in baseball." O'Neill, trying to work both sides of the street on the Williams issue, told reporters, "My only problem with Williams is his trying to work too hard." But he also mentioned that he, O'Neill, would decide when to play him. The next day the sparring match continued in a different format. Williams was asked by a local Sarasota radio man, Phil Harris, if he would be on a show broadcast from the Sarasota Terrace, the Red Sox hotel. Williams, who lived in the Florasota Arms, an apartment complex (complete with fishing boats) about a mile away, said sure. But when he arrived he found the broadcast was to be conducted from a platform in the hotel's hot night spot, the Jungle Room. The actress Betty Hutton was on the scene as well. Williams wanted out of the whole deal and particularly objected to the glitzy atmosphere. He hated to be gawked at with no means of escape. Phil Harris ended up getting his interview by sitting with Williams privately in a side booth right near the exit door, which Williams intended to make use of in short order.

Short order it was. Harris asked the almost obligatory spring question, and one for which O'Neill and the Red Sox front office had primed the pump. "Do the Red Sox have better spirit this year?" Precious little reflection or easy clichés were forthcoming from Williams: "No. I know you would like me to say yes, but no." "And how's your arm?" "Not good," said Williams. "It hurts. It's sore." Interview over. Williams was out the door. A few days later, on March 14, he played all 10 innings of a game against the Braves and doubled twice to left field. In the clubhouse afterwards he ran into an elderly gentleman, one Dr. Jones, a friend and colleague of Dr. Shortell, who had operated on his elbow. Williams was eager to meet him and talk about his arm. Within earshot of the *Globe*'s Roger Birtwell, Williams asked the doctor, "What's the time for a full recovery?" "Usually, a year," Dr. Jones replied. Williams nodded his head. Every move, every comment, every gesture this spring was part of a public relations chess match.

The New York and Boston baseball writers were at it again this spring, as usual. Tom Meany did a piece, "Baseball's Hottest Seat," in which he claimed that the writers in the Boston area weighed "like an anchor around the neck of the Red Sox." Their expectations for the team year in and year out were more hindrances than anything else, putting pressure on the entire organization from the word go. Jerry Nason of the *Globe* responded that the writers in Boston were only in accord with the oddsmakers in Vegas. In 1948 the odds were even for a Boston pennant; in 1949 the odds were 8–5; and in 1950, 7–5. Besides, the real problem derived from Boston's front office, deeply influenced by stalwart players, especially Williams and Dom DiMaggio, to protect them from the press before and after the games. On its own, the Red Sox front office was ready to put a lid on information of any kind whenever possible and to lie, distort, and deny whenever desirable. As a result, the competitive newspapers in the area scrambled for confirmed and unconfirmed stories from whatever source they could get. Many of the breaking stories were from out of town and wildly inaccurate. The whole business of poor press relations was a team-induced mess, according to Nason.

On March 17 rumors floated around the press corps of a tape recording made with sportswriter Bill Keating, from Holyoke, Massachusetts, about Williams quitting after the 1952 season. The *Globe*'s Hy Hurwitz, that feisty ex-marine, called Williams at the Florasota Arms to confirm. Williams wouldn't take the call. At the park next day, he told Hurwitz: "I'm here at the ballpark every day. You want to ask me questions, then ask me here. Don't bother me at home." Hurwitz responded, "I've got my job to do." "Ask me here," demanded Williams. "Okay," said Hurwitz, "I'm asking. Did you tell Keating you were through after 1952?" Williams saw an opening for another jab at O'Neill for taxing his arm: "If my arm is not 100 percent, yes, I will quit." The message was clearly directed to Yawkey and general manager Cronin: protect the merchandise.

The writers were beginning to enjoy all of this. O'Neill made the next move. He ordered Williams to hit to left, restating his case that the in-blowing wind would put a strain on Williams's elbow if he tried to pull. Moreover, the team had been keeping stats. Williams could put the ball in play to left with consistency—well over 80 percent of the time. If so, his chances for base hits against the shift were astronomical. O'Neill demanded he try for the sake of the team.

That day Harold Kaese arrived to dispatch some stories for the *Globe*. "Did you miss me?" Kaese asked as he crossed Williams's path on the field. "No," Williams replied, without breaking his step. That was the longest interview Kaese had gotten from Williams in years. He then watched Williams take some cuts in the cage, getting angrier and angrier at Kaese's silent shadow. The tag on Kaese's column: "Nobody could have hit with such abandon as Williams did today and be dying from a pain in the elbow."

A couple of days later, Williams was saddened to learn of the sudden illness and subsequent death of Eddie Collins, the great Hall of Famer and Red Sox front office man who signed him from San Diego. He wanted to travel to Boston for the funeral and asked O'Neill, who said of course Williams could attend. Indeed, the rest of the team in Florida "would all like to attend." O'Neill left it for Williams and the press to draw whatever conclusions they wished.

When Williams returned by plane from Boston he remained in Sarasota while the Red Sox traveled for a few road exhibition games. He hit for twenty minutes off Chuck Stobbs and Maury McDermott before calling it quits. His elbow hurt, he had shin splints, his neck was stiff, and he was coming down with a cold. He didn't know it yet, but maybe he was getting himself in shape for the Korean War. Earlier, at the Detroit Tigers' camp in Lakeland, Florida, Dizzy Trout presented Williams with a letter "B" insignia, a reference to the well-known distinction between a varsity and a B-team school letter. Trout was joking, and Williams took it in good spirits because the papers were so filled with stories about Williams not wishing to travel with the A squad for spring exhibition games. But when Williams begged off the St. Pete trip, someone taped the B letter on his locker. He was furious.

From late 1950 and through this year's spring training, Williams's fellow Red Sox were beginning to irritate him and sending stronger signals that he was beginning to irritate them. Only in 1940 had the feelings on the club run so strong. Later in the season, Williams wanted it known that he never shirked a minute: "I played more innings in exhibition games than anyone on the team." Billy Goodman said, "No, you didn't, Ted. I played more." "Want to bet?" asked Williams. Goodman thought a minute, and then said, "Nope. You never lost a bet in your life. You probably kept an exact count. Anyhow, I must have come in a close second."

The season began shortly after Truman and General MacArthur split publicly on the Korean War, MacArthur favoring the use of Chinese Nationalist troops in opposition to the current policy of the United States and the United Nations. In April, Senator Joe McCarthy was hard at what passed for work, smearing with the widest brush available anyone who came within the purview of his investigation. He would say anything for a headline, claiming that Truman was slipped bourbon and benedictine by his Red advisors before they coaxed him to dump MacArthur in Korea. The smear campaign, in all its phases, was getting help from the House Un-American Activities Committee, whose members had just grilled actor Sterling Hayden for names of other Hollywood actors, writers, directors, and front-office people deemed members of communist organizations. Hayden was more than ready to help. The paranoid xenophobe he later played in the movie *Dr. Strangelove* was perhaps a kind of ironic penance for this earlier House committee performance.

On April 14, the Red Sox were in Boston for the last game of their city series with the Braves, and Williams looked ready as ever. He homered and drove in six runs in the 15–8 Red Sox win. But in the season opener in New York against Vic Raschi, the Red Sox could barely scratch for a few hits, and Williams scratched for none, as the Yankees won 5-0. The Sox lost again, 6-1, the next day, and O'Neill was already considering a shakeup. The Red Sox manager was suffering from gout, an irritable disease in itself, and his team wasn't doing much to ease his pain. As for the writers, some of them listened to General MacArthur's "old soldiers just fade away" speech on April 19 and thought he was talking about the Red Sox. The columnist and future variety show host Ed Sullivan wrote: "Why drop him when we're winning?" Sullivan then claimed the Red Sox wouldn't dump Williams if he keeps hitting home runs even if they were not entirely happy with him.

Though the season began poorly, the Red Sox started turning things around, and Williams began to stroke with some power by the end of April. But in May the home runs stopped and the average sagged. The boo birds in left were already out, and Williams said they would get only smiles this year, "but what I say under my breath is another thing." Even though Williams was hitting only .231 by mid-May, Paul Richards, the tactically innovative manager of the Chicago White Sox, did not want to lose a ball game because of Williams's bat. In a game on May 15, Richards let his pitcher, Harry Dorish, hit with the bases loaded in the top of the ninth with his team holding a 7-6 lead. In the bottom of the ninth, Billy Pierce showed up on the mound in relief to pitch to Williams, leading off the inning. If Richards intended to take Dorish out, why had he let him hit with the bases loaded a half inning earlier? Because the right-handed Dorish wasn't out. He was playing third base while Pierce pitched to Williams and put him away. Dorish then returned to the mound. He allowed the Red Sox to tie the game anyway, but the White Sox won it in the 11th, 9-7.

Ty Cobb was in Boston in late May and took another swipe at Williams for not hitting to left. Harold Kaese, whose relations with Williams were abysmal since his man-on-the-street poll in 1948 about Williams's rotten potential as a father, came to Ted's defense in an insulting sort of way, striking a rhetorical pose that at once stood by Williams and humiliated him: "So now is the time to pick on Williams? He is in the worst slump of his career. His average is a puny .226. He cannot hit to left, right, or center." That day at Fenway Williams was steaming mad, and tore into the ball, lashing three hits for Kaese's benefit off Dizzy Trout and Gene Bearden, one of them out of the park, and making sure for Cobb's particular pleasure that all three were to left field. Kaese said in his column the next day, "This game makes you humble."

Williams slammed out three more hits the next day. He was on a rampage. In his next 10 games he hit .537 with 4 home runs and 22 runs batted in. By May 27 he had pushed his previously anemic average over .300, and during the Memorial Day doubleheader with the Yanks at Fenway he got seven hits, five of them for extra bases. The Red Sox were winning game after game and creeping toward the top. By June 1, Williams was hitting .321 and leading the league in home runs and runs batted in. Ty Cobb and Harold Kaese would do well to get together for a chat more often as far as the Red Sox leftfielder was concerned.

On June 16, Williams started another run of 14 games in which he would hit .531, bang out a couple more home runs, and drive in another 20. These streaks made his season, and though they were enough to lift a sagging Red Sox team near first place by July, they were not enough to carry the Sox through to the end. Bobby Doerr said of Williams at this time of the year that he had never seen him play so well. He was making catches and throws in the outfield and running the bases like a revived man; on June 26 it even took the A's Joe Astroth, a catcher, to sneak out from his position to make the tag at second on a hustling Williams trapped in a rundown. All of this had to do with a sustained hurt he was carrying from another article in the *Globe* just before his second incredibly hot run began in mid-June. Retired Red Sox Manager Joe McCarthy, at the urging of local writers, picked a personal all-star team of players he had managed and, surprisingly, he left Williams and Babe Ruth off the list. He argued that the complete ballplayer is the one who helps his team win pennants. He only won one pennant with Ruth and none with Williams.

Before the All-Star break, the Red Sox made a real run at first. They beat the Yanks at Fenway 6-2 on July 6 and again on July 7, 10-4, with Williams homering. They were tied for the lead, but the second game was more notable for a move made by Casey Stengel in the middle innings. He benched Joe DiMaggio. Joe left the field seething. Later, Stengel spoke about the incident and about the rumored feud between the inscrutable manager and the aging ballplayer as if DiMaggio had already died on the field and gone to baseball heaven: "DiMaggio made me a winner. I lost plenty until I came to New York. He made me. For 15 years he's been the best. And he played in a park not suited to him. If he played in Fenway, he'd break every hitting record on the books." Perhaps that's why Stengel pulled him from the game at Fenway? Harold Kaese, having taken his shots at Williams, couldn't resist one for DiMaggio. He got off a sharp but cruel line on the theme of the aging gamer: "The solution has become the problem."

Williams made it to the All-Star break in one piece with a healthy average of .341, a creditable 16 home runs, and a more-than-creditable 76 runs batted in. The Red Sox were trailing the first-place White Sox by a game, with the Yanks another game behind in third. An item in the back pages of *The Sporting News* in early July before the All-Star Game picked up what would later be a first for the majors: organized ball signed a former softball ump to a contract in the Southwest International League. He was the first black umpire in professional baseball: Emmett Ashford.

The 1951 All-Star Game was easily won by the National League 8–3, their second straight victory, on home runs by Musial, Kiner, Bob Elliott, and Gil Hodges; Williams tripled in the eighth inning. Williams was happy enough to go home intact, a notable improvement from the previous year. After the break, the Red Sox and White Sox had themselves quite a series vying for first place. Boston swept a doubleheader on July 12, winning the second game 5–4 in 17 innings. The next day they lost in 19 innings by the same score. As the western swing continued, Boston began losing ball games. This was a pattern so familiar that O'Neill just threw up his hands in despair when the writers spoke to him about it. Williams added to his manager's irritation on July 19 in a tie game against Cleveland: Bobby Avila seemed to slow down around third on Sam Chapman's bloop single to left but turned on his burners after Williams feinted a throw to second to hold Chapman. This was the bottom of the 11th inning, and Williams's play had *bonehead* written all over it. The Indians won it 5–4. Later, the writers waited 15 minutes to get in the clubhouse to ask for Williams's explanation. His honesty was refreshing: "I got slickered."

O'Neill blew a fuse when the Sox continued to lose, especially in a late-July game to the ancient Satchel Paige, hired by Bill Veeck of the lowly St. Louis Browns. "That goddamn hesitation pitch must be illegal," O'Neill said. Bill Veeck had all sorts of things up his sleeve in 1951. Not only was Satchel on the mound for him, but later, on August 19, he brought Eddie Gaedel to the plate in the first inning of game two of a doubleheader against the Tigers. Gaedel was 3'7" tall, a midget whom Veeck employed through Standard Entertaining Services of Chicago. Browns manager Zack Taylor had to bring a copy of his contract out to the batter's box for umpire Ed Hurley to peruse before he would let Eddie step in. The midget walked against Tiger pitcher Bob Cain, and then Taylor put in a pinch runner. Soon enough the commissioner's office banned Gaedel. "This is a conspiracy against short guys," Gaedel complained, "I need the work."

The Red Sox couldn't draw close enough to have a shot at the very end of the race, as they had in the last three seasons. O'Neill managed to keep them in shooting distance through August, but he was under increasing strain. Bob Holbrook of the *Globe* wrote that O'Neill was not sleeping well; he was beginning to make screwy moves on the field; and he was upset "at a great Red Sox team disintegrating before his eyes." Dropo was hurt and out, and Bobby Doerr's chronically bad back was betraying him. Doerr had broken in a year before Williams and jokingly summed up his now-fading career hitting behind Ted for so many years: "Williams hits home runs. Doerr hits dirt."

Boston's troubles highlighted what for years the players around the league and the fans in the two cities saw as an essential difference between the Sox and the Yankees, who were so close in talent and so unbalanced in pennants. Tommy Henrich put it most bluntly: the Yankees allow no broken cogs in the gears; their replacement rate is cold and relentless. On the other hand, the Red Sox were notorious for running on worn or damaged gears. The benevolent despotism of the Yawkey regime made it difficult for the team to function at top capacity. Too much patience coddled the part at the expense of the whole. The Red Sox made impetuous moves that were often badly timed. They rarely brought in a player for the kill, as the Yanks did Johnny Mize or Johnny Sain late in the season. Yawkey's regime was marked by leniency and indecision. It was impossible to tell what the Red Sox intended to do, and the odds were just as likely that they would make the wrong move as the right one.

Dom DiMaggio later offered a different point but one just as telling. He said the Red Sox, even under Joe McCarthy, were never properly managed. They were left alone, which made them, in DiMaggio's estimation, too predictable a ball club. Players developed habits and patterns and were under no pressure to break them. DiMaggio said that what the Sox needed, even in their best years, was a hands-on manager like Lefty O'Doul, whom he remembered from his minor league days with the San Francisco Seals. O'Doul would roll his players' socks if it helped him keep control of the game.

The Red Sox were still clawing away but could not move up in the standings from third, especially after losing two to the A's on September 9. The fans seemed to sense they were not going to make any kind of grab for the pennant; on September 13 Harold Kaese parodied his usual "What's the Matter with the Red Sox?" diatribes with a column called "What's the Matter with the Red Sox Fans?" He couldn't believe that Boston was only 3½ out of first and a mere 7,789 showed up for a crucial Tigers game; even fewer showed up for the Browns—5,281 for one game and 5,466 for another, in which Williams splintered his bat over the dugout railing when Satchel Paige got him with a piece of junk in the eighth inning.

On September 17, the Red Sox were still hanging close after a 12-5 win over Chicago; Williams went 4 for 4, including his 30th home run. But they lost two to Cleveland and fell back. Williams gave a deep-source story to Holbrook in the *Globe*: The vets on the team thought O'Neill and the Sox management were betraying them. The Yankees picked up Johnny Sain for the pennant run, but who was helping Boston? Rumors were floating around that Lou Boudreau would take over the team next season. Williams then spoke on the record: "There'll be a lot of sore guys around here if he doesn't."

The Red Sox swooned to end the year. They could barely win a game. Allie Reynolds even threw a no-hitter at them on the last day of the season. Williams got new life when Yogi Berra fumbled his foul pop that would have nailed the no-hitter in the ninth. Then he obliged by popping another in virtually the same location, and Yogi snapped this one up. Williams ended the year hitting .318 with 30 home runs and a league-leading 144 bases on balls. But he faded where the Red Sox faded—on the road. His .232 road average was the lowest in his career so far. At Fenway he hit .403.

The real excitement at the end of the season was in the National

League, where the Dodgers seemed to have a lock on the pennant before the Giants made an incredible run at them in September. All but forgotten in that race were two Brooklyn games in Boston at the end of the year. On September 26 the Dodgers were rolling over the Braves 10–1 when Jackie Robinson stole home. Tommy Holmes, the Braves' manager, felt his club was getting its nose rubbed in it and pulled all the stops to win the next day's game. The Braves managed the victory by scoring the winning run on a grounder to Robinson. Umpire Frank Dascoli's safe call threw the Brooklyn bench into pandemonium. Fifteen Dodgers were heaved from the game for furiously protesting the call. After the game, catcher Roy Campanella, the arch-protester, began to pound on the umpires' wooden door under the stands. This episode could have been ugly, but the Dodgers genuinely felt they had been robbed.

The Dodgers were a frustrated ball club. They got beat again the next day by the Phils, forcing them into a playoff game with the Giants, which culminated in Bobby Thomson's famous "shot heard round the world." Thomson would soon get a bevy of promotional endorsements for his efforts, everything from cigarettes to Bromo Selzer, though the better gimmick for the Bromo Selzer people would have been to recruit Ralph Branca of the Dodgers, who tossed up the ball for Thomson's stomach-churning three-run homer.

The Yankees polished off the Giants four games to two in a World Series notable for Monte Irvin's hot hitting in a losing cause and for the controversial play in which Eddie Stanky drop-kicked the ball out of a startled Phil Rizzuto's glove to begin a game-winning Giants' rally. The Series was the last for the great Joe DiMaggio, who quit in December after one brief but quickly quenched rumor of a trade to Boston. As for the Red Sox, it was back to the drawing board. Management was readying plans to dump Steve O'Neill and elevate their superannuated part-time shortstop, Lou Boudreau, to manage the club. Boudreau's fertile baseball mind was already brimming with ideas, some of which he included in a magazine article he was preparing for the *Saturday Evening Post*. Boudreau would rattle Boston before he, too, would end up shaken.

◇ 14 ◇
To Hell and Back
1952-1953

LOU BOUDREAU TOOK UP THE challenge of managing the Boston Red Sox in 1952. In an article he wrote, or had ghosted, for the *Saturday Evening Post* in February, he set out the tasks before him. Boudreau played against the Red Sox for years and with them for one season in 1951. The problems were classic: Boston's great sluggers were not fused into a team; they lacked a competitive edge; they were not encouraged to run; and they benefited in the past without proper gratitude from an owner whose benevolence was legendary. Lou might as well have signed on for Harold Kaese's yearly column, "What's the Matter with the Red Sox?"

One thing the new manager intended, indeed had already accomplished, was to relocate his office at Fenway so writers could get to him without going through the players' clubhouse. Instead of cooling their heels waiting out the obligatory delay before talking to the players after games, they were invited in by Boudreau to a holding cell of sorts. This was not an ideal compromise to a situation that, over the years, had grown onerous, but it would do.

Boudreau knew, or would know soon enough, that he might have to break in as Red Sox manager without Williams in left field. Rumors were drifting into Boston in February that the marines wanted Williams for the Korean War. The very nature of the draft was controversial, precisely because of the wholesale recall of veterans from the last war while a generation of college students was exempted under provisions of the draft code formulated in March of the previous year. Later that spring, Congress refused to grant President

239

Truman his request for a universal draft, and even Republicans complained that over 1,000,000 men might "test" out of the war on the basis of a government-designed aptitude exam for college. The poor and ill educated would end up fighting. This was not the last time such an issue would surface.

One thing was clear though: aerial support and strategic aerial combat missions were essential to the war effort, and the United States did not have enough pilots to fly fighter jets. It became necessary to dip into the fighter-pilot reserve from World War II and to set up retraining programs with dispatch. Many of the veteran fliers, if they were in the inactive reserve, were drawn into the Korean War to fly active missions. At the same time, enlisted career fliers were doing predominantly instructional work in flying the new jet aircraft. The assignments were, perhaps, inescapable, but a healthy proportion of air force and navy fliers felt their injustice. To pull 30-year-olds out of their jobs and away from their married lives to train them for the dangerous missions when the most experienced and crafty pilots were stateside seemed unaccountable.

Moreover, the notion that those who fought in World War II would go back for a second run while college-age kids escaped on exemptions irritated the reserve forces. The newspapers began picking up the resentment and its pathos. A forlorn picture of a flier's wife with two kids appeared on the front page of the *Boston Globe* with the caption, "Wife of Missing Pilot Asks U.S. Call Students." The story recounted how Mrs. May Elise Thomas grieved for her missing husband, who had flown bombing runs over Japan in World War II and was now missing in Korea. She was "tired of hearing mothers complain that their sons' educations should not be interrupted for military service while reservists were actually the ones doing the fighting. Reservists should be kept in this country as instructors."

Whatever their ages, men with flying skills such as those possessed by Ted Williams were sorely needed, regardless of the availability of untried draftees and temporary exemptees. General Hoyt S. Vandenberg, Air Force Chief of Staff, complained in the spring that "we are having trouble getting enough new pilots and in persuading experienced fliers to continue flying." Vandenberg was particularly worried about the resistance of reservists and inactive reservists who were taking subtle measures against being rushed dangerously into the fray while already-experienced careerists were avoiding combat. There were actually slowdown strikes at some bases and several cases in which fliers risked courts-martial to avoid aerial missions. In one Boston case a flier, Verne Goodwin, refused training missions near the end of his wife's pregnancy, claiming that they made her so nervous it posed a medical threat. Her doctors agreed, but Goodwin was court-martialed and sentenced to two years in military prison. The air force prosecutor told the court-martial board, "If you don't sentence this man, there will be a general exodus from the military service."

All this provides something of the context for Ted Williams's activation in 1952. He was not the only one who questioned the system. At Randolph Air Base in Texas, eight reserve officers met secretly to file a complaint that they were recalled to fill in for those serving in Korea while their air base was "stacked with high-ranking, free-loading regulars who never had any overseas time. It's a boy scout camp." These officers were giving back some of the flak they thought they were set up to take: "At the time we were recalled we thought the reason was to replace regulars who had gone to war. When we got here we found some of the same ones we ran into during the last war when we were sent over, waiting here to send us overseas again."

In the very month that Williams was recalled to the marine fliers, the April 20 *Globe* featured a story headlined "AIR FORCE MORALE UNBELIEVABLY LOW." Psychiatrists at Truax Field in Wisconsin were warning of breakdowns by fliers. Regulation 35-16 allowed any flier to ground himself and request an evaluation by a board of fellow pilots. Hundreds had done so, bogging down the system in a procedural quagmire. The action was more than psychological; one flier admitted, "Nobody thought there would be a war, let alone a police action." The airmen said their action was "not a strike. It's legal. Our best pilot composed a three-page typed, single-spaced letter asking relief from duty." It was an angry, bitter letter complaining about the reserve corps fighting in Korea while the regulars goldbricked: "Why should men be called out of civilian life while others get the breaks? For Christ's sake, haven't we had enough?"

The resentment toward the draft policies was so high in the air services of the army and navy that reservists were calling for a full-scale congressional investigation of the disposition of personnel. Reserve officers claimed that the military pay was so low that enlistments were down before the Korean War but that drawing older men out of their professional and marital lives was the wrong solution to a previous blunder: "It's rank discrimination against reservists." It was in the midst of this general resentment that Ted Williams spoke to a friend of Senator Taft, then running for the Republican slot on the presidential ticket against Eisenhower, about the possibility of congressional action on cases such as his own. There were promises of help but none forthcoming. Remembering the hullabaloo surrounding his previous procedural sparring with the draft laws in 1942, Williams was savvy enough to keep his back-stage efforts out of the news this time.

These were not exhilarating and glorious times in America. Few were happy about the status or the nature of the Korean War— indeed, a powerful antiwar film, Marlon Brando's *The Men*, reflected some of the sentiment in the land—and no one ought to have been happy about the frenzy of activity orchestrated by Joseph McCarthy and several congressional investigative committees against suspected communists. The State and Defense departments, the university faculties of Harvard and MIT, and the film industry in Hollywood were under something of a state of siege. McCarthy was the most-feared witch hunter since the townsfolk of Salem, a notion that later struck Arthur Miller as the inspiration for his powerful play *The Crucible*.

Early in 1952, there were high government officials who tried to face down McCarthy and some of his allies in the Senate, but to little avail. Newbold Morris, Truman's corruption investigator in the Senate's Permanent Investigations Subcommittee, accused McCarthy of "mental brutality" and treating people "like dogs." "No man with red blood in his veins could sit here and take the innuendos and insinuations left by the diseased minds in this chamber," he charged, continuing, "You have created an atmosphere so vile that people have lost confidence in their government." When McCarthy asked Morris if he felt that he, McCarthy, and fellow Senators Mundt and Nixon had been unfair to him, Morris replied, "That's an understatement." Responding to Nixon's charges that Morris was indirectly involved in shipping aviation fuel to China, Morris turned to Nixon and nailed him: "You are a young man. Maybe in 10 or 15 years you will behave like a Senator."

Williams arrived for spring training on March 1 in none too good a political mood himself. He said openly, in response to the draft rumors, that he would play until a scheduled medical exam revealed his call-up status. He seemed to sense that his days were numbered, and, as Bob Holbrook of the *Globe* put it, "this was a rare day in a Red Sox training camp—for the first time since 1938, Ted didn't ask for additional batting practice as he held his initial workout." The writers were already depressed. Hy Hurwitz wrote that Williams was the highly seasoned "meat and potatoes" of the club, and without him the Sox could call it a year.

Boudreau was prepared to begin his new regime with a kind of panache. He had an idea in mind as controversial as the infamous Williams shift he devised in 1946. This time he wanted to position Williams in the lineup in such a way as to cut down on his walks without decreasing his run production. He would bat Williams second, a position that discouraged walks, the bane of Ted's life. Boudreau would then round out his experiment by pulling his pitcher from the customary last spot in the lineup, and replacing him with a decent on-base hitter. Williams might then still bat, during the course of the game, with men in front of him likely to get on base. Boudreau would place his pitcher in the seventh position. He actually tried the lineup in seven straight exhibition games, and the Red Sox lost every one. Back to the drawing board. The next game Boudreau put Williams in his customary third spot; he hit one out of the park and Boston won 10–6.

The talk of spring training in late March was a series of articles in *Life* magazine by Ty Cobb on the state of modern baseball, "They Don't Play Baseball Anymore." This was the most scathing attack on the moderns that the ancients ever launched. Cobb's insistent theme was the paucity of versatile ballplayers who could and would do anything on the field to win. He wrote that only Phil Rizzuto and Stan Musial could hold a candle to the old-time greats. DiMaggio "limped along on one cylinder," and Williams never thought enough of the game to learn to hit to left against the shift. Casey Stengel was the only manager who won by getting a maximum effort from each player.

None of this would have surprised Williams, who had been going head-to-head with Cobb on this and other issues for five years. But players around the majors were clearly upset. It was rumored that the largely ghostwritten piece brought Cobb $25,000 and that he was paid to be nasty. Stanley Woodward wrote, "Having once received a letter from Tyrus, I can guarantee he is no Anatole France." Harold Kaese, who had grown tired of Cobb's complaining and his temperament, lashed back, "You'd think that the talent in this league had been on the wane ever since the battle of Thermopylae." Grantland Rice, who walked both sides of the ancient-modern beat, blamed Cobb's ire on a career-long envy of Babe Ruth. Cobb never forgave Ruth for revolutionizing the game, turning it into a slugfest of long balls and high scores. That's why he attacked DiMaggio and Williams, successors to Ruth's fame and to his game. Cobb's game was gritty and dirty, much like his personal life. One day he showed up in the Detroit clubhouse all bloody and beaten around the face. "What happened to you?" was the chorus from the players. "Ah, nothing much," said Cobb, "I got tired of waiting for a phone booth so I reached in and yanked this guy out. Turned out he was a professional fighter. He was real good."

Cobb had some support from persuasive voices. Connie Mack did not exactly join the fray, but his knowledge of the game was archaeological. Surely Cobb was right about one thing, according to Mack: he could beat a team singlehandedly a different way every day of the month. Casey Stengel pointed out that whereas "Cobb was not a very popular fellow" either then or now, most everything he said about baseball as a team sport was right. Pennants are won over the long haul by adjustments that individual players make in light of the nature of their team and in light of the circumstances that crop up in games they have to win. As Dom DiMaggio pointed out, this was not exactly the strong suit of the Boston Red Sox.

Spring training moved into its April phase with no clear indication of Williams's draft status but with an appointment for him to pay an examination visit to one Captain Julius C. Early, the head of the marine medical board at the Jacksonville training center. Early was a friend of another ex-marine, Hy Hurwitz, and he told writers that Williams's bum elbow was by no means an automatic exemption. Much more important were muscle balance and the depth of perception in his vision, matters subject to change as a man enters his mid-30s. On April 2, Early and Commander Lewis Sims, Jr., conducted a two-hour examination of Williams, promising an orthopedic consult if there was any doubt about the elbow.

Williams passed his physical. So did Jerry Coleman, Yankee second baseman and fighter pilot who flew 57 missions during World War II and would fly another 63 in Korea before his discharge in August 1953. The *Globe* of April 2 headlined the story: "TED WILLIAMS IN MARINES." After the exam, Captain Early introduced Williams and Jerry Coleman of the Yanks as Captain Williams and Captain Coleman, which signaled to reporters the results of the physical before Early said another word. Williams was good-humored enough: "I'm praying for a quick truce." He would begin a 17-month hitch in May, reporting to Pennsylvania for an eight-week refresher course at Willow Grove, and then on to Cherry Point, North Carolina, for operational training. Joe DiMaggio was having a much better time of it this very day. The newspapers carried a picture of Joe in Hollywood with a new interest on his arm—Marilyn Monroe. The caption implicitly drove home the message by explicitly denying it: "We're just friends."

The Red Sox were not happy about Williams's new job at $7,000 a year for the United States Marines. But Tom Yawkey, at least, remembered the swirl of controversy around Williams and the draft in 1942 and said nothing. Don Lenhardt, the penciled-in replacement for Williams in left field, would have preferred a different sort of burden to bear: "Boy, when they take a fellow Ted's age, and a married man with a family, it's murder." All Williams could do was continue tuning up with the team and see what the future would bring. "TELL IT TO THE MARINES," a local headline blared when he hit a monstrous home run in Tulsa against the Tulsa Oilers. But the fans of High Point, North Carolina, who hadn't seen a major league exhibition game in 20 years, got all over Williams, marines or no, when he loped to first on a grounder to Bobby Shantz of the A's with the Red Sox down by two in the sixth inning. The ball bounced off Shantz's glove, but Williams turned on his accelerator too late and was nipped at first when he should have easily beaten the throw. Boudreau had to take Williams out of the game because of the boos.

On the northern swing into Boston before the season, the Red Sox warmed the home turf with their annual city series with the Braves. Williams hit two out in one game, merely adding to the impression that the Sox were going to feel his loss. On opening day in Washington, with Williams's future commander in chief, Harry Truman, taking in the game, the Red Sox beat the Senators 3-0. Williams tripled, but Boston's tempestuous and talented rookie Jimmy Piersall stole the show with his hitting and fielding. Piersall was a "can't miss" prospect, according to those in the Boston farm system, if he could keep his almost-preternatural bursts of temper under control.

Piersall was one of the last of Eddie Collins's projects before the Red Sox executive died in 1951. Collins had marveled at Piersall's defensive ability in camp back in 1950, though Piersall did not know then whether he was a shortstop or an outfielder. Collins knew. The kid was the most instinctual ball hawk in the outfield that he had seen since the days when Johnny Mostil patrolled center for the 1925 White Sox. On one occasion, Mostil waived off leftfielder Bibb Falk and caught a long fly on the other side of the foul line near the seats in left. Ty Cobb said of that White Sox outfield that "it consists of Mostil and two traffic cops."

Williams's triple in the opener was the most running he did during his brief season. He pulled a muscle in his calf and strained a knee; he would do nothing but pinch hit until the end of April. The Sox got off to a fast start, but already there were doubts about the season. When the Senators came into Boston and got pasted by the Sox, Bobo Newsom stopped by the Red Sox clubhouse and asked a few Boston players, "What are you going to do when you lose half your ball club?" "Huh?" said one of the Red Sox. "I mean Ted Williams," said Bobo. "He's half your ball club, ain't he? For 10 years I've heard how much better you'd be without him. Now I guess I'll see." Newsom's sarcasm was thick. And he was right. The Red Sox faded to the second division and finished sixth in 1952. They had not yet suffered such an indignity with Williams in the lineup, though during his World War II years the Sox finished seventh in 1943 and 1945.

As Williams's own season wound to a close, Mayor John B. Hynes of Boston set Wednesday, April 30, as Ted Williams Day. Williams tried halfheartedly to discourage the event, but he relented when Fire Commissioner Michael Kelleher promised that gifts would be limited to a bike for Ted's daughter, Bobbie Jo, and an aviator's watch for Williams. But that wasn't to be, and Williams was embarrassed by the barrage of gifts showered on him before the game, especially the powder-blue Cadillac. But his embarrassment did not impede his flair for the dramatic. After a first-inning single through a vacancy left by the Tigers' shift on the left side of the infield, Williams came up in the seventh inning with two down and Dominic DiMaggio on first. He broke a 3-3 tie with a blast off Dizzy Trout into the right-field seats.

Williams crossed home plate to the absolute delight of the Fenway crowd and called it a season. His lifetime batting average edged up to .347 as the result of this, his second .400 season; of course, on the year he had but 10 at-bats and 4 hits. He was off to Pennsylvania for an eight-week refresher course. He would then begin operational training on the prop Corsair fighter jet for 90 hours before beginning on F-9 Panther jet fighters in North Carolina. For cold-weather training, he would head to the Sierras. By winter he would be attached to Marine Air Group 33, flying aerial reconnaissance in Korea.

Williams told Robert Cramer in an *Esquire* profile in June 1986, that he had the first sequence of shots of a movie about his life all blocked out. The opening frames would project onto a blue-sky pilot's-eye view; then a cut to a F-9 Panther jet streaking across the wide screen; then an explosion, flames, and a black screen. The next shot would be a widening panorama from the green grass of a ball park to Fenway Park filled with screaming, cheering fans. Perhaps Williams was not exactly William Holden in *The Bridges at Toko-Ri*, which was filmed in the spring of 1952 with the cooperation of the navy, but he nonetheless had a good grasp on what passed for drama in his life.

In a syndicated article for the Scripps-Howard chain that appeared in the *Boston Herald* in the spring, John Lucas tracked Williams down in Korea at Pohang in Hut I-C, a prefabricated job that Ted shared with Major Jim Mitchell of San Francisco and Captain Lee Scott from Washington state. The fliers had plenty of spare time, and Williams spent a good deal of it fiddling with a new hobby, photography, more than fitting for his aerial photographic reconnaissance unit. But the officers weren't short on horseplay, either. Williams sacked out one evening in his bunk only to find himself belly-to-belly with dozens of frozen orange juice cans. He screamed out, and his hut mates queries: "What's the matter, Bush, a bit chilly?" Thinking about that incident, among others, Williams sighed to Lucas, "I got to the top of the Big Time, and these bums call me Bush."

Mitchell and Scott were on Williams all the time. They told him they had already purchased reserve seats for 1954 in Fenway's left field. Nothing would make them happier than conversing with Williams as part of the wolf pack: "We're going to give you hell, Bush." Williams wasn't even sure he had a career in baseball any more, though he said he couldn't turn down a request from Yawkey: "I'd do anything for him, but I've got a little fishing-tackle business that cleared a million and a half last year. Maybe I've had it." He then took out a letter from a teammate he wouldn't identify, though it was from Dom DiMaggio, his conspirator in barring the Boston writers from the clubhouse after the war in 1946. He began reading: " 'We don't vote on anything any more. The scribes come into the clubhouse whenever they want to.' " Williams chortled, "That's what's happening. You know who it was who kept 'em out whenever the front office weakened. Old Number One. Old TSW."

Dom DiMaggio would quit playing ball in May, but not before recommending that the players hire a lawyer to represent them in dealings with the leagues. DiMaggio was the American League player representative, and he left in a snit about everything: minimum wage, night ball, salary negotiation. He told Williams that the game was on the verge of radical changes, and, as it turned out, DiMaggio was right. Expansion, reserve-clause reform, free agency, and media contracts (nearly $20 million a year were now at issue over television rights) were to mark the post–Korean War years in baseball.

When Lucas spoke to him Williams had been grounded with a bad ear infection, which he had had treated in Japan and aboard a Danish medical ship, the *Jutlandia*. This virus would eventually be his ticket out of the marines via Hawaii, but he had plenty to tell Lucas about events in Korea prior to his illness. Williams liked to fly the F-9 jet, but ever since his training days he had felt uneasy about the fit of his body in the cockpit. The thought of ever having to bail out of one spooked him: "They say they build those jets for guys up to 6'3", but when I used to put on my chute, life raft, and survival kit, my head would scrape the canopy top, and my legs would be doubled up under the instrument panel. I used to be convinced that if I had to bail out with the pilot's ejection device, I'd leave both my shin bones in the ship."

By then he had flown 39 reconnaissance missions over enemy lines and insisted that heroics were not for him. He flew his missions as best he could and made no bones about wanting out of there before an unscheduled trip in his ejection seat. Getting fired on was less fearful to him than trying to squeeze his frame out of a cockpit. He told Lucas that he had written a friend that he felt he was in for it, that he had some kind of premonition that he was going down. But he was irritated that the press had picked up the story as a death wish. It was nothing of the sort and he dismissed it summarily: "Made me sound like a fool."

Most of Williams's missions in Korea took place after his most harrowing one. He began with a simple flight along the bombing line with no flak thrown up at him; and his second mission, though deeper into enemy territory, was still unimpeded. But on February 16, 1953, on a run to scout out the tank and infantry training school near Pyongyang, he met with big trouble. As he swooped in for a pass his airplane was hit by small-arms fire from the ground: "I was the only guy hit. I still don't know what happened. We've gone over that plane with a fine-tooth comb. It was small arms. No wonder they didn't hit anyone else. I got it all." The ground fire knocked out his radio, his compass, and disabled his landing gear. He flew back toward base at Suwon with his plane in trouble and its handling capacity severely jeopardized.

A fellow pilot, Lawren R. Hawkins of Pine Grove, Pennsylvania, picked Williams up on his wing, and Williams struggled with his stick the best he could to follow Hawkins in. Hawkins could see the flames flaring from Williams's plane and prayed that he would bail out; he didn't see how Williams could bring the plane in without crashing in a fireball. But bailing out wasn't in Williams's handbook for the science of flying. He couldn't shake the picture of getting wedged in the cockpit like a sardine. He was able to keep Hawkins in view, control his plane in the air, put it on the ground without landing gear, leap out of the fiery craft like a guy with a hotfoot, and scamper across the field before the plane was completely engulfed in flames. In spite of Williams's repeated attempts to discount his heroism, it was a nifty piece of flying.

The rest of Williams's runs were duck soup compared to this one.

Information began to circulate in June 1953 that he was on his way stateside. The Korean War was near settlement as the pace of peace talks increased. Queen Elizabeth had just been crowned on June 2; Julius and Ethel Rosenberg were electrocuted at Sing Sing on June 19; and Lucille Ball, of all people, was facing congressional investigation for having registered to vote as a communist in 1936, a gesture to please her aging socialist grandfather. The baseball highlight of the year so far was a now-famous prodigious home run by Mickey Mantle on April 17 at Griffith Stadium in Washington. He blasted one right-handed 565 feet, over the center-field seats. Billy Martin, camped on third, waited for Mantle to circle around. "What the hell you standing here for?" Mantle yelled. "Just tagging up," smiled Martin.

On July 14 in Cincinnati, Williams showed up at the All-Star Game after a short stay in the naval hospital at Bethesda, Maryland, for a checkup. He was introduced by Ford Frick, and, following a huge ovation from the crowd, he threw out the first ball to Roy Campanella. Williams began talking with Yawkey and Cronin about next year's contract or, possibly, about returning to finish out the 1953 season. He was pale and looked tired, but after consulting with his business manager, Fred Corcoran, and the Red Sox management he ultimately decided to play to boost the chances of the Sox in a pennant run. Corcoran told his client, "You're not a fisherman, Ted; you're a ballplayer."

Despite a light-hitting outfield, the Red Sox were not entirely out of the race (10 games from first place) and had been playing hot ball since before the All-Star break. Williams could sign on in 1953 for a healthy percentage of a yearly salary, close to $40,000. That would get him on the payroll months before the 1954 season. The Red Sox had themselves a deal, and Williams let the writers know: "Okay, boys, tell the fans to get their lungs warmed up. It looks like I'll be back." The last sounds he heard from Boston's fans were the tremendous cheers for him on his "day" before leaving to rejoin the marines. But Williams expected the worst; he even counted on it to sharpen his skills.

Williams began limbering up at Fenway, taking some batting practice off George Susce on July 29, the very day a truce was formally enacted in Korea. He had been discharged from the marines the day before, by Colonel K. G. Chappel at the barracks of the Naval

Gun Factory in Washington, D.C. He then immediately drove to Boston. With reporters clustering around the cage, he donned a pair of golfing gloves given him by pro Claude Harmon and sprayed line drives all over the field. He finally muscled up for a home run on the 53rd pitch and another on the 78th. Everyone had been waiting and counting in a kind of informal lottery. The question for Williams was not so much his hitting stroke as his legs. Many remembered Hank Greenberg's early return to Detroit in 1945 for half a season. He had no trouble powdering the ball, but his legs were so sore toward the end of the year and into the World Series that he could barely suit up.

Williams faced a similar prospect. His illness in Korea did not allow him to keep in top shape, and he was weak and untoned when he came out to hit. At most, he had shagged a few fly balls in Korea off the bat of Lloyd Merriman, who played for Cincinnati. But he had lost little of his feel for the batter's box. About halfway through the day's session he told Joe Cronin that the plate at Fenway was out of line a fraction of an inch. Cronin had the groundskeeper check it out, and Williams was right. The part of the game that took place in Williams's head and engaged his instincts would always be the source of his genius. Only the body plotted its subtle betrayal as the seasons rolled on.

The Red Sox, having clawed their way to within seven games of first place with a sequence of wins in July, lost three straight games after the news that Williams would get himself in shape to return. They would lose five more in a row. Harold Kaese wasted little time in setting Williams up before he even donned a uniform. He wrote a column, "FANS DISCUSS LOSSES OF RED SOX FOLLOWING RETURN OF WILLIAMS," in which he spoke to the man on the street about Ted and the pennant race. A bus driver buttonholed him: "I got nothing against him, mind you, but he seems to bring tough luck to the team. Everything's going to pieces." As for Williams, he was not insensitive to the effect his return was having on the media, hence on his teammates: "I don't want to disrupt the team—after all, they've won 21 out of 24—so I'll practice at odd hours."

Some of the younger Red Sox were eager to hang around with him. Ted Lepcio spoke to Clif Keane of the *Globe* about Williams on hitting: "It isn't that Williams is critical in what he says to you. It's the way he makes you feel you have to be a hitter that makes him so good at instructing. He'll never say 'why do you do it like that?' when he's talking. Instead, he'll tell you that your stance is all right, but you're just a little slow with your hands and wrists. So you try what he says and the first thing you know the ball is being stung pretty good."

A week later Williams was ready to do some pinch hitting. On August 6 he popped out against Oriole screwball pitcher Marlin Stuart in an 8–7 Sox loss. He appeared again as a pinch hitter on August 9 with the Sox down by three in the seventh inning to Cleveland and Mike Garcia. Garcia had the count 3-1 against him and didn't want to walk Williams while protecting a lead. So he came in with a fastball, and Williams got into it. He drove the pitch 420 feet into the right-field seats at Fenway. "Brother," said Ted, "if that ball isn't in the seats, I'll never hit a home run again as long as I live." Bob Feller, the old veteran of the Indian staff, was as excited as a kid for his long-time nemesis. "It made me feel young again."

Al Rosen was surprised by the expression on Williams's face as he rounded third in his brisk home-run trot: "I'll bet maybe he was trying to hold back tears or something." Williams was always grim as he rounded the bases so Rosen may have been projecting a little bit of his own emotional sense of the moment. Cleveland catcher Joe Tipton remembered the other side of the at-bat, the moment before the dramatic pinch homer. " 'All right—sing your song,' Ted said to me as he came up. See, I used to hum 'Good Night, Irene' whenever he came to bat. I just happened to think of it one day, and I sang it to him every time. But not today. I kept quiet. I just said, 'Hello, Ted.' "

The Sox were losing, and the reappearance of Williams still did not sit well with all. Bill Cunningham of the *Herald* recorded a bit of conversation at the park: "He always could hit 'em when they don't mean nuttin'. I don't say he chokes. I just say he doesn't change. He'll hit 'em, but you can't be sure he'll hit 'em when you need 'em." Cunningham took the occasion of Williams's home run to damn him with faint praise:

> I think Williams is wonderful, but there are no heights and depths to him. He's like a perfect machine, smoothly functioning but with his gears meshed and locked in a speed that can be neither accelerated nor retarded. That brings it back to "the clutch," which is another way of saying "the ability to rise to the

occasion." The Babe Ruths, the Ty Cobbs, the Joe DiMaggios could, and when they failed, they died trying. I'd say that Williams is a competitor, but that his blood is ice cold. Furthermore, I think that's the way he was born to be, that, as a ballplayer, nothing, not even Korea, has changed, nor could change him, and that, like religion, you can't argue with him. There he is and that's it. Take him or leave him.

A week later, after a road trip in which Williams pinch hit four more times without any success, he would start his first game on August 16 at Fenway. The ovation lasted for nearly five minutes when the 25,000 fans heard Williams's name in the starting lineup. He responded with a double and a home run. In the same game, against Washington, rightfielder Jimmy Piersall made the finest catch Joe Cronin had ever seen. Mickey Vernon hit a line drive that, for all purposes, was already over the low right-field barrier when Piersall, at high speed, dove over the wall, speared the ball, and rebounded back onto the field in an acrobatic move that had Cronin sputtering: "Hell, that wasn't just the best catch I ever saw, it was the best catch ever made." Less than a month earlier, on July 20, Piersall made two memorable catches back-to-back: a spectacular charging grab of an Al Rosen blooper and a daredevil leaping catch of a Bob Lemon line drive down the foul line. Lou Boudreau said it was the best inning of outfield play he had ever witnessed.

Piersall was both a find and a problem for the Red Sox. He could go on tears with his bat and then slump almost into a state of depression. He would fight at the drop of a hat. Several players in the American League thought him a lunatic; they would resist fights with him on the legitimate theory that his behavior was a sickness. Chico Carrasquel of the White Sox summed it up: "He's crazy guy." On the other hand, Piersall's play was electric. He could track down balls in the outfield faster than early-warning radar; his arm was strong enough to throw out runners at first from right field on grounders; and his base running was a treat to which Red Sox fans were seldom exposed. Boston had not seen the last of the controversy that surrounded this extraordinary ballplayer, nor had the rest of the league.

Williams's home run in his first complete game since his return made the annual Jimmy Fund Dinner—the charity closest to Wil-

liams's heart and the one to which he devoted a considerable amount
of his time over the years—a pleasure. Williams was the honored
guest for this August 17 event at the Statler. Ted Kennedy was the
bearer of the largest donation, $50,000, in honor of his brother, Joe,
who had been killed in World War II. Ed Sullivan, the master of
ceremonies, made a point of putting on Williams's tie for the presen-
tations, and Ted made a point of taking it off on the dais after he
spoke. Of the fund and the kids it supported, Williams said, "We're
all a bunch of boys cheating the calendar."

In the next month, the Red Sox faded in their quest for the
pennant, but it would be difficult to argue that Williams's return
stifled the team. First off, they began losing regularly before his
return to the lineup; and second, he hit .462 the first three weeks he
played. In just under a month he hit 11 home runs and drove in 27
runs. His slugging percentage was a gargantuan 1.017. Casey Stengel
was asked in September whether Williams looked different to him
this year: "Yeah, he looks bigger, more powerful, and more dangerous."

The 1953 American League season ended on a day of considerable
controversy, but it had nothing to do with Ted Williams. On the last
day of the year, Cleveland's Al Rosen, in a dogfight with Mickey
Vernon for the batting title, failed to touch first base on a deep
grounder to third that he would have surely beaten out for a base hit.
Rosen already had three hits on the day, and his lapse in baserunning
lost him his fourth, a hit he absolutely needed to win the title from
Vernon. Meanwhile, in the ninth inning of their game the Senators
were falling all over themselves to avoid another Vernon at-bat and
a chance that their first baseman's average would slip a notch.
(Vernon could have left the game, but he felt funny about doing that.)
One Senator was picked off second, another was out stretching a
single, and Pete Runnels took a pathetic half swing at a third strike.
Vernon did not come to the plate, and his average held at .337, while
Rosen's dipped to .336. Rosen's baserunning blunder also cost him
the Triple Crown: he already led the league in home runs and runs
batted in.

This was not the most bizarre ending to a batting-title race in the
American League, though it came close. That honor belonged to
1910, when Napoleon Lajoie and Ty Cobb fought it out. Cobb sat out

the doubleheader against Chicago with what he figured was a comfortable lead in average. Lajoie had to go at least 9 for 9 in a doubleheader against the Browns to surpass him. Incredibly, he went 8 for 8 and missed tying for the title by a hair, .3841 to Cobb's .3848. The story had another twist. Six of Lajoie's hits were bunt singles, with the Brown's third baseman playing so deep he might just as well have been penciled in for left. Cobb had his enemies around the league and several of them played for the Browns. Ty screamed to the commissioner's office about this stunt; had Lajoie gotten one more hit, he would have taken the case to the Supreme Court.

The Red Sox finished the year in fourth, 16 games behind the Yankees, who would win the World Series, led by Billy Martin and Mickey Mantle, against the Dodgers. Williams finished with his highest average ever, .407, though far short of the necessary at-bats for the title. He averaged .455 for 18 games on the road and .362 for 19 at Fenway. In a mere 91 at-bats he hit 13 home runs, slugged at a phenomenal .901, and walked 19 times. He told Jerry Nason of the *Globe*, that he expected 200 walks next year, a ballplayer's way of hinting to the front office that he was unprotected in the lineup. So he was.

◇ 15 ◇

Cold Shoulder
1954

THE MARRIAGE OF THE FORMER Doris Soule to the present Ted
Williams hit the permanent skids in January 1954. It was not exactly
as if their marriage before then was on solid ground—the contrary
was, in fact, the case—but matters had reached separable proportions
by this year. In the midst of the divorce proceedings Doris delivered
the line that pegged the marriage even in its earlier stages and
forecast Ted's increasingly diffident behavior in regard to it: "I don't
think Ted wanted to be married." One can look at these matters in a
dozen different ways from a dozen different angles, but Doris Soule
trusted her memory. In essence, she was right.

So Doris filed for separate maintenance, complaining of "mistreat-
ment and abuse" and constant subjection to "profane and obscene
language." The almost formulaic quality of the charges would have
struck baseball writers around the Boston clubhouse as perfectly
plausible. It would be hard to imagine Williams denying them. He
simply complied with her request for $125 a week pending negotia-
tion for settlement under provisions of Florida law. Williams was
faced with an accounting dilemma as the year progressed. He had to
play to settle up with Doris; but too much money in his pocket made
him vulnerable. Later, his strange remarks about playing in 1955 were
intricately connected to his negotiated marriage settlement, though
these matters were kept quiet by the Red Sox and by what still passed
for the code of honor among baseball writers.

Over the years it was hardly a well-kept secret that Ted Williams
worked Fenway Park for possible postgame entertainment; he and

256

park personnel set up a simple and efficient messenger service for whenever the urge struck. Eddie Waitkus's unfortunate run-in with a love-crazed fan in 1950 had discouraged Williams's road whims, though Mike Epstein, who played for Williams on the Washington Senators in 1969, tells a marvelous story about Ted on the road.

The Senators were waiting in the team bus that would take them from the hotel in Chicago to Comiskey Park; Williams, as manager, was always last to board. At the very last beckoning honk of the horn, he emerged from the lobby in his characteristic ganderlike trot, face alive, body active in a million different ways. Just before he stepped on the bus two women, clearly in their fifties, excitedly ran toward him, one panting, "Oh, Ted Williams! It's Ted Williams! Yoo-hoo, Ted, Ted. You do remember us, don't you? Here? In Chicago? Oh-h-h, you remember! Don't you, Ted?"

With the younger ballplayers trying to stifle their laughter, Williams paused for what seemed an eternal moment, one foot on the bus step, darting his eyes at the women and through the bus windows at his players. "Oh, Ted, surely you remember?" Williams gave the ladies one lingering look, then swung his body onto the bus. "No," he said tersely, more to his wide-eyed players than to his admirers. The entire Senator squad, aching with suppressed laughter, finally burst out in a roar. Williams remained glum for a while and then smiled almost imperceptively.

But these matters were not for public consumption in 1954. Williams was trying to get out of a marriage as quietly and discreetly as he could. Most of his energies would be directed toward accommodating his wife's lawyer. If Doris had complaints about Ted's conduct, Ted reserved his complaints in 1954 for the Red Sox brass. He wanted more protection in the lineup. One answer to Williams's plea had been a trade for Jackie Jensen. At the annual Sportsman's Show in February Williams told Hy Hurwitz that he liked the trade: "To say we're going to win the pennant is silly, but we will be an improved ball club." Joe Cronin got to Williams and tried to tone him down: "You're taking us out of the race before it even begins." On the other hand, Williams simply might have taken a look at the rosters of the Indians and Yankees for 1954 and drawn some sensible conclusions. The Yankees were stocked with talent. Their lineup was in the prime of its collective career. Cleveland had a chilling pitching staff; some argue it was the best ever assembled in the history of baseball: Feller, Wynn, Lemon, Garcia, Houtteman, Mossi, Narleski, and Newhouser.

Harold Kaese was also down on the Red Sox from the start: They had the wrong mix of players, and their youth movement needed seasoning. To win, a team has to have "first-division stars," a collection of proven money players with enough time logged to stir things in ways commensurate with the internal rhythms of baseball. It is a matter of knowledge, confidence, timing, plus the subtle ways of getting to the opposition, interrupting *their* rhythm, feeling the pulse of the game. The Red Sox of the late 1940s came close. Not this team.

While the local writers were busy figuring just how low Boston would plunge in the standings for 1954, the nation itself, for the first time in years, was roused out of its oppressive McCarthyite doldrums. With the confidence of a year in office behind him and with the Korean War folded into history, President Eisenhower finally drew the line on the blustering Senator McCarthy, whom he personally detested. He reacted violently to McCarthy's taunting of Secretary of the Army Robert T. Stevens: "I will not tolerate the browbeating or humiliation of Army personnel before the investigating committee." McCarthy was said to have boasted to friends that he had the armed services in the palm of his hands. Exactly who had whom in the palm of whose hands turned out to be the very issue that led to McCarthy's downfall. Little did the senator know that he was heading for trouble because of the favors granted by his aide Roy Cohn to Dave Schine of the United States Army, Cohn's private obsession.

Public opinion lined up behind Eisenhower slowly but surely. It remained for Edward Murrow, during a famous "See It Now" show of May 9, and a folksy army counsel, Joseph Welch, to finish McCarthy off. McCarthy seemed desperate after his sad showing with Murrow. He was reduced to fulminating on the Fulton Lewis, Jr., radio show that the young Murrow, as head of the International Study Institute, was a communist: "I hold here in my hand a clipping from the Pittsburgh *Sun-Telegraph* of February 18, 1935." The clipping revealed that Murrow has been an advisor for the summer session of Moscow University. The charge was almost pathetic.

Finally the tables were turned, and, in a series of dramatic confrontations, McCarthy's tactics became the object of investigation. Army counsel Welch had evidence that McCarthy's aides had doctored a photo featuring Cohn's friend, Private Schine. "Who cropped the photo?" asked Welch. "A pixie?" McCarthy interrupted: "Will the counsel for my benefit define—I think he might be an expert on that—what a pixie is?" Welch said, "Yes, I should say, Mr. Senator, that a pixie is a close relative to a fairy. Shall I proceed, sir? Have I enlightened you?" These snide and nasty exchanges were dynamite, given the appearance of homosexuality implicit in Cohn's actions.

On March 1, the opening day of spring training, an infamous paramilitary operation of sorts took place in the Congress of the United States. A group of Puerto Rican nationalists led by Lolita Lebron opened fire on the U.S. House of Representatives and wounded five of its members. That same day Ted Williams was getting ready to enjoy his first appearance on the practice field at Sarasota, but he met with trouble of his own. He began by jogging in the outfield and then chatting with Jimmy Piersall while moving, every once in a while, to shag a batting practice fly. He wanted to gauge his senses and just loosen up. He had been on the field for 10 minutes.

Hoot Evers was taking his cuts at the plate, and he lined one toward left center. Williams started in, then reached low for the liner falling fast with topspin. He stumbled on shaky first-day legs and crash-landed on his shoulder. Williams heard the snap of his collarbone and told Piersall on the spot, "I broke it." Right he was: a displaced and comminuted fracture at the juncture of the outer and middle third of the left clavicle. Even this piece of bad luck was grist for the mill of the Boston press corps; Williams had to endure not only the pain of his freak injury but the back-handed compliment of Harold Kaese: "At least he was hustling."

Williams had actually arrived in training camp that day with Dr. Russell Sullivan, an orthopedist from Boston General, who had been fishing with Ted in the Keys. Little did the doctor know he would step out of the car, stretch his legs, and then, a few moments later, render his professional services to the man who just chauffered him to camp. Sullivan's medical decision was definitive. Surgery was necessary to pin the collarbone. Williams would travel to Boston for the operation on March 8.

Up to this point in his career, Williams had missed almost a season's worth of games, 138, with injuries or illnesses. For 35 additional games he could only pinch hit. But as prone as he was to injury, his healing processes were extraordinary. Williams insisted, "I'll play in the opener. I've fooled the doctors before and I'll fool them again." Dr. Sullivan operated on March 9 and found a detached triangular fragment of bone 1½ inches long and about half the thickness of the collarbone from which it had come. He had to remove the fragment and connect the fracture with a six-inch stainless steel pin. Williams responded very quickly. In a little over a week his cast was off and replaced with a brace; but his collarbone was so fragile that he couldn't even run to keep his legs in shape without jarring it. He would not play until mid-May.

Williams used his free time to put together a series of articles for the *Saturday Evening Post* with Joe Reichler and Joe Trimble, Associated Press baseball writers. The magazine paid him $30,000 for the effort, and he shuttled off $10,000 of that for Reichler and Trimble. For this kind of money, the magazine wanted something hot, and they got it: "This Is My Last Year in Baseball." Williams was unabashed: "Even before I broke my collarbone on my first day of spring training last month, I had made up my mind to quit at the end of this season." His military hitches cost him $500,000 in salary and endorsements. The only reason he remained in the game at all now was for money. He had a financial timetable, and this year it balanced on the favorable side: "A fellow has to look out for his future."

Williams was growing weary of abuse from the press and the fans:

> Let's face it. I know when they're cheering and I know when they're booing, and anyone would be crazy to prefer the boos to the cheers.
>
> I believe I have the best pair of "rabbit ears" ever developed in the majors. There might be 30,000 people in the stands, some of them cheering and some of them talking to their neighbors, but if there are a half dozen giving the old razoo, I can spot them in a matter of seconds. I know who they are before a half inning is over. A lot of the regulars at Fenway Park make a practice of giving me the business every time they come out to see a game. I'm the guy they love to hate. For these "sportsmen," I can only extend my heartiest contempt.

About his refusal to tip his cap to the crowd when he hit one out,

Williams tried to make the most telling point he ever made on the subject, one that the almost painfully boastful players of this present generation would do well to heed. "Do the pitchers tip their cap to the crowd when they strike me out?" The crowd didn't deserve his acknowledgment, and the pitchers might resent it.

But Williams had his conventions confused. It's customary for hitters to tip their caps to cheering fans; it's not customary for the pitcher to tip his cap after a strikeout. Feller, Sandy Koufax, and Nolan Ryan would have gotten arm weary had they done so. On the other hand, the whole business was full of casuistry for Williams. He tipped his cap like a doorman in 1939 when he was the golden boy of the bleachers at Fenway. When he hit fewer homers in 1940 and the fans and writers let him have it, he stopped.

With his article hot off the press in early April and with the Boston writers, counterinsurgents of a sort, laying in wait for him, Williams began to work out gently in Fenway Park. He ran a bit and played light pepper, but he still would not be available for pinch-hitting duties until May 15. Lou Boudreau took one look around the league this season and told the writers the Sox hadn't a chance without Williams.

On opening day the Red Sox lost to the A's 6-3, with their ace Mel Parnell taking the defeat. An old baseball custom went the way of television sanitization on this day. The commissioner's office issued a directive stating that gloves could no longer be left near the foul lines between innings, even though few players still did so. Most fans remembered this convention from old baseball movies, but fewer and fewer of these personal touches remained as the sport was neatened up over the years under the influence of television and its prying cameras.

Williams joined several of his old teammates, among them Lefty Grove, Jimmie Foxx, and Bobby Doerr, to honor Tom Yawkey at a B'nai Brith Dinner on April 16. Yawkey wished all of those present could have played together in their prime for him, implying that such an imaginary team might have been the only way he could win pennants consistently. Of course, the baseball writers in attendance snickered that even such a team would have found a way to lose.

By early May the Red Sox were floundering in last place, and Williams was anxious to resume play. He began traveling with the club on May 4: "I can't sit on the bench any longer in these 1-0 and

2-1 games." The Red Sox needed a boost, especially in that they would begin periodic telecasts of their road games, commencing with a WBZ broadcast from Baltimore to the New England area on May 13. The Red Sox on the road were not always the prettiest of sights, and now that the home fans would get an occasional look, the club would, at the very least, like Williams's bat in the lineup. Two days later, on May 15, Williams pinch hit and stayed in the game for the late innings. He flied to left center and grounded to short in his two official times at bat.

But the next day in Detroit was a marvel, one of Williams's best efforts in the major leagues. In a doubleheader on May 16 he came to the plate nine times and chalked up eight hits, two home runs, a double, and seven runs batted in. His second home run in the nightcap off righty Ray Herbert landed in the third tier of the right-field stands. And his collarbone? Williams said "it hurt like hell all day." The Sox were no longer losing 1-0 and 2-1. This day they lost 7-6 and 9-8 and were still wiping up the bottom of the league.

By the end of May the Sox began winning some ball games. Williams was still stroking well, though he wanted the pin out of his shoulder. Dr. Sullivan wanted it to remain. It remained. When the Red Sox arrived in New York with Williams hitting close to .500 Casey Stengel remarked, "If they take that pin out of his shoulder, they can give it to me because I can use it on about three of my players." It was during these late-spring days that America exorcised its resident demon. Early June marked the downfall of Senator Joseph McCarthy and the effective end of his haunting power. After a desperate final attack on army counsel Joseph Welch's young colleague, Frederick Fisher, McCarthy faced the wrath of Welch, who spoke his famous words: "Until this morning, Senator, I think I never really gauged your cruelty or your recklessness. . . . If there is a god in heaven, it will do neither you nor your cause any good. You have done enough. Have you no sense of decency, sir, at long last? Have you no sense of decency?"

Williams could watch these televised proceedings from a sickbed. He was out of the lineup with viral pneumonia. Throughout his career he was plagued by upper-respiratory viruses, and there wasn't much to be done except rest and recover. This bout hit him for over two weeks. Boston had plunged deep into the cellar when Williams returned on June 23. About all he had to look forward to was the All-Star Game, and he did little in the American League's 11-9 win but convince Al Rosen to shorten up on the grip of his bat. Rosen ripped two home runs to contribute to the win. A couple of weeks earlier, Lou Boudreau had thrown a fit when Boston catcher Sammy White picked up Rosen's bat during a game and found five nails driven in. The ump tossed it out; Rosen exclaimed, "Well, I'll be damned! Would you look at that!"

Things kept getting worse for the Red Sox. By the end of July their record was truly abysmal—30 wins and 58 losses. The team was 28½ games out of first place behind a Cleveland Indians squad destined to win 111 games. What made it worse for the rest of the league was that the Yankees were also competitive right to the end of the season. So there were not many wins left over to distribute around the league. Williams was stroking consistently at .356 and would up it to .367 the next day with three hits, but he was still the butt of local jokes. Harold Kaese said Williams's best move these days was craning his neck to watch balls sail over the Green Monster in left field.

In the National League, the last day in July saw Joe Adcock of the Milwaukee Braves hit four home runs and a double against the Dodgers. That in itself was a baseball rarity, but the next day was more fun. Adcock came up in the fourth inning and blasted another double. The Dodgers had seen enough. When the Braves batted around that inning and Adcock came to the plate the second time, Clem Labine promptly beaned him. The Braves' Lew Burdette rushed to the mound to pounce on Labine, and Jackie Robinson arrived to contribute his bit to the fray. After the donnybrook, Robinson was struck by the irony of the situation: "Can you imagine Burdette upset about throwing at somebody? That's how he makes his living." The bad blood between these two players would last. A couple of years later, in 1956, Burdette taunted Robinson in infield practice: "Hey, watermelon." Robinson asked Gil Hodges if he was, indeed, hearing right. Hodges said "Yep," and Robinson heaved a ball at Burdette in the dugout: "He didn't even have the guts to come out and fight," said Jackie. "Hell," said Lew, "I was just referring to a bit of extra weight he's carrying around. If he's going to be a redneck about this, I'll quit agitating him."

When the Red Sox tried to finish out the year by simply showing up they found the fates were still against them. Their gloves were stolen from the Chicago clubhouse—all of them, that is, except Piersall's, which was so tattered the thief didn't want it, and Billy Consolo's, which had a hole cut in the palm. At the end of their road swing they passed through Baltimore and played at the new Municipal Stadium. Jimmy Dykes and the Orioles were on Williams all day to hit his first out of the new ball park. In the 10th inning he belted the game-winning homer off Bob Chakades into the right-field seats. He smiled at the Baltimore dugout as he rounded the bases, and the crowd gave him a hearty ovation. The Baltimore-Washington area was one of Williams's favorites, and his decent reception there throughout his career helped influence his later decision to manage for Bob Short's Washington Senators in 1969.

Boudreau had by now put Williams second in the lineup because he wanted to try to force the pitchers to throw to him, a notion he had had in spring training of 1952. With the Red Sox so far out, Boudreau could try just about anything with impunity. He also wanted to get Williams some extra at-bats in his pursuit of the career home-run totals of Johnny Mize and Joe DiMaggio. It was uncertain whether Williams would play the next year, and his old nemesis Boudreau was trying to boost him a bit. With 358 home runs, he trailed Mize by one and DiMaggio by three. He would easily surpass both before the year was out.

Against the Yankees in New York on August 14, Williams, who had walked, displayed some real fire on the base paths. He moved from first to third on a shallow single and just made it with a fine hook slide. Then he tagged up on a relatively short fly to right and, testing Hank Bauer's rifle arm, beat the throw to the plate by a whisker. "What's he steamed about?" wondered a baseball writer in the press box. Then a friend pointed to the box seats behind the Yankee dugout, where several Hall of Famers, having been honored before the game, were seated: George Sisler, Rogers Hornsby, Paul Waner, Bill Terry, and Gabby Hartnett. "Oh, give him the right audience, fit though few, and he'll play a little baseball for you."

Williams slumped for the next few games, but he broke out of it in time to help the Red Sox hang five straight defeats on the Yanks at Fenway. This was a crunching blow to Yankee pennant chances in a year when Cleveland was virtually unbeatable, though the Yanks were staying close. This run of losses at Fenway deep-sixed them, and they had to endure their fifth defeat in a row on the day that Williams tied DiMaggio's career home run total at 361 by taking one of Bob Turley's fastballs to never-never land. After the game Williams joked, "Only 130 to go to catch Gehrig," and everyone had a good laugh. Few, including Williams, realized that the joke would end up a distinct possibility.

On September 3 Williams went ahead of his long-time rival DiMaggio. He hit a monster of a home run off the A's Arnold Portocarrero in the midst of an 11–1 win. The ball sailed 40 feet over the fence at the 375-foot sign in right and hit the chimney of a home across North 20th Street. To a certain extent this season rejuvenated Williams. He had recovered from a broken collarbone and was hitting .361 with 26 home runs. Bing Miller, a former Sox player, told Roger Birtwell of the *Globe* that Williams had been quizzing him: "If Williams is going to quit, he's going about it in a funny way. He's asking all us old-timers what we did to keep playing as long as we did. Any time Ted asks for information about baseball, he's doing it to help himself."

But Williams was so physically exhausted near the end of the season that he repeated what he had said earlier in the year: "I'm through. No more." Jerry Nason of the *Globe* wrote his eulogy: "We never had it so good when he came along. We may never have it so good when he is gone. Guys like him can happen, maybe, once in a sportswriter's life, if he is lucky. We were lucky."

The season had indeed worn Williams down. His shin was sore from foul tips ripping into it, and he began wearing a protective shin guard to the plate, looking odder than he usually did in his unstylishly rolled baseball trousers. His average dipped nearly 30 points from September 6 to September 17, but he put some of those points back again by hitting .484 over his last nine games to finish at .345, very near his lifetime average. Because of all his injuries, illnesses, and walks, Williams was shy of the at-bats he needed to challenge Bobby Avila, who hit .341, for the batting title. Williams hit 29 home runs but failed to drive in 100, topping out at 89. His best road work for the year was at Briggs Stadium in Detroit, .433 with four home runs, and at Yankee Stadium, .424 but with only one home run.

After the season Williams headed to Maine for a fishing vacation, taking a whistle-stop train on the Bangor and Aroostook Railroad that stopped all along the way for kids to see him and get his autograph. Williams was gracious enough but adamant about next year: "I've had enough. This is the end." Yawkey all the while had been working on him to consider the idea of managing, perhaps with a mentor in the dugout to boost his confidence, but Williams wasn't buying. He had the feeling the Sox were trying to ease him out. He remained adamant, and Yawkey instead dumped Lou Boudreau as manager and went to Pinky Higgins. For the Red Sox, it was any port in a storm.

The New York–based sportswriter Tom Meany thought all of the Williams talk was a smoke screen, and he wrote a piece for *Collier's* in October that explained why: Williams would not leave in 1955 precisely because the long-sought Red Sox youth movement had so badly fizzled in 1954. Besides, Williams felt his reflexes were there and wanted to go out on a season in which he got at least enough at-bats to vie for the batting title. Meany was sure that Boston had not seen the last of Williams. He turned out to be prescient.

For all anyone knew, though, Williams was through. He said so in his article for the *Saturday Evening Post* at the beginning of the year, and he had said nothing since that changed anything. In the off-season he became harder and harder to reach. On December 10 near Cabo Blanco, off the coast of Peru, he caught the eighth-largest black marlin ever taken by rod and reel, a 14-foot, 1,235-pound beauty of a fish. This made Ted Williams a happy man. What he was avoiding—a looming and murky divorce imbroglio in Florida—most assuredly did not. Nonetheless, he would fight through the world of experience—the mess of his upcoming divorce—before he would rejoin the baseball world of innocence, where, as he had said the year before, men cheated the calendar to remain boys.

◊ 16 ◊
Hiatus
1955

MIKE HIGGINS TOOK OVER AS Red Sox manager in 1955 and told the local Boston press in February that Boston's chances were excellent if he could count on the services of one Theodore Samuel Williams. Shall we dance? The wonder of baseball is that hope does indeed spring eternal. Williams wasn't coming to Boston or to spring training just yet. And excellent was not the way Boston's chances could be described in 1955, whether Williams donned his uniform or not.

Battle Cry was on the silver screen; the Quemoy-Matsu crisis was brewing near China; Princess Margaret and her sex life were stealing headlines; *Peter Pan* was broadcast on television; mass inoculations with the brand new Salk antipolio vaccine were being planned; an incredible schoolboy sensation, Wilt "the Stilt" Chamberlain, was burning up the court at Philly's Overbrook High in his senior year; and Ted Williams was living in Florida but not exactly living the good life. He told the Red Sox that his affairs were a mess and that he would not play until it became clear to him what the nature of his pending divorce settlement would be. For the last few years he had readily admitted to playing primarily for the money; he liked to hit as much as he ever did, but the daily grind wore him down.

Nonetheless, he would play at some time during the season, as soon as it became clear to him that he could do so without putting this year's coins in last year's purse. He needed to recoup some of his finances, but he surely didn't want to benefit his estranged wife at this point. There was also the matter of the fishing business and equitable distribution of proceeds. Williams had his own rod-and-tackle concern, Ted Williams, Inc., and a part interest in a larger tackle consortium, Southern Tackle Distributors, of Miami, with 1,500 dealers. Most of the ready funds were inventory, which did not exactly add up to proceeds, but Doris and her attorney were in there counting.

The local Boston press couldn't get a thing out of the Red Sox on this one. And they were frustrated. When they ran into Williams in West Palm Beach he told them enigmatically that "I've signed contracts to compete in fishing expeditions in May and June." Spring training in Sarasota arrived without Williams's name on his locker, but his name was notably on the Red Sox roster. Cronin simply would not tell the writers—as part of an agreement the Red Sox cut with Williams—what this meant, only that "it's the strangest thing ever." What if he never shows? was the natural question asked again and again by all. Boston had until May 12 to keep Williams on the roster or place him on the voluntary retirement list. If on the voluntary list, he could reapply in 60 days or on the roster expansion date of August 16. The Red Sox were stonewalling on Williams but talking dates and deadlines as a smoke screen, aided by a technical provision that allowed clubs roster spots for players still being drafted into military service. That wasn't Williams, of course, but he balanced another credited spot.

The Yankees and Indians both looked strong again. New York added a brilliant black player, Elston Howard, to the roster; he would get his first major league hit against the Red Sox on April 14. The Cleveland Indians looked better than ever this year; they added the great but fated Herb Score to their mound staff. And the White Sox were also tough, with excellent pitching, including Pierce, Donovan, and Trucks among their front liners. On opening day in Baltimore the Red Sox took the field with nothing but a piece of paper from Williams. He telegrammed Mike Higgins a simple "Good luck." It worked. Ted Lepcio hit a couple of home runs and the Sox took a 7-1 opening-day victory.

The Red Sox were hot in the beginning of the year, led by the hitting of Faye Throneberry, who had the locals talking about the new Ted Williams. Such talk usually lasted until the first serious slump of the season, and, soon enough, Throneberry obliged. This Red Sox team was not going to hold its own in a brutally tough American League without Williams. A local chef offered a solution of sorts: John Tennyson, of the Hotel Charles in Springfield, entered a seven-foot, 200-pound statue of Williams made of beef suet in an original-dish cooking contest at the New England Hotel and Restaurant Convention in Boston. He won.

Unfortunately, the beef-suet Williams was not driving in runs for Boston when the Cleveland Indians faced the Red Sox on May 1. Bobby Feller, at the end of his career, beat them 2–0 in the first game of a doubleheader and Herb Score, at the beginning of his career, beat them 2–1 by striking out 16 in the second game. This was the story of the decade for the Red Sox; they came up short against the old *and* the new. As Lefty Grove used to say of Boston's teams during the pre-Williams era, they "hit with one foot in the American Association." Harold Kaese implored Mr. Yawkey to get on the phone and bring back Number 9.

The divorce story finally broke. With the settlement negotiation complete in Williams's divorce case on May 9, the Sox were ready to release information and get back on track with their leftfielder. Frank Lane of the White Sox had just complained on behalf of the whole league that a missing Williams added up to about $500,000 in gate losses. What was going on? The *Globe* headlined the answer on its first page: "WILLIAMS' WIFE GETS DIVORCE." Doris R. Soule, of Princeton, Minnesota, was currently working as a hotel cashier in Miami. This was precisely what she was doing years ago. Her career had not been meteoric.

The divorce was granted by circuit court judge George E. Holt on May 9. Williams, in a gesture of relief, walked over to his former wife's attorney and shook his hand: "I want to thank you for being big league all the way." On some occasions Williams could turn a phrase. This wasn't one of them. But he was out of a bind and refocused for the first time in months. The most salient piece of testimony in the divorce hearing was an exchange with Doris and her lawyer: "Has Mr. Williams made any attempt at reconciliation?" Doris answered with an emphatic "No." She walked with a $50,000 lump-sum settlement plus the $42,000 family house, full custody of seven-year-old Barbara Joyce, $100-a-month child support payments, and temporary alimony of $125 a month until the lump sum kicked

in. As for the baby-blue Cadillac that Williams received from the
fans of Boston before he reentered the marines in 1952, it remained
in the former Mrs. Ted Williams's family garage.

Williams called Joe Cronin on the phone: "It's been a tough day.
I'll give you another ring and we'll talk." Phil Bissell's cartoon in the
Globe showed Williams arriving in a tow truck to pull Mike Higgins's
battered Cadillac out of a ditch: The club was in seventh place, 9½
out of first. Two days later, on May 13, Williams joined the Red Sox.
He would earn over $60,000 for two-thirds of a season, or over $600
for every game. Put that way, as the papers were glad to do, Boston's
fans got a sense of what the Red Sox thought he was worth. Every
home run cashed in at over $2,000 in this scheme, but so did every
strikeout. For every dollar paid to Williams the Red Sox expected to
get over four back in home attendance alone. The road cut extended
the profits. Keeping him on the roster was good business.

Phil Bissell's cartoon in the May 13 *Globe* told the social side of
the Ted Williams story: a comfortable father in his easy chair glowed
with satisfaction, a teenage son pounded his baseball glove, a wife had
stars in her eyes, and a little tot prodded Dad: "Who's Ted Wiw-
yums?"

On May 14 Williams hit a few at Fenway. He was 10 pounds
overweight, a pin was still in his collarbone from 1954, and his hands
were uncallused and unroughened. The first questions he asked were
to teammates Willard Nixon and Grady Hatton: "How fast is Score?
Is he faster than Newhouser?" Pete Cerrone, a lefty batting-practice
pitcher, hurled a few to him, as did coach Dave Ferriss. He got into
a couple of Ferriss's fat tosses and put them into the bleachers.

The Red Sox were 7½ back when Williams began working out. On
May 18 he got his first look at Herb Score, but from the radio booth
with Curt Gowdy on WHDH. Score beat the Red Sox 19-0. Williams noticed something that impressed him more than Score's speed.
He curved Sammy White on the first pitch when he was way ahead
in the game: "That impressed me. He's not just a thrower. That jug
he threw White! His curve's much better than everyone says." By
May 23 Williams was ready. Boston beat the New York Giants in a
charity exhibition game at Fenway 4-3, and Ted homered into the
right-field bleachers.

On May 28 he started his first game of the year and singled to center against Camilo Pascual of the Senators on his first at-bat. He was off to what would be one of his best seasons after a long layoff with no spring training. But the Red Sox were working from a deficit of 12 games when Williams returned and that's about the way the season ended, though the team made a gutsy run that got them a lot closer than anyone dreamed. In a sense, Williams played the Yankees to a tie for the last hundred games of the year.

In Elton, Kentucky, a couple of weeks after Williams's return, two kids got in a fight at the local drugstore. One of them, Luke Hollingsworth, 11, was an avid Red Sox fan, and he took a licking when his friend challenged him over whether Al Rosen or Ted Williams was a better ballplayer. The town figured Luke had suffered enough for his convictions. They chipped in and paid $36.40 for a round-trip bus ticket to Boston. He saw the Sox win two from Chicago with Williams out with a strained back. But Ted took the kid to dinner and gave him a Red Sox number 9 jersey. He figured there weren't that many experts in the country who would fight to preserve his honor. At this point the Red Sox public relations squad got in on the action. They made sure Luke rode on the team plane at least as far as a stopover in Pittsburgh on his way back to Kentucky to gloat over any of Al Rosen's fans that might be left in Elton.

A couple of days later, on June 27, the Red Sox were stunned by the sudden death of Harry Agganis, who had been the regular Sox first baseman in 1954 and for the opening month of 1955 before he was hospitalized for lung cancer. Williams had been calling the 25-year-old regularly in the hospital. He was distraught and near tears at the memorial service held by the team on the road in Washington, D.C. But Williams kept stroking at the plate. At the All-Star break he was hitting .394 with 12 home runs. Moreover, the Red Sox were winning, pulling up to within 6½ games of first place early in July.

The National League took the All-Star Game on July 12, with Musial hitting a crucial home run in the 12th inning and with Willie Mays making a spectacular leaping catch of a drive by Williams that would have cleared the fence in right center at Milwaukee's County Stadium. Mantle's three-run homer had given the American Leaguers a lead, which they later expanded to 5–0, but they frittered it away until Musial's blast did them in for the day.

Williams's poor conditioning was beginning to show a little after the break. His back was bothering him, he was tiring easily, and his average was precipitously losing points. But the Red Sox, surprisingly enough, were winning. They crept up to within three on July 23 when Williams broke out of his slump with a home run on the roof at Comiskey Park about 450 feet from home plate. And then they returned to Fenway for a 20-game home stand. This would make or break the club, and the fans were roused. There were long lines for tickets at the park. No one could believe it, but the feeling was something like the late 1940s. Could this ball club do it in a tough league?

The front-page *Globe* headline for July 27 captured the renewed spirit of the times: "33,423 SEE SOX BEAT INDIANS." Williams hit one out in Boston's 5-1 win. The Sox won again that day but lost on July 28 with Williams's daughter in the stands for the first time in her young life. The seven-year-old watched her dad take the collar, 0 for 5. Williams said he was pressing. On July 31, Boston took a pair from Detroit. Williams hit the 12th grand slam home run of his career in the first game; when he came to the plate late in the second game with the score tied 2-2, shortstop Harvey Kuenn tried to distract Williams by playing a roving shift. He simply ran like a mad man from one side of second base to the other while Williams stood at the plate. Only Eddie Stanky in the National League thought this sort of thing kosher. Mike Higgins ran onto the field: "What's that bush-league crap?" he asked umpire Ed Rommel. Rommel stopped the game, told Kuenn to keep still, and, for good graces, threw two abusive Tigers in the dugout out of the game.

By August 4 the Red Sox were creeping even closer to the top. They beat the White Sox 7-3 and found themselves two out, scrapping with the Yanks, the Indians, and Chicago for first. This race was a doozy. A big 16-12 win over Kansas City on August 7 put Boston within 1½ games of first as they cruised into Yankee Stadium for a big series. Though the Yanks won two of three, Williams got his 2,000th hit on August 10, a blooper behind second, off Bob Turley: "Cheapest of the year," he said, ruefully, and then: "What the hell, I'll take it."

It was all the Red Sox could do to hang in. On August 14 the Yankees, with a barrage of 30 hits, took two from Baltimore. They

Williams batting against a version of the famous shift in the third game of the 1946 World Series at Fenway Park. St. Louis Cardinals manager Eddie Dyer has removed an infielder and positioned a fourth outfielder in shallow right field near the foul line. *(National Baseball Library, Cooperstown, N.Y.)*

Ted's first wife, Doris, with their daughter, Barbara Joyce, in the summer of 1950. *(Boston Globe Photo)*

Williams is tagged out at the plate on September 21, 1951, by a diving Yogi Berra of the Yankees, who has just taken Hank Bauer's throw from right field. *(Wide World Photos)*

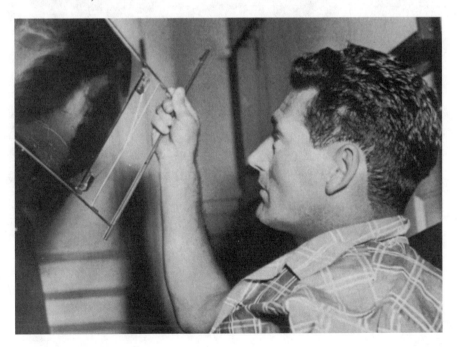

Williams in his hospital room looking at an x-ray of his broken collarbone in March 1954. He was injured in the outfield on the first day of spring training. *(Boston Globe Photo)*

Williams raps a base hit against the Yankees in a game on April 27, 1957, a year in which he would hit a remarkable .388 at the age of 39. *(Wide World Photos)*

Williams checks his swing on a called strike by Detroit's Jim Bunning on September 16, 1957. (Note the location of the pitch.) He hit the next pitch for a home run. *(Frank Scherschel,* Life *magazine* © *Time Warner, Inc.)*

Williams going haywire after throwing his bat 75 feet during a game against the Washington Senators on September 21, 1958. The bat landed in the stands and hit Joe Cronin's housekeeper, who was taking in the game on her day off. *(National Baseball Library, Cooperstown, N.Y.)*

The changing faces of Ted Williams—from left to right: a serious-faced kid of 19 in 1937, with the San Diego Padres but soon to be signed by the Boston Red Sox; a wide-eyed but brash Red Sox rookie in 1939 who hit .327 with 31 home runs in his first season in the majors; a cocky, unpredictable star in 1941, his .406 season; and a mature but still outspoken veteran nearing his 40th birthday in 1958. This photo was reproduced from the front page of the August 27, 1958, issue of *The Sporting News*, under the headline "THE FOUR FACES OF TED . . . FROM TEEN-AGER TO VET OF FORTY." *(The Sporting News)*

Williams still swinging in 1960, the last year of his career. *(Wide World Photos)*

Crossing the plate after hitting his 521st home run on the last at-bat of his career on September 29, 1960. Williams hit it in the eighth inning off Baltimore's Jack Fisher. Red Sox catcher Jim Pagliaroni greets Williams. *(Wide World Photos)*

won another doubleheader from the Orioles the next day. Boston wasn't losing; they just weren't winning enough. On August 15 Williams hit his 20th home run of this truncated year against the Senators, which was also the 13th grand slam of his career, and helped the Red Sox stay within shooting range of the Yankees.

This was a scrapping and courageous Boston club, something that the home fans appreciated. But pennants are not won by the home fans. The Red Sox faced a long road trip, and it was crunch time. They faltered at first and then, lo and behold, untrue to their history, they held their own on the road. By August 26, they were five games out after losing a tough ball game in Detroit, 5–4. Williams fanned looking against left-hander Billy Hoeft in the ninth with men on base, and Dave Egan of the *Record* went to his files for the standard "Never hits when you need 'em" column. Williams always had the Boston newspapers mailed to him on the road. There was time to kill; as he put it, "I always kept up with my critics." Never was he so furious at Egan. It was an extraordinary baseball ignorance that assumed a hitter, any hitter, never got fooled at the plate. Egan was bad enough when he attacked Williams's moral character; he was worse when he took after Ted on how simple it was to hit tough lefties.

The next game at Detroit Williams came to the plate again in the ninth with the Red Sox behind 3–0. Boston had three men on with two out and there was no place to put him. So Al Aber tried throwing the ball over the plate on a 2–1 count. He should have tried something else. Williams put the pitch on the roof at Briggs Stadium for a 4–3 Red Sox win and the 14th grand slam of his career. Al Aber took the long view when asked about the effect on him of losing such a ball game so suddenly: "With Williams hitting it doesn't pay to get too depressed."

When the Sox returned to Fenway they were still only five out, but they took two from Washington on September 5 to crawl back to within 3 of the Indians and 2½ behind the Yanks. Williams was hitting .352 with 27 home runs. And then disaster: the Sox could not win at home. They lost seven of their next nine games and then had to face the league-leading Yanks in New York with Williams in severe pain from a foul ball off his ankle. They couldn't pull a miracle in New York and faded even further after a couple of tough losses.

The Red Sox gave it their best run in 1955 from June 5 to

August 9, when they won 44 of 60 games and pulled from 14½ to 1½ games out of first. But they flagged at the end and the Yankees ended up winning it by three over the Indians, with the White Sox 5 out and Boston 12 out. Williams finished at .356 with 28 home runs. At Fenway he hit .390, his best since 1951, when he hit .403 at home. For 1955 he hit .318 on the road, sustaining his above-.300 career average in every rival park but Cleveland's, where he fell to .286, and Baltimore's, where he had only 34 at-bats in two years and a battery-dead .211 average.

Williams was exhausted as usual at the end of the season but was playing to put money in his own pocket after resolving his divorce woes. He was clear on his plans: "I'm gonna rest and then play next year." He was on vacation when the Yankees and the Dodgers fought it out in a classic seven-game World Series, with Johnny Podres shutting down the Yankees 2–0 in the clincher on Sandy Amoros's tough catch of Yogi Berra's slicing liner to left. Podres's success in the Series, in a convoluted way, ended up getting Williams in trouble during spring training of 1956. He was ingenious in figuring ways to throw himself into the national limelight, and he would use the draft status of the classy young Dodgers' lefty to do so.

◇ 17 ◇

Rivalries
1956

THERE MAY HAVE BEEN NO MORE Joe McCarthy, junior senator
from Wisconsin, in America of 1956, but the Cold War still raged.
Never would either side miss a chance. The Russians spread rumors
that Americans ate dogs at baseball games, making the vernacular
speak literally, and the Americans rubbed it in with headlines such as
this one in the *Globe*: "GOOD NEWS FOR RED HANGED 7 YEARS
AGO; HE'S INNOCENT."

Williams started 1956 frisky. He signed in early February for
$100,000 plus bonuses and a promise not to field balls the opening
day of spring training. Everyone remembered the collarbone fiasco of
1954. On the first day of training in Sarasota he coaxed a young
writer into taking a $25 bet on whether he could clear the fence in
deep right at Payne Field within five pitches. It was a long way for a
rusty old man. Williams had tried this scam before. Frank Sullivan,
on the mound, was in on the proceeds from the bet and planned to
set one up right in his wheelhouse. The action on the field stopped.
All eyes focused on Williams at the plate. He hit Sullivan's fourth
fastball like a bullet over the center-field fence. "There," said Williams, "right into that lousy trailer camp." "Another," he beckoned.
Sullivan's pitch came and Williams rammed it near the same spot
but more toward right center. Only then did the action resume from
every corner of the field, but the writer was out $25 and the year
began well.

But two things hadn't happened to Williams yet in 1956. One was
Mickey Mantle, who would be the first in the American League to

win the Triple Crown since Williams himself managed it in 1947. And the other was an episode in Fenway Park that marked the single greatest humiliation of Williams's career in baseball, an outburst that almost cost him $5,000 and what good will he had left with the Boston press. But at the beginning of the year things were looking up. It was spring. Grace Kelly was planning to marry a prince; *Picnic* opened on the silver screen; and there were good ballplayers in the Red Sox camp. Mickey Vernon had joined the squad. Don Buddin would steady the Sox at short. A rookie Frank Malzone would come up for a bit and play some games at third. And the veteran pitching staff could hold its own in the league.

Williams was coasting along with the calmest spring training of his life—that is, until March 13 at 10:45 A.M. in the locker room at Sarasota. A few reporters from the *San Francisco Chronicle* following the Red Sox minor league affiliate, the San Francisco Seals, training at De Land, dropped by to chat with "Broadway" Charlie Wagner, the Red Sox farm director. Wagner was Williams's former roommate on the road and was sitting near Ted's locker in the clubhouse. The talk turned to Williams's own minor league career and the last homer he hit in the Pacific Coast League back in 1937. Was it off Osborne of the Missions on the last day of the season? Or off Tony Freitas of Sacramento in the playoffs? Williams was having a good time.

One of the writers then asked him about the army's drafting Johnny Podres, who had done such a remarkable job for the Dodgers in the 1955 World Series. It was as if someone had set Williams's ass on fire: "Podres is paying the penalty for being a star. If he lost those Series games he would probably still be with the Dodgers. A politician probably said, 'Why isn't a big strong kid like that in the Army?' The draft boards and the sportswriters didn't have the guts to stick up for him." At the end of his tirade he looked up at the San Francisco writers and realized from the expression on their faces that they had some hot copy. And there wasn't a Boston writer in sight. "Hey, fellas," Williams slyly remarked as they edged out, just dying to break into a gallop toward the nearest phone, "Good luck."

When the story broke, it broke big. Headlines in San Francisco preceded others all over the country. "You really hosed us," a local Boston writer said to Williams. Ted had a ready reply: "Good." Then he took off again, this time to everyone in sight.

Go ahead, make a big story out of it. That's exactly how I feel. Wait until a guy's famous and then, whambo, they take 20 percent of his earning life, his best earning years. . . . You get into college and you can hide behind a book until Hell wouldn't have you. Couple of hours a week rifle drill or something and the college kid never gets touched. But they make good object lessons out of guys like Podres. They make me sick. Guys who work for big corporations, too. What a crock of [shit]. The president of the corporation goes to the draft board, pleads his man is indispensable, and whambo, the guy is deferred. No one is indispensable.

Williams was onto one of his jags and there was no stopping him. But Podres had as little luck stopping the draft as well. So the Dodgers' lefty signed up with the navy on his own March 19. Edward L. Kelly of Schroon Lake, New York, and chief of Podres's local draft board in Northeast Essex County, New York, said that Podres was called up for random reclassification before the 1955 Series. It was just a freak of the statistical draw. Two days later Williams was asked about Kelly's explanation: "Yeah, sure. I'm staying put with what I said—100 percent."

For the most part, Williams calmed down after this and kept himself out of trouble for the rest of spring training. The season opened April 17 with the Red Sox winning their first game at Baltimore 8-1 behind big Frank Sullivan. Williams doubled twice. But the contours of the 1956 season fairly much defined themselves for Williams a few miles down the road at Griffith Stadium. On opening day Mickey Mantle hit two monumental home runs, both over the 31-foot barrier in center and both over 500 feet. Neither, of course, was as far as the 565-foot job off Chuck Stobbs he hit at Griffith on opening day 1953. Mantle began to take over the headlines early this year, and Ted Williams would silently seethe at what writers more and more often considered his waning powers in contrast to Mantle's waxing ones.

On the second day of the season, the Sox won again, 8-4, but Williams, after a base hit and a couple of walks, was removed from the game, having bruised a tendon in his instep. This one was a slow healer. Nothing worked—diathermy, cortisone, whirlpools—and he simply could not run. For the next month he only pinch hit, and everyone, except Williams, was getting restless. He may have remembered 1941, when he broke a small bone in his foot early in the year and nursed it along through a .406 season. He claimed that not forcing the issue in the cold of early spring was one of the reasons he ended up hitting .400. On April 27, Clif Keane wrote a column in the *Globe* that Williams remembered only selectively later. For a good while he simply stopped talking to Keane, but there was obviously more here than met the eye.

Mantle and Williams were both hurting for a Yankee series in New York, but Stengel had penciled Mantle in for the day. Keane wrote a column on the whys and wherefores of playing hurt. Williams brooded over the opening remarks of that column for years: "Unless Mickey Mantle changes his mind this afternoon he will limp out to center field for the Yankees—and unless Ted Williams decides otherwise he will just limp for the Red Sox." Later, Williams told Keane that his piece "was so damn lousy it was brutal. . . . You didn't know how bad my instep was. Is there any doubt in your mind that I would have been playing if I could have? When you wrote that article about me, you made me want to punch you right in the nose."

What Williams forgot to do was read on or, more likely, recall exactly what he had read. Keane made his observation precisely because he wished to praise the wisdom of Williams's decision: "Each day while he shakes his head and says 'no' Williams's sore instep gets better. Mantle may be a gamer, but is Williams wiser? Ten days of inactivity being wise by Williams may yet turn out far better than a possible Mantle stretch of inactivity of 30 days by being game." Williams's irritation at this piece suggested his state of mind. For the rest of the year he couldn't shake Mantle, and he felt the press was feeding itself on unflattering comparisons.

Of course, Mantle was providing the inducement. By early May he had already hit 10 home runs. There was talk of the new Ruth, just as Williams, in 1939, had been nicknamed Baby Ruth around the league. Moreover, there was talk of Williams passing the torch (in the shape of a bat) to the Mick. Williams kept his own counsel, but his feelings were hurt. Even his most worshipful admirer, Casey Stengel, began to make comparisons that, although true, were troubling to Williams: "Your Williams fella, he's a better hitter. But my man can run, field, and throw better. My man will beat out bunts."

Williams resumed playing again regularly on May 29, but he

didn't hit his first home run of the year until June 22. This was extraordinary. "Washed up" was the phrase whispered around the Boston press box. But it was also joined to the old standby that Williams couldn't hit home runs in the clutch even when he did put the big numbers on the board. At issue was the same old paradox. Williams had cultivated a theory of hitting that enabled him to drive the pitches in his zone high and hard. But he was less likely to get such pitches late in the game. If he didn't take the walks given him— that is, if he cut at bad pitches—he was then less likely to get any pitches he could drive at any time. This last point was a complex one, but Williams held onto it. Pitchers become better, looser, more confident, and sharper if hitters made them so by widening the strike zone at the plate.

Harold Kaese came to Williams's defense along a statistical salient. He produced a spread sheet to make his case, going back over the personal stats he kept in his own files and arguing that Williams hit an almost equal number of home runs in the early, middle, and late innings. The majority of his home runs were with men on base, though that statistic slanted toward the early innings when pitchers were less likely to walk him. A hefty 77 percent of his late-inning home runs were game winners, a higher percentage than Babe Ruth's. Kaese had gone so far as to figure out that Williams's game-winning-home-run percentage was .184 (almost 2 in 10) to Ruth's .176. In 1956 Williams would hit nine more game-winning home runs despite a modest season total of 24. Kaese reasoned, "Some people can't be objective when they are reading a thermometer, let alone reading Ted Williams."

When Williams resumed play in New York, Dale Long of the Pittsburgh Pirates had just set the major league record for consecutive home-run games at eight, but Mantle had cooled off a bit and was striking out with enough consistency that Casey Stengel put on a bit of a show for the roving press corps. He took a big whiff in imitation of his great new star, stomped down the dugout steps in fury, still holding the bat, wandered the length of the bench looking for something to smash, smashed it, and turned to an imaginary pitcher, screaming, "Put something on the fucking ball!" The writers and the rest of the Yankees were in stitches, including Mantle. A day later Mantle hit his famous Yankee Stadium blast off Pedro Ramos of the Senators, one that hit the high facade of the roof 370 feet from home and 117 feet from the ground. The ball just missed leaving the Stadium, the closest any ball has ever come to doing so.

In June Lou Boudreau, then managing Kansas City, put on a version of the Williams shift for Mantle whenever he hit left-handed. He brought his leftfielder to play third base and spread the rest of his fielders all over the right side. Mantle began bunting on the shift immediately. With his speed, the choice had to be whether to allow him to hit near 1.000 or chance the long ball. The Yankees would force the issue for Mantle in ways the Red Sox could not, or would not, for Williams. Bunting, after all, was already part of Mantle's arsenal.

Williams was still looking for his first home run on June 18 when Mantle hit his 25th of the year, dynamiting one off Paul Foytack that blew the ball clear out of Briggs Stadium in Detroit. In 1939 Williams had become the only other player to hit the ball completely out of the park onto Trumbull Avenue. Clif Keane, already in Williams's doghouse, wrote on June 19: "When the ballplayers start to talk about another player like the Sox were talking about Mantle tonight, you know he's great. They're talking about him the way they used to talk about Williams years ago." Williams must have felt that he was playing this season of 1956 in the past tense.

When Mantle drove two more out of the park on June 20, Kaese headlined his column "RED SOX NEED HOMERS FROM TED TO WIN." Mantle was now both a nemesis and a challenge. Boston was by then in fourth place, 9 ½ out. Sure enough, Williams hit his first homer of the year the next day off Art Ditmar of Kansas City. In late June and early July, he began swinging a hot bat, and he was fighting it out with Mantle for the league lead, hitting .366 to Mantle's .371. At that time *The Sporting News* came out with its first Player of the Decade poll for 1945-55, and Stan Musial took 97 first-place votes, followed by DiMaggio at 87, and Williams at 52. Garnering votes for these sorts of polls was not Williams's forte, though arguably Musial deserved to beat him. But DiMaggio, for that particular sequence of years, surely did not. With Williams chasing Mantle, this nasty vote haunted him with the ghost of DiMaggio behind.

In the All-Star Game of July 9, Williams hit one out in the sixth off Warren Spahn and Mantle followed with another. But the National

League, led by Ken Boyer, won it 7-3. When regular-season play resumed the next week Williams reached a career milestone. On July 17 at Fenway against the A's he hit his 400th home run, a game-winning shot off Tommy Gorman in the nightcap of a doubleheader. And he warmed up for a more sustained exhibition later in the year by feigning a contemptuous spit at the writers in the press box as he crossed home plate. He had been thinking about this as a payback gesture for their season-long comments about his lack of power, and Mickey Vernon, on deck at the time, recalls that Williams was so intent that "as I put out my hand to congratulate him he didn't even see me." Williams was now up to six home runs on the year; surely the writers were not totally deceived. Contempt was mixed with charity, however, in Williams's heart. He intended to auction his 400th home-run ball for the Jimmy Fund and was glad to get it back from an excited fan, Peter Hickey, of Waltham, who caught the ball in the stands and returned it for a new ball and a couple of Red Sox tickets.

By the last week of July Mantle had hit 32 home runs and was still the talk of the majors. By August the Red Sox were 13½ games back and going nowhere. Williams's own frustration was obvious in batting practice in Detroit on August 2, when he flung his bat and almost coldcocked writer Bob Holbrook by the dugout. "Jeez, I'm sorry," Williams said, "I wasn't trying to hit you. Hell, there's three or four other of you guys hanging around. Why should I just aim at you?" And another Red Sox outfielder was beginning to feel the strain. Jackie Jensen, just off a game in Detroit where he racked up nine runs batted in, was asked why he couldn't hit consistently in Fenway. His answer sounded as if it had run into complaints from time past.

> For me it's easy to explain. It's those wolves in the stands at Fenway that make me hit less at home. The first thing, they start riding me, and I start pressing. I force myself to try harder to come through and, as a result, I get worse. As I get worse, the riding gets worse. I'm ruined for the whole home stand. But when we go out on the road everything is different. I relax and start swinging at the ball naturally. It's a new lease.

Williams had endured much the same, though his average at Fenway never seemed to suffer from it. He even knew some of his

more faithful antagonists by name, including a particularly obstrep-
erous Mr. McLauglin, who drove him berserk. Williams would walk
on the field sometimes from the clubhouse and ask Johnny Orlando
whether McLauglin was out there that day. "Damn," he'd say if
Orlando nodded. The only respite Williams got was the year
McLaughlin was in prison for activities related to organized crime in
Boston.

Now it seemed to be Jensen's turn for a while, but only a while.
Jensen was home at Fenway for what would be a fateful game with
the Yanks on August 7 before a jammed ballpark—36,350 fans.
During batting practice he was shagging balls in right and he heard
a fan yell over from the stands, "Hiya, Mr. Doubleplay." Jensen
walked over and beckoned the fan down the aisle to normal speaking
distance near the fence. "I just wanted to find out why he did this to
me. I asked, 'Are you a Red Sox fan? Do you think this will help the
team or me?'" After the game he told this story to some writers, "You
know what the fan said? He said he didn't actually come to the games
that often but he read the 'Mr. Doubleplay' business in the papers.
Can you imagine that?"

If Jensen resorted to calm reason with genus fanaticus before this
particular game, Ted Williams ended up in one of his horrendous
frenzies during it. The game was tense enough on its own merits
when trouble started in the 11th inning. Neither the Sox nor the
Yanks had scored. In the top of the 11th Williams dropped a routine
fly by Mantle because he got confused about whether Don Buddin
was coming out from short to get it. This was the sort of play that
makes an outfielder look awful. But there is that moment in the field
when the trajectory of the ball, the approach of the infielder, and the
angle of access all seem to converge. An outfielder tries to keep his
head still when approaching a ball, even if his legs are on the move.
But if he slows or hesitates or simply breaks rhythm, he can lose the
line of the ball's flight. It shouldn't happen, but on occasion it does.
It did this time to Williams.

The fans let loose their fury as Mantle coasted in to second base.
Berra followed with a tough fly to left center, but the wind held it and
Williams faded back against the scoreboard to grab it to end the
inning. As he neared the dugout steps, he was fuming. His decent
play on the Berra fly didn't seem to count for much. Williams also

figured that his error counted for little since he had just speared the third out. But the fans around the dugout were having too much fun with all this by now. They were still on him. He exploded. He began spitting in the direction of the fans behind the dugout, pursing his lips like a Mussolini of the Fens. At the top of the dugout steps he turned toward the press box. The writers could use a few lugies themselves. He obliged.

Once a tantrum takes whatever form it does, it is already out of control. Williams became his own worst nightmare; he could not free himself from the outrageous. He spat everywhere, waving his glove now at the fans across the field behind the third-base dugout. And when things seemed to have calmed a bit in the bottom of the 11th— the Red Sox had loaded the bases before Williams came to the plate—he stepped up and spat again, this time in the direction of the Yankees, who were also on him pretty hard. Tommy Byrne didn't know exactly what to do on the mound. He used to taunt Williams good-naturedly about what and where he wanted it at the plate. Williams would listen for a while and finally say, "Just throw the damn ball." But this time Byrne was dead quiet.

Williams focused. He was going to demolish anything that came near the plate. Byrne did not take the challenge. He figured Williams would be anxious, so he threw a couple of balls, getting far enough behind in the count that he was at risk of walking him. Williams waited. Byrne couldn't turn it: ball four—the winning run walked home. Williams flung his bat in disgust and walked to first for form's sake before he bolted to the clubhouse.

Tom Yawkey was at his suite in the Hotel Pierre on Fifth Avenue in New York. He heard Mel Allen's call of the game on the radio and was on the phone with Cronin and Mike Higgins in a minute. Yawkey was incoherent when speaking to reporters later that afternoon: "I can't put myself in his spot out on that field. If I could, I might have the answer. Oh, I might feel certain ways about what goes on with Ted. But I can't come to a final answer on the thing. It's too bad, I know that. You know, every day behind closed doors awful things are done. I know I sit across the table with men in business and what happens? I say something awful. A man across the table says something awful. Why, if people knew what was said, they'd be shocked. But here's a man in front of the public, and everything he does and says gets into print. It's got to stop, that's all." Yawkey remembered the words of his father, which had served him well, he thought, and which only rarely served Williams: "Think logically and keep your mouth shut."

His own thoughts might not have been in perfect logical order this afternoon, but Yawkey had already told Cronin to give Williams a call at his Boston hotel and let him know this filthy escapade was going to cost him $5,000. Worse, Williams would have to read the afternoon and morning papers. Mike Gillooly of the *Boston Herald* tried to get the scoop by following Williams to the Hotel Somerset, where he lived in Boston. But Ted just shouted at him through the closed door: "You son of a bitch, this is invasion of privacy." Williams continued the strange closed-door interview, nonetheless: "I'd spit again at those booing bastards. I just can't help it. You writers are responsible for this shit. The whole thing. If it didn't bother me, I wouldn't still be as fired up as I am right now. And if I could afford the $500—I mean $5,000—and other fines, I wouldn't be at the ballpark tomorrow."

A few weeks later, Williams had had enough time for a considered response to the incident. He gave an interview to a writer from *Sport* magazine, Joan Flynn Dreyspool. It was poignant in its way, and it made some points about why Williams reacted to the fans and writers the way he did.

> They're interviewing psychiatrists now on me. I am the spitting cobra. I never had any trouble in any other town, only Boston. The big thing is the writers in any town educate the fans to their reactions pretty much. You can go and write about Andy Gump and praise him for a week, and before you know it the fans will be clapping for him; or you can write nasty things about him and the fans will boo.
>
> There's 10 percent up there, the baboon type, who's always got his lungs ready to explode. I make a bad play or do something, and right away they start to yell vile names at me and boo all out of proportion, and even though they're only 10 percent they sound like they were five times as many because they're so much more vigorous than those who applaud. If someone could tell what I could do to show my disgust without spitting or making a vulgar

gesture—which I certainly am not going to do—I would be grateful.

I know I'm not right, spitting, but gee, it's the only thing I can think of doing. I don't want to smile at them. I don't want to wave my hat at them. I don't want to give them a fist job. All I can do is let a big heave, take in a lot of air and go *phooey*! It's the best way I can relieve my tension, to spit at them, and I am only spitting at 10 percent of them. It's something that happens, and I'll probably do it again.

In his more detached moments, Williams was well aware that a screaming fan was not a debating partner, not a perfectly rational entity. Most hostile fans come to the game with morsels of precooked opinions and dish them out. But ballplayers are not so ready to forgive fans who know not what they do, nor to forgive those writers whose columns prime the fans' pumps. The situation was irremedial. A response from Williams in kind was, by his own admission, absurd. But he knew he needed a release; and he knew his anger did not hurt him at the plate.

Harold Kaese was less charitable about all this. He checked in early and offered Williams a bit of advice: "Ted Williams should do himself a favor. He should quit baseball before baseball quits him. His body is wearing out and so, apparently, is his nervous system." Williams could get mad as hell at the writers, said Kaese, but "they didn't drop Mantle's easy fly." He was a child, a petulant child, and the edge was off his game. Kaese, who was a champion squash player in Massachusetts as well as a premier writer for the *Globe*, knew that pressure and temperament mix in funny ways. He, too, was a high-strung and emotional competitor. But vulgarity was another thing entirely.

That Mantle's fly was at the root of the problem was not lost on those who had been watching Williams closely this season. Kaese thought the lionization of Mantle was conducted primarily at Williams's expense, whether openly acknowledged or not. Williams well knew that he was not hitting for power, and the hometown jeers focused so squarely on him while Mantle was standing idly at second base contributed to the ugly scene that followed. The screw turned all the more painfully with seemingly innocent comments on Mantle that implicitly dug into Williams. Jimmy Cannon wrote slant-wise: "What did Mickey do today? A question wondrous and fine. It turns men into ecstasies and reminds some others that they are no longer young. They're the doomed and they know it."

Bill Corum of the *New York Journal-American* took another angle: he had Williams chasing not the home-run-hitting Mantle but the ghost of a raucous Babe Ruth: "Ted Williams finally caught up with Babe Ruth. He got fined $5,000." Corum's reference was to Miller Huggins's blowing a gasket at Ruth's hostile behavior during an infamous Yankee train trip. Williams's display was worse; he even got the Boston watch and warders into the act. On August 8 State Representative James F. Condon, Democrat of South Boston, filed a House bill prohibiting profane, obscene, impure language, or slanderous statements directed at or uttered by participants in a sports event. The fine would be $50, and Williams, at that point, might have settled for the law rather than Yawkey's heftier fine of five grand.

The inflammatory Dave Egan of the *Record American* wanted Williams out of baseball: "No grown man in full possession of his faculties would make the vile gestures that he made." Apparently, Egan hadn't seen enough grown men or enough gestures. When he invited his readers, as was his custom, to write in and sound off, many surprised him by defending Williams from the hostility of the fans, their mindlessness, and their bear baiting. Williams's reaction was mild, given the circumstances; besides, as many fans responded, "It's just his way."

As was almost always the case with Williams, the fans loved to bait him but not to ride him out of town on the rails. The next home game was billed as "Family Night." Yawkey wanted no trouble with a surplus of women and children in the stands, especially from a volatile Williams in left. He put a huge security force to work and roped off the wolf-pack seats near the fence so Williams would not have to face the savagery of loudmouths at extra-close range. On the other hand, loyalists were at work. A group of fans had opened an account at the Rockland Atlas National Bank to pay for Williams's fine. They had already raised $1,000. Williams said he would donate it to the Jimmy Fund and pay the fine himself. Eventually, Yawkey relented and simply failed to deduct the amount from Williams's paycheck. The matter was dropped.

On Family Night Williams atoned in the best way he could. Before over 30,000 watching the game against Baltimore, most of them cheering him, he hit one into the right-field seats in the sixth. As he crossed home plate he put his hand over his mouth to make sure no untoward gesture or action slipped out. It should be remembered that Williams was hitting .348 at the time of the spitting incident; and just after it he hit three home runs in four games. Rarely did a controversy, even one so dramatic as this one, shut him down. In fact, he hit as many home runs from this point on in the season as he had during the first four months.

Going into the next Yankee series at the Stadium in mid-August Williams and Mantle were both hot: Williams was cruising at .352 and Mantle at a gargantuan .376. but Mantle also had 42 home runs and Williams a mere 15. Williams managed to get through this series, however, without incident. Jimmy Piersall, whose book *Fear Strikes Out* was then being made into a movie at Fenway Park, took up his slack, throwing a tantrum in center field that made Williams look like Dink Stover. Piersall, on his way to his position in center, was furious at scorer Dan Daniel, who had given Jerry Coleman an error on the hard grounder he hit in the Boston half of the inning. He went berserk just beyond the infield grass, violently kicking up divots with his spikes. Mantle passed him coming in from center and observed, "Hey, you oughta play barefoot." This merely inspired Piersall to greater trench work. After the game, Casey Stengel told Dan Daniel, who quit the scorer's table in disgust at this exhibition, "I thought he was digging your grave out there."

In August the Yankees made one of their typical late-season moves, the kind that had gained them their reputation as heartless and savvy at the same time. They gave Phil Rizzuto his release on August 25. On the same day they picked up the aging but still productive Enos Slaughter. Tom Yawkey could never operate in such a way, and therein, according to those who thought about these things for years on end, lay one major difference between the two ball clubs. Boston ran on hunch and sentiment; the Yankees on calculation and cold logic.

The Red Sox had little to think about for the last month of the season. They were near the bottom of the first division, 13 games out. But there was a different sort of excitement for New England when the *Globe* featured a story on August 29 that set the fussy modern-day Puritans on their collective ear: "WIFE'S GOSSIPY NOVEL COSTS TEACHER JOB: Spicy Book Has Town Agog." The story centered around the prepublication release of a novel about the goings-on in Gilmanton, New Hampshire, fictitiously named Peyton Place. The grammar school teacher (and principal) fired was George Metalious, whose wife, Grace, it seems, filled her leisure hours embellishing local scandal in a way that would enthrall half of America and appall the other half when *Peyton Place* hit the bookstores.

Williams was having a good month. He was hitting consistently for average, and midway through September he actually passed Mantle, who was hurt and slumping. Williams was up to .353 and Mantle had fallen to .351, though the Yankee slugger had already hit a prodigious 50 home runs. When the Yankees arrived for a series in Boston on September 22 Don Larsen tried an experiment that would serve him well in the World Series that year: he pitched without a windup—and won the game. Williams could hardly buy a hit in the series, going 2 for 11 and fading to .350. Mantle got hot again, went 6 for 9 in the series, and took over the lead in the race for the batting title at .356. Stengel told the Yankee staff to help Mantle in his Triple Crown quest by making Williams hit bad pitches, and for one of the few times in his career Ted took some cuts in this series that he knew were low-percentage swings. He wanted the batting title badly, and the spate of Mantle hits unnerved him a bit.

The same teams closed the season at Yankee Stadium, and Williams again met with difficulty, especially from Larsen, who collared him in the final game as Mantle took the batting title, .353 to Williams's .345. A disappointed but gruffly gracious Williams said of Mantle: "If I could run like that son of a bitch, I'd hit .400 every year." Head-on against the Yanks in 1956 Williams hit but .196 with one home run. Mantle won the home-run and runs-batted-in titles easily to take the Triple Crown in 1956, the only time he did so. Indeed, 1956 was the only year Mantle won the batting title. Eddie Mathews took the home-run crown in the National League, and he looked, at this point in his career, as potent as anyone with the bat. A breakdown of early-career home runs—those hit by the age of 25— was interesting: Mathews, 190; Ott, 176; Foxx, 174; Mantle, 173; DiMaggio, 137; Williams, 127; Ruth, 49. Of course Ruth had been doing some pitching, and Williams donated his 25th year to World War II.

There was no thought in Williams's mind about hanging them up. More than any other year, 1956 revved him for the next season. He played with a bad foot early in the year and through a barrage of adverse press reaction to his fading run-production power. Not only was his home-run output off but so was his runs-batted-in total, 82. He knew that he was a better percentage hitter than Mantle, and he simply wanted to atone in his own mind for losing the batting title in a head-on late-season confrontation with the Yankees. Mantle was the only hitter in the American League to beat him in a batting race since 1951. Even in those years when Williams didn't have the requisite number of at-bats he beat the league leader. At the end of the 1956 season he gave his customary large tip to Johnny Orlando on the way out of the clubhouse: "See you in Florida." Orlando later told Clif Keane: "He's gotta come back. I gotta eat."

◇ 18 ◇
Comeback Kid
1957

WILLIAMS WAS IN TOWN FOR THE annual Sportsman's Show in Boston at a time when the current rage in America was the phenomenal television quiz show "21," with Jack Barry. Charles Van Doren, a particularly nervous contestant who was in the midst of his stint on the program, had already surpassed Williams's yearly salary and was still going strong. Commentators were aware of the almost-cultivated drama of the spectacle and noted "it was a nervous, nearly trembling Van Doren who kept wiping his face with a handkerchief as he answered the questions." "Nervous" sells soap. Nervous also cons, and the scandal that would break the next year over this particular quiz show would rock the television industry.

At their February baseball dinner the Boston writers were tracking down rumors that Williams was going to take a pay cut for 1957. He was too old and too injury prone to play a full season. A salary cut, however, was not on Williams's agenda. He was going after the batting title that had eluded him the year before. This year he would not only be up against Mickey Mantle but up against BIZMAC, the world's largest computer, which digested bits of information and calculated that Williams would hit .322 to Mantle's .342. BIZMAC factored in such things as the curve of improvement over the years. But in Williams's case, it forgot to factor in revenge.

Williams's salary would remain in the vicinity of $100,000 in 1957, including special bonus clauses. Williams had now earned $1,223,000 with the Red Sox, putting him well ahead of Ruth's total of $980,000 during his career. Williams had made another $250,000 from ghostwritten work, plus lesser amounts from instructional films. One of his ambitions when he first began playing ball in 1939 was to make more money than Ruth. On that score, he could now hang them up whenever he felt like it.

Once Williams put to rest the public negotiation of his salary, other personal matters made their way up the Boston post road. Midway through February a New York model, Nelva Moore, claimed that Williams had proposed marriage to her and was now backing out. She had called him in Boston, and he supposedly rescinded an offer to have her join him for the Sportsman's Show. When Nelva threatened to go on television and tell her sad story, Williams held firm. He knew the ways of the press, and he had taken everything they could muster. He gave Moore a bit of advice: "Go ahead, make a jackass out of me. But be sure you get enough money for it." This effectively put a lid on things.

Williams met fire with fire when the press sought confirmation of the story: "I've gone that route before and I've H-A-D I-T, had it." After he had shut down Nelva, the writers tried to tick him off about Jackie Jensen's deal with the Red Sox to train in California and not join up with the squad until March 22, three weeks into spring training. Williams looked askance at this deal: "Well, isn't that something! Maybe I'll meet up with the Sox on their swing through Miami on March 15."

In fact, Williams showed up on the opening day of spring training, February 27, looking rested and strong. During the winter he had been exercising with 25-pound weights for wrists and forearms and doing fingertip pushups—he just couldn't come in cold any more at 38 years of age. He was amiable enough with the press corps: "Just let me know what I'm supposed to do—I want you guys to be happy." He told the writers that he had given Ted Lepcio a call when he was in Boston earlier that month. Lepcio was threatening a holdout for more money, and Williams pretended to be a United Press reporter asking for details: "You signed yet?" "No," said Lepcio. "You a holdout, then?" "I wouldn't say that," said Lepcio. "What about Williams? Has he signed?" "Yeah," said Lepcio. "The club floated a loan so they could pay him." Williams did not blow his cover until spring training; he and Lepcio roared over the gag.

The talk of spring training came from the National League and the

Pittsburgh Pirates organization, where Bobby Bragan seemed to be
nurturing some kind of monster, a 24-year-old rookie named Dick
Stuart, who had hit 66 homers for Lincoln in the Western League.
Bragan told the story of a Stuart at-bat with two outs in the ninth
inning of a game. The manager, coaching from third, had his base-
runner on first steal second to get in scoring position. Stuart stopped
the game and walked toward the coaching box: "How could you send
the man with me hitting? Are you nuts?"

Williams loved these upstart home-run hitters. As for himself this
year, he made a strategic decision. In the early weeks of the season he
would choke up a touch on the bat and sacrifice some power for
range. He finally decided, for a variety of reasons, that the time had
come to use a bit more of the field against the shift. For one thing, his
speed was negligible and infielders were playing him even deeper on
the grass; for another, his reflexes slowed with age—whether he
wished them to or not. Widening his range on the field was to mimic
what was happening naturally to his swing. Over the course of the
year his all-fields hitting in the early season produced an even fuller
effect. Managers were not shifting so extensively on him anymore,
and by the time of the summer heat he reversed the process and was
pulling more effectively than he had for years because the bunch-up
effect of the shift was mitigated, if not eliminated. With any attempt
by the defense to compensate, he began to use more of the field yet
again.

Yawkey made a move in late spring to bolster his ball club for a
pennant run that looked hopeless even before it began. He offered
$1,000,000 for the contract of Herb Score. This would have been one
of the biggest of nearly 100 trades and deals concocted by Yawkey
since purchasing the Red Sox on February 25, 1933. For a man
whose personal fortune, even after some of his thin years with the
Red Sox, registered around $75,000,000, the offer was mere pocket
money. But the deal wasn't to be. Though tempted, the Cleveland
Indians finally backed off. They did not want to lose their wonderful
young property. Little could anyone foresee the baseball tragedy that
loomed in Score's future.

In late March the Red Sox took a swing west and played three
exhibition games in San Francisco. Jackie Jensen was to join the Sox

there and continue spring training with them. Still a little edgy about Jensen's sweet deal, Williams wondered aloud why the team was schlepping all the way across the country: "a fourth-place team won't draw flies in that city." San Francisco, of course, was pumping for major league ball that year, and the local citizenry took offense. Williams was in hot water yet again. He eased the strain by personally addressing the fans in Seals Stadium on March 22: "I first played here 21 years ago. It was a great baseball town then. And looking at today's crowd, it's a great baseball town now. I hope you get major league ball here real soon."

Crowds totaling 57,345 for a three-game set saw the Red Sox play their Seals farm club, and they even played on the day of a 5.5 earthquake that had the eastern writers in a panic about the future of baseball for the area. Hy Hurwitz was adamant: "No team in their right mind would move here." All Hy wanted to do was go home, not an unusual response to an earthquake from an easterner. It took more than a quarter of a century for earthquake-prone San Francisco to meet up with baseball on the wrong day again, but when it did—the third game of the 1989 World Series—it was with a vengeance.

Williams escaped California with minimum damage, but he could not let the travel issue rest. A week later, in New Orleans, as the Red Sox were still playing what seemed to him cross-continental exhibitions at a time when he would rather not be traveling so excessively, he ruptured under his own self-imposed strain. The scene was reminiscent of a Tennessee Williams play. The Red Sox were trying to get out of town on a Sunday night in a torrential southern downpour that the prolix Bill Cunningham of the *Herald* called "tornadic." The whole club and its entourage of attendants and writers grabbed a bite before driving to the New Orleans airport, where they set in for what looked like a long delay. The planes that were scheduled to go out hadn't even been coming in.

Williams was restless and a bit claustrophobic under the best of conditions. These were not the best of conditions. He had been eating with Billy Goodman before the ride to the airport when Hy Hurwitz brought the sports editor of the *New Orleans States*, with the colorful local name of Crozat Duplantier, to their table for an introduction. Duplantier, an ex-marine like Hurwitz and a Korean War vet like

Williams, was used to these Bayou rainstorms, and he planned to wait this one out the way he waited them all out—by drinking it into submission. He was already tanked before the trip to the airport.

Hurwitz and Duplantier were supposedly working on Williams to say something nice about the Marine Corps Reserves, but all that transpired at the dinner table was some banter about pensions. Duplantier joked that his 1952 recall boosted his military retirement pension. Williams said, "Well, I don't think it's going to affect *my* retirement all that much." On the way to the airport, Hurwitz and Duplantier decided to pursue their prey. When they arrived, they kept at Williams to boost the marines. At least that was Hurwitz's story the next day, when he wrote that Duplantier told him on the way to the airport, "I hope I can get Ted to say something nice which will help encourage the Corps." Williams was in no mood to say pleasant things about his wartime home away from home or any other institution or human being. Furthermore, he was growing uncomfortable with Duplantier, whose three sheets were increasingly blowing in the tornadic winds.

Hy Hurwitz knew full well that there were two surefire ways to get Williams going: ask him why he took so many close pitches, or ask him how he felt about being drawn from the inactive reserve to fight in Korea. They chose the latter, and it worked. Williams's fuse blew. He was the "Rider of the Purple Rage," in Harold Kaese's phrase. He rolled in for a full reprise of 1952. He was not the only one in the country, he informed his companions, who felt at the time that the selective service selections were selective with a fury: "Most of us hadn't flown a plane for many years, but they wanted to make a good show. That's why they got a big name like myself. I got a raw deal from the marines, and as I've said before, I've got no use for them."

At the time of the 1952 draft Williams was at the height of his earning power, and he had already served in World War II. But his presence in the Marine Corps was a good ad for the inactive reserve call-up. He knew the politics of the decision were as much domestic as strategic. The military wanted an appropriation of $450 million from the government for airplanes, and they needed pilots to fly them. So they recalled 11,000 pilots who hadn't flown planes for years.

Williams claimed that every one of these 11,000 probably had a story to tell. He then told one of a friend who appealed to Senator Robert Taft to help him out of the Korean call-up: "I used to admire Senator Taft. I thought he was a wonderful man. But a friend of mine was called back for Korea as I was. He knew Senator Taft. He went to him and asked if he could help him get a deferment. Do you know what Senator Taft told him? He said, 'I can't touch you. If you were just an ordinary person I could help you, but because you are pretty well known, I can't do a thing for you.'"

Hurwitz and Duplantier began to smell a scoop. Williams's friend was like one of those "friends" who has hemorrhoids and is too embarrassed to talk straight to his doctor. The "pretty well known" man may well have been Williams himself. Ted then spat contemptuously on the floor of the airport lobby—his all-purpose gesture for helpless frustration—and invited former President Harry Truman into his pantheon of gutless politicians: "We've got a lot of gutless politicians in this country." Williams could hardly be drawn and quartered for originality. This country, as is the case for most, could feed its poor on gutless politicians.

The next day the weather in New Orleans calmed but the tempest continued around Ted Williams, at least as far as the efforts of the press were concerned. Reporters tried to get Harry Truman to respond to the gutless politician remark, but Harry wasn't biting: "No. He's a great ballplayer. I like to watch him." Casey Stengel, who always felt protective toward Williams, especially ever since the 1950 All-Star Game when Ted played eight innings for him with a broken elbow, said that this sort of incident was precisely why the Yankees "have twenty-five public relations people to clean up the mess," a point that Williams had been making for years in relation to the penchant of the Red Sox to let him twist in the wind. Of course, this was also the year when a host of Yankees got themselves in a brawl on May 16 at the Copacabana in New York for Billy Martin's birthday party, and Hank Bauer found himself charged with felonious assault. All the public relations men in the world couldn't put that one back together.

As for Williams's airport tirade, the press tried to stir up matters even more. They wanted to know what the marines thought of Williams's charges. Like their commander in chief, the marines wanted no part of it: "Williams is a private citizen. He can say what

he wants to. We call up a man and use him as we see fit." But Jerry
Nason had another angle on the story. He figured that Williams was
getting itchy for a controversy, that Jackie Jensen had taken over as the
Red Sox problem child, and Williams felt deprived: "Of this you may
be sure: On the day Ted isn't getting much mileage in the press he
will choose one of the hundreds of topics he likes to pop off on."
Nason had in mind spring training of 1956, when the Boston writers
made a conscious effort to ignore Williams because he simply insulted them at the drop of a hat. That's when he exploded, out of
hearing range of the Boston writers, on the drafting of Johnny Podres.

Damage control from the Williams camp was quick and terse. He
issued a press release.

> For the first time in my career I am concerned about publication
> of alleged remarks I made during a discussion at the airport in New
> Orleans last Sunday night.
> I have too many friends and I have spent too much time in the
> Marine Corps not to know that that organization is tops.
> I want to apologize to anyone I might have offended by remarks
> alleged to me by a drinking reporter.
> I have learned, as a result of this so-called interview, that I
> should never again discuss anything with reporters who have been
> drinking excessively . . . or have a gripe of some sort of their own.

But there remained some brass to polish for Williams and he was
good about it. He sent the following telegram on April 5 to Marine
Corps General Randolph Pate in Washington, D.C.: "This pertains to
the statement I was reported to have made in New Orleans. My four
years spent in the Corps are the proudest of my life. I would never say
anything nor suffer anything to be said which would detract one iota
from the Corps and the wonderful men who compose it. Even though
I am no longer a member of the Corps I will always be a Marine at
heart." This was not entirely true, but Williams was delivering a
different kind of message with the last sentence of his telegram. He
would have wished to have been able to utter its sentiments before his
recall in 1952.

Williams denied nothing in his statements; he just reset the circumstances. And he reset them with some accuracy. He claimed he
was set up by a drunk. Three weeks later Duplantier was arrested by

the Louisiana State Police for weaving all over the Jefferson Highway in his car in the middle of the night. He posted bail after spending the wee hours of the morning and a good deal of the next day drying out in a Jefferson Parish jail cell.

As for Hurwitz, Williams was steamed at him for weeks. One day in mid-May Red Sox catcher Haywood Sullivan was sitting forlornly at his locker after having just been farmed out. Williams walked by and pointed to Hurwitz, who was about to talk to Sullivan: "Be careful what you say to that shit." Then to Hurwitz: "If you were ten years younger and ten inches taller, I'd kick the shit out of you, you little bastard. If Yawkey and Cronin had any guts they'd ban you and the rest of you gutless assholes from the park." Dave Egan, catching wind of this little exchange, wrote on May 30 that Hurwitz proved his guts in Guadalcanal, implying that Williams's goal in 1942 was to beat the draft. This infuriated Williams even more.

When the season began on April 16 it was almost as if Williams already had played half of it in the columns of the local papers. The episode in the New Orleans airport was two weeks old, but Bill Cunningham still couldn't resist a bit of preseason advice: "Ted Williams should have learned from the fish that they never get into trouble as long as they keep their mouths shut." A revved-up Williams got out of the blocks fast. He was hitting .408 at the end of the first week, though when the Sox lost two in a row to the Yanks early in the season a *Globe* headline read, "SHORT SEASON, WASN'T IT?"

Williams kept rolling early. Two weeks into the season he was hitting .474 with nine home runs, three of which he picked up in one game on May 8 off a shell-shocked Bob Keegan at Comiskey in a 4-1 win over the White Sox. This was the first time he had hit three in one game in a decade, the last being July 14, 1946, the day Lou Boudreau, managing the Indians, first employed the Williams shift. Characteristically, after the game Williams was less interested in talking to reporters about his home runs than he was intent on explaining how he upset his rhythm at the plate by swinging at a bad pitch on a 3-1 count in the sixth. "That wasn't right. I should have taken the walk."

Williams's strong opening this season could be attributed to many things: his strengthening program during the winter, his selective playing in spring-training games, and the intensity of his will to

outhit the league at the age of 38 (he would be 39 in August). But
Harold Kaese reached for another reason: the sheer knock-me-down
fury that Williams harbored in his soul, a fury he let go in that
incident in the New Orleans airport, and one centered however
arbitrarily on "that New Orleans sportswriter with the smell of Old
Mulekick on his breath."

At the beginning of the year the Red Sox had been ready to
purchase the contract of Herb Score for $1,000,000. But after one
shocking pitch during a game on May 7, Score's career would, for all
purposes, be over. In the first inning of a game in Cleveland against
the Yankees, Score took a Gil McDougald line drive flush in the eye
socket. He was felled from the force of the drive. The sight was
devastating for the ballplayers and the fans, and the majors had seen
nothing so horrific since Hank Greenberg's savage liner nearly killed
Jim Wilson of the Red Sox in 1945. But Score was talking in the
clubhouse, joking that he felt just like Gene Fullmer, who a few days
earlier had walked into a vicious Sugar Ray Robinson left hook in the
fifth round of their championship fight and crumpled in the middle
of the ring. Later, after Score was admitted to the hospital, Mc-
Dougald, Berra, and Hank Bauer were in the waiting room with the
Cleveland contingent. McDougald was distraught: "If he loses his
sight, I'll quit this game." Score's eye had hemorrhaged severely, but
he had some light perception. The bones around the eye, the cheekbone, and the bridge of the nose absorbed the shock of the batted
ball, and the eye itself was intact.

As the season progressed, Williams could not keep up his extraordinary hitting and, indeed, slumped almost immediately after his big
game against Bob Keegan and the White Sox. He hit .200 for a week
and his average dipped to .392, but he did not despair. When Tiger
catcher Frank House tried to help him out in mid-May—"Ted,
you're swinging too hard"—Ted replied, "No, I'm not." "But I hear
you gruntin' and groanin'," House said. "Only when I miss," said
Williams.

Williams would ride through this slump and avoid the usual
controversy that attended his slides. He broke out soon enough and
was back up to .409 by June 1, though the Sox were struggling in fifth
place, 7½ games out. Roger Birtwell took a characteristically cheap
shot: "Williams's average is right up there with the Red Sox winning

percentage." A couple of days earlier, on May 29, the Brooklyn Dodgers and New York Giants had been given permission by the league office to pick up stakes and move to the West Coast. Harold Kaese's reaction to the move proved prophetic. He predicted the possibility of a 3-million-per-year attendance figure in Los Angeles, and he also suggested that travel schedules and general interest in baseball throughout America merited expansion and divisional play: "Let the two existing leagues expand to 10, 12, 14 teams each, if necessary. But, to maintain interest, have two divisions in each league." He could not have hit the nail more squarely on the future's head.

A few days after the announcement that the Dodgers and Giants were likely to leave New York, the Yankees gave their scrapping second baseman, Billy Martin, a one-way ticket out of town for his part in the Copacabana fiasco of May 16. They also levied fines totaling $5,500 against Hank Bauer, Mantle, Berra, Martin, Ford, and Johnny Kucks. Berra summed up the brawl: "Nobody ever touched nobody." He was commenting on the result rather than the intent. When Martin shipped out to Kansas City the magnanimous Yankee brass rescinded the $1,000 fine, but, as Billy pointed out, the kickback wouldn't substitute for the $7,000 he might have expected from his World Series check. Harry "Suitcase" Simpson, bags presumably packed, came to the Yanks in exchange.

Williams continued to roll in early summer en route to a fabulous year. On June 13 he enjoyed another three-home-run game, this one against the Indians in Cleveland—two off Early Wynn and another 435 feet off Bob Lemon. His average was still hefty at .392. More important, he tied Mickey Mantle for the league lead in home runs at 17. This was a sweet season. Even quality pitchers were in awe of him. Early Wynn showed up for a Fenway game and remembered Williams's last outing against him. He walked up to him during batting practice, took a book of matches out of his pocket, and said, "Hey, Ted. This is your strike zone tonight."

Williams had other things to think about. He was going after Mantle in the batting race this year. Mickey was on fire, hitting .446 for the month of June. As the Yanks made a move to wipe the White Sox from the league lead, Mantle raised his average to .381 while at the same time surging ahead in the home-run race, 20 to 17. Williams felt himself choking on the young star's dust for the second year in a row, and he did not like it. But he would have to wait until after the All-Star Game to attend to matters.

National League Commissioner Ford Frick had to overturn the results of the voting for the 1957 All-Star team when it became clear that Cincinnati fans had stuffed the ballot boxes with the names of their hometown favorites. Frick took it upon himself to insert Mays, Musial, and Aaron for George Crowe, Gus Bell, and Wally Post, which seemed the right thing to do. Exactly how to pick the players had always been a matter of concern, and the issue has not been entirely resolved to this day. For the first two years of the game's existence (1933–34) *Chicago Tribune* readers picked the team; for the next three years (1935–37), the rival World Series managers of the previous year chose; for the next nine years (1938–46) all the managers in the league voted; and fan ballots began in 1947. This year the ballot-box stuffing was so obvious that the Reds bat boy almost hit lead-off for the National League squad.

Just before the All-Star break Williams's friend Joe Reichler, an Associated Press reporter, asked Yankee pitcher Don Larsen, who had tied Williams in knots the previous year and thought him to be washed up, what he thought of Ted now. Larsen did not want to go on record but said he still thought Williams's swing was slowing down. Come the real heat of late season and the man will be too tired to take the bat out of the rack. Then Larsen suffered a hot flash: "Something tells me I shouldn't say this, because it would be just like the big son of a bitch to make me eat my words before the day is over."

The All-Star Game was not Williams's best, but the American League won a cliff-hanger 6–5 on Minnie Minoso's clutch double in the ninth. Minoso had replaced Williams after Ted got zapped 0 for 3, though he hit the ball hard, once on a line to Musial and once a long way to center before Mays flagged it. Williams said to Stengel after the game: "Nice going, Casey. I guess you got me outta there just in time."

Williams restarted slowly after the All-Star break, and the vultures began circling overhead. Bob Holbrook wrote a column, "Barometer Dropping," about those "clinical observers looking for telltale signs that Number 9 is reaching the end of the trail." His average had plummeted more than 60 points in a month, and his swing looked terrible. This, as always, was Williams's kind of tonic. The next day he ripped two home runs against the Tigers' Jim Bunning and was off again on a tear in which he stroked 13 hits in 19 at-bats, including 6 home runs in 5 games to bring him up to 26. His average soared back to .367.

The Red Sox were floundering in third place about 12 games out in late July, and Williams was the whole show. On July 26 the Indians came into Boston for four games. Williams had 8 hits in 12 at-bats, including a couple of home runs. On July 28 he went 4 for 4 in a 9–8 Sox win, with a double, a towering bleacher-seat home run off Early Wynn, and three runs batted in. Late in the game Ned Garver was actually ordered to put him on intentionally with runners on first and second, loading the bases. Then Jensen came up and hit into a double play. Garver summed up the zen of pitching: "If Williams can hurt you, walk him."

In his last five games against Cleveland, Williams had gone 12 for 16 with four home runs; he was hitting nearly .700 against Early Wynn. His average had climbed to .379, compared to Mantle's .352; and he was two ahead in the homer derby, 29 to 27. For good measure, Williams went 3 for 4 his next game, against the Tigers, raising his average to .384. In his last five games he was hitting .687; in the last three weeks he was hitting .550; and for the month of July, .440, the highest since his .460 average in June 1948.

Williams's three-hit game against the Tigers, a night game at Fenway, involved a controversial play. Hy Hurwitz, the reporter responsible for part of the fiasco in the New Orleans Airport back on March 31, was official scorer for the game. Harvey Kuenn had moved from his position at short to a spot in right center behind second base. Williams smashed one right at him, and Kuenn couldn't handle it. Hurwitz signaled error. After the game Kuenn told Hurwitz that he lost the liner in the lights and jumped instinctively; it ought to go as a base hit because the topspin was brutal. Hurwitz had the right to change his call, and he did. Williams kept his mouth absolutely shut through all this and took the base hit. But he valued what Kuenn had done. No doubt Kuenn earned one less error for the year, but that is not why he made his point to Hurwitz. He did it for Williams and in honor of a great season.

Williams did not cool off in early August. By August 9 his average was .391, and he had been hitting .516 for the past 30 days. This was an amazing streak for a man his age in the middle of the summer heat. His conditioning before spring training was paying off. By the end of August his average dipped to .377, but he was still just ahead of Mantle, then surging to .376. Williams had 33 home runs and Mantle, 34. The competition could not have been more intense nor, to Williams, more satisfying.

Williams would have to hit around .500 during most of September's games to reach .400 for the year; instead, he was felled by a severe upper-respiratory virus—one of the worst of his career—and missed more than half of September. Williams was so ill—in effect, he had pneumonia—that Hy Hurwitz wrote that he was through: Not only wouldn't he play for the rest of 1957, but he wouldn't come back at all. The illness was simply a signal that time had caught up with him and that the rigors of the season were too much.

After reading Hurwitz's piece in the *Globe*, Williams was ready to get back on the field if he had to be carried out in an iron lung. And his return to the lineup in late September was, indeed, one of those legendary moments in baseball history. On September 17 he pinch hit at Fenway against Kansas City and put one out of the park off Tom Morgan in the eighth to help rally the Sox to a 9–8 win. The next day he pinch hit and walked. The Red Sox then traveled to New York for a series at Yankee Stadium, and Williams took the first game off. On September 19 he hit another pinch home run, off Whitey Ford in the ninth inning of the first game; in the second game he played regularly getting a grand-slam off Bob Turley and three walks for the rest of the day. In the last game of the series he walked against Tom Sturdivant and then homered, singled, and walked again. Against the Senators on September 23 Williams singled, walked three times, and was hit by a pitch.

In effect, after suffering a horrendous case of pneumonia, he put his flannels back on and reached base the first 16 times he came to the plate: he had six hits—four of which were home runs on four consecutive at-bats, tying a record—nine bases on balls, and was hit by a pitch. And after finally grounding out to end the streak, he hit another one out of the park in his very next at-bat. That gave him five home runs in eight official at-bats.

An event that took place several years later is an addendum, of sorts, to this tremendous exhibition of hitting. In June 1971, when Williams was in his third year of managing the Senators, his team was playing the Oakland A's. Mike Epstein, whom the A's had picked up in a trade with the Senators only a few weeks earlier, had hit four home runs in four consecutive at-bats and was going after Williams's 1957 record. He had already teed off twice against Denny McLain in the first and third innings and had two in a row from the game before. Williams ran out to the mound to replace McLain with a tough lefty, Paul Linblad. He was convinced Epstein couldn't hit lefties. But he took Linblad's first pitch far and high down the right-field line and into the seats—foul. To this day Epstein swears it hooked around the foul pole fair.

Linblad then struck out Epstein on a curve low and outside. Epstein heard an unmistakable voice from the lip of the dugout: "Hot damn!" It was Ted Williams. The competitive juices were still flowing. At batting practice the next day, Williams told Epstein that what he had just done was the best exhibition of power hitting he had ever seen. He said nothing about his own four consecutive home runs in 1957.

Williams played out the season against the Yanks in Fenway and added a couple of doubles and a single to his stats. The single was not without controversy. He pounded a grounder that almost took Joe Collins's kneecap into short right field, but Yankee pitching coach Jim Turner screamed to the press, "An error if there ever was one. If the run had been unearned, we'd have been under 3.00 for the season." Everybody has an angle. In this case Turner was thinking about the look of a staff earned run average of 2.999. It's a game of numbers, but Casey Stengel had the better perspective on the call: "Well, the ball went right between Collins's legs. Then again, it might have killed him." Stengel was still a great Williams fan, and this year he had particular reason. Williams hit .453 against the Yanks on the season.

From mid-September to the end of the season, Williams hit .647, which boosted his final average to .388 and gave him a lock on another batting title. Mantle hit .365, his highest average ever. If Williams had had eight more hits in eight at-bats, or five more hits within the 420 at-bats he did register, he would have hit .400.

Pneumonia prevented Williams from an excellent shot at the home-run title to go along with his batting title; ironically, he didn't lose that chance to Mantle, who was also injured, with excruciating shin splints, but rather to Roy Sievers of the Senators, who finished with 42. Williams ended up with 38. Mantle had to settle for 34.

Harold Kaese wrote after the season that the Red Sox, though 16 games out of first, finished higher than expected in third. Moreover, they drew 1,181,067, "that is, the Red Sox drew the 181,087 while one of their players, Ted Williams, drew the million."

Williams hit for much more power on the road, 26 home runs to a mere 12 at Fenway. His road average was .374 and his Fenway average, .410. He tore up Cleveland's Municipal Stadium, hitting .481 with 7 home runs. At Fenway against the Indians he hit .467. The pulse of his season was irregular. There were genuine Jekyll-and-Hyde rhythms to it. In fact, one could put 62 games together in which Williams failed to hit .300. But in another collection of 70 games culled from his season he hit over .500. To string these games together and register their cumulative range of averages is to plot the variances in his year: .474 on May 8, .382 on May 14, .413 on May 30, .342 on July 7, .391 on August 9, .376 on September 1, and .388 at season's end. Perhaps this is what an old man's batting title would have to look like. A younger Williams had put together a season in 1941 during which he fell under .400 for only a few games.

Ted Williams was king of the geriatrics. In 1927 Harry Heilmann led his league at .398 when he was 34 years old. Mickey Vernon led the American League at .337 in 1953 at the age of 35; and Honus Wagner hit .334 at age 37 to take the title in 1911. Ty Cobb won the batting title in 1919 with a .397 average, but he was only 33 years old. Cobb was the only player to come close to Williams's great year at Williams's age, though his .378 average when he was 39, in 1925, did not take the title.

The previous year *The Sporting News* had put out a list of the greatest achievements in the history of baseball. They were ranked in the following order:

Ty Cobb's 12 batting championships
Ed Walsh's 40 wins in 1908
Joe DiMaggio's 56-game hitting streak in 1941

Rogers Hornsby's .424 season in 1924
Babe Ruth's 60 home runs in 1927
Cy Young's 510 career wins
Grover Cleveland Alexander's 16 shutouts in 1916
Jack Chesbro's 41 wins in 1904
Christy Mathewson's 3 shutouts in the 1905 World Series
Bob Feller's 348 strikeouts in 1946
Johnny Vander Meer's back-to-back no-hitters in 1938
Rube Marquard's 19 straight wins in 1912
Walter Johnson's 56 scoreless innings in 1913
Harry Stovey's 156 stolen bases in 1888
Lou Gehrig's 2,130-consecutive-game streak

Of course, some of these great efforts have been superseded, notably Ruth's 60 home runs by Roger Maris, and Johnson's scoreless-inning streak by Don Drysdale and Orel Hershiser. But one more record would have to be added to the list to make it distinctive: Ted Williams's batting title at .388 at the age of 39. He could begin savoring his achievement in its full glory the day after the season ended. Williams turned down a five-figure offer to do television commentary for the World Series, in which the Milwaukee Braves beat the Yanks in seven games, and headed for Labrador for some of the best salmon fishing in North America.

◇ 19 ◇
Life Begins at Forty
1958

LATE IN JANUARY 1958 TED WILLIAMS graciously declined—by telegram—an invitation to attend a New York press dinner honoring him
for his great season in 1957. As in a similar episode at a 1948 Boston
dinner, no one bothered to read the telegram from the dais, and the
New York writers were all over Williams in the papers the next day.
Of course, he was under no compunction to attend the dinner, and
his response was exactly correct. But abuse followed Williams around
as naturally as night follows day.

In early February he showed up in Boston for the Sportsman's
Show and his contract signing. Yawkey simply opened his coffers and
signed his star for $125,000 plus attendance clauses. Musial was
earning in the neighborhood of $100,000 for 1958, and Mantle,
$72,000.

Williams approached this year's spring training with the same
rigor as last year's. He was taking ultrasonic treatment for a bone chip
in his ankle, which he injured slipping on the rocks fishing in Canada
at the end of the 1957 season. He wanted to do everything he could
to play in top shape, and he intended to do so by toning his 220-
pound body rather than by logging playing time in the Grapefruit
League. As always, he began anew with the press, explaining that he
did better in spring because during the off-season he didn't "have to
read that garbage you write." And as always, he made it clear that he
set the rules—he was judge, prosecutor, and jury: "I'll be nice. You
be fair. If you write an unfair piece, don't bother coming around me."
"What, exactly, is unfair?" a writer asked. "Well, let me tell you,"

answered Williams. "If I'm hitting .280 in May, don't write that they ought to bench me."

Williams would turn 40 late this year, and those old bones had a mind of their own. His ankle was not healing as quickly as he might have wished; his elbow injury from 1950 was acting up; and in mid-March he strained a muscle in his ribs sliding, which he aggravated again merely by helping ex–Red Sox Wally Moses coach some young Phillies on the sideline during an exhibition game. Williams's spring batting average by early April, a month after training commenced, was .000, no hits and no at-bats. He finally pinch hit in a game with the Memphis minor league club. His totals on the spring training season were, however, impressive: three official at-bats and three hits for an average of 1.000.

"CALIFORNIA HERE WE COME," read *The Sporting News* headline for the opening week of the 1958 season. Major league baseball had gone west. San Francisco beat the Dodgers on Opening Day 8–0 behind Ruben Gomez, but when the teams moved down the coast to Los Angeles on April 18, the Dodgers returned the favor, 6–5, before 78,672 fans at the massive Coliseum, refitted for baseball. There was a strange, looming screen in short left field that made Fenway's Green Monster look respectable. During a game on April 24, Dodger Lee Walls popped three balls over the screen in a 15–2 win. If he cultivated the same swing all year, he might hit 90 for the season. Whether that was good or bad for baseball, there was no doubt it was good for West Coast attendance. The Dodgers drew 377,601 during their first home stand. The old St. Louis Browns would have considered that a successful season.

Back on the East Coast, Williams had a case of ptomaine poisoning or stomach flu (it never was diagnosed) and missed the opener. He would have done better to forget about all of April. And May was no solace, either. He didn't look ready, and his average took a beating the first month. The Boston writers were already perched on tree branches over Williams's dying corpse. Harold Kaese's *Globe* header for May 20 whispered, "WILLIAMS SLOWED? DON'T DARE SAY IT." Hy Hurwitz's column on May 22 made his worries interrogatory: "EVERYBODY ASKING, 'WHEN'S TED GONNA HIT?'" And the out-of-town press in Kansas City sang the usual Boston refrain with a slightly different lyric: "WHAT'S WRONG WITH TED WILLIAMS?"

This seemed to be the spark he needed. On May 20 Williams went

0 for 5 against Cleveland lefty Dick Tomanek and his average bottomed out at .225. Then he read the papers in Kansas City before the May 23 game and went 4 for 4 to raise his average to .260, gracing his day with a grand-slam home run off Jack Urban, a drive that left the park at the 363-foot sign and smashed into the base of a light tower. Hurwitz came back with a lead, "DON'T EVER CALL TED WASHED UP, OR YOU WILL EAT YOUR WORDS." Billy Martin, who had been shipped to Kansas City in 1957 for his part in the Yankees' Copacabana escapade, told Williams: "Ted, it's going to be tough to move from .220 to .350. I know, I've been trying to do it all my life."

Williams was feeling much healthier than at the beginning of the season. By early June he was stroking .276 and inching up. He also was leaping around like a gazelle in the outfield, diving and sliding on his rear for a Minnie Minoso line drive on June 5. Minoso got to him in batting practice the next day: "Williams, why you hustle so against old Minnie? Do you want to catch ball so bad you kill self?"

The Red Sox slipped within range of the pennant leaders in June, at a time the nation was absorbed with the troubles of Eisenhower's chief of staff, Sherman Adams, who had received gifts from financier Bernard Goldfine at a time in Adams's career when he was head of the Federal Trade Commission. Eisenhower would hold onto Adams as long as he could before the political pressure became unbearable and he had to dump him later in the year.

Williams was hitting around .300 in late June, but for the first time since 1939 he was not picked for the All-Star team, nor did he expect it. Stengel added him to an expanded roster, and in a flurry of gratitude before the break Williams brought his average up to .308 with five home runs in five games. He played in the All-Star Game in Baltimore and took the collar in two at-bats during the American League's 4–3 win. Before the season resumed, several star ballplayers, including Williams, testified in Washington before the Senate committee investigating baseball's monopolistic practices. This was Casey Stengel's most wondrous performance ever.

Stengel told the Kefauver committee nothing they particularly wanted to know but almost everything under the sun they might have been amused to hear, from the playing conditions in Japan—"In Tokyo they are trying to play baseball over there with small fingers"—to the fine points of hiring and firing managers—"discharged means there is no question you have to leave." Following Stengel,

Mickey Mantle told the bewildered Kefauver, "My views are just about the same as Casey's."

Williams's natural distrust of politicians surfaced in his questioning. He held no great stake in management, but he was going to give the Senate little. (They were getting an earful from the more militant Bobby Feller, Robin Roberts, and Eddie Yost.) Senator Kefauver asked, "What would have happened if you didn't want to go to the Red Sox?" And Williams played dumb: "I've never heard of a ballplayer who didn't want to go from the minors to the major leagues." That this was not exactly Kefauver's question didn't seem to matter to Williams. He was playing the artful dodger, a talent he never exhibited to the Boston press. In reference to a question about further expansion of baseball, he responded, "That would be nice." The committee might just as well have been talking to Cowboy Bob.

The Senators got information more to their liking from Robin Roberts, of the Phillies, who staked out a position that was radical for its day but sounds tame now: Baseball indeed should be placed under antitrust restrictions, but the nature of the game was such that exempting certain key areas—contract options, trades, college drafts, territorial rights, and media broadcasts—was essential. That is, most everything unique to baseball would be exempted. The owners could surely live with this. Of course, to lump the reserve clause under contract options was to lose the needle in the haystack.

When play resumed, and with the Red Sox still in the race, the Boston fans got greedy. Jackie Jensen was hitting up a storm; Williams was coming alive; and everything might be fine if manager Mike Higgins only removed a pathetic Don Buddin from his position at short. Joe Cronin concurred. Of the fans, Cronin simply said, "We can't subject him to this; Boston's a rough town." When asked about the Buddin situation, Williams smiled: "Hey, sometimes they're none too sociable out there." Endurance had made Williams a figure of strength.

By late July, the Red Sox were in second place, though a distant 11 games out. Williams was less happy than in early July. He was tired and slumping, and after bouncing one slowly to first in a game in Kansas City, he ran halfway down the line and just stopped. The crowd let him have it, and he feigned a swan dive, a graceful pirouette, into the dugout before issuing a stream of spit in the direction of the fans. The gesture cost him $250 by edict of the league office, and a terse apology: "I lost my head. Sorry. Principally, I'm sorry about the $250."

Swinging through Detroit, things got worse. Huck Finnigan, a former *Globe* writer, printed a piece in *Cavalier* magazine that detailed a scene in the Boston Sheraton Hotel when the talk turned to gambling stories involving Dutch Leonard of the Senators. Williams told a group of writers that he, too, had been approached by gamblers once and shut them down. Williams blew a fuse when he read Finnigan's account. This was the sort of thing that should never hit the league offices, whatever Williams may or may not have said to Finnigan. The writers knew the rules of the game. Williams was threatening to go to the courts on a libel charge. Even Hy Hurwitz, who was at the table and who, from Williams's point of view, would trample his grandmother for a juicy personal story on Ted, came to Williams's defense on this one. "Funny," wrote Hurwitz, "I was right there and never heard anything like this."

Williams's response to the gambling story was to come out and hit two monstrous homers in Detroit during an 11–8 Sox win, including the 17th grand slam of his career, off Jim Bunning, against whom he had been 0 for 9 on the year. Finnigan's gambling story made the rounds to Leo Durocher, one baseball veteran who had been through an experience of his own when Happy Chandler suspended him for the year in 1947 in part for consorting with gamblers. Durocher came to Williams's defense. "It's always the writers. I have yet to hear any ballplayer knock this man, from either league. This is the most likable guy in baseball. He's one of a kind."

As the baseball season wound down, a big story broke in America: the fixing of the network quiz shows "21" and "Dotto." It all began when a contestant on "21" claimed the show wouldn't employ him, as promised, after he participated in the fix. And an investigation was already underway when another contestant noticed a woman backstage rehearsing the answers to questions that had not yet been asked. The most ridiculous figure in all of this was Charles Van Doren, a junior professor from Columbia University, whose theatrics in the answer booth rivaled those of the great Barrymore on the stage.

The Red Sox moved into late September in fourth place, fighting it out with Cleveland for first-division honors, but the live contest was between 40-year-old Williams and teammate Pete Runnels for the batting title. The lead kept shifting, with Harvey Kuenn of Detroit hovering nearby if either should falter; and, indeed, on September 19 the three players were tied at .316. Runnels then spurted in the next few days as Williams slumped. During a game at Fenway on September 21 Williams was so upset at an anemic pop that he heaved his bat from home plate in the direction of the dugout. The shillelagh sailed high, flying 75 feet into the dugout seats before it conked Joe Cronin's cleaning lady, Gladys Heffernan, on the forehead above the eye. When Williams saw what happened he was genuinely distraught, stomping the ground and salaaming like a figure out of the chorus of the *Oresteia*. Gladys went to the first-aid station in the park, and the game was held up for a few minutes while Williams followed her there between innings. He said he "felt ready to die."

That he almost took out Cronin's loyal cleaning lady helped put things in perspective for Williams. His anger, on this occasion solely at himself, refocused him. He began a run of hits in the last days of the year that brought him near Runnels, whose 2 for 9 in a September 26 doubleheader in Washington sent him plunging. The next day against the Senators Runnels went 3 for 5 and Williams 3 for 4, and they were within decimal points of each other before the last game of the year. But Williams homered and doubled in a 6–4 Red Sox win over the Senators as Runnels took the collar, 0 for 4. Williams won the title, .328 to .322, hitting .411 in September and .636 in his last four games. In the equally exciting National League batting race, Richie Ashburn edged Willie Mays, .350 to .347.

Runnels counts the race to the title the top thrill of his career. Williams claimed he would not have minded losing, but only if Runnels remained as hot at the end as he. Williams kept joking with Pete that if he had had more meat on a bigger frame he would have won it: "Got to be strong at the end."

Williams went fishing while the Yanks and Milwaukee fought it out in the Series, the Yankees winning it after being down three games to one. Could an old man, having just turned 40, be back to play for the Red Sox in 1959? Why not? He had just won the league batting championship two years in a row. At 40 Babe Ruth hit .181; Honus Wagner, .252; Nap Lajoie, .246; Rogers Hornsby, .208; and Ty Cobb .339. Cobb's figure was a little high for Williams's tastes. He would try to do something about it.

◇ 20 ◇

Pain in the Neck
1959

ROGER KAHN TOLD A STORY of a reporter asking Williams in spring
training of 1959 about Billy Klaus's bad year at short for the Red Sox
in 1958. "Me?" snapped Williams, "you're asking me about a bad
year?" Williams went on to point out that the horde of Boston
reporters around the batting cage would give their right arms if he
had a bad year, "but old T. S. W. don't have bad years." Unfortunately, 1959 would prove an exception.

Williams signed early for a slim boost, with attendance clauses,
over his $125,000-plus salary of the previous year, and Jackie Jensen,
the league's Most Valuable Player in 1958, began a quiet stew in
California. "I'm only in baseball for the money," he told several West
Coast writers, in preparation for demanding more of it than the Red
Sox were, at least early in the negotiations, prepared to offer. "After
all, there's not much incentive," Jensen added, "when your team
doesn't have a chance." If Williams had said this, all hell would have
broken loose, as it did in 1951 when he merely noted that it didn't
seem to him that the club had any more spirit than the year before.

Meanwhile, in New York the Yankee brass had a better idea in
regard to the issue of contract squabbles. Their scheme was to insert
a behavior clause in the contracts of Whitey Ford and Mickey Mantle
to cover off-the-field shenanigans. Because of the Copacabana and
other incidents in 1957, the Yankees had hired private investigators to
follow the players around town in 1958. The gumshoes returned
exhausted, and the Yankee front office cooked up a special deal.
Without a behavior clause in his contract, Ford could take a salary

312

cut to $27,000 from $32,000 and Mantle to $67,000 from $72,000. With the clause inserted, Ford could climb to $35,000 and Mantle to $75,000. The players were aghast. It soon occurred to the Yankees that blackmail was not the best approach to winning the pennant. Ford ended up with his higher figure for the year, and Mantle even edged his up to $80,000. Neither contract carried the behavior clause.

The Red Sox had cut a deal with the San Francisco Giants for 1959 to train in Scottsdale, Arizona. Yawkey had spoken with Giants' owner Horace Stoneham, and Arizona looked good to both clubs— the Red Sox, because they wanted to angle for better conditions in Sarasota; and the Giants, because of proximity to the West Coast. The situation was not ideal for Williams, but the choice was not his. He arrived a day late on March 1 with a pain in his neck. Before he left Florida he had picked up a bat in his Islamorada home to make a point to a visitor about hitting and had felt a twinge in his neck. He planned to work it out in the dry Arizona sun.

Something new and important took place in the Red Sox camp this spring. The club was ready to bring up a black ballplayer. Jerry "Pumpsie" Green played short the season before in Minneapolis, with a not-altogether-impressive .253 average, but he had been stroking at .365 in winter ball in Panama. Because of restrictive real estate and rental covenants, Green had to live on the outskirts of Phoenix, 10 miles from the facility in Scottsdale. The Sox had to hire a driver to transport him back and forth. But he was ready to bear the indignity if he could cut it with the parent club as its lone black player. Pumpsie was even amused when he overheard a fan in the stands asking a companion, "Which one is Green?"

Green would hang in there until the first week in April, when the Red Sox sent him back to Minneapolis. They had their reasons. He was 2 for 19 in his last few spring training games, and he was having trouble at short. The decision was made to make him into a second baseman and to try him again, perhaps in the middle of the season. But the Boston press corps was not that easily appeased. The Red Sox past was littered with dicey-fielding shortstops. Why not extend the same opportunity to a black man? Whatever answer the Red Sox might provide, the Massachusetts Commission Against Discrimination planned an inquiry into the full range of Red Sox hiring practices. Yawkey threatened to sell the team or to leave Boston.

Williams was taking it very easy in Arizona and nursing his strained neck. But he did travel with the club for two exhibition games against the Cleveland Indians in San Diego on March 13 and 14. This was the first time in 22 years that he had played organized ball in the city of his birth. He enjoyed a reunion with some of his Hoover High teammates, including Roy Engle, a catcher once idolized by the rail-thin Williams because of his huge torso and powerful arms.

Ted came to the plate twice in the first exhibition game, received the warming cheers of the crowd, and dribbled out. But the next day he drove a ball 390 feet to deep right center for a massive double off the wall. He also strained his already-aching neck. When the squad got back to Scottsdale, Williams figured he might be able to loosen the tightness by throwing batting practice during a training session. Bad idea: discomfort turned to excruciating pain.

Late in March Williams flew back to Boston for treatment on his neck and shoulder. He checked into the hospital for a few days of traction. There was, as yet, no diagnosis other than myalgia. But he was not set to play. The Red Sox floundered through the opening of the season, but they had company this year; the Yankees were behind them in seventh place in the early weeks of the season. Williams began light workouts the last week in April.

On May 12, in a night game at Fenway against Chicago, Williams decided to play, setting a course for his worst season ever. He took the collar that night against Dick Donovan, 0 for 5, and was philosophic enough about the experience: "Hell, I saw the ball; I just couldn't hit it." Williams played steadily for a week, and at the end of it he had been to the plate 22 times with one scratch single, a grounder through short against the shift. His average, .045, was a sorry sight. As the season progressed, he added a groin pull to his aching neck. He would get a few base hits and then sink into another batting slough. With the Sox in the cellar, Williams blasted the 2,500th hit of his career, a solid double to left center off Tom Sturdivant in Kansas City. "Might be 3,500 now," he told the writers in the clubhouse, and then, "Oh, don't quote me. I didn't say that." Williams was thinking about his two hitches in the military, and he had learned by now that any remarks on that subject could set off a fire storm.

A month into his season Williams was hitting .176 with two home runs. He felt the strain deeply, all the more so when the writers kept up with their chorus of "hang 'em up, Ted." Hy Hurwitz wrote that the good ones knew when to quit, not merely because their reflexes were on the wane, but because they were a burden to their teammates in the field and on the bases. He hinted that Williams ought to take note.

On June 16 Mike Higgins said he was going to rest Williams for a week. He might pinch hit him, but he wanted him out of the lineup, ostensibly to nurse his ailing neck. Williams was playing out the year with one goal left, his 500th home run. He reentered the lineup on June 23 and got one notch closer with a home run off Dave Sisler in Detroit. He was at 485 career homers and managed to break the .200 average barrier, pulling his up to a paltry .202.

For the next three weeks Williams hit with some consistency and some power, cranking up to .244, but he would dip again until a bit of streak hitting at the end of the year helped him out. Tom Yawkey had a talk with Mike Higgins about the play of the Red Sox generally and the fate of Ted Williams specifically. "I think you're in the wrong place," Yawkey said to Higgins. There was hardly any contesting the point. Last place was wrong by any measure. Before the All-Star break Higgins was out and Billy Jurges was in as manager.

Casey Stengel picked Williams for the two All-Star games that year, in Pittsburgh and Los Angeles. Williams commented only on the honor of the choice, not its merit: "I appreciate the gesture." The National League won the first game on Willie Mays's triple in the eighth. Williams took a walk with two men on in his only at-bat. The *Globe* ran side-by-side photos of Williams hitting the game-winning home run in the 1941 All-Star Game and Williams looking like Father Time at the plate in this year's game. "Then . . . Now," read the cruel caption.

After the All-Star break the Red Sox swept the Yanks in five straight games at Fenway and ruined their year. It was "Funway" Park again. A week later the Red Sox went way out on a limb: they brought up shortstop Pumpsie Green to play a little baseball in Boston. When he took the field on July 22, in the eighth inning of a ball game against the White Sox, he became the first black man to play for the Red Sox; Boston was the last team in the league to be integrated.

The new Red Sox manager got his first real taste of life in Boston after the honeymoon. On July 25, a day after Richard Nixon and Nikita Khrushchev slugged it out in the famous kitchen debate at the American exhibition in Moscow, Jurges blew sky high at a meeting with the Boston press over a story by Ed Rummil in *The Christian Science Monitor*. An unnamed player (actually named Jackie Jensen) told Rummil that the Red Sox were dogging it, "just going through the motions." This was hardly news. Jurges didn't know in which direction to strike, so he put a curfew on the players' road activities and insisted that the Boston press write some good news once in a while. Where was Jurges when the lights went out? The press was merciless. Rummil wrote the next day: "I cover the club. I don't do publicity releases." One of the more remarkable things about this turn of events was Williams's absence from it. It was all he could do to salvage an anemic .234 average at this time in the season.

Sixteen games out and in last place, the Red Sox brought up Earl Wilson, a black pitcher. The talk around the clubhouse and in Boston was that the Sox were also trying to figure out something for Williams to do the next year. Managing was not out of the question. Williams's response was coy: "Does it occur to anyone that I'll play next year?" He was thinking he didn't want to go out with a plummeting average; everyone watching him play was thinking that it was fated to plummet even further.

The last lap around the league in September was a somber experience for Williams. He struck a chord that was new for him, a combination of humility and inadequacy. The cheers that he heard in visiting cities were memorials: "Maybe they feel sorry for me. They know I can't hurt their teams any more." The sad valedictory spirit overwhelmed the writers who had followed his career from the beginning. Harold Kaese finally wrote that "the image he leaves has passed beyond the realm of mere number." Williams fell ill again with a typical late-season upper-respiratory ailment, and it seemed as if the baseball gods were just clearing space. Clif Keane reported that the Red Sox organization was ecstatic over an 18-year-old shortstop hitting .377 for Raleigh: his name was Carl Yastrzemski.

But Williams wasn't done yet. He had pinch hit in a game on August 28 just about the time he was beginning to feel under the weather. He doubled in a run and won the game. When he could play a bit again on September 11 he pinch hit in eight straight games, coming through with base hits four times and walking twice. Then he played in the last two games of the year, doubling twice and singling. So in his last burst of at-bats he went 8 for 13 and brought his average from .239 to .254. With 18 seasons behind him, he was fortunate that this disaster—by his own standards—brought his lifetime average down only three points, from .349 to .346. He had put numbers on the board this year that he preferred to forget: .091 at Yankee Stadium; .158 at Griffith Stadium; .143 at Comiskey Park. His road average was a feeble .232 and his average at Fenway, .276.

The White Sox took the American League pennant, and Boston finished in fifth place, 19 games out of first, the only time so far in Williams's career that the ball club finished out of the first division while he was on the roster. It was small consolation that the Yankees finished 15 games out in third. The Dodgers had to fight their way past the Braves in a playoff series, coming from behind to win it on a Gil Hodges tapper in the 12th inning, before beating Chicago in an exciting World Series. The three West Coast games were played before huge crowds in the Los Angeles Memorial Coliseum; the fifth game, for example, drew a record 92,706.

The last word from Williams on calling it quits was almost plaintive: "I don't want to give up something I love." He wouldn't just yet, and he had his reasons. Primarily, he wanted 500 home runs and was 8 short. But in the back of his mind he kept recirculating a statistic that cheered him. He hit nearly .300 (.295, to be exact) in what amounted to the second half of his season. The .212 he hit in his first half was bad history.

◇ 21 ◇

Last but Not Least
1960

THIS WAS A STRANGE YEAR for two Red Sox stars. Jackie Jensen sat it out because he was plumb tired of the seasonal grind; and Ted Williams took a $35,000 pay cut, a cut intentionally larger than that taken by Babe Ruth from his high of $80,000 in 1930 to the mid-$50,000 range toward the end of his career in New York. The Red Sox front office was a partner but not an instigator in Williams's pay cut. In fact, Dick O'Connell was ready to sign Ted for his last year's base $125,000 salary, but Williams thought, with good reason, that Yawkey and the Red Sox management would have preferred that he retire. He preferred to strike himself a deal that he could live with. Williams felt good and wanted to come to spring training, but he also wanted an escape hatch if things went as poorly as they had the previous year. He made a large purchase on his own magnanimity.

The psychological reasons behind Williams's pay cut were important to him. He knew that based on his 1959 numbers he was burdening the ball club with his own desire to play. He also knew from the flurry of activity to employ him in areas not directly related to the starting lineup that he would not go hungry. Mostly, he knew that a pay cut of such dimension focused the intensity of his desire to go around one more time. Williams wanted to avenge 1959 even more than he wanted to avenge what he thought was a second-rate power hitting performance in light of Mickey Mantle's career year in 1956. And he wanted to hit a milestone 500 career home runs.

In late February the Red Sox were heading back to Scottsdale for their second spring training in Arizona. The disc jockey payola hearings were hot news in Washington; Jack Paar had just walked off his late-night show because of a furor surrounding a joke about an English water closet; the movie *On the Beach* opened in New York; Caryl Chessman was facing execution in California; Dr. Bernard Finch and Carol Tregoff, accused of finishing off the good doctor's wife, were facing a jury in one of the juiciest murder trials of the century; a dramatic and flashy Boston politician, John Fitzgerald Kennedy, was fighting it out with Hubert Humphrey in the West Virginia presidential primary; and actress Angie Dickinson, at Cape Cod working on the set of a racy movie called *The Bramble Bush*, was in hot water for a comment that, given her subsequent dalliance with that same dashing Boston politician, had curious implications: "People in some sections of the Bay State are not as straitlaced as church people believe."

On March 1 Williams took a 14-hour flight from Miami and arrived in Arizona with another sore neck. This did not augur well, and the Red Sox management already had a new wrinkle for him. He would work out in the morning and then share batting instructor duties with Rudy York in the afternoon. Williams was half on the team and half off. Red Smith called him Arizona's "Chief Pain-in-the-Neck" and more than strongly hinted that Yawkey would like to mothball him and make an outfielder out of that kid Yastrzemski, who "cost the Red Sox $10,000 a consonant to get that last name on their roster."

On March 9 Williams got into his first intersquad game of the spring and put the first pitch thrown to him under game conditions into orbit. The *Globe* headlined the at-bat on their front page: "RED SOX OFFICIALS JUBILANT." This must have been the first time a single swing of the bat in a practice game caused such commotion. For years fans had been criticizing Boston's front office for holding onto veterans too long, and here was a classic case. But if Williams could do a little damage with his bat in spring training, the whole ball club could breathe easier. And Williams? He was the old warrior, sheathing up in the cold air of a desert morning: "I keep thinking, 'Williams, you're dying hard.' I keep saying, 'your ankle hurts, your neck hurts, and your back hurts and you are dying so damn hard.'"

The St. Louis Cardinals and the Red Sox played an exhibition game in Phoenix on April 6, and all the young players on both squads crowded around the cage to watch two ancient left-handers take their cuts: Ted Williams and Stan Musial. Musial, too, had had a woeful year in 1959, hitting .255 at the age of 38. But he would hang in another four years, reaching a high of .330 in 1962 at almost 42 years of age. The old vets had a brief conversation. Musial asked Williams how he felt. Ted responded, "Lousy."

Lousy or no, Williams readied himself for the opening game of the year and made his presence felt on his first at-bat of the season, just as he would on his last. He came to the plate in the first inning against Camilio Pascual of the Senators in Griffith Stadium. The count edged to 3-2 before he took a gargantuan cut at a fastball and put it high and far to the right of the flagpole in center. The blast was over 450 feet from the plate, and it tied Williams with Lou Gehrig at 493 home runs. That was it for the Red Sox on the day—they lost 10-1—and Pascual was in a good enough mood to savor the home run he delivered up: "Ted's like old wine. He gets better with age." In the second game of the season at Fenway, against the Yankees, Williams passed Gehrig on the home-run list with an eighth-inning shot off Jim Coates in a losing cause, 8-4. But his age was showing; he pulled a muscle in his calf on his home-run swing and slowed to a sad hobble around the bases.

For the next month Williams was consigned to pinch hitting. Early-season injuries were a perpetual nuisance for him but often a disguised blessing. They kept him out of games in the cold of spring when his body rarely functioned with the snap he felt was necessary at the plate. Williams pinch hit 11 times and reached base only on three walks. Manager Billy Jurges was having a tough time of it in Boston, and he didn't know what to do. The press howled at him for pinch hitting Williams with no one on base late in one donnybrook of a game on April 24, one that the Sox finally lost 11-10 to the Senators. But Jurges claimed that sending Williams in was a difficult decision with or without men on base. Ted was double-play bait; he could barely walk to first base.

The season rolled into May with the Red Sox readying to fall into the league's cellar and with the world agog over the shooting down of a United States U-2 spy plane over the Soviet Union. Khrushchev angrily canceled the Paris summit meeting scheduled for later that month, and he staged a show trial to highlight the confession of

Francis Gary Powers, the plane's pilot. Williams returned to the lineup on May 21 for two days and then caught cold as the team, having lost 10 straight, headed for Kansas City. Rumors were afloat that Billy Jurges was all but gone from the helm of the club and that Yawkey wanted Williams to take over as manager. That would be the neatest switch, with the added benefit of opening a spot on the roster.

Boston management was not in agreement on this, or on anything, in May. As a rule, Yawkey did not like to change managers in the middle of the season. It seemed to him that such a gesture fed the press vultures with more carrion than was good for them. On June 1 he called a rare meeting with Boston's writers to tell them off. He informed them that he was in the game as a sportsman, not as a press agent. He ran his team the way he wanted to, and if he stopped enjoying his time in Boston he would move the team rather than cave in to press opinion: "I hold the last ace and I won't hesitate to use it. It's as simple as that." This is a position Yawkey had taken with equal fervor when the Massachusetts Fair Employment Practices board questioned his commitment to minority hiring.

Yawkey wasn't about to let the writers go without blasting them from the spot they seemed to hold in his raging consciousness: "I could take every one of your stories and find 30 mistakes in it every day. People who couldn't run trolley cars are telling me how to run a $6 or $7 million dollar ball club." The club's front-office personnel had by now talked him out of turning to Williams as manager. As for Williams, whatever interest he had in managing was stifled by his truculence. One little glimmer of doubt from the team was enough for him to relegate his managerial ambitions, as he told Joe Reichler of the Associated Press, "to San Diego's Junior Legion team." "Manage in Boston?" Williams pondered. "Yeah, I'd consider it if the writers considered not writing." Then he had another thought, one pointed in the direction of the left-field seats: "But, you know, Boston is still a great baseball town. Even the writers can't keep the fans away."

Williams returned to the lineup again on June 5 and hit a monstrous home run off Ralph Terry in Yankee Stadium, the 495th of his career. The next day Jurges platooned him only against right-handed pitching, saying that he could not play every day—he just didn't have enough gas left in his tank. That was the last thing Jurges said. His managerial life had come a cropper. Yawkey relieved Jurges of his duties after the Red Sox manager wrote his boss a letter demanding field control of the ball club. The Red Sox announced Jurges was suffering from stress. Del Baker would handle the club until former manager Mike Higgins could take over.

Gene Stephens, the player who would have platooned with Williams, was traded to Baltimore on June 10. Stephens had been with the squad for most of the decade and was known around town as "Ted Williams's caddy." He played a journeyman left field for the Red Sox, primarily filling in the interstices of Ted's injury time. In Baltimore Stephens let go with a career's worth of feelings. He liked Williams—he had nothing but fondness for the big guy—but Ted stole his desire from him: "Every time I saw him putting on a uniform I got red-eyed. Something boiled up inside of me. I kept thinking, he took everything away from me. He's even made me so that I don't care."

The new regime was a tonic for Williams's aging bones. In the next two weeks he got red hot, hitting .421 and belting seven home runs. In Briggs Stadium on June 16 he hit number 499 and then asked Higgins for a day off as the club moved on to Cleveland. But Higgins said a rookie right-hander, Wynne Hawkins, was going for the Indians, and he would rather sit Williams the next day with a lefty penciled in. Hawkins made a mistake with a fastball away but up, and Williams blasted it over the left-field wall. He had achieved one of the goals that drove him to play this one last year: 500 major league home runs.

After the game Williams did something he hadn't done for years: he broke the club's 15-minute delay on interviews and spoke privately to Cleveland writer Hal Lebovitz. He was all sweetness and light, leading Lebovitz to wonder "how this friendly, charming person ever got the rap that he hates sports writers." Lebovitz got himself a scoop. Williams firmly announced that he would retire at season's end. He showed Lebovitz the 500th home-run ball that had been returned to him: he would donate it for a Jimmy Fund auction. He had kept only three baseballs as personal souvenirs: one with Babe Ruth's signature, one with the signatures of every living .400 hitter, and a third was the ball he hit for his first home run off Bob Feller. At his Hall of Fame induction, Enos Slaughter would give him another one: the ball that

Williams bounced off the facade of Detroit's Briggs Stadium for a dramatic last-inning All-Star Game win in 1941. Slaughter had held onto it for years.

Talking to Lebovitz was a calculated move on Williams's part. He was delivering a message to the Boston press. He knew that the hometown editors put all kinds of pressure on their writers to generate stories and that they hated nothing more than getting beaten by rival-city dailies. Williams was tough prey, and the Boston writers were constantly on the hunt. That Lebovitz got a sweetheart scoop on retirement was precisely the sort of thing that set local writers' teeth on edge.

Williams was nobody's fool. He said disingenuously on any number of occasions that a writer's job was merely to record the accomplishments of a ballplayer and record them accurately. He spoke about facts as if they were the only stories, and as if they were always ascertainable. But anyone who pursues facts knows that they are not. They are often not even exactly definable as facts. They are versions, twists, or, as the physicists put it, quarks. Facts have characteristic spins. The spin is what the writer needs to satisfy an editor, and that was what, on this occasion, Williams gave to the lucky Lebovitz and withheld from the Boston corps.

By June 21 it looked as though the Red Sox had made themselves a good deal in taking Williams for $35,000 less than in 1959. He was hitting .333, though the Red Sox were as hapless a bunch as they had ever been in the Yawkey era. They were losing regularly under Higgins just as they had under Jurges. In the last week of June the club had fallen 17 behind in dead last with a horrendous 22–42 record. Consolations were small, indeed. On June 30 Williams took his daughter Bobbie Jo, now 12, to Fenway and pumped a long drive into the grandstand seats in deep right. Usually he pressed when she was there and got collared. But this day he popped one, giving him 11 for the month of June. This was his best power effort since the 13 home runs he hit in June 1950.

On the season Williams, nearing 42 years of age, was hitting one out of the park every 7.38 at-bats, an extraordinary ratio that would not get much worse—one every 10.62 at-bats—by season's end. Moreover, after another batting spurt prior to the All-Star Game, he was leading the league in average at .346. He was feeling old but mighty good. He pinch hit in both All-Star games in 1960, grounding out in the first game in Kansas City, and, after a tremendous ovation in Yankee Stadium, singling off Larry Jackson in the seventh inning of the second game. Stan Musial also had pinch hit and homered in the top of the seventh. This was a poignant inning for longtime baseball fans; it would be the last time these two great stars played in the same game.

After the break, Williams went into a bit of a tailspin at the plate, but toward the end of July he cranked up for 4 more home runs, raising his total to 18. But his most interesting at-bat of the month turned out to be inconsequential. Cleveland was at Fenway on July 23 for a nationally televised game on NBC. Jimmy Piersall, by then playing for the Indians, was in center—sort of. With Williams at the plate and Jim Perry on the mound, Piersall began jumping around like a human neutron. He moved from left to center, in and out, leapt into the air, and glided in front of other fielders.

Williams, as he later put it, happened to be "a nut about distractions at the plate," and this business simply wouldn't do. "Put the chains on him," he told ump Ed Hurley, who walked toward the mound and gestured to Piersall. Piersall merely aped Hurley's gestures. The scene was out of hand, so Hurley gave him the heave. Bad move: Piersall had a first-class fit on the field. Joe Gordon and Mel Harder moved to calm him, but Hurley was so ticked that he gave them the heave as well. Later, Joe Gordon threatened to quit as Cleveland manager if General Manager Frank Lane didn't do something about Piersall. A week before, Jimmy had been forced to apologize to the entire Cleveland squad for erratic and embarrassing behavior: "Can't help it—I'm high-strung," was the gist of Piersall's excuse.

These were the days for baseball's bad boys. A week later, on August 4, Billy Martin, then playing for Cincinnati, threw his bat near the mound after Chicago's Jim Brewer put one a little too close to Martin's head. On the way to pick up his bat, Billy detoured and checked in with Brewer for a savage right hand that broke the pitcher's orbital cheekbone just under his eye. Brewer needed surgery, and Martin needed a lawyer for the lawsuit the Cubs and Brewer planned to lay on him for damages totaling $1,040,000. "Would they take cash or check?" wondered Martin.

Williams was trying as hard as he could to hold on to his .300 average, but he also wanted to move a notch up the all-time home-run list and pass Mel Ott, at 511. In Cleveland on August 9 he tied him, hitting a meaty Jim Perry 3-1 fastball over the fence in right center. The next day he surpassed Ott with a fifth-inning shot off Barry Latman on a line into the left-field seats, and in the ninth he added another off Johnny Klippstein over the right-field fence for his 21st home run of the year. He was hitting .318. On the plane to Baltimore after the game, Williams bought the writers a bottle of champagne. The *Globe* the next day acknowledged the gesture with a brief article headed simply, "THANK YOU."

As he eased into his last active months Williams was almost beyond controversy, but it still sought him out. Before a game on August 15 at Griffith Stadium, his friend J. Taylor Spink of *The Sporting News* sent a photographer to ask him to pose with President Eisenhower, who was at the park taking in the ball game. Williams asked if Ike was agreeable, at which point press secretary Jim Hagerty told the photographer, Don Winfield, to "let the president just enjoy the game." The day's papers had Williams ducking the photo session.

Hagerty read the same papers and tried to play Mr. Fix-It. Williams was asked to drop by the White House for a photograph, but by now he was miffed. A small matter had mushroomed. Posing at the ball park was one thing; making a political pilgrimage was another. At least *The Sporting News*, the prompter of the episode, took no offense. The next day they named Williams the Player of the Decade, though their decade, 1956–1960, was a few years short. Stan Musial was the first winner, but that poll was for 1945–1955. Now *The Sporting News* wanted to recycle the award at the head of the decade. So Williams edged in for the abbreviated honor.

Williams had one more goal for the year: he wanted to hit .300, and he agonized as points were whittled away in the exhausting heat at season's end. As wilted as he was, he enjoyed a brief spurt early in September at two of his favorite parks, in Detroit and Kansas City, with 7 hits in 12 at-bats to bring him up to .321. He was going to make it, a sweet thought given the horrendous personal news that reached him at the same time: Hurricane Donna had battered his Islamorada home in the Keys on September 11, tearing down walls, flooding his rooms containing priceless trophies and photographs, and delivering his stove and refrigerator to the other side of the island.

Williams took what solace he could from his last games. Mike Higgins would pinch hit him in 3 of his 13 remaining games, giving him some needed rest. But he would go out hitting .500 in his last four-game series at Fenway for a solid .316 on the year, including an excellent road year in Cleveland (.364) to bring his average there over 19 years to .301. His .167 average at Chicago's Comiskey Park in his final season knocked his lifetime average there below .300, to .298, making it the only park where he did not hit at least .300 for his career. His best on-the-road power park was Briggs Stadium in Detroit, where he hit .330 for his career with 55 home runs and 164 runs batted in. The full breakdown of Williams's performances on the road and at home against the American League is provided in Appendix B.

On the final day of the 1960 season, Tom Yawkey fired Boston's general manager, Bucky Harris. Yawkey handed him his pink slip as a testimonial to the firm lock the Red Sox held on seventh place. On the other hand, the hibernating Jackie Jensen, who had relaxed at home for the entire 1960 season, picked the day of Williams's finale to announce he was coming back for 1961. Readiness is all.

Ted Williams's last game at Fenway remains one of baseball's most stirring moments, brilliantly chronicled in John Updike's famous essay "Hub Fans Bid Kid Adieu." On September 28, two days after the first historic Kennedy-Nixon television debate, Ted Williams said good-bye in his inimitable way. At the ceremonies before the game on a bleak Wednesday afternoon, with a crowd of 10,454 on hand, Boston's Mayor Collins presented Williams a check for his beloved Jimmy Fund. Williams's speech was brief.

> It is awfully hard for me to speak on an occasion like this. In spite of all my differences and disagreements with the "knights of the keyboards" upstairs, I must say my stay in Boston has been the most wonderful thing in my life. If I were ever asked what I would do if I had to start my baseball career over again, I'd say I would want to play in Boston for the greatest owner in the game and the greatest fans in America.

Despite all, Williams had won a firm place in the hearts of most Bostonians, and with one more swing of the bat that day he would cement that place even more firmly. Steve Barber started the game for the Orioles but only got one man out, walking Williams in the first inning. Jack Fisher replaced him. In the third Williams flew out to Jackie Brandt; in the fifth he backed Al Pilarcik against the visitors' bullpen for a fly-ball out. The fall air was hanging damp and heavy, and this might be the limit for Williams today. In the eighth inning he came to the plate for the last time. With the count 1-0 he took a big cut and missed. But then Fisher came in with a fastball over the heart of the plate, and Williams launched it on a trajectory that finally placed it on the canopy over the bench in the Red Sox bullpen to help the Sox win the ball game 5-4.

Williams ended the season as he began it—with a glorious home run. The crowd was jubilant, and Ted, as was his custom, broke into his loping home-run trot. He kept his head down, almost a submissive ritual practiced over the years to leave the pitcher whatever remained of his dignity. Williams went to his position in left for the acknowledgment of the fans at inning's end, but Higgins replaced him with Carroll Hardy before the ninth began. With the game still in progress, Williams sent his bat upstairs to Tom Yawkey via batboy Bobby Sullivan. Mrs. Eddie Collins was sitting in the box seats. "My husband brought him here, and I'm seeing him off." The motion, as Shakespeare put it, is ended.

Epilogue

IN WHAT AMOUNTED TO A eulogy on Williams's last game at Fenway Park, John Updike marked the change in Williams over the years: "In the two decades since Williams had come to Boston, his status had imperceptibly shifted from that of a naughty prodigy to that of a municipal monument." A New England wordsmith such as Updike could not help seeing in Ted Williams's relation to Boston another of the knotty marriages he plotted so often in his own fiction: "The affair between Boston and Ted Williams was no mere summer romance; it was a marriage composed of spats, mutual disappointments, and, toward the end, a mellowing hoard of shared memories."

I have centered on a somewhat different configuration in describing the Williams era in Boston. Updike may have mellowed while watching Williams over the years, but there is little that is mellow in Williams or little in his partly French ancestry that could be referred to as *mou*, or soft. His career, if monumental, was monumentally troubled. The year after he retired, a decidedly unmellowed Williams traveled with the Red Sox to spring training in Scottsdale as batting coach. Larry Claflin, of the *Boston Record American*, a paper that Williams truly detested, was on the field with Dick Young of the *New York Daily News*. As soon as Williams sighted Claflin he let go with a tirade against him for calling his ex-wife to ask what he, Williams, got his daughter for Christmas. "A pretty rotten thing to do," screamed Williams, "but you're up to your neck in shit anyway."

Claflin was furious. He had nothing to do with this, and he felt so ill used that he tried to get Williams to go to the local sheriff's office

328

so he could prove his innocence by taking a lie-detector test. Williams stormed away. It didn't really matter to him whether Claflin or someone else had telephoned Doris. Claflin was the part that stood in for the whole. The notion that had entered Williams's head was fixed there. This is what frustrated those dealing with Williams, and this is why *mellow* could never be the right word for him.

But other qualities emerged in Williams over the years that seem exactly right. He hated what can only be called a kind of foreclosure, a judgment made upon him that appeared unalterable. Life for Williams was opportunity, and baseball, like life, was a game of recurring chances. He raged when chances were denied him, when his turn was taken away. When he was inducted into the Hall of Fame on July 25, 1966, he tried to set the record straight. He thanked the 280 writers who voted for him because he knew that he didn't have anything like 280 friends among them. In a characteristic gesture, he at once acknowledged that life is not a democracy, that the inferior deserve no special note, but that even the best need a chance. He took the occasion of Willie Mays's surpassing Williams's own career home-run totals to remind his audience that baseball offers the chance to excel at something very, very difficult, "not just to be as good as someone else, but to be better. This is the nature of man and the name of the game." For Williams, accomplishment was the measure of excellence, but opportunity was the measure of fairness: "I hope that someday the names of Satchel Paige and Josh Gibson can be added as a symbol of the great Negro players who are not here only because they were not given a chance."

Many years later Williams returned to Cooperstown to honor the induction of Billy Williams and Ray Dandridge into the Hall. The late Bart Giamatti, then president of the National League, told a story of Williams speaking before the invited Hall of Famers at a private dinner. This was shortly after the unfortunate remarks of Al Campanis, of the Dodgers, about blacks in baseball. Williams had the usually raucous collection of immortals transfixed with a story of his own son and Ray Dandridge's grandson playing pool late into the night in the game room of the lodge at Cooperstown. He was not making a point about brotherhood but about generations. What had been so difficult for one generation could be, with tolerance, natural for another. Williams felt that Billy Williams's chance and Dan-

dridge's belated chance for the Hall of Fame spoke more eloquently
for baseball's future than for its past. All his life Ted Williams
demanded two things he thought everyone deserved: to be judged by
his achievements and to be given a fair chance. He had few personal
regrets on either score, but he thought that many, especially black
ballplayers, had not been accorded those basic rights.

◇

As for raw achievements in baseball, Williams would have liked to
have won one more batting title—the one he lost to George Kell in
1949. And he would have liked a few more leg hits in 1957 to inch his
average to .400. But Kell had the higher average at the end; nothing
was to be done about that. As for Williams's speed to first in the last
years of his career, he invariably looked, as Joe Garagiola used to say,
like he was loping to high tea at Lourdes.

If Williams regretted that Yawkey had not turned to him as
manager in 1959—a matter of deep ambivalence even if the best spin
be put upon it—he got his chance a decade later to manage in the
major leagues. An unlikely employer asked him to take the helm of
the Washington Senators in 1969. Bob Short, a millionaire trucker,
bought the still-struggling expansion club for $9,400,000 in De-
cember 1968. He hired Ted Williams while denying that he hoped
his manager's famous name would draw the attention of the fans
away from the wretched quality of his team: "I just didn't want to
hire someone to remind them of it." On opening day Short distributed facsimile versions of the pen with which he signed Williams, a
gambit that seemed conventional in comparison to Sweetheart Night
in 1970, when Short gave away panty hose.

Bob Short and Ted Williams were strange bedfellows, as Jack
Mann described it: "This is Bob Short, professional Democrat (he was
national treasurer when the party ran up a $6 million debt during the
Humphrey campaign), knocking Richard Nixon with the same breath
that adores a manager whose politics make Honor America Day
sound like an SDS rally."

Williams did a remarkable job his first season, pulling a ragtag
club 10 games over .500 and increasing attendance by 400,000. But
managing had its sober realities. The superb job he did with the
Senators in 1969 didn't count for much in 1970. Bob Short was still

looking at a ledger soaked in red ink. Against Williams's advice he traded away, as Williams put it, "half the fucking ball club" and got Denny McLain, a whole lot of trouble. "You don't buy an expansion club," protested Short, "and get a bunch of gentlemen who can also play baseball. If the merchandise weren't tainted, who'd sell it to me?"

Williams's three subsequent years managing were never much fun, surely never as much fun as his first. He began his managing career in 1969 the way he began playing, with tremendous enthusiasm. Mike Epstein, one of Williams's big sluggers his first year, recalls getting a letter from the club telling him to be sure to come to camp at a decent playing weight—210 pounds. But when he showed up at the desired weight—on the dot—Williams was aghast; he took one look at Epstein and blustered. "Come on, let's get something to eat." Williams took Epstein to Howard Johnson's and plied him with milk shakes. His first impulse as a manager was to do what he tried to do as a youth—put some meat on those bones.

Epstein told another story about Williams that, in its way, bridges two eras. Williams never could understand how Epstein could hit at all wearing eyeglasses with lenses thick enough for the telescope at Mt. Palomar. One day in Cleveland he and Epstein were walking down the street in the vicinity of the municipal courthouse. "So, how far in yards or paces is the building from right here?" Williams asked. Epstein could barely see the courthouse; he had to blink to tell if it was night or day. "Come on, how far in yards or paces? You're a hunter. You gotta know these things," prodded Williams. "Damned if I know," said Epstein, "maybe 500 paces." "No—you're way off," Williams shot back, "641 paces."

They paced it off, and Epstein ended his count on 640. "Good God," Epstein exclaimed, and then he wondered whether he'd been had, whether Williams had taken him on a fool's count-off, having numbered the paces the day before, or perhaps three decades before, on his first trip to Cleveland in 1939. But Epstein had to wonder. As he looked at Ted Williams, he knew he was walking with a legend; there never would be another like him.

Afterwards

There is something deeply paradoxical about America's love for the game of baseball and the admiration accorded its great players. For one thing, baseball is one of the few team games played by individuals of relatively normal size and stature. Some of its players even look fallible—a bit oddly shaped, slow of foot, paunchy. Fans watching football or basketball players deplane at an airport see monstrous forms in front of them, forms implying that only a group of similarly gigantic athletes could even think of testing these behemoths on the field of play. But baseball players rarely look so awesome or so forbidding. They look much more like us, or at least like younger versions of us.

Yet the actions performed on the baseball field are among the most difficult in sport: hitting a ball traveling more than ninety miles per hour, pitching a hardball even close to that speed, hauling in a long fly at full clip, throwing deep from the hole at short, fielding a hot grounder, making the pivot at second, pegging a runner out on an attempted steal. Anyone who has tried these feats usually reaches a level of frustration more quickly than dignity ought to allow.

Baseball is inordinately difficult, and that is why we are so fascinated with those who play the game at a level approaching brilliance, and why we are equally fascinated with those who reflect the game's frustrations and pressures. Ted Williams did both. Moreover he began playing in the 1930s, and his active career lasted until 1960. He is a monument to the midcentury. To drive into downtown Boston, one must pass through the Ted Williams Tunnel, and I suspect there is something fitting about the grandeur of the entrance and the likelihood that in a traffic jam Boston fans are still hurling deprecatory curses toward the heavens at Williams's expense.

The scope of Williams's major league career, touching four decades, inscribes the golden age of baseball in America. In the first week of his rookie season, Ted played a game at Yankee Stadium in which ten of the players on the field that day eventually made the Hall of Fame: Joe Cronin, Bill Dickey, Joe DiMaggio, Bobby Doerr, Jimmie Foxx, Lou Gehrig, Lefty Gomez, Lefty Grove, Red Ruffing, and Ted Williams himself. By any standards, that was a golden day in a golden age. Williams outlasted all those players from the 1930s, and his stature seems to grow and grow, as one after another legendary player departs not only the field of dreams but the mortal flesh to which life is heir.

In the decade since the original publication of this book, Ted Williams has not taken many swings at a baseball—and I venture that he has not done much deep-sea fishing either, his other great love in life—but he has done something more glorious, something even Joe DiMaggio just missed doing: Ted Williams lived to the year 2000. He helped baseball usher out one millennium and hail a new one. Time and illness may have slowed him down, but if the relentless rat-a-tat-tat of Williams's conversation has dimmed in decibels, it has not waned in enthusiasm. Hitting is his life, as Ted has said on any number of occasions, and talking about hitting is a kind of perpetual reincarnation. Almost anything can set him off on what the body, mind, and soul do while swinging a bat at a baseball. He still believes that the arc of a hitter's swing should be upward, that it is supreme folly to let go of the bat with the top hand even beyond the apogee of the swing, and that a hitter is consistently in the pitcher's hip pocket if he foolishly swings again and again at pitches outside the strike zone.

Any baseball fan tuned in to television's broadcast of the 1999 All-Star game at Fenway Park, the last such game of the millennium, could have heard over the din of the crowd and the buzz of those standing on the field Williams talking about hitting. The occasion that July before the All-Star game was the appearance of the century's best living ballplayers, perhaps the greatest collection of players ever assembled in one place. Old timers and newly minted stars hovered in small groups on the field near the positions they played—stacked, it seemed, three or four deep the way we as kids used to arrange the disks for the board game All-Star Baseball before selecting our own teams.

As the players stood at their positions, Williams was the last intro-duced. The roar of the crowd was predictable, but the rush of the players, old and young, leaving their places on the field and swarming around Williams was spontaneous, almost as if all these stars were attending the *couché* of a king. Ted appeared to bless all baseball in his good-natured and effusive way, the television network simply leaving the microphone open as he chatted with the players milling about him, complimenting both those he had played with and many whom he had merely watched. Nomar Garciapara was almost in tears after Williams singled him out and told him he was a terrific talent. Ted asked Mark McGwire whether he could see smoke come off the bat on a foul-tip. Williams was old. He was ill. But he was irrepressible.

No one who saw Ted Williams at Fenway that day will forget the moment, just as no one who ever saw him hit will forget the image of his twitching left elbow, the lightning hip pivot, and that marvelous swing of the bat. It is no small part of the pleasure in writing about Williams, especially Williams the hitter, that the written record tries to recapture part of the visual one by drawing on a resource instantly available to each of us: memory.

When I researched the material for this book in the late 1980s, I hounded Ted Williams for months with what must have seemed to him an annoying stream of questions. He was generous with his answers but finally reached a limit of sorts. In one letter his tone grew dismissive, but then he couldn't resist a simple and winning signoff, although I sensed a bit of the irony as well: "I'm glad you're such a fan." Here I was trying to get volumes out of him, and in the end he was right. To be a historian of baseball and a chronicler of one of its greatest players is to be, above all, "such a fan." *Confiteor.*

◇ Appendix A ◇

Sweet Science:
Williams on Hitting

IN 1986 *SPORTS ILLUSTRATED* BROUGHT Ted Williams, Wade Boggs, and Don Mattingly to Fenway Park for a colloquy on hitting. The issue was the hitting theories of Charlie Lau and Walt Hriniak versus the hitting practices of Ted Williams. To Williams, Lau and Hriniak made little sense. Williams was less interested in getting Boggs and Mattingly to change the way they hit than to change the notions each had about what happened when they did hit: "They don't know as much as they think they know about hitting."

Williams was fighting a losing battle, though he insisted that Lau's weight-shift theory of hitting was bunk. "He set back hitting 25 years," Williams blustered to Boggs and Mattingly. Power is not generated from a to-and-fro rocking at the plate. Its source is more lever and pulley: a pivot at the hips and a bat that makes contact on a slight upswing just before complete extension.

When Williams looked at Boggs and Mattingly (or especially at another Red Sox hitter, Dwight Evans) practicing exaggerated down-swings in the on-deck circle, with the head down and the chin tucked in at the neck, he wanted to, as he so delicately put it, "puke." No one ever hit that way; why should anyone swing that way? He compared the swing to a blow in boxing. The most powerful blow is produced by fast hip rotation. Weight shift is not primary. One wants to pivot and smash, boom. "The boxer," said Williams, "will generate most power if he doesn't do a thing, then goes umphph with the hip." He rotated his own sizable hips and lashed out with a short cross.

Boggs looked at Williams and told him he was shifting weight right then. He repeated, "Sure, you have to shift some weight in a swing, but the pivot is the important thing." Boggs wanted to know about the bat. Does Williams let it go with one hand after the swing? "Never." Boggs hounded him: "Well, you gotta let go sometime." Williams was equivocal: "Sure, sometime."

When Mattingly claimed that the Lau "rock" got him topspin drive off the ball and, consequently, a more stinging swing, Williams scoffed. Topspin or backspin have to do with where the bat hits the ball in the swing and the angle of contact, he argued, not how a hitter rocks to swing at it. "There's a great thing in life called logic," he told Mattingly insistently. Besides, a hitter doesn't really want topspin if he can help it. And backspin can only occur without chopping down when the bat hits the ball slightly upward at the extension of the swing. A hitter can only do that by getting hips and butt into the action. Williams said that he always tried to hit the ball in the air because a groundball swing was generally an overanxious one and a bit out in front. Many of his mis-hits, even his hardest ones, were vicious top-spinning ground balls and low line drives, including one that Gene Woodling complained "really sunk hard" and broke his big toe. Williams preferred to launch balls differently, with an explosive last-minute swing. He always tried to hit it late, hard, long, and high in the air.

Boggs marveled at a distant bleacher seat that had been painted red: it marked where Williams had driven the longest ball he ever hit at Fenway, a monstrous home run that he had pasted off of Fred Hutchinson. Williams and Mattingly then had a little go at the Red Sox third baseman. Williams told Boggs that on a couple of occasions he had swung so hard that he had smelled smoke from a foul tip. Boggs couldn't believe it, but Mattingly said the same thing had happened to him. One could imagine the gears engaging in Williams's brain—"Not on a Charlie Lau swing, it didn't"—but he kept quiet and took solace in the fact that to smell the smoke of a foul tip is to swing a Williams swing.

Much of that 1986 colloquy repeated notions Williams had held for ages. Two decades earlier he had serialized what was to become his primer, *The Science of Hitting*, in issues of the same magazine, *Sports Illustrated*. These articles were accompanied by dramatic stop-action shots of Williams swinging at the plate. The images are still evocative for those who saw him hit and transfixing for those too young to have borne witness.

There he stands before the pitch: Feet are balanced, 15 inches between insteps, 6 inches from the back of the box; front foot extends just a touch toward the plate; knees are slightly bent. Williams grips the bat as if, in Updike's words, he wanted to wring the resin out of its handle. The back elbow is in tight at the beginning of the swing and then flaps out just before the hands do a slight dipping hitch—a triggering, timing move something like a conductor's downbeat right before starting the piece.

The position of the elbow snaps in again when the split-second decision is made to swing; the elbow sets the arc of the bat along its trajectory. The right knee dips slightly; the hips open on a pivot from a tense, cocked position. The rotating hips pull the hands around as the bat trails, first with sweeping and then flattened force on an upward swing. Shoulders open; hips and butt are at top rotational speed; the stride is a precise eight inches; the hands are first in front of the arc of the bat, the bottom one pulling through. The bottom hand then rotates to a higher position at the apogee of the swing, pulling the bat through the arc of the swing at contact. There is no break of the wrists at contact but just after, as a coda to full extension of the swing. Nor do the eyes remain glued to the spot where bat and ball make contact—"pretty much impossible," argued Williams, if the swing is right.

This was what it looked like; the only change during the almost 17 full seasons (plus loose change) Williams played was a wider stance and a slightly shorter stride toward the end of his career. How to make it happen was another matter. Lou Fonseca, the famous sports technician who photographed the speed of Bobby Feller's fastball, took some stop-frame photos of Williams's swing. The head of his bat was traveling close to 200 miles per hour, twice as fast as Feller's fastball. That was, indeed, a faster swing than that of most ballplayers—a few milliseconds faster, for instance, than Joe DiMaggio's. Fonseca calculated that a ball traveling 100 miles per hour would reach the plate in less than half a second. Williams's swing thus uncoiled in an incredible .25 seconds.

No matter how fast the swing, there is still no guarantee that the bat will hit the ball. Williams said this was the toughest thing to do in any sport, and he spent more time thinking about it than anyone in the history of the game: "I feel in my heart that nobody in this game ever devoted more concentration to the batter's box than Theodore Samuel Williams, a guy who practiced until the blisters bled, loved batting anyway and always delighted in examining the art of hitting the ball."

A man who refers to himself in the third person and uses his middle name in the bargain is staking out a real claim. So be it. Williams was ready. He set down the terms for hitting with three cardinal rules that he preached and practiced all his life: get a good pitch to hit; think productively at the plate; and be quick. The last was the catch. It is every bit as important as the other rules but not exactly learnable. "Be quick" is a bit like saying "be beautiful." On this last point, at least, Williams settled for finding ways to increase quickness rather than to produce it.

To begin with the principal rule—get a good pitch to hit—is to imagine the central agon, or struggle, that constitutes the game for Williams: the battle for physical and psychological advantage at the plate. In 1940 Joe Cronin, the Red Sox manager, benched Williams for a game because he said the kid had to realize baseball was a team sport. The next day Cronin put Williams back in: "Hell, it really isn't. It's the individual with a bat in his hands that makes the game what it is."

Williams chose to focus, as he had from the time of his repeated contests with a strong-armed young pitcher named Wilbur Wiley on the playgrounds of San Diego, on the individual at-bat. That, for him, was the essence of baseball: "It's so important, the real crux of baseball, and so many hitters seem to miss it. You're not playing the Cincinnati Reds or the Cleveland Indians, you're playing that pitcher—Johnny Vander Meer, Bob Feller, Bob Lemon, whoever he is—and he's the guy you concentrate on."

"Get a good pitch," Rogers Hornsby told Williams in spring training camp of the Minneapolis Millers in 1938, and Williams always said this was the most intelligent thing the garrulous Hornsby ever said. But how? The pitcher's job is to make the batter swing at what is known as the pitcher's pitch, so called because the odds of the batter hitting it well are remote. Yogi Berra, a hitter who was famous for making the most outrageous pitcher's pitch into his own delight, nonetheless praised Williams's working the pitcher into an almost legal submission. Berra called Williams's pitch selection at the plate his "ultimate prerogative," a nifty phrase for a man whose love for words skirted perilously close to what those words didn't mean.

To get a good pitch was not merely to wait for a pitch you liked, though that entered into it on some at-bats. More subtly, it was to put the pitcher in a position where he could not raise the odds of getting you out by throwing the pitch *he* liked. Williams always believed that the advantage lay with the pitcher because the pitch dictated the swing and because, under even ideal conditions, hitting a baseball was so frustratingly difficult.

What Williams tried to do with pitchers who faced him over and again, and who were savvy about it, was to put himself in position to hit pitches that were the result of marginal pitching errors. Williams wanted to close the gap between the mistakes he allowed a pitcher and the mistakes he would smash. He was convinced that most major league pitchers with experience had an actual and statistical advantage over the hitter. Three out of ten times, even with good hitters, they would win the struggle by merely showing up. The odds against a perfect swing were too high; the calculated or fortunate positioning of the defense took away too many potential hits; the antagonism of the elements—wind, sun, lights—figured against the hitter to a greater extent than against the pitcher. The aches and pains of a long season took their toll on the hitting reflexes.

If a pitcher was on, if his ball was moving, if he was consistently putting pitches in zones where it was simply more difficult to make proper bat contact, or if conditions were poor, the hitter found it almost impossible to do the thing he must do: get a good pitch to hit. Williams was ready to waive on the percentages—take your 1 for 4 on the day, consider yourself lucky, and hope the next game's pitcher will be a bit off. But never, if you can avoid it, give the pitcher an advantage beyond those he already has.

Williams always set himself the same distance from the plate in the batter's box. He wanted to know exactly where every pitch was in relation to his strike zone. In certain instances, he would move up or back, but never in or out. Strikes in parts of the hitting zone were difficult enough to hit; he would not swing at balls. Herein lay the longest-running controversy of his career. Perhaps it began that memorable day in 1939, his rookie season, when he hit one clear out of Briggs Stadium.

Rudy York, catching that day for the Tigers, recalled the game: "The first time I caught him in Detroit I noticed how he took pitches that were just off the plate. Not by much. Maybe an inch. And yet he took them without the least doubt in his mind. I went home that night and looked up his record in Minnesota." York knew that impatience was fatal for most hitters. Only those who made a special living as bad-ball hitters—in later decades, Yogi Berra or Roberto Clemente—spooked pitchers who counted on the edge they usually gained by a hitter's impatience. Williams said that "giving the pitcher an extra two inches around the strike zone increases the area of the strike zone 35 percent. Don't believe it? Give a major league pitcher that kind of advantage and he'll murder you."

Al Kaline described Williams with an unusual phrase, a ballplayer's phrase: "Williams had a great strike zone." More important, he sensed that pitchers and catchers assumed as much. The moves they made to compensate for Williams's ingrained selectivity ended up benefiting him. Pitchers who faced him learned soon enough they would have to throw strikes to get him out or he would take the walk. "A great hitter should walk three times for every strikeout," Williams said. If not, he's swinging too often at the pitcher's pitch.

If a pitcher was proficient at throwing tough strikes, Williams would try to work the count until he saw a strike he could hit with more authority. He figured it was strategically undesirable to walk him every time. The pitcher's pride also came into play. Some pitchers simply did not like to give walks for free again and again. It made them look bad. At some point a major league pitcher wants his go at getting any hitter—even a .400 hitter—on strikes or on a feeble pop or on a double-play ball. He is not in the big leagues to give in.

There is another important variable in Williams's commitment to the hittable pitch. Over the course of time pitchers knew that if they were going to throw what they considered a good strike to Williams—one in a tough hitting zone—they had little margin for error. As a result, they worked with a special fineness. There is a risk for pitchers working too fine: they lose that extra bit of confidence a wider margin for error brings, and they end up putting more pitches exactly where they would prefer not to put them. Williams's refusal to swing at pitches difficult to hit gave him many more opportunities to swing at pitches he could hit. Further, he saw more pitches every at-bat because he would not nibble at fine pitches just outside the strike zone. He consequently hit with the counts against him strung out. A strung-out count means that a pitcher is more likely to come in with a hittable pitch. All hitters know this, or they *ought* to know it.

The most stinging charge against Williams by baseball writers and by some players was that he was too measured and too predictable a hitter. He would have done better to hack away every once in a while at a pitch off the plate or out of a preordained hitting zone. The Red Sox needed him to drive in runs, and if pitchers knew they could limit the damage by avoiding the strike zone, they accommodated what they figured were better long-run odds of walking him.

Those who criticized Williams for taking too many walks and too many close pitches rarely understood the full effect of his patience at the plate. For every run batted in he may have missed by refusing to swing at a pitch early in the count or just outside the strike zone late in the count, there were scores of runs batted in on decent pitches because the pitcher—still trying to get him out—knew the futility of throwing him bad ones.

It seems so simple to say, as players often did, that a great hitter picks his moments and varies his approach. Dom DiMaggio said it in comparing Williams to his brother: "Joe would swing at a bad pitch if the situation called for it. Not Ted, who was always the perfectionist." Dominic implied that the situation sometimes called for it. Jim Hegan, the great defensive catcher for the Indians, said the same thing: "Joe DiMaggio was more dangerous than Williams with men on base. Williams will take a ball or balls with men on even if the pitch is just a fraction of an inch off the plate." The *Globe* writer Jerry Nason was more colorful on the same subject: "There's too much artist in him. Ted would no more think of taking out after a bad pitch than Picasso would think of framing and exhibiting the rag on which he wipes his brushes." (Actually, if Picasso wouldn't think of it, his friends and heirs surely would.)

But Williams replied that no hitter gains an advantage by doing something on a Friday that he wouldn't do on a Tuesday. If pitchers know they can put the ball just off a corner of the plate outside the strike zone and get hitters to swing, they will find ways to do so exclusively. If a hitter begins swinging at balls off the plate, those pitches begin to look as if they are in his hitting zone. That is precisely what the pitcher wants them to look like. Williams said it this way in *The Science of Hitting*: "As soon as you start going for the pitch that's one or two inches off the plate, you've automatically widened the strike zone for the pitcher. Pitchers like Eddie Lopat and Ned Garver will start pitching a little farther out of the strike zone. Before you know it, you're swinging at pitches three or four inches off. Where does it end? You're playing right down the pitcher's alley, and you wind up hitting .250 instead of .450."

There is even more to it. Hitters coach the umpires by their hitting style. Williams earned close calls because the umpires over hundreds of at-bats knew he knew the strike zone. This could be frustrating to pitchers. Bobby Shantz said that he consistently put curves on the low outside corner of the plate—the toughest pitch for Williams to hit, even over the strike zone—at which Williams and the ump would just stare with scarcely a movement between them. "I thought they caught the corner," Shantz complained, "but the ump figured it had to be a ball."

One answer to those who claimed Williams should have cut more often at marginal pitches is statistical. And Williams would always point to a number that proved him right in his own mind: his ratio of at-bats to runs batted in, calculated as an average, was .239 to DiMaggio's .225. Williams was ready with this sort of information because he saw the charge of his selectivity as going to the heart of his approach to team play in baseball. When he protested, as he always did—"I couldn't have helped the team any more than I have; I know that in my heart"—he meant that getting the pitch he wanted to hit was the best contribution he could have made to the success of the Boston Red Sox.

Williams's second cardinal rule—proper thinking—touched upon much encompassed by his first rule—getting a good pitch to hit. But it also involved the rigorous mental discipline prior to the instantaneous response at the plate that made a great hitter great. One of the true strengths of Williams as a hitter was that he thought about his turns at bat all the time. Every at-bat was both memorial and anticipatory. Sometimes he would have to wait one turn to make sense of a pitcher, sometimes a turn around the league, sometimes a turn of seasons. But he knew that turns were the name of the game, and his notion of hitting was to refine *his* at-bats into a fine science. Ted Lepcio said of Williams that he would walk down the bench after a fly out or ground out and ask the rest of the Red Sox about his swing. In a way, he already knew the answer but wanted another perspective, another angle. "I was honest," said Lepcio, "and told him the truth—I think that's what he liked about me—I told him when he had a lousy swing. Even he had some. Well, some. Not many."

Williams had little truck with the natural hitter, the unthinking hitter, and nothing drove him crazier than to talk with those whom he figured could improve just by giving a moment's thought to what they were doing. Mickey Mantle remembers the first conversation he ever had with Williams about hitting: "You're a switch hitter, Mantle, so which hand do you grip the bat with and which hand do you guide it with?" A young Mantle looked puzzled: "How the hell do I know?" Williams was just warming up: "Pay attention. You gotta grip the bat with one hand and guide it with the other, see?" Mantle was neither humble nor absorbed: "I gotta do this? Shit, I won't get a hit for two weeks." By the time Williams was done Mantle said he "didn't know which end was up." Mantle, who just shattered whatever air molecules happened to get in the way of his swings, said that Williams got him "crazy just thinking about it."

Memory, recall, the very physics of the swing—all were essential for Williams as a hitter. The more he knew, the better he guessed. Williams always acknowledged the importance of guess hitting because the reaction time at bat was so short on a pitched ball— sometimes a quarter of a second—that a hitter was lost without some notion of what he was likely to see and where. Dennis Galehouse remembers a game at Boston, when he pitched for St. Louis, in which he got Williams on a "mediocre fastball down the middle which he took for a called third strike. That evening we were out to a Kiwanis dinner meeting and rode in the same car. He questioned me about the pitch, noting that I had done something different which made him think it would be a curve low and in. That was how observant he was. Of course I could never come at him like that again with two strikes on him."

Williams insisted that an intelligent guess at the plate was not an option so much as a necessity. It enabled the hitter to cut down the pitcher's natural advantage. In taking his sign and spotting his delivery, the pitcher had something even better than a guess—he had an idea he could carry out if properly executed. A hitter's mode was inevitably reactive, but a good guess could cancel the effectiveness of a particular pitch, and even, in some lucky circumstances, make the pitcher's pitch into the hitter's pitch.

When Williams managed he used to ask his hitters to imagine pitching to themselves. How would they do it? What kind of patterns and sequences would they set up? What would they consider an out pitch? "You gotta learn something about pitching," he told his players, "if you're ever going to learn something about hitting." So his big first baseman, Mike Epstein, asked him, "Okay, how would you pitch Ted Williams?" Williams was quick with an answer: "I'd pitch him down. I wouldn't give him the same pitch twice in a row. I'd give him more breaking balls than fast balls, and I'd change my delivery just a little so he couldn't zero in on that window all the time."

Throughout his career, Williams had a consistently high respect for the skill, if not the intelligence, of pitchers, and not only for the ones he considered toughest for him—Feller, Newhouser, Trout, Trucks, Ford, Lemon, Lopat, Raschi, Reynolds—but even for rookies he had never seen. Ray Boone, an old friend and ex-teammate, said that when Williams would ask about rookies coming into the league he would pursue any compliment, such as "the kid's got a good curve," with a host of qualifying questions. ("Like Brewer's curve?") And if the comments were negative, he would ask someone else until he got a more challenging answer. He never denigrated an opposing pitcher the way he would do the press; he rarely walked back from an out saying that rag arm couldn't break a dish, that he's got nothing, that his curve wasn't worth a plugged nickel.

Williams's generosity to pitchers certainly belied his reputation as an overbearing and undergiving ballplayer. But always with an agenda. He wanted reasons to bear down, to play focused, and, if need be, play scared. To build up the challenge that faced him as a hitter was one way to increase the intensity of his response. Mickey Vernon remembers one Williams at-bat against the Yankees when

Stengel brought in Tommy Byrne to pitch to Ted with the bases loaded. Williams gestured to Vernon, who was on deck, to come with him near the batter's box to gauge Byrne's pitches. He wanted a quick consult. Byrne figured he'd show the two of them what they came to see. So he fired his first warm-up pitch right at them. Low bridge. Williams looked at Vernon with fire in his eye, squeezed his bat handle, stepped in to hit, and shot one on a line right through the box for the winning hit of the ball game.

Obviously, Williams's open admiration for the talent of major league pitchers did not dissuade him from the challenge of hitting them. He counted on the fact that he could consistently outthink a pitcher, and he would begin as he walked into the batter's box. Tommy Byrne recalled his encounters with Williams: "He came up to the plate like he was the only man in town. He wouldn't breathe until everything was all right." Byrne would try to engage him: "What're you hittin'?" Silence from Williams. "Don't you know, Ted?" Byrne persisted. Williams wouldn't lose concentration: "Just throw the ball." Pitchers were often amusing on the subject of Williams at the plate. They gave themselves little chance of outfoxing him. Billy Pierce spoke for most: "I hope for minimum damage." Virgil Trucks described his "out" pitch for Ted: "I throw it behind his back."

When Williams walked into the box he remembered virtually every time he had hit against the pitcher he was facing. He thought his powers of concentration better, and he thought the reactive mode of the hitter less arrogant than the creative control of the pitcher, whose patterns or sequences were susceptible to discovery and anticipation. "Most pitchers," Williams wrote in *The Science of Hitting,* "are hardheaded enough not to realize you have figured them out." For Williams, to have figured out a pitcher did not mean a pitcher couldn't get him out; it simply meant that he would get a productive swing from a productive guess a healthy percentage of the time: "You can't outsmart the pitch," he said, "but you can outsmart the pitcher."

Preparation and a sense of history are the prelude to guesswork at the plate. "Guessing is thinking," Williams insisted. When he had a miserable World Series against the Cardinals in 1946, he guessed badly on a preponderance of at-bats. For one thing, he had no history on their pitchers, especially Harry the Cat Brecheen; and for another, the Cardinals planned their approach to him by understanding the principles upon which he planned his approach to them. Eddie Dyer, the Cardinals' manager, neutralized Williams's anticipation at the plate by adapting a strategy that had a chance of working in a short series. He instructed his pitching staff to think about likely pitches to throw Williams in certain situations and then to throw the exact opposite pitch: curveballs behind in the count and fastballs in his zone ahead of the count. Williams, Dyer figured, would assume pitchers with little firsthand experience against him would pitch by the book. But they most militantly wouldn't. Dyer and the Cards figured right. They shut Williams down.

For Williams, guessing well took time; for the most part, baseball provided it. Thinking and guessing at the plate got easier over longer sequences. But even at the microlevel of the game Williams would try to buy time for thought; he would try to stretch out an at-bat. Rarely would he swing at a first pitch on his first at-bat of the day. Too much was at stake—the pitcher's rhythm; his release point; the rotation, movement, speed of the ball. "You figure to face a pitcher at least three or four times in a game. The more information you log the first time up, the better your chances the next three. The more you make him pitch, the more information you get."

Mike Epstein recalls popping out one day on the first pitch his first time up when he played for Williams on the Senators. "No, no, no," Williams greeted him in the dugout. "You must be stupid. Why did you swing at that pitch?" "Because it looked good," said Epstein. "But you missed the chance to get a real look. The first strike is not important. Try to learn something on the first strike your first time up, maybe even your first two times up. The third time the pitcher will guess you're taking and slip one in fat. Then you pounce."

The greatest challenge to Williams as a guess hitter occurred in 1946 with the Lou Boudreau shift. The disposition of so many fielders on the right side of the diamond changed the nature and effectiveness of Williams's thinking at the plate. In a sense, it could be argued that Boudreau was eliminating the need for Williams to guess, and consequently the advantage he gained from guessing. It was clear that Boudreau was giving Williams the outside hitting lane if he wanted it and instructing his pitchers to give him balls he could pull into the teeth of the shift. Boudreau would take his chances with home runs, and he would force Williams to alter his swing to go to left. Further, Boudreau knew that Williams's bat speed even enabled him to swing naturally on an outside pitch and take it up the middle or up the middle deep. The middle was therefore clogged in the shift he put on.

Williams, it seemed, was at an impasse. Of course Ty Cobb and Paul Waner were telling him almost immediately to adjust his position in the box and to adjust the arc of his swing. But he wouldn't hear of it, and here was a second major controversy about the clash between his theory of hitting and the virtue of team play. Again, Williams's position turned on what he thought was the necessary preparation for a productive at-bat. When he disturbed the natural arc of his swing through the zone he disturbed the advantage he derived from anticipating and guessing the pitch and its location. He never was as severe a pull hitter as some thought, because that would have involved taking some pitches where nature and physics never intended them to go. But under no conditions would he become a spray hitter.

One day in spring training of 1951 he was arguing with Eddie Mayo about repositioning his feet in the box. "No," said Williams. "You can hit the ball wherever you want by changing the position of your hands and the arc of the swing." "Impossible," said Mayo. "Cobb said that, too," Williams returned, "but Hornsby, Ruth, Simmons all agree with me. The hands adjust, not the feet. Here, look." Then he proceeded to spray hit all over the place, no matter where the pitch was. Harold Kaese, who witnessed the exchange and demonstration, said it was the most stunning exhibition of bat control he had ever seen. But then Williams told Mayo: "Yeah, but this is not the way to do it for me. It's not my best swing."

Williams tried to beat the shift by sticking with his theory of hitting: he would keep guessing location and drive balls as deep and as high as he could, with that degree of underspin necessary for distance. Teams had always played him with an outfield shift of sorts—it was the array of infielders Boudreau realigned—and Williams would continue to look for balls he could drive. Ultimately, Williams's position on the shift was the same as that on selectivity at the plate. The thinking hitter does not cave in. It was as unwise to alter the structure of the swing through the hitting zone as it was consistently to hit the pitcher's pitch. Both assumed a defensive posture in the struggle with the pitcher that constituted the essence of the game.

Williams's third cardinal rule was the toughest of all: be quick. A hitter could select his pitches with the gusto of an art critic; he could think his way through the theory of relativity; but if he could not whip his bat through the hitting zone, forget it! The quickness of the swing was the grace beyond the reach of art. But there were swing mechanics that could help, and, insofar as Williams's own use of the word *science* applied to his principles, he hammered away all his life on the mechanics of the swing to ensure its speed. Foot positioning, bat weight, arm strength, hip rotation, wrist rolling (never before bat contact) all entered in. So, too, did certain strategies to gain more bat speed at appropriate times. For example, Williams argued that a hitter can choke up slightly with two strikes, cut down the arc of the swing, gain better bat control, and do his team a service. Why a hitter would not do so was a mystery to him. He did, and he hit hundreds of two-strike home runs in the bargain.

Most of his advice to ballplayers over the years centered on generating bat speed—at least as much of it as they were capable. Those who listened heard the same things: face the bat label down to avoid distraction on the swing; place the feet the same distance from the plate on every swing; cock the elbow; wait on the swing until the eyes, at the last second, okay the cut; generate bat speed from the pivot, butt following hips; hit within a 15 degree tolerance either side of the right angle that the bat forms with the plate on the swing; roll the wrists after contact with the ball; keep the top hand on the bat through the swing.

When Williams wrote about the modern ballplayer he detailed a litany of complaints, all centering on his three rules. Hitting in the majors was in danger of becoming a lost science, if not a lost art.

> They don't protect themselves with two strikes—they don't shorten up with the bat, they don't think about hitting through the box, getting wood on the ball. They're still up there swinging from their rear end. They think about that big, powerful swing, but not about being quick with the bat. They don't do their homework— on the pitcher, on the situation, on the game. They're not selective.

They swing at bad pitches, and that's the first rule in the book: *Get a good ball to hit*. Most of all, they don't have any idea what that little game between pitcher and hitter is about.

Even after all the rules were laid down and all the rules were heeded or broken, there was something else. There would have been a fourth cardinal rule if Williams could have figured a way to describe it. That rule would not and could not have been framed as a theory. It was a matter of soul. And it was not explicable; it could only be felt. George Kell, who had beaten Williams in the batting race in 1949 and later played with him in Boston, interviewed Ted for a Chicago television station in 1958. They were trying to name the precise difference between a good hitter and a great hitter. Kell said the great hitter is the one "who goes three for three in a ball game and then wants the fourth hit so bad he can taste it." "That's it," said Williams, "that's it for sure." That same year Williams ran into Tommy Henrich, and the two disagreed on the roll of the wrists in the swing. "We argued for a few minutes," Williams remembered, "and then I said, 'Hell, you got to have it right here,' and I pointed to the heart."

◊ Appendix B ◊
Playing by the Numbers

COMMON LORE HOLDS THAT a calmer Williams in a town less hostile than Boston—which suffers from, as Henry Adams put it, chronic irritability or "Bostonitis"—would have done much better. But it's doubtful.

Many who remember Williams and many who write about him ask the wrong questions—those beginning with "what if?"—or surmise the wrong surmises—those beginning "if only!": What if he played for the Yankees? If only his career were not interrupted by service in the nation's wars or by injury. The better questions and surmises are actual, not putative. How did he hit? How did he hit in the various ballparks around the league?

The seasonal résumés in this appendix answer the basic questions season by season and month by month.

CAREER TOTALS

	G	AB	H	HR	R	RBI	BB	SO	Avg	Slug- ging Avg
1939	149	565	185	31	131	145	107	64	.327	.609
1940	144	561	193	23	134	113	96	54	.344	.594
1941	143	456	185	37	135	120	145	27	.406	.735
1942	150	522	186	36	141	137	145	51	.356	.648
1946	150	514	176	38	142	123	156	44	.342	.667
1947	156	528	181	32	125	114	162	47	.343	.634
1948	137	509	188	25	124	127	126	41	.369	.615
1949	155	566	194	43	150	159	162	48	.343	.650

351

	G	AB	H	HR	R	RBI	BB	SO	Avg	Slug-ging Avg
1950	89	334	106	28	82	97	82	21	.317	.647
1951	148	531	169	30	109	126	**144**	45	.318	**.556**
1952	6	10	4	1	2	3	2	2	.400	.900
1953	37	91	37	13	17	34	19	10	.407	.901
1954	117	386	133	29	93	89	**136**	32	.345	**.635**
1955	98	320	114	28	77	83	91	24	.356	.703
1956	136	400	138	24	71	82	102	39	.345	.605
1957	132	420	163	38	96	87	119	43	**.388**	**.731**
1958	129	411	135	26	81	85	98	49	**.328**	.584
1959	103	272	69	10	32	43	52	27	.254	.419
1960	113	310	98	29	56	72	75	41	.316	.645
Career	2,292	7,706	2,654	521	1,798	1,839	2,019	709	.344	.634

*League-leading totals in boldface

The tables below chart Williams's career performance against individual teams on the road and at Fenway Park. During some of his abbreviated seasons he did not play in one or another city, and there were two franchise moves, the St. Louis Browns to Baltimore in 1954 and the Philadephia A's to Kansas City in 1955. The teams are listed in descending order of Williams's highest combined (home and away) career batting averages against them. Career totals appear in **bold-face** at the end of each listing.

VERSUS ST. LOUIS BROWNS   1939–1953

		G	AB	H	HR	RBI	Avg
1939	At St. Louis	11	50	20	4	23	.400
	At Fenway	11	41	12	1	9	.293
	On Year	22	91	32	5	32	.352
1940	At St. Louis	11	44	17	2	6	.386
	At Fenway	11	45	12	1	7	.267
	On Year	22	89	29	3	13	.326
	Totals						
	At St. Louis	22	94	37	6	29	.394

		G	AB	H	HR	RBI	Avg
	At Fenway	22	86	24	2	16	.279
	2 Years	44	180	61	8	45	.339
1941	At St. Louis	10	28	13	7	15	.464
	At Fenway	11	33	13	2	11	.394
	On Year	21	61	26	9	26	.426
	Totals						
	At St. Louis	32	122	50	13	44	.410
	At Fenway	33	119	37	4	27	.311
	3 Years	65	241	87	17	71	.361
1942	At St. Louis	11	34	16	4	8	.471
	At Fenway	11	41	18	2	15	.439
	On Year	22	75	34	6	23	.453
	Totals						
	At St. Louis	43	156	66	17	52	.423
	At Fenway	44	160	55	6	42	.344
	4 Years	87	316	121	23	94	.383
1946	At St. Louis	9	25	7	1	5	.280
	At Fenway	12	47	27	4	13	.574
	On Year	21	72	34	5	18	.472
	Totals						
	At St. Louis	52	181	73	18	57	.403
	At Fenway	56	207	82	10	55	.396
	5 Years	108	388	155	28	112	.399
1947	At St. Louis	10	34	17	5	14	.500
	At Fenway	12	48	22	6	19	.458
	On Year	22	82	39	11	33	.476
	Totals						
	At St. Louis	62	215	90	23	71	.419
	At Fenway	68	255	104	16	74	.408
	6 Years	130	470	194	39	145	.413
1948	At St. Louis	11	42	19	2	9	.452
	At Fenway	7	20	7	2	4	.350
	On Year	18	62	26	4	13	.419

		G	AB	H	HR	RBI	Avg
	Totals						
	At St. Louis	73	257	109	25	80	.424
	At Fenway	75	275	111	18	78	.404
	7 Years	148	532	220	43	158	.414
1949	At St. Louis	11	41	15	4	11	.366
	At Fenway	11	38	13	2	15	.342
	On Year	22	79	28	6	26	.354
	Totals						
	At St. Louis	84	298	124	29	91	.416
	At Fenway	86	313	124	20	93	.396
	8 Years	170	611	248	49	184	.406
1950	At St. Louis	9	38	15	2	11	.395
	At Fenway	5	22	9	4	12	.409
	On Year	14	60	24	6	23	.400
	Totals						
	At St. Louis	93	336	139	31	102	.414
	At Fenway	91	335	133	24	105	.397
	9 Years	184	671	272	55	207	.405
1951	At St. Louis	11	40	11	2	5	.275
	At Fenway	11	34	13	3	11	.382
	On Year	22	74	24	5	16	.324
	Totals						
	At St. Louis	104	376	150	33	107	.399
	At Fenway	102	369	146	27	116	.396
	10 Years	206	745	296	60	223	.397
1952	At St. Louis	—					
	At Fenway	—					
1953	At St. Louis	—					
	At Fenway	3	9	0	0	0	.000
Career Totals							
	At St. Louis	104	376	150	33	107	.399
	At Fenway	105	378	146	27	116	.386
	12 Years	209	754	296	60	223	.393

VERSUS KANSAS CITY A's 1955-1960

		G	AB	H	HR	RBI	Avg
1955	At Kansas City	7	29	12	2	4	.414
	At Fenway	8	29	14	2	8	.483
	On Year	15	58	26	4	12	.448
1956	At Kansas City	9	34	13	4	9	.382
	At Fenway	11	27	8	2	4	.296
	On Year	20	61	21	6	13	.344
	Totals						
	At Kansas City	16	63	25	6	13	.397
	At Fenway	19	56	22	4	12	.393
	2 Years	35	119	47	10	25	.395
1957	At Kansas City	10	32	13	4	6	.406
	At Fenway	11	28	13	3	6	.464
	On Year	21	60	26	7	12	.433
	Totals						
	At Kansas City	26	95	38	10	19	.400
	At Fenway	30	84	35	7	18	.417
	3 Years	56	179	73	17	37	.408
1958	At Kansas City	10	36	14	2	7	.389
	At Fenway	9	30	9	2	9	.300
	On Year	19	66	23	4	16	.348
	Totals						
	At Kansas City	36	131	52	12	26	.397
	At Fenway	39	114	44	9	27	.386
	4 Years	75	245	96	21	53	.392
1959	At Kansas City	9	22	6	1	5	.273
	At Fenway	9	25	6	0	1	.240
	On Year	18	47	12	1	6	.255
	Totals						
	At Kansas City	45	153	58	13	31	.379
	At Fenway	48	139	50	9	28	.360
	5 Years	93	292	108	22	59	.370

		G	AB	H	HR	RBI	Avg
1960	At Kansas City	7	26	7	2	6	.269
	At Fenway	6	13	5	1	7	.385
	On Year	13	39	12	3	13	.308
Career Totals							
	At Kansas City	52	179	65	15	37	.363
	At Fenway	54	152	55	10	35	.362
	6 Years	106	331	120	25	72	.363

VERSUS PHILADELPHIA A's 1939–1954

		G	AB	H	HR	RBI	Avg
1939	At Philadelphia	10	37	16	3	9	.432
	At Fenway	12	51	25	3	15	.490
	On Year	22	88	41	6	24	.466
1940	At Philadelphia	9	42	16	2	10	.381
	At Fenway	13	48	17	2	13	.354
	On Year	22	90	33	4	23	.367
	Totals						
	At Philadelphia	19	79	32	5	19	.405
	At Fenway	25	99	42	5	28	.424
	2 Years	44	178	74	10	47	.416
1941	At Philadelphia	10	35	15	4	11	.429
	At Fenway	9	28	13	4	11	.464
	On Year	19	63	28	8	22	.444
	Totals						
	At Philadelphia	29	114	47	9	30	.412
	At Fenway	34	127	55	9	39	.433
	3 Years	63	241	102	18	69	.423
1942	At Philadelphia	11	40	10	4	14	.250
	At Fenway	11	35	11	6	15	.314
	On Year	22	75	21	10	29	.280
	Totals						
	At Philadelphia	40	154	57	13	44	.370

		G	AB	H	HR	RBI	Avg
	At Fenway	45	162	66	15	54	.407
	4 Years	85	316	123	28	98	.389
1946	At Philadelphia	11	41	14	3	9	.341
	At Fenway	9	29	5	0	4	.172
	On Year	20	70	19	3	13	.271
	Totals						
	At Philadelphia	51	195	71	16	53	.364
	At Fenway	54	191	71	15	58	.372
	5 Years	105	386	142	31	111	.368
1947	At Philadelphia	10	34	10	5	10	.294
	At Fenway	12	35	12	4	12	.343
	On Year	22	69	22	9	22	.319
	Totals						
	At Philadelphia	61	229	81	21	63	.354
	At Fenway	66	226	83	19	70	.367
	6 Years	127	455	164	40	133	.360
1948	At Philadelphia	7	27	10	1	4	.370
	At Fenway	11	39	14	0	3	.359
	On Year	18	66	24	1	7	.364
	Totals						
	At Philadelphia	68	256	91	22	67	.355
	At Fenway	77	265	97	19	73	.366
	7 Years	145	521	188	41	140	.361
1949	At Philadelphia	11	41	15	1	6	.366
	At Fenway	11	35	11	4	14	.314
	On Year	22	76	26	·5	20	.342
	Totals						
	At Philadelphia	79	297	106	23	73	.357
	At Fenway	88	300	108	23	87	.360
	8 Years	167	597	214	46	160	.358
1950	At Philadelphia	5	22	8	3	11	.364
	At Fenway	3	9	5	2	7	.556
	On Year	8	31	13	5	18	.419

		G	AB	H	HR	RBI	Avg
	Totals						
	At Philadelphia	84	319	114	26	84	.357
	At Fenway	91	309	113	25	94	.366
	9 Years	175	628	227	51	178	.361
1951	At Philadelphia	13	48	14	4	12	.292
	At Fenway	9	31	12	3	12	.387
	On Year	22	79	26	7	24	.329
	Totals						
	At Philadelphia	97	367	128	30	96	.349
	At Fenway	100	340	125	28	106	.368
	10 Years	197	707	253	58	202	.358
1952	At Philadelphia	—					
	At Fenway	1	1	0	0	0	.000
	Totals						
	At Philadelphia	97	367	128	30	96	.349
	At Fenway	101	341	125	28	106	.367
	11 Years	198	708	253	58	202	.357
1953	At Philadelphia	3	4	2	1	1	.500
	At Fenway	2	5	2	1	2	.400
	On Year	5	9	4	2	3	.444
	Totals						
	At Philadelphia	100	371	130	31	97	.350
	At Fenway	103	346	127	29	108	.367
	12 Years	203	717	257	60	205	.358
1954	At Philadelphia	10	34	13	3	10	.382
	At Fenway	9	29	12	2	7	.414
	On Year	19	63	25	5	17	.397
Career Totals							
	At Philadelphia	110	405	143	34	107	.353
	At Fenway	112	375	139	31	115	.371
	13 Years	222	780	282	65	222	.362

VERSUS WASHINGTON SENATORS   1939–1960

		G	AB	H	HR	RBI	Avg
1939	At Washington	9	38	2	1	5	.053
	At Fenway	11	43	19	3	12	.442
	On Year	20	81	21	4	17	.259
1940	At Washington	8	32	13	1	5	.406
	At Fenway	11	44	14	2	13	.318
	On Year	19	76	27	3	18	.355
	Totals						
	At Washington	17	70	15	2	10	.214
	At Fenway	22	87	33	5	25	.379
	2 Years	39	157	48	7	35	.306
1941	At Washington	11	32	9	0	3	.281
	At Fenway	11	31	15	3	10	.484
	On Year	22	63	24	3	13	.381
	Totals						
	At Washington	28	102	24	2	13	.235
	At Fenway	33	118	48	8	35	.407
	3 Years	61	220	72	10	48	.327
1942	At Washington	10	38	17	0	7	.447
	At Fenway	11	35	18	1	7	.514
	On Year	21	73	35	1	14	.479
	Totals						
	At Washington	38	140	41	2	20	.293
	At Fenway	44	153	66	9	42	.431
	4 Years	82	293	107	11	62	.365
1946	At Washington	11	35	14	2	9	.400
	At Fenway	11	37	14	2	10	.378
	On Year	22	72	28	4	19	.389
	Totals						
	At Washington	49	175	55	4	29	.314
	At Fenway	55	190	80	11	52	.421
	5 Years	104	365	135	15	81	.370

		G	AB	H	HR	RBI	Avg
1947	At Washington	11	37	13	2	6	.351
	At Fenway	11	38	16	0	8	.421
	On Year	22	75	29	2	14	.387
	Totals						
	At Washington	60	212	68	6	35	.321
	At Fenway	66	228	96	11	60	.421
	6 Years	126	440	164	17	95	.373
1948	At Washington	12	50	18	3	8	.360
	At Fenway	11	37	11	1	3	.297
	On Year	23	87	29	4	11	.333
	Totals						
	At Washington	72	262	86	9	43	.328
	At Fenway	77	265	107	12	63	.404
	7 Years	149	527	193	21	106	.366
1949	At Washington	11	33	9	0	5	.273
	At Fenway	14	51	17	2	9	.333
	On Year	25	84	26	2	14	.310
	Totals						
	At Washington	83	295	95	9	48	.322
	At Fenway	91	316	124	14	72	.392
	8 Years	174	611	219	23	120	.358
1950	At Washington	3	14	4	0	1	.286
	At Fenway	9	33	7	1	5	.212
	On Year	12	47	11	1	6	.234
	Totals						
	At Washington	86	309	99	9	49	.320
	At Fenway	100	349	131	15	77	.375
	9 Years	186	658	230	24	126	.350
1951	At Washington	11	44	10	2	10	.227
	At Fenway	9	34	17	3	14	.500
	On Year	20	78	27	5	24	.346
	Totals						
	At Washington	97	353	109	11	59	.309

		G	AB	H	HR	RBI	Avg
	At Fenway	109	383	148	18	91	.386
	10 Years	206	736	257	29	150	.349
1952	At Washington	2	4	1	0	0	.250
	At Fenway	2	2	1	0	1	.500
	On Year	4	6	2	0	1	.333
	Totals						
	At Washington	99	357	110	11	59	.308
	At Fenway	111	385	149	18	92	.387
	11 Years	210	742	259	29	151	.349
1953	At Washington	5	12	7	2	7	.583
	At Fenway	3	4	2	1	1	.500
	On Year	8	16	9	3	8	.563
	Totals						
	At Washington	104	369	117	13	66	.317
	At Fenway	114	389	151	19	93	.388
	12 Years	218	758	268	32	159	.354
1954	At Washington	8	28	7	0	4	.250
	At Fenway	9	29	13	3	6	.448
	On Year	17	57	20	3	10	.351
	Totals						
	At Washington	112	397	124	13	70	.312
	At Fenway	123	418	164	22	99	.392
	13 Years	235	815	288	35	169	.353
1955	At Washington	3	10	3	1	2	.300
	At Fenway	10	37	16	2	8	.432
	On Year	13	47	19	3	10	.404
	Totals						
	At Washington	115	407	127	14	72	.312
	At Fenway	133	455	180	24	107	.396
	14 Years	248	862	307	38	179	.356
1956	At Washington	9	29	11	2	2	.379
	At Fenway	10	22	9	3	11	.409
	On Year	19	51	20	5	13	.392

		G	AB	H	HR	RBI	Avg
	Totals						
	At Washington	124	436	138	16	74	.317
	At Fenway	143	477	189	27	118	.396
	15 Years	267	913	327	43	192	.358
1957	At Washington	10	29	13	3	7	.448
	At Fenway	9	28	6	0	3	.214
	On Year	19	57	19	3	10	.333
	Totals						
	At Washington	134	465	151	19	81	.325
	At Fenway	152	505	195	27	121	.386
	16 Years	286	970	346	46	202	.357
1958	At Washington	9	28	11	3	7	.393
	At Fenway	11	32	12	5	14	.375
	On Year	20	60	23	8	21	.383
	Totals						
	At Washington	143	493	162	22	88	.329
	At Fenway	163	537	207	32	135	.385
	17 Years	306	1,030	369	54	223	.358
1959	At Washington	5	19	3	0	0	.158
	At Fenway	6	16	5	0	3	.313
	On Year	11	35	8	0	3	.229
	Totals						
	At Washington	148	512	165	22	88	.322
	At Fenway	169	553	212	32	138	.383
	18 Years	317	1,065	377	54	226	.354
1960	At Washington	8	23	6	2	3	.261
	At Fenway	8	14	4	0	1	.286
	On Year	16	37	10	2	4	.270
Career Totals							
	At Washington	156	535	171	24	91	.320
	At Fenway	177	567	216	32	139	.381
	19 Years	333	1,102	387	56	230	.351

VERSUS NEW YORK YANKEES   1939-1960

		G	AB	H	HR	RBI	Avg
1939	At New York	9	30	10	1	5	.300
	At Fenway	9	30	11	5	12	.367
	On Year	18	60	21	6	17	.350
1940	At New York	11	36	11	4	9	.306
	At Fenway	8	32	13	2	5	.406
	On Year	19	68	24	6	14	.353
	Totals						
	At New York	20	66	21	5	14	.318
	At Fenway	17	62	24	7	17	.387
	2 Years	37	128	45	12	31	.352
1941	At New York	11	33	16	0	7	.485
	At Fenway	11	35	16	2	6	.457
	On Year	22	68	32	2	13	.471
	Totals						
	At New York	31	99	37	5	21	.374
	At Fenway	28	97	40	9	23	.412
	3 Years	59	196	77	14	44	.393
1942	At New York	11	38	12	4	9	.316
	At Fenway	11	39	11	2	7	.282
	On Year	22	77	23	6	16	.299
	Totals						
	At New York	42	137	49	9	30	.358
	At Fenway	39	136	51	11	30	.375
	4 Years	81	273	100	20	60	.366
1946	At New York	11	34	5	2	5	.147
	At Fenway	11	35	8	1	5	.229
	On Year	22	69	13	3	10	.188
	Totals						
	At New York	53	171	54	11	35	.316
	At Fenway	50	171	59	12	35	.345
	5 Years	103	342	113	23	70	.330

		G	AB	H	HR	RBI	Avg
1947	At New York	11	36	9	2	5	.250
	At Fenway	11	38	8	0	2	.211
	On Year	22	74	17	2	7	.230
	Totals						
	At New York	64	207	63	13	40	.304
	At Fenway	61	209	67	12	37	.321
	6 Years	125	416	130	25	77	.313
1948	At New York	11	41	13	3	9	.317
	At Fenway	11	42	16	2	21	.381
	On Year	22	83	29	5	30	.349
	Totals						
	At New York	75	248	76	16	49	.306
	At Fenway	72	251	83	14	58	.331
	7 Years	147	499	159	30	107	.319
1949	At New York	11	35	13	1	8	.371
	At Fenway	8	28	12	4	9	.429
	On Year	19	63	25	5	17	.397
	Totals						
	At New York	86	283	89	17	57	.314
	At Fenway	80	279	95	18	67	.341
	8 Years	166	562	184	35	124	.327
1950	At New York	8	28	7	3	6	.250
	At Fenway	10	31	13	1	10	.419
	On Year	18	59	20	4	16	.339
	Totals						
	At New York	94	311	96	20	63	.309
	At Fenway	90	310	108	19	77	.348
	9 Years	184	621	204	39	140	.329
1951	At New York	7	22	6	1	2	.273
	At Fenway	11	45	18	2	11	.400
	On Year	18	67	24	3	13	.358
	Totals						
	At New York	101	333	102	21	65	.306

		G	AB	H	HR	RBI	Avg
	At Fenway	101	355	126	21	88	.355
	10 Years	202	688	228	42	153	.331
1952	At New York	—					
	At Fenway	—					
1953	At New York	3	7	3	0	1	.429
	At Fenway	4	10	5	1	5	.500
	On Year	7	17	8	1	6	.471
	Totals						
	At New York	104	340	105	21	66	.309
	At Fenway	105	365	131	22	93	.359
	12 Years	209	705	236	43	159	.335
1954	At New York	10	33	14	1	7	.424
	At Fenway	9	24	9	2	8	.375
	On Year	19	57	23	3	15	.404
	Totals						
	At New York	114	373	119	22	73	.319
	At Fenway	114	389	140	24	101	.360
	13 Years	228	762	259	46	174	.340
1955	At New York	8	21	6	1	1	.286
	At Fenway	6	15	7	1	3	.467
	On Year	14	36	13	2	4	.361
	Totals						
	At New York	122	394	125	23	74	.317
	At Fenway	120	404	147	25	104	.364
	14 Years	242	798	272	48	178	.341
1956	At New York	10	29	6	0	1	.207
	At Fenway	10	27	5	1	5	.185
	On Year	20	56	11	1	6	.196
	Totals						
	At New York	132	423	131	23	75	.310
	At Fenway	130	431	152	26	109	.353
	15 Years	262	854	283	49	184	.331

		G	AB	H	HR	RBI	Avg
1957	At New York	9	21	7	3	7	.333
	At Fenway	11	32	17	3	6	.531
	On Year	20	53	24	6	13	.453
	Totals						
	At New York	141	444	138	26	82	.311
	At Fenway	141	463	169	29	115	.365
	16 Years	282	907	307	55	197	.338
1958	At New York	5	14	7	2	6	.500
	At Fenway	9	28	12	1	7	.429
	On Year	14	42	19	3	13	.452
	Totals						
	At New York	146	458	145	28	88	.317
	At Fenway	150	491	181	30	122	.369
	17 Years	296	949	326	58	210	.344
1959	At New York	7	11	2	0	0	.182
	At Fenway	7	20	10	1	8	.500
	On Year	14	31	12	1	8	.387
	Totals						
	At New York	153	469	147	28	88	.313
	At Fenway	157	511	191	31	130	.374
	18 Years	310	980	338	59	218	.345
1960	At New York	5	10	3	2	4	.300
	At Fenway	9	30	11	1	5	.367
	On Year	14	40	14	3	9	.350
Career Totals							
	At New York	158	479	150	30	92	.313
	At Fenway	166	541	202	32	135	.373
	19 Years	324	1,020	352	62	227	.345

VERSUS DETROIT TIGERS   1939–1960

		G	AB	H	HR	RBI	Avg
1939	At Detroit	11	44	14	4	14	.318

		G	AB	H	HR	RBI	Avg
	At Fenway	11	36	10	0	7	.278
	On Year	22	80	24	4	21	.300
1940	At Detroit	8	28	10	1	7	.357
	At Fenway	11	45	17	0	8	.378
	On Year	19	73	27	1	15	.370
	Totals						
	At Detroit	19	72	24	5	21	.333
	At Fenway	22	81	27	0	15	.333
	2 Years	41	153	51	5	36	.333
1941	At Detroit	10	38	13	3	10	.342
	At Fenway	11	36	12	2	9	.333
	On Year	21	74	25	5	19	.338
	Totals						
	At Detroit	29	110	37	8	31	.336
	At Fenway	33	117	39	2	24	.333
	3 Years	62	227	76	10	55	.335
1942	At Detroit	11	43	15	5	13	.349
	At Fenway	11	37	16	2	9	.432
	On Year	22	80	31	7	22	.388
	Totals						
	At Detroit	40	153	52	13	44	.340
	At Fenway	44	154	55	4	33	.357
	4 Years	84	307	107	17	77	.349
1946	At Detroit	11	38	18	6	11	.474
	At Fenway	11	39	12	4	10	.308
	On Year	22	77	30	10	21	.390
	Totals						
	At Detroit	51	191	70	19	55	.366
	At Fenway	55	193	67	8	43	.347
	5 Years	106	384	137	27	98	.357
1947	At Detroit	12	42	12	1	10	.286
	At Fenway	11	40	15	3	9	.375
	On Year	23	82	27	4	19	.329

		G	AB	H	HR	RBI	Avg
	Totals						
	At Detroit	63	233	82	20	65	.352
	At Fenway	66	233	82	11	52	.352
	6 Years	129	466	164	31	117	.352
1948	At Detroit	9	37	8	1	7	.216
	At Fenway	7	29	12	1	5	.414
	On Year	16	66	20	2	12	.303
	Totals						
	At Detroit	72	270	90	21	72	.333
	At Fenway	73	262	94	12	57	.359
	7 Years	145	532	184	33	129	.346
1949	At Detroit	12	50	17	6	17	.340
	At Fenway	13	53	17	5	10	.321
	On Year	25	103	34	11	27	.330
	Totals						
	At Detroit	84	320	107	27	89	.334
	At Fenway	86	315	111	17	67	.352
	8 Years	170	635	218	44	156	.343
1950	At Detroit	8	23	5	3	7	.217
	At Fenway	6	26	7	2	7	.269
	On Year	14	49	12	5	14	.245
	Totals						
	At Detroit	92	343	112	30	96	.327
	At Fenway	92	341	118	19	74	.346
	9 Years	184	684	230	49	170	.336
1951	At Detroit	11	37	7	1	5	.189
	At Fenway	11	39	12	1	7	.308
	On Year	22	76	19	2	12	.250
	Totals						
	At Detroit	103	380	119	31	101	.313
	At Fenway	103	380	130	20	81	.342
	10 Years	206	760	249	51	182	.328

		G	AB	H	HR	RBI	Avg
1952	At Detroit	—					
	At Fenway	1	3	2	1	2	.667
	On Year	1	3	2	1	2	.667
	Totals						
	At Detroit	103	380	119	31	101	.313
	At Fenway	104	383	132	21	83	.345
	11 Years	207	763	251	52	184	.329
1953	At Detroit	2	4	2	0	1	.500
	At Fenway	1	4	1	1	2	.250
	On Year	3	8	3	1	3	.375
	Totals						
	At Detroit	105	384	121	31	102	.315
	At Fenway	105	387	133	22	85	.344
	12 Years	210	771	254	53	187	.329
1954	At Detroit	8	30	13	4	13	.433
	At Fenway	8	28	6	1	3	.214
	On Year	16	58	19	5	16	.328
	Totals						
	At Detroit	113	414	134	35	115	.324
	At Fenway	113	415	139	23	88	.335
	13 Years	226	829	273	58	203	.329
1955	At Detroit	8	26	11	4	11	.423
	At Fenway	9	27	11	4	13	.407
	On Year	17	53	22	8	24	.415
	Totals						
	At Detroit	121	440	145	39	126	.330
	At Fenway	122	442	150	27	101	.339
	14 Years	243	882	295	66	227	.334
1956	At Detroit	10	28	9	1	4	.321
	At Fenway	9	32	10	1	4	.313
	On Year	19	60	19	2	8	.317
	Totals						
	At Detroit	131	468	154	40	130	.329

		G	AB	H	HR	RBI	Avg
	At Fenway	131	474	160	28	105	.338
	15 Years	262	942	314	68	235	.333
1957	At Detroit	9	28	10	5	7	.357
	At Fenway	9	36	13	1	4	.361
	On Year	18	64	23	6	11	.359
	Totals						
	At Detroit	140	496	164	45	137	.331
	At Fenway	140	510	173	29	109	.339
	16 Years	280	1,006	337	74	246	.335
1958	At Detroit	11	35	9	5	13	.257
	At Fenway	9	28	7	1	2	.250
	On Year	20	63	16	6	15	.254
	Totals						
	At Detroit	151	531	173	50	150	.326
	At Fenway	149	538	180	30	111	.335
	17 Years	300	1,069	353	80	261	.330
1959	At Detroit	8	23	7	2	8	.304
	At Fenway	7	23	4	1	3	.174
	On Year	15	46	11	3	11	.239
	Totals						
	At Detroit	159	554	180	52	158	.325
	At Fenway	156	561	184	31	114	.328
	18 Years	315	1,115	364	83	272	.326
1960	At Detroit	10	31	13	3	6	.419
	At Fenway	9	28	10	3	7	.357
	On Year	19	59	23	6	13	.390
Career Totals							
	At Detroit	169	585	193	55	164	.330
	At Fenway	165	589	194	34	121	.329
	19 Years	334	1,174	387	89	285	.330

VERSUS BALTIMORE ORIOLES   1954–1960

		G	AB	H	HR	RBI	Avg
1954	At Baltimore	8	24	4	1	2	.167
	At Fenway	7	20	7	4	6	.350
	On Year	15	44	11	5	8	.250
1955	At Baltimore	4	14	4	2	2	.286
	At Fenway	7	18	6	3	8	.333
	On Year	11	32	10	5	10	.313
	Totals						
	At Baltimore	12	38	8	3	4	.211
	At Fenway	14	38	13	7	14	.342
	2 Years	26	76	21	10	18	.276
1956	At Baltimore	10	33	10	2	10	.303
	At Fenway	10	32	16	3	11	.500
	On Year	20	65	26	5	21	.400
	Totals						
	At Baltimore	22	71	18	5	14	.254
	At Fenway	24	70	29	10	25	.414
	3 Years	46	141	47	15	39	.333
1957	At Baltimore	11	39	14	0	3	.359
	At Fenway	7	27	9	1	4	.333
	On Year	18	66	23	1	7	.348
	Totals						
	At Baltimore	33	110	32	5	17	.291
	At Fenway	31	97	38	11	29	.392
	4 Years	64	207	70	16	46	.338
1958	At Baltimore	6	19	6	0	2	.316
	At Fenway	8	24	5	0	2	.208
	On Year	14	43	11	0	4	.256
	Totals						
	At Baltimore	39	129	38	5	19	.295
	At Fenway	39	121	43	11	31	.355
	5 Years	78	250	81	16	50	.324

		G	AB	H	HR	RBI	Avg
1959	At Baltimore	5	14	5	0	3	.357
	At Fenway	4	12	5	1	3	.417
	On Year	9	26	10	1	6	.385
	Totals						
	At Baltimore	44	143	43	5	22	.301
	At Fenway	43	133	48	12	34	.361
	6 Years	87	276	91	17	56	.330
1960	At Baltimore	5	10	3	0	2	.300
	At Fenway	9	24	8	3	8	.333
	On Year	14	34	11	3	10	.324
Career Totals							
	At Baltimore	49	153	46	5	24	.301
	At Fenway	52	157	56	15	42	.357
	7 Years	101	310	102	20	66	.329

VERSUS CHICAGO WHITE SOX   1939-1960

		G	AB	H	HR	RBI	Avg
1939	At Chicago	11	44	11	1	7	.250
	At Fenway	12	44	17	1	4	.386
	On Year	23	88	28	2	11	.318
1940	At Chicago	11	44	16	3	11	.364
	At Fenway	11	44	14	0	2	.318
	On Year	22	88	30	3	13	.341
	Totals						
	At Chicago	22	88	27	4	18	.307
	At Fenway	23	88	31	1	6	.352
	2 Years	45	176	58	5	24	.330
1941	At Chicago	9	27	9	3	9	.333
	At Fenway	11	42	17	4	9	.405
	On Year	20	69	26	7	18	.377
	Totals						
	At Chicago	31	115	36	7	27	.313

		G	AB	H	HR	RBI	Avg
	At Fenway	34	130	48	5	15	.369
	3 Years	65	245	84	12	42	.343
1942	At Chicago	10	31	8	1	6	.258
	At Fenway	10	36	8	1	6	.222
	On Year	20	67	16	2	12	.239
	Totals						
	At Chicago	41	146	44	8	33	.301
	At Fenway	44	166	56	6	21	.337
	4 Years	85	312	100	14	54	.321
1946	At Chicago	10	36	10	2	6	.278
	At Fenway	11	40	12	0	8	.300
	On Year	21	76	22	2	14	.289
	Totals						
	At Chicago	51	182	54	10	39	.297
	At Fenway	55	206	68	6	29	.330
	5 Years	106	388	122	16	68	.314
1947	At Chicago	10	36	16	1	5	.444
	At Fenway	13	44	13	3	10	.295
	On Year	23	80	29	4	15	.363
	Totals						
	At Chicago	61	218	70	11	44	.321
	At Fenway	68	250	81	9	39	.324
	6 Years	129	468	151	20	83	.323
1948	At Chicago	10	29	14	3	13	.483
	At Fenway	7	29	13	1	18	.448
	On Year	17	58	27	4	31	.466
	Totals						
	At Chicago	71	247	84	14	57	.340
	At Fenway	75	279	94	10	57	.337
	7 Years	146	526	178	24	114	.338
1949	At Chicago	11	51	19	6	18	.373
	At Fenway	11	36	12	6	21	.333
	On Year	22	87	31	12	39	.356

		G	AB	H	HR	RBI	Avg
	Totals						
	At Chicago	82	298	103	20	75	.346
	At Fenway	86	315	106	16	78	.337
	8 Years	168	613	209	36	153	.341
1950	At Chicago	6	25	6	0	0	.240
	At Fenway	5	19	9	3	10	.474
	On Year	11	44	15	3	10	.341
	Totals						
	At Chicago	88	323	109	20	75	.337
	At Fenway	91	334	115	19	88	.344
	9 Years	179	657	224	39	163	.341
1951	At Chicago	11	31	5	1	3	.161
	At Fenway	11	42	20	4	15	.476
	On Year	22	73	25	5	18	.342
	Totals						
	At Chicago	99	354	114	21	78	.322
	At Fenway	102	376	135	23	103	.359
	10 Years	201	730	249	44	181	.341
1952	At Chicago	—					
	At Fenway	—					
1953	At Chicago	3	11	4	0	2	.364
	At Fenway	3	7	4	1	3	.571
	On Year	6	18	8	1	5	.444
	Totals						
	At Chicago	102	365	118	21	80	.323
	At Fenway	105	383	139	24	106	.363
	12 Years	207	748	257	45	186	.344
1954	At Chicago	8	28	7	3	9	.250
	At Fenway	9	32	12	2	4	.375
	On Year	17	60	19	5	13	.317
	Totals						
	At Chicago	110	393	125	24	89	.318
	At Fenway	114	415	151	26	110	.364
	13 Years	224	808	276	50	199	.342

		G	AB	H	HR	RBI	Avg
1955	At Chicago	8	26	7	1	7	.269
	At Fenway	5	12	5	0	1	.417
	On Year	13	38	12	1	8	.316
	At Chicago	118	419	132	25	96	.315
	At Fenway	119	427	156	26	111	.365
	14 Years	237	846	288	51	207	.340
1956	At Chicago	8	27	11	1	4	.407
	At Fenway	10	24	8	0	2	.333
	On Year	18	51	19	1	6	.373
	Totals						
	At Chicago	126	446	143	26	100	.321
	At Fenway	129	451	164	26	113	.364
	15 Years	255	897	307	52	213	.342
1957	At Chicago	11	38	10	5	9	.263
	At Fenway	7	25	11	1	5	.440
	On Year	18	63	21	6	14	.333
	Totals						
	At Chicago	137	484	153	31	109	.316
	At Fenway	136	476	175	27	118	.368
	16 Years	273	960	328	58	227	.342
1958	At Chicago	11	37	10	1	5	.270
	At Fenway	10	31	11	1	4	.355
	On Year	21	68	21	2	9	.309
	Totals						
	At Chicago	148	521	163	32	114	.313
	At Fenway	146	507	186	28	122	.367
	17 Years	294	1,028	349	60	236	.339
1959	At Chicago	8	28	4	2	3	.143
	At Fenway	9	18	4	0	2	.222
	On Year	17	46	8	2	5	.174
	Totals						
	At Chicago	156	549	167	34	117	.304
	At Fenway	155	525	190	28	124	.362
	18 Years	311	1,074	357	62	241	.332

		G	AB	H	HR	RBI	Avg
1960	At Chicago	9	24	4	0	3	.167
	At Fenway	9	23	6	3	4	.261
	On Year	18	47	10	3	7	.213
Career Totals							
	At Chicago	**165**	**573**	**171**	**34**	**120**	**.298**
	At Fenway	**164**	**548**	**196**	**31**	**128**	**.358**
	19 Years	**329**	**1,121**	**367**	**65**	**248**	**.327**

VERSUS CLEVELAND INDIANS 1939–1960

		G	AB	H	HR	RBI	Avg
1939	At Cleveland	11	36	11	3	12	.306
	At Fenway	11	41	7	1	11	.171
	On Year	22	77	18	4	23	.234
1940	At Cleveland	10	38	9	1	5	.237
	At Fenway	11	39	14	2	12	.359
	On Year	21	77	23	3	17	.299
	Totals						
	At Cleveland	21	74	20	4	17	.270
	At Fenway	22	80	21	3	23	.263
	2 Years	43	154	41	7	40	.266
1941	At Cleveland	7	20	6	1	3	.300
	At Fenway	11	38	18	2	6	.474
	On Year	18	58	24	3	9	.414
	Totals						
	At Cleveland	28	94	26	5	20	.277
	At Fenway	33	118	39	5	29	.331
	3 Years	61	212	65	10	49	.307
1942	At Cleveland	11	37	15	2	12	.405
	At Fenway	10	38	11	2	9	.289
	On Year	21	75	26	4	21	.347
	Totals						
	At Cleveland	39	131	41	7	32	.313

		G	AB	H	HR	RBI	Avg
	At Fenway	43	156	50	7	38	.321
	4 Years	82	287	91	14	70	.317
1946	At Cleveland	11	39	10	4	9	.256
	At Fenway	11	39	20	7	19	.513
	On Year	22	78	30	11	28	.385
	Totals						
	At Cleveland	50	170	51	11	41	.300
	At Fenway	54	195	70	14	57	.359
	5 Years	104	365	121	25	98	.332
1947	At Cleveland	11	32	12	0	1	.375
	At Fenway	11	34	6	0	3	.176
	On Year	22	66	18	0	4	.273
	Totals						
	At Cleveland	61	202	63	11	42	.312
	At Fenway	65	229	76	14	60	.332
	6 Years	126	431	139	25	102	.323
1948	At Cleveland	11	44	18	3	11	.409
	At Fenway	12	43	15	2	12	.349
	On Year	23	87	33	5	23	.379
	Totals						
	At Cleveland	72	246	81	14	53	.329
	At Fenway	77	272	91	16	72	.335
	7 Years	149	518	172	30	125	.332
1949	At Cleveland	11	43	11	2	8	.256
	At Fenway	9	31	13	0	8	.419
	On Year	20	74	24	2	16	.324
	Totals						
	At Cleveland	83	289	92	16	61	.318
	At Fenway	86	303	104	16	80	.343
	8 Years	169	592	196	32	141	.331
1950	At Cleveland	7	24	4	1	5	.167
	At Fenway	5	20	7	3	5	.350
	On Year	12	44	11	4	10	.250

		G	AB	H	HR	RBI	Avg
	Totals						
	At Cleveland	90	313	96	17	66	.307
	At Fenway	91	323	111	19	85	.344
	9 Years	181	636	207	36	151	.325
1951	At Cleveland	11	41	8	1	8	.195
	At Fenway	11	43	16	2	11	.372
	On Year	22	84	24	3	19	.286
	Totals						
	At Cleveland	101	354	104	18	74	.294
	At Fenway	102	366	127	21	96	.347
	10 Years	203	720	231	39	170	.321
1952	At Cleveland	—					
	At Fenway	—					
1953	At Cleveland	2	6	2	2	4	.333
	At Fenway	3	8	3	3	5	.375
	On Year	5	14	5	5	9	.357
	Totals						
	At Cleveland	103	360	106	20	78	.294
	At Fenway	105	374	130	24	101	.348
	12 Years	208	734	236	44	179	.322
1954	At Cleveland	7	23	6	1	5	.261
	At Fenway	7	24	10	2	5	.417
	On Year	14	47	16	3	10	.340
	Totals						
	At Cleveland	110	383	112	21	83	.292
	At Fenway	112	398	140	26	106	.352
	13 Years	222	781	252	47	189	.323
1955	At Cleveland	6	22	4	2	9	.182
	At Fenway	9	34	8	3	6	.235
	On Year	15	56	12	5	15	.214
	Totals						
	At Cleveland	116	405	116	23	92	.286

		G	AB	H	HR	RBI	Avg
	At Fenway	121	432	148	29	112	.343
	14 Years	237	837	264	52	204	.315
1956	At Cleveland	9	19	7	4	9	.368
	At Fenway	11	37	15	0	6	.405
	On Year	20	56	22	4	15	.393
	Totals						
	At Cleveland	125	424	123	27	101	.290
	At Fenway	132	469	163	29	118	.348
	15 Years	257	893	286	56	219	.320
1957	At Cleveland	9	27	13	6	12	.481
	At Fenway	9	30	14	3	8	.467
	On Year	18	57	27	9	20	.474
	Totals						
	At Cleveland	134	451	136	33	113	.302
	At Fenway	141	499	177	32	126	.355
	16 Years	275	950	313	65	239	.329
1958	At Cleveland	11	35	10	3	4	.286
	At Fenway	10	34	12	0	3	.353
	On Year	21	69	22	3	7	.319
	Totals						
	At Cleveland	145	486	146	36	117	.300
	At Fenway	151	533	189	32	129	.355
	17 Years	296	1,019	335	68	246	.329
1959	At Cleveland	9	21	5	2	3	.238
	At Fenway	10	20	3	0	1	.150
	On Year	19	41	8	2	4	.195
	Totals						
	At Cleveland	154	507	151	38	120	.298
	At Fenway	161	553	192	32	130	.347
	18 Years	315	1,060	343	70	250	.324
1960	At Cleveland	9	22	8	5	10	.364
	At Fenway	10	32	10	4	6	.313
	On Year	19	54	18	9	16	.333

	G	AB	H	HR	RBI	Avg
Career Totals						
At Cleveland	163	529	159	43	130	.301
At Fenway	171	585	202	36	136	.345
19 Years	334	1,114	361	79	266	.324

The line summary below lists Ted Williams's road and Fenway numbers over the course of his career.

	G	AB	H	HR	RBI	Avg
Road	1,126	3,814	1,248	273	872	.327
Fenway	1,166	3,892	1,406	248	967	.361

Month-by-month breakdowns are another informative method of examining Williams's career. Such tables chart a path through the course of the years and respond in some way to the charge that Williams faded in the late-season pennant runs. The fact is, he was often wearied during the latter part of the year and subject to the upper-respiratory ailments that repeatedly felled him. His body never did adjust to the chill of the northeastern spring and fall. But the numbers reveal something other than poor late-season hitting. In fact, Williams's highest-percentage month was September.

In the table below, averages in **boldface** indicate the months Williams hit at least .400 *and* played at least 20 games. Figures in parentheses are the number of games played during that month, excluding postseason play.

	April	May	June	July	Aug.	Sept.	Oct.
1939	.344	.257	.318	.372	.289	.394	
	(7)	(25)	(24)	(33)	(32)	(28)	
1940	.302	**.408**	.294	.336	.354	.367	
	(11)	(21)	(26)	(32)	(27)	(27)	
1941	.389	**.436**	.372	**.429**	**.402**	.397	
	(9)	(26)	(28)	(22)	(35)	(23)	
1942	.269	.376	.326	.388	.330	**.431**	
	(15)	(28)	(26)	(29)	(32)	(20)	

	April	May	June	July	Aug.	Sept.	Oct.
1946	.346	.344	.369	.350	.272	**.400**	
	(14)	(27)	(30)	(30)	(29)	(20)	
1947	.342	.272	.289	.383	.383	.356	
	(13)	(25)	(26)	(32)	(30)	(30)	
1948	.344	.383	**.460**	.317	.320	.355	.500
	(9)	(28)	(24)	(17)	(28)	(28)	(3)
1949	.306	.343	.304	.390	.383	.301	.200
	(11)	(26)	(30)	(31)	(31)	(24)	(2)
1950	.450	.265	.362	.263	—	.262	.800
	(6)	(29)	(29)	(6)		(18)	(1)
1951	.297	.330	.363	.303	.303	.299	
	(11)	(26)	(30)	(29)	(30)	(22)	
1952	.400	—	—	—	—	—	
	(6)						
1953	—	—	—	—	.429	.388	
					(19)	(18)	
1954	—	.408	.237	.385	.333	.323	
		(16)	(12)	(33)	(30)	(26)	
1955	—	.333	.397	.293	.386	.369	
		(3)	(18)	(27)	(27)	(23)	
1956	.500	.238	.363	.350	.330	.345	
	(7)	(15)	(27)	(31)	(29)	(27)	
1957	.426	**.402**	.295	**.440**	.355	.632	
	(12)	(25)	(27)	(28)	(28)	(12)	
1958	.219	.287	.345	.311	.371	.411	
	(11)	(26)	(26)	(28)	(21)	(17)	
1959	—	.190	.229	.296	.236	.538	
		(18)	(24)	(27)	(24)	(10)	
1960	.222	.364	.329	.315	.313	.310	
	(6)	(10)	(26)	(23)	(25)	(23)	

The table below breaks down Williams's monthly home runs and runs batted in. The highest monthly career figures are in **boldface**.

	April HR	RBI	May HR	RBI	June HR	RBI	July HR	RBI	Aug. HR	RBI	Sept. HR	RBI	Oct. HR	RBI
1939	1	5	7	31	2	22	6	28	6	36	9	23		
1940	1	5	3	16	5	23	5	21	4	25	5	23		
1941	1	5	6	22	8	29	6	19	10	26	6	19		
1942	3	14	12	**41**	2	18	6	25	4	19	9	20		
1946	1	10	8	27	11	27	8	29	6	21	4	9		
1947	3	9	8	20	2	13	10	29	4	18	5	25		
1948	3	6	8	36	5	27	0	13	7	20	1	21	1	4
1949	1	9	11	32	7	38	7	25	10	34	7	21		
1950	3	12	8	29	13	40	1	2	—	—	3	11	—	3
1951	4	10	7	32	3	28	7	20	6	22	3	14		
1952	1	3	—	—	—	—	—	—	—	—	—	—		
1953	—	—	—	—	—	—	—	—	7	17	6	17		
1954	—	—	4	15	2	7	11	29	7	24	5	14		
1955	—	—	1	4	8	20	10	24	6	25	3	10		
1956	0	3	0	3	2	14	7	23	8	15	7	24		
1957	4	8	7	14	9	21	9	21	4	14	5	9		
1958	3	7	3	13	5	16	6	21	4	15	5	13		
1959	—	—	1	5	4	10	3	16	2	9	0	3		
1960	2	2	—	1	11	24	5	12	6	20	5	13		

The table below provides the totals of Williams's regular-season career broken down by month.

	G	AB	H	HR	RBI	Avg
April	148	468	156	31	108	.333
May	374	1,297	434	94	341	.335
June	433	1,500	504	99	377	.336
July	458	1,541	545	107	357	.354
August	477	1,601	543	101	360	.339
September	396	1,279	462	88	289	.361
October	6	20	10	1	7	.500
Totals	2,292	7,706	2,654	521	1,839	.344

Notes

Preface

Page viii. **"At the hotel"**: Carl T. Felkner, *The Sporting News*, June 19, 1941.

Page viii. **"He's like a lightning bug"**: Stan Baumgartner, *The Sporting News*, July 17, 1946.

Page x. **And the only other creditable full-length biography**: Ed Linn, *Ted Williams: The Eternal Kid* (New York: Bartholomew, 1961). Linn's book was published soon after Williams's retirement and shows signs of the haste necessary to get it into the public eye.

Introduction

Page xiii. **"I never met you"**: Lou Miller, *New York World Telegram*, August 8, 1951.

Page xiii. **"It's all very staccato"**: Roger Kahn, "Salute to Baseball's Elder Statesmen," *New York Times Magazine*, July 26, 1959.

Page xiv. **"You buy every newspaper"**: Roger Birtwell, *Boston Globe*, June 20, 1950.

Page xiv. **"They knew I hit better mad."**: Ted Williams, correspondence with the author dated February 3, 1987.

Page xiv. **"I prefer a kid"**: Clif Keane, *Boston Globe*, February 9, 1958.

Page xiv. **"Kid, there's only one way"**: Bob Holbrook, *Boston Globe*, March 21, 1951.

Page xiv. **"I hit better when I'm mad"**: Ted Ashby, *Boston Globe*, June 25, 1949.

Page xv. **"I fly better mad"**: John Cory, "The Return of Ted Williams," *Harper's*, 238 (June 1969): 73–78.

Page xv. **"Williams nurtured his rage"**: Kahn, "Baseball's Elder Statesmen."

Page xv. **"some ham-and-eggs writer"**: Clif Keane, *Boston Globe*, February 9, 1958.

Page xv. **"forty-nine million newspapers in Boston"**: Ted Williams and John Underwood, *My Turn at Bat: The Story of My Life* (New York: Simon and Schuster, 1969), 161.

Page xv. **"The boos stir me up."**: Harry Brundidge, *The Sporting News*, April 10, 1957.

Page xvi. "we're the poor fish": Harold Kaese, *Boston Globe*, February 1, 1960.
Page xvi. "Ted wants to look good": Ibid., September 6, 1946.
Page xvi. "you made them eat their words": Ibid., March 27, 1947.

1
Country of the Sun

Page 2. "mother was gone all day": Williams, *My Turn at Bat*, 19.
Page 3. "Here, let the Army buy you one": Joe Hamlin, "Salvation May," *San Diego Union*, July 7, 1980.
Page 4. "I was embarrassed": Williams, *My Turn at Bat*, 33.
Page 6. "I'm not even sure where I got my name": Ibid., 33.
Page 6. "I tagged after Rod Luscomb": Ibid., 24.
Page 8. "from the time I was old enough": Ted Williams and John Underwood, *The Science of Hitting* (New York: Simon and Schuster, 1971), 60.
Page 9. An old playground acquaintance: Cf. Bob Holbrook, *Boston Globe*, August 14, 1958.
Page 10. "My, he could hit 'em high": Telephone conversation with the author, June 10, 1988. Ray Boone's son, Bob Boone, still plays in the majors.
Page 12. "he didn't have much choice": This and the following material are from a letter from Elmer Hill to Mr. Ernest Lannigan, dated March 5, 1957. The letter is in the archives of the Hall of Fame Library in Cooperstown, New York.
Page 13. "Let this kid hit": Bobby Doerr, in a telephone conversation with the author, February 22, 1990.

2
Minor Key and Major Talent

Page 18. "A wonderful, wonderful man": Williams, *My Turn at Bat*, 39.
Page 19. "Young Ted Williams, Padre recruit": Monroe McConnell, *San Diego Union*, August 11, 1936.
Page 20. Lane was a gruff old coot: Doerr's telephone conversation with the author, February 22, 1990.
Page 21. "a sad little ditty for Shiver": *San Diego Union*, September 1, 1936.
Page 22. All the while Desautels was serving Eddie Collins: Gene Desautels, correspondence with the author, January 20, 1990.
Page 26. "too high-strung for New York": On July 7, 1966, Ted Williams wrote a letter to the Baseball Hall of Fame in response to this story told by Heinie Groh to baseball historians present for the induction of Williams into the Hall. He claimed he was unaware of these early dealings for his contract but intrigued because of his respect for Bill Terry.
Page 27. "he's going to like Boston": Monroe McConnell, *San Diego Union* January 15, 1938.
Page 28. Eddie Collins called Doerr at his home in Los Angeles: Doerr's telephone conversation with the author, February 22, 1990.
Page 31. "Ted 'Babyface' Williams will be farmed out": Hy Hurwitz, *Boston Globe*, March 18, 1938.
Page 32. "Donie Bush announced Thursday": *Minneapolis Tribune* March 18, 1938.

Page 33. "Ted Williams became the first Miller": Dick Hackenberg, *Minneapolis Star*, March 25, 1938.
Page 35. "forget about Dusty Cooke in right field": Ibid., April 15, 1938.
Page 35. "with his age on his back": Ibid., April 14, 1938.
Page 37. "It's no ordinary slugger": Bob Beebe, *Minneapolis Star*, April 22, 1938.
Page 38. "sailed the proverbial mile in the air": George Barton, *Minneapolis Star*, May 2, 1938.
Page 39. "the Kid made an inglorious muff": Ibid., June 5, 1938.
Page 42. "A merciless official campaign against the Jews": *Minneapolis Star*, June 19, 1938.
Page 43. "It is pleasing to see": George Barton, *Minneapolis Tribune*, August 8, 1938.

3
Baby Ruth
1939

Page 50. "Seldom have we seen Gehrig": Gerry Moore, *Boston Globe*, March 18, 1939.
Page 53. "Tommy, you're full of shit": Hy Hurwitz told an edited version of this story the next year (February 1, 1940) in the *Boston Globe*.
Page 54. "greatest ovation we have ever heard": *Boston Globe*, May 4, 1939.
Page 55. "I fanned three times on nine pitches": Ted Williams and Joe Reichler, "This Is My Last Year in Baseball," *Saturday Evening Post*, April 10, 1954.
Page 55. "We got all good pitchers": *Boston Globe*, April 29, 1952, just after Williams was redrafted into active duty for the marines.
Page 56. "he could just hit everything": Bob Feller, in a telephone conversation with the author, March 20, 1988.
Page 57. "three lengths of barbed wire": Ring Lardner, *Boston Globe*, June 10, 1939.
Page 59. "well—Foxx and DiMaggio": Ted Williams, correspondence with the author, February 3, 1987.
Page 59. "That Foxx": Williams, "This Is My Last Year."
Page 60. the pained expression: Doerr's telephone conversation with the author, February 22, 1990.
Page 60. settle the matter with their fists: Gene Desautels, correspondence with the author, January 20, 1990.
Page 60. "some outside circumstances": Gerry Moore, *Boston Globe*, August 10, 1939.
Page 61. "Whew! The kid has lived up to": Ibid., August 29, 1939.
Page 61. "A drenched Williams screamed": Ibid., *Boston Globe*, August 29, 1939.
Page 63. "He thought of everything": Recollection by Kaese in the *Boston Globe*, April 7, 1954.

4
"Williamsburg"
1940

Page 64. "That stuff about breaking up the Yankees": *Boston Globe*, February 2, 1940.

Page 65. "the real virus": David Halberstam, *The Summer of Forty-Nine* (New York: Morrow, 1989), 133.

Page 68. "anyone who comes along good enough": Grantland Rice, *Boston Globe*, March 23, 1940.

Page 69. "Gehrig could wait and wait": Gerry Moore, *Boston Globe*, April 2, 1940.

Page 71. "My decision is the result": *Boston Globe*, May 21, 1940.

Page 72. "Twenty-one is pretty young": Victor O. Jones, *Boston Globe*, June 4, 1940.

Page 72. "It ain't that he don't want to be friendly": Joe Reichler, *Boston Globe*, June 19, 1950.

Page 74. "Dom DiMaggio played a gorgeous left field": *The Sporting News*, July 4, 1940.

Page 75. "Hitting is Ted's life": Hy Hurwitz, *Boston Globe*, July 15, 1940.

Page 77. "Ted Williams is a grown man": Austen Lake, *Boston Evening American*, August 13, 1940.

Page 77. "If his noodle swells": Jack Miley, *New York Post*, August 19, 1940.

Page 80. "Foxx never bad-mouthed anybody": Williams, *My Turn at Bat*, 62.

Page 80. "You've sat sullen and aloof": Austen Lake, *Boston Evening American*, August 18, 1940.

5
The Last .400
1941

Page 86. "Where civilization is laid aside": Bill Cunningham, *Boston Herald*, April 27, 1941.

Page 86. "There is a 'lost, strayed, or stolen' sign": Melville Webb, *Boston Globe*, March 1, 1941.

Page 87. "Boston may or may not win": *Boston Globe*, March 6, 1941.

Page 87. "The misanthropic Ted Williams": Tom Meany, *Boston Globe*, March 12, 1941.

Page 88. "Too many Negro ballplayers": Ibid., February 20, 1941.

Page 89. "That's just the kind of guy I am": Arthur Sampson, *Boston Herald*, March 10, 1941.

Page 90. "Anything that is unusual": Melville Webb, *Boston Globe*, March 21, 1941.

Page 91. "the cleverest ways to cork bats": Johnny Sturm, correspondence with the author, January 24, 1990.

Page 91. "Ode to the Red Sox": *Boston Globe*, April 10, 1941.

Page 92. "The dugout was a cozier": Ted Williams, correspondence with the author, February 3, 1987: "I was so hot at the plate pinch hitting that I had established a .400 average by the time I started to play."

Page 93. "the homer was one of the longest": Melville Webb, *Boston Globe*, May 7, 1941.

Page 94. "Say, you should have seen": Dan Daniel, *New York World Telegram*, June 9, 1941.

Page 94. "Lyons was tough": Williams, *My Turn at Bat*, 68.

Page 97. "Hell, no. I played": Hy Hurwitz, *Boston Globe*, June 25, 1941.

Page 97. "He's loose and easy": Ibid., July 1, 1941.
Page 98. "When I got up to the plate . . .": J. G. Taylor Spink, *The Sporting News,* July 17, 1941.
Page 99. "a wallop which for altitude": Kyle Crichton, *Collier's,* September 28, 1946.
Page 99. ambled from his position in right: Enos Slaughter, correspondence with the author, January 19, 1990.
Page 99. "Hardened veterans and more publicized stars": Gerry Moore, *Boston Globe,* July 9, 1941.
Page 101. ended his streak at 56 games: The saga of DiMaggio's streak is chronicled in Michael Seidel's *Streak: Joe DiMaggio and the Summer of '41* (New York: Penguin, 1988).
Page 102. Could this be the man: Victor O. Jones, *Boston Globe,* August 7, 1941.
Page 102. "As soon as this campaign closes": Gerry Moore, *Boston Globe,* August 11, 1941.
Page 104. "Umpire Eddie Rommel disclosed yesterday": Ibid., September 18, 1941.
Page 104. "Remember 1941, when I hit over .400?": *The Sporting News,* August 7, 1946.
Page 104. "I figure a man's a .400 hitter, or he isn't": Maxwell Stiels, *Boston Globe,* July 28, 1957.
Page 105. "most disappointed guy in the world": Ibid., September 29, 1957.
Page 106. "a hundred percent poison": Grantland Rice, *Boston Globe,* February 23, 1942.

6
Draft Bait
1942

Page 109. "So I think I'm one helluva hitter?": Cleveland Amory, "I Wanna Be an Immortal," *Saturday Evening Post,* January 10, 1942.
Page 109. "If Uncle Sam gives Ted a uniform": *The Sporting News,* January 29, 1942.
Page 110. "Baseball and sports in general": Hurwitz, *Boston Globe,* February 3, 1942.
Page 111. "hasn't a chance of being deferred": Ibid., February 3, 1942.
Page 111. "To replace Greenberg, Williams, or Feller": Ibid., February 13, 1942.
Page 112. "if one sportswriter was his enemy": Cunningham, *Boston Herald,* March 1, 1942.
Page 113. his advisor . . . "got mad": Williams, *My Turn at Bat,* 98.
Page 115. "If Uncle Sam says fight, he'll fight": *Boston Globe,* February 27, 1942.
Page 115. "some common meeting ground": Williams, *My Turn at Bat,* 9.
Page 116. "The first reaction from all sides": Kaese, *Boston Globe,* February 27, 1942.
Page 116. "The case seems black": Ibid., February 28, 1942.
Page 116. "this is a matter between Williams and his draft board": Cunningham, *Boston Herald,* February 28, 1942.
Page 117. America wasn't then at war: Jerry Nason, *Boston Globe,* March 3, 1942.
Page 117. "If you went off to the war": Jones, *Boston Globe,* March 4, 1942.
Page 117. "If I had Yawkey's millions": Cunningham, *Boston Herald,* March 7, 1942.

Page 118. "Sgt. Hank Greenberg": Ibid., March 10, 1942.
Page 118. "The quickest route to a solution": *Boston Globe*, March 7, 1942.
Page 120. "the white of his eyes?": Cunningham, *Boston Herald*, March 24, 1942.
Page 120. "Jeez, I can't hit": Ibid., March 24, 1942.
Page 121. "Safe at home": *Boston Globe*, April 10, 1942.
Page 122. "Yeah, everyone was for me except": Ibid., April 12, 1942.
Page 123. "And what've you got against him?": Cunningham, *Boston Herald*, April 29, 1942.
Page 123. "Ted, you think everybody's a good hitter": Kaese, *Boston Globe*, May 5, 1942.
Page 124. "Most of the fans": Webb, *Boston Globe*, May 22, 1942.
Page 125. "He was always near the top": Johnny Pesky, correspondence with the author, January 21, 1990.
Page 126. "I can't get over those marine fliers": *Boston Globe*, June 11, 1942.
Page 129. "There is no understanding": Ibid., July 28, 1942.
Page 129. "flopped all over the park": Nason, *Boston Globe*, August 17, 1942.

7
Interlude
1943-1945

Page 139. "It's a damned shame": *The Sporting News*, June 14, 1945.
Page 140. "He is not now major league stuff": This and the following remarks from Branch Rickey are from a feature story in *The Sporting News*, November 1, 1945.

8
The Real Thing
1946

Page 141. chattered about "baseball and Ted Williams": Hurwitz, *Boston Globe*, September 15, 1945.
Page 143. "Can I do this?": Mel Allen, in a telephone conversation with the author, August 1, 1988.
Page 143. Berra always begged Williams: Correspondence with the author, January 25, 1990. Berra tried to get Williams thinking about fishing while at the plate. It never worked, but Yogi claimed he never stopped trying.
Page 144. "He'll always hit the ball": Hurwitz, *Boston Globe*, February 20, 1946.
Page 144. "I could have led the league": Rice, *Boston Globe*, April 7, 1946.
Page 146. Dick Wakefield had bet him $1,000: Williams, "This Is My Last Year in Baseball," *Saturday Evening Post*, April 10, 1954.
Page 146. "I'm always nice enough": From a profile in *Time*, April 10, 1946, with a deleted expletive reinstated.
Page 146. The postgame time was an especially vulnerable period: Dom DiMaggio, in a telephone conversation with the author, February 1, 1990. DiMaggio recalled that he had to ask Joe McCarthy for the same policy on behalf of the players in 1948 and was relieved at the promptness with which McCarthy agreed to it.
Page 147. "closing his team off from the press": George Barton, *Minneapolis Star*, March 11, 1938.

Page 147. **"a team with the resources"**: Kaese, *Saturday Evening Post*, March 23, 1946.

Page 148. **"maybe Cronin's got a few faults"**: *Boston Globe*, March 24, 1946.

Page 148. **"funny business for America?"**: Roger Birtwell, *Boston Globe*, August 3, 1950.

Page 149. **"A man is free to work"**: *Boston Globe*, April 6, 1946.

Page 152. **"The ordinary ballplayer"**: Nason, *Boston Globe*, May 12, 1946.

Page 153. **"Ted hit a balloon?"**: *Boston Globe*, July 10, 1946.

Page 155. **the outfielders played him to pull anyway**: John Chamberlain, *Life*, September 23, 1946.

Page 155. **"hit where his power was"**: John Lardner, *Newsweek*, July 22, 1946.

Page 158. **the courts eventually**: on October 2, 1950, Williams's insurance company agreed to a $16,000 settlement awarded to George and Shirley Doncaster.

Page 159. **He wanted Williams to play**: Feller claimed in correspondence with the author, February 8, 1990, that Williams had signed a contract with him and then reneged.

Page 160. **"When I look at a guy"**: Russell Owen, "It's All in Your Eyes and Timing," *Time*, August 4, 1946.

Page 161. **venom with a democratic zeal**: In his *Summer of Forty-Nine* David Halberstam draws a wonderful verbal portrait of Egan.

Page 161. **"Who up there in the press box"**: Ted Williams (as told to Leslie Lieber), "Let's Talk Things Over!" *Sport*, May 19, 1957.

Page 163. **"I could have told you"**: *Boston Globe*, October 5, 1946.

Page 163. **"He ain't a money player"**: Kaese, *Boston Globe*, October 5, 1946.

Page 165. **"The Kid's bunt was bigger"**: Red Smith, *Boston Globe*, October 10, 1946.

Page 165. **"As matters stand"**: Kaese, *Boston Globe*, October 14, 1946.

9
Triple Crown Redux
1947

Page 169. **Feller agreed to pitch**: Feller said that Williams was so good a hitter he didn't even worry about making a mistake pitching to him. "He didn't need you to make a mistake in order to hit you." (Correspondence with the author, February 8, 1990.)

Page 169. **"served as scoutmaster"**: Red Smith, *Boston Globe*, May 23, 1947.

Page 169. **"It is about time"**: *Boston Globe*, February 14, 1947.

Page 171. **Infielders hated a hard Williams shot**: Phil Rizzuto claimed that an infielder could misjudge a Williams grounder because of the topspin, and line drives were even more brutal. He remembered one shot that he thought he had speared for a potential triple play until he felt the ball spin off his glove into short left. (Telephone conversation with the author, January 21, 1990.)

Page 171. **"I can hit to left field"**: *Boston Globe*, March 6, 1947.

Page 172. **"Did Williams hit to left?"**: Kaese, *Boston Globe*, March 17, 1947.

Page 174. **Rickey informed Durocher**: Kaese, *Boston Globe*, April 10, 1947.

Page 177. **"all that sort of advice"**: *Time*, September 15, 1947.

Page 179. **"you big 600-pound gorilla!"**: Kaese, *Boston Globe*, March 19, 1947.

Page 182. **"They sure were dead game"**: *Boston Globe*, March 1, 1948. From an interview with Heath conducted the following spring.

10
Daddy-O
1948

Page 186. **"In Boston, a man"**: Kaese, *Sport*, May 1949. Kaese went on to note the productive debility that so marked the man: "Super-sensitiveness is probably Ted Williams's greatest asset, connected as it is with his lightning quick reactions. Yet it probably is also his greatest torment."

Page 187. **"What Ted does in his spare time"**: Nason, *Boston Globe*, February 5, 1948.

Page 189. **Williams was so shaken**: Williams, *My Turn at Bat*, 16: "I will never forget the day I hit Lou Brissie with a line drive. It was 1946, and he had come out of the service a great war hero with part of his leg blown off."

Page 192. **"pitching me outside"**: Birtwell, *Boston Globe*, June 25, 1948.

Page 194. **"Here's to the Land"**: Rice, *Boston Globe*, September 13, 1948.

Page 196. **"Galehouse can't explain"**: In correspondence with the author, February 26, 1990, Galehouse was still reluctant to tell the whole story and perhaps doesn't even know it completely, but he insists there was some strange business going on, at best a loss of nerve and at worst a kind of shirking.

11
Close but No Cigar
1949

Page 201. **"Without faking himself"**: Nason, *Boston Globe*, April 8, 1949.

Page 204. **His performance was and still is**: For a full and wonderful account of these games, indeed of the entire 1949 season, see David Halberstam's *Summer of Forty-Nine*.

Page 205. **"That is *not* the way to pitch him"**: Jim Bagby's wife remembers her husband's friendship with Williams. He venerated the big guy and used to talk about him all the time. On the field Bagby, with a noticeable harelip, used to kid rival first basemen when they held runners on with Williams up: "Stand there, Meatball, and you'll be sporting a lip like mine." (Correspondence with the author, March 19, 1990.)

Page 206. **"Greatest left-hand hitter"**: Clif Keane, *Boston Globe*, August 9, 1957. Keane was reminiscing about conversations with DiMaggio through the 1940s.

Page 208. **"no logical reason"**: Kaese, *Boston Globe*, September 12, 1949.

Page 208. **"Screwy game, ain't it?"**: Nason, *Boston Globe*, September 13, 1949.

Page 209. **Pesky said he beat the tag**: Correspondence with the author, January 26, 1990.

12
Elbowed Out
1950

Page 213. **potential effects of television**: The minors were at their height in the late 1940s; the Dodgers, for example, boasted 22 affiliates; the Cardinals, 21; the Yankees, 15, and the Red Sox, 8.

Page 217. **"dirty little man"**: Austen Lake, *Boston Herald*, May 12, 1950.

Page 217. **"Why's Ted doing that?"**: Kaese, *Boston Globe*, May 12, 1950.

Page 217. **Yawkey's benevolent dictatorship:** Jack Maloney, *The Sporting News,* May 1, 1950.
Page 217. **"Boston's hostile and abusive":** Jimmy Cannon, *New York Post,* June 1, 1950.
Page 218. **"Possessed of more natural ability":** Dan Parker, *New York Daily Mirror,* June 1, 1950.
Page 219. **"fifth-place Senators":** Birtwell, *Boston Globe,* June 20, 1950.
Page 219. **"When I retire":** Ibid., June 26, 1950.
Page 220. **"They'll never get me out":** *Life,* September 23, 1946.
Pages 223–224. **"no such reception parties":** Nason, *Boston Globe,* September 16, 1950.

13
Boston Fade
1951

Page 227. **"go fishing like I planned":** *Boston Globe,* February 3, 1951.
Page 230. **In 1948 the odds were even:** Nason, *Boston Globe,* March 15, 1951.
Page 231. **"Nobody could have hit":** Kaese, *Boston Globe,* March 23, 1951.
Page 233. **"Why drop him":** Ed Sullivan, *Boston Globe,* April 26, 1951.
Page 233. **"So now is the time":** Kaese, *Boston Globe,* May 21, 1951.
Page 234. **"This game makes you humble":** Ibid., May 22, 1951.
Page 236. **"disintegrating before his eyes":** Holbrook, *Boston Globe,* August 17, 1951.
Page 237. **a hands-on manager like Lefty O'Doul:** These remarks came from a Hy Hurwitz profile on Dom DiMaggio later in the decade. Cf. *Boston Globe,* August 16, 1959.

14
To Hell and Back
1952–1953

Page 240. **"Reservists should be kept":** *Boston Globe,* April 24, 1952.
Page 241. **"It's a boy scout camp":** *Boston Globe,* April 17, 1952.
Page 243. **"this was a rare day":** Holbrook, *Boston Globe,* March 2, 1952.
Page 244. **"You'd think that the talent":** Kaese, *Boston Globe,* March 18, 1952.
Page 244. **Cobb never forgave Ruth:** Rice, *Boston Globe,* March 27, 1952.
Page 251. **"I got nothing against him":** Kaese, *Boston Globe,* July 30, 1953.
Page 251. **"It isn't that Williams is critical":** Keane, *Boston Globe,* August 4, 1953.
Page 252. **"He always could hit 'em":** Cunningham, *Boston Herald,* August 11, 1953.

15
Cold Shoulder
1954

Page 260. **"Even before I broke":** This and the following citations in the text are from "This Is My Last Year in Baseball," *Saturday Evening Post,* April 10, 1954.

Page 265. **"If Williams is going to quit"**: Birtwell, *Boston Globe*, September 7, 1954.

Page 265. **"We never had it so good"**: Nason, *Boston Globe*, September 23, 1954.

Page 266. **Williams would not leave**: Tom Meany, "Williams Will Be Back," *Collier's*, October 15, 1954.

17
Rivalries
1956

Page 275. **"HE'S INNOCENT"**: *Boston Globe*, March 29, 1956. On 1949, Stalin executed one Laxzio Rajk, Hungarian foreign minister, and now Budapest radio rehabilitated his career but, unfortunately, could do nothing for the stone-dead minister.

Page 277. **"Go ahead, make a big story"**: *Boston Globe*, March 14, 1956.

Page 278. **"so damn lousy it was brutal"**: Keane, *Boston Globe*, February 9, 1958. This was nearly two years after the original column.

Page 279. **"Some people can't be objective"**: Kaese, *Boston Globe*, March 16, 1956.

Page 281. **"he didn't even see me"**: Mickey Vernon, correspondence with the author, February 24, 1990.

Page 281. **"For me it's easy"**: *Boston Globe*, August 2, 1956.

Page 284. **"They're interviewing psychiatrists"**: Joan Flynn Dreyspool, *Sport*, August 20, 1956.

Page 285. **"Ted Williams should do himself a favor"**: Kaese, *Boston Globe*, August 8, 1956.

18
Comeback Kid
1957

Page 291. **"The club floated a loan"**: Ted Lepcio, correspondence with the author, February 10, 1990.

Page 294. **"I hope I can get Ted"**: Hurwitz, *Boston Globe*, April 2, 1957.

Page 296. **"Of this you may be sure"**: Nason, *Boston Globe*, April 2, 1957.

Page 297. **"Be careful what you say"**: An edited version of this encounter appeared in *The Sporting News*, May 29, 1957.

Page 297. **"Ted Williams should have learned"**: Cunningham, *Boston Herald*, April 16, 1957.

Page 298. **"that New Orleans sportswriter"**: Kaese, *Boston Globe*, May 9, 1957.

Page 299. **"Let the two existing leagues"**: Ibid., June 2, 1957.

Page 300. **"Something tells me"**: Larsen claimed in a recent letter that he never said anything about Williams on the record precisely because he didn't want to rile him. (Correspondence with the author, January 20, 1990.)

Page 300. **"clinical observers looking"**: Holbrook, *Boston Globe*, July 11, 1957.

Page 303. **To this day Epstein swears**: Mike Epstein, correspondence with the author, September 5, 1988.

Page 304. **"the Red Sox drew the 181,087"**: Kaese, *Boston Globe*, September 30, 1957.

19
Life Begins at Forty
1958

Page 306. **"I'll be nice. You be fair"**: *Boston Globe*, February 5, 1958.
Page 311. **Runnels counts the race**: Pete Runnels, correspondence with the author, January 19, 1990.

20
Pain in the Neck
1959

Page 312. **"But Old T. S. W."**: Kahn, "Baseball's Elder Statesmen," *New York Times Magazine*, July 26, 1959.
Page 316. **"the image he leaves"**: Kaese, *Boston Globe*, August 30, 1959.

21
Last but Not Least
1960

Page 318. **took a $35,000 pay cut**: Williams's salary for 1959 was at that time the highest ever in baseball. By way of comparison at the other end of the historical scale, the Cincinnati Red Stockings of 1869 had a combined payroll of $9,500, with high salaries of $1,400 to George Wright and $1,200 to brother Harry.
Page 319. **"cost the Red Sox"**: Red Smith, *Boston Globe*, March 8, 1960.
Page 319. **"I keep thinking"**: *Boston Globe*, March 25, 1960.
Page 323. **Slaughter had held onto it**: Enos Slaughter, correspondence with the author, January 19, 1990.

Epilogue

Page 328. **"In the two decades since"**: John Updike, "Hub Fans Bid Kid Adieu," *New Yorker* 36 (October 22, 1960): 109-110.
Page 329. **the usually raucous collection**: Bart Giamatti, interview with the author, June 10, 1988.
Page 330. **"This is Bob Short"**: Jack Mann, "The Return of No. 9," *Time*, May 2, 1969.

Appendix A
Sweet Science: Williams on Hitting

Page 332. **"They don't know as much"**: "A Real Rap Session," *Sports Illustrated*, April 14, 1986.
Page 333. **Many of his mis-hits**: Gene Woodling, correspondence with the author, January 19, 1990: "His drives really sunk hard. One ball game in Fenway Park he hit a line drive to me I thought I had in perfect range when the ball sunk and hit my big toe and broke it."

Page 333. **Two decades earlier:** *Sports Illustrated*, June 10, 1968, was the first installment, and four more followed, through July 8. These articles were collected and expanded to Williams's *The Science of Hitting*, with John Underwood.

Page 335. **"I feel in my heart":** *Sports Illustrated*, July 8, 1968.

Page 335. **"It's so important":** *My Turn at Bat*, 23–24.

Page 336. **Berra called Williams's:** Yogi Berra, correspondence with the author, January 15, 1990. "He could pick any pitch *he* wanted. That was his ultimate prerogative."

Page 337. **Al Kaline described:** Al Kaline, correspondence with the author, January 15, 1990.

Page 338. **"There's too much artist":** Nason, *Boston Globe*, September 11, 1953.

Page 339. **"I thought they caught":** Bobby Shantz, correspondence with the author, January 22, 1990.

Page 339. **"I couldn't have helped":** Keane, *Boston Globe*, February 9, 1958.

Page 340. **"I was honest":** Ted Lepcio, correspondence with the author, February 10, 1990.

Page 340. **"mediocre fastball":** Dennis Galehouse, correspondence with the author, February 26, 1990.

Page 342. **Williams gestured to Vernon:** Mickey Vernon, correspondence with the author, February 24, 1990.

Page 342. **"I throw it behind":** Virgil Trucks, correspondence with the author, February 19, 1990.

Page 343. **"You must be stupid":** Mike Epstein, correspondence with the author, September 5, 1988.

Page 344. **"Cobb said that, too":** Kaese, *Boston Globe*, March, 23, 1951.

Index

395